DATE			
DEC 0 2 1995			
MAY - 5 1998			
5 - 4			
APR 2 2 '02			
MAY 1 ? 02			

WHAT
REALLY
MATTERS

WHAT REALLY MATTERS

Searching for Wisdom in America

TONY SCHWARTZ

BANTAM BOOKS
NEW YORK · TORONTO · LONDON · SYDNEY · AUCKLAND

WHAT REALLY MATTERS
A Bantam Book / April 1995

Library of Congress Cataloging-in-Publication Data
Schwartz, Tony, 1952–
What really matters : searching for wisdom in America /
Tony Schwartz.
p. cm.
Includes index.
ISBN 0-553-09398-3
1. United States—Religion—1960– 2. Spiritual life. 3. Wisdom.
4. Schwartz, Tony, 1952– . I. Title.
BL2525.S344 1995
128—dc20 94-31033
CIP

Published simultaneously in the United States and Canada

Bantam Books are published by Bantam Books, a division of Bantam Doubleday Dell Publishing Group, Inc. Its trademark, consisting of the words "Bantam Books" and the portrayal of a rooster, is Registered in U.S. Patent and Trademark Office and in other countries. Marca Registrada. Bantam Books, 1540 Broadway, New York, New York 10036.

PRINTED IN THE UNITED STATES OF AMERICA
BVG   0 9 8 7 6 5 4 3 2 1

For
Deborah, Kate and Emily
always

CONTENTS

Contents

INTRODUCTION

A Longing in the Heart

*What does a life of total dedication to the truth mean?
It means, first of all, a life of continuous and never-
ending stringent self-examination. We know the world
through our relationship to it. . . . The life of wisdom
must be a life of contemplation combined with action.*
    —M. SCOTT PECK

*One does not become enlightened by imagining figures
of light, but by making the darkness conscious.*
    —CARL JUNG

THE party in the pink marble atrium of Trump
Tower began shortly after ten on a cold Saturday
evening in December 1987. Klieg lights illuminated
the Fifth Avenue entrance as guests pulled up in stretch limousines,
stepped out onto a red-carpeted sidewalk, and entered the lobby,
where they were greeted by a dozen strolling violinists and scores
of white-jacketed waiters serving champagne in fluted glasses.
Crowds of everyday folks stood behind police barriers to gawk at
the arriving celebrities. Although the party was being held in
honor of a book I had written—ghostwritten, to be precise—I,
too, felt like an outsider. After all, this was the sort of event I was
used to attending solely as a reporter. Instead, dressed in a tuxedo,
sporting a new haircut, and wearing an uncharacteristically social
smile, I found myself standing with my wife on a receiving line,
wedged between Donald Trump, Ivana Trump, and Si Newhouse,
the owner of Random House.

Together, we were greeting guests who had come to help
celebrate the publication of *The Art of the Deal*, which I'd written

with Trump. Most people shaking our hands had no idea who we were, but that didn't bother us a bit. Instead, we reveled in this glamorous fairy tale. The book was about to reach number one on the *New York Times* best-seller list. Trump himself was fast emerging as the embodiment of 1980s success: an entrepreneurial deal-maker, an unabashed self-promoter, a very conspicuous consumer, and a high-voltage celebrity. Whether you loved or hated him, there was something fascinating and seductive about the life that he was leading.

Determined to make the most of this unique event, I'd invited every friend, family member, and acquaintance in my address book, including our baby-sitter, our accountant, and my tennis teacher—each with their spouse. My brother was in charge of videotaping. My sister handled the still photography, although it was our baby-sitter who managed to get the greatest number of pictures of herself alongside famous people—among them heavyweight boxing champion Leon Spinks and his manager Don King; New Jersey governor Tom Kean; model Cheryl Tiegs; socialite Anne Bass; former Miss America and CBS anchorwoman Phyllis George and her husband, ex-Kentucky governor John Y. Brown; writer Norman Mailer and the actor Michael Douglas— who had just appeared as a Trump-style billionaire in the movie *Wall Street.*

Shortly after midnight, with hundreds of guests hanging over the railings at each of the atrium's five levels, comedian Jackie Mason introduced Trump, who spoke rhapsodically about the book's success and even joked that part of his challenge had been to teach me how to make money. Afterward, an immense cake sculpted in the shape of Trump Tower was wheeled in, followed by a parade of men and women carrying red sparklers. As the cake was cut, hundreds of red balloons were released from the top of the atrium. I spent the next several hours dancing, drinking and laughing with my wife, family and friends. We didn't leave until shortly after three A.M.

It was a heady celebration of an extraordinary moment. I was thirty-five years old, and by many measures, I was riding the crest of the American Dream. I'd been a reporter for *The New York Times,* a writer for *Newsweek,* and a successful magazine journalist. Even so, I'd never earned much money, and like most people I knew, I spent a lot of time worrying about how to make ends meet. Now, with *Art of the Deal,* I was about to earn more in a few weeks than I had in the whole of my working life, giving me a financial cushion that few people are ever lucky enough to enjoy. Publishers were eager to sign up whatever book I chose to do next. My marriage of ten years was strong and stable. My wife had her own challenging career, and our two young daughters, ages two and six, were healthy and mostly happy. I jogged several miles a day and played tennis at least twice a week. I had several close friends, and I felt I contributed usefully to my community.

Why, then, wasn't I happier?

In the weeks after the Trump party, as the book continued to command huge attention, I remained on a giddy high. But I also noticed that when a day went by without some new piece of exciting news about the book, I experienced a certain vague anxiety. I'd spent two years seeing the world through Trump's eyes, and I'd grown accustomed to living at his dizzying pace, cramming my days full of action and activity. But now suddenly, I wasn't under the same external pressures that had fueled me for so long. I didn't have to jump immediately into a new project in order to pay the next month's bills. Beyond that, something more subtle began to change. All my life, I'd been driven to achieve in my work and to be recognized and appreciated for my efforts. Now I'd written a book that was highly visible and undeniably successful—and yet something was still missing. It was a privilege even to have the time to consider these issues, but that didn't make them feel any less pressing or significant.

At first, I wondered if the answer might simply be in the nature of the success I'd achieved. After all, *The Art of the Deal* wasn't truly *my* book. And even as it climbed the best-seller list, it prompted some backlash. Trump himself was criticized as a symbol of the acquisitive, self-promoting spirit of the times, and I was sometimes judged guilty by association. I was accused of selling out. I told myself that I'd done a good, honest job on the book and that the proof was not just in its popularity but in the mostly positive reviews it received. Still, I cringed when I found myself characterized in terms so at odds with the way I longed to be seen—and to see myself.

I wanted not just recognition but respect. My journalistic heroes had been writers such as David Halberstam, Gay Talese, and Tom Wolfe. I'd always wanted to write books like theirs: ambitious, resourceful reporting on large, visible topics of the day. Perhaps by turning now to that dream, I thought, I'd find a way to fill the gnawing emptiness I felt inside. But even as I began to cast about for the perfect book, I sensed that the answers I was after weren't going to be found simply by achieving a more prestigious success. I'd done a lot of good journalistic work over the years, yet somehow it hadn't translated into a sense of depth, or richness, or passion in my life. Above all, I lacked the experience of meaning—that I was here for some reason beyond succeeding in work and building a comfortable, close-knit life with my family and my friends. Both of these were honorable, important goals. They simply felt insufficient. What I longed for was to feel more at home with myself, more deeply comfortable in my own skin, more connected to something timeless and essential, more real.

For all my outer focus, I'd always been a seeker. Beneath the veneer of my smooth-sounding success story and the tough, confident persona I often presented to the world, I'd long felt an inner turbulence and discontent, a muted but chronic sense of anxiety. I sought acceptance and love but easily became angry, impatient, and judgmental. I was often deeply drawn to people, yet I felt myself holding them at a distance or even pushing them away. I had enormous energy but frequently had to struggle to focus my attention. I was torn between a drive to succeed and the sense that this intense desire often prevented me from simply enjoying my life day to day. I gave endless thought to resolving my conflicts yet felt best when I simply became absorbed in an activity or got engaged with another person. And while I often experienced turmoil in the present, I was expansively hopeful about the future. I felt certain that there was more to life than I'd experienced so far. I sensed that I was living only a piece of the life I'd been given, a pale reflection of my potential. I was searching for a more complete life, an experience of my own essence, something I came to call wisdom.

Unlike many Americans, I was never drawn to organized religion as a route to meaning. Born Jewish, I was raised by parents with virtually no religious beliefs themselves. Instead, values such as honesty, rationality, objectivity, and hard-headed skepticism were prized above all. We never discussed the possibility that there might be a God, or a higher power, or even a form of deeper, unseen intelligence in the universe. My limited experiences in synagogues left me unmoved, even numb. When I attended Sunday school classes, services at the Jewish high holidays, or Passover celebrations at my grandmother's apartment, I was unable to connect to the rituals and traditions in any heartfelt way. As I grew older, I became increasingly mistrustful of the dogma, hierarchy, and rigidity that seemed to characterize most organized religions. I also viscerally resisted *any* absolute authority—something I viewed, through the prism of my own experience growing up, as often abusive, narrow-minded, and hypocritical. Looking back, I realize that I longed for faith—but not at the cost of blindly accepting beliefs that didn't resonate for me in my own experience.

The one route to meaning that was accorded value in my family was service to others. My mother spent her life as a social activist and made it clear that she considered this work the highest calling. Dutifully—and sometimes even enthusiastically—I spent time in my teenage years volunteering in political campaigns, tutoring disadvantaged kids, and working in opposition to the war in Vietnam. In my early twenties, I turned my activism to writing about causes that interested me. But as I grew older, got married, and had children, my focus shifted to advancing my career and my family's well-being. Only later did I begin to recognize that this was also a way of rebelling against my mother. Her obsessive commitment to causes had occurred, I felt, at considerable expense to me and my siblings. In reaction, I became determined to take a different route.

To a large extent, I placed my faith in two modern American paths to a better life. The first was success. If only I had enough, I told myself—enough achievement, recognition, and money, a sufficiently comfortable home, more exciting vacations, a good marriage, beaming kids, a wide circle of friends—then eventually I'd feel satisfied. Ironically, it was by finally realizing this dream that I ran up against its limitations. In the aftermath of the Trump experience, I couldn't say for sure what role external success played in a complete life, but I felt certain that at most, it was only one piece in a much larger puzzle.

I also invested considerable faith in psychotherapy. Toward the end of college, the woman I'd been involved with for three years left me. She had been my first true love, and I felt devastated. I turned to therapy for answers and ended up in a long and traditional Freudian psychoanalysis. Over time, I began to understand better the conflicts from my childhood that still deeply troubled me in the present, and to see the defensive patterns that I'd developed to protect myself from pain. After several years, I fell in love with the woman I eventually married, and my difficulties in bringing focus and discipline to my work began to ease. I never knew, however, whether these changes would have occurred by themselves, in the natural course of growing up.

Whatever the answer, it finally dawned on me that there was something arid and one-dimensional about my experience in therapy. My analyst was a decent and intelligent man, but our relationship was oddly casual and detached. I rarely felt any strong emotions during sessions—I don't ever remember crying or feeling intense anger—and my analyst never pushed me to dig deeper. Instead, he kept a neutral distance, and our relationship remained largely intellectual. While the circumstances of my life improved over time, I didn't *feel* fundamentally better. Even so, when I finally decided to quit therapy, I did so with mixed emotions. I knew I hadn't yet found the answers I was looking for. I continued to hunger for a more satisfying life. I still felt that something was missing.

I t was in the aftermath of *The Art of the Deal* that I became interested in meditation. The lure was not spiritual. I'd never been much interested in a practice that seemed so utterly removed from the everyday world. I was drawn to meditation purely as a way to relax. I felt I was living in a state of chronic overdrive, forever hungry for the next adrenaline fix, and rarely able to relax. I started meditating simply to slow down.

To my surprise, the practice of letting go of my thoughts and resting in a place of inner quiet proved both exhilarating and moving. For the first time, I found that it was possible to get beyond my gnawing everyday concerns and to experience instead a sense of calmness, clarity, and deep well-being. In time, I became convinced that I'd found the answer I'd been searching for—a way to fill up what was missing in my life. I concluded that many people had overlooked and even disparaged meditation merely because it seemed mystical—an activity that made sense only for those prepared to renounce their material lives and leave the workaday world behind.

Very quickly, I realized that meditation had practical uses. Learning to quiet my mind reduced my tension, helped me to concentrate better, and made it easier to absorb information. Beyond that, I found myself experiencing a broader sense of awareness and clarity, opening to a more expansive view of the world that didn't lend itself easily to words. I began to sit for at least twenty or thirty minutes every day and often for as much as an hour. There were times, alone in meditation, when I felt more present, more alive, more open, and more connected to others than I ever remembered feeling before. In these moments I started to apprehend a new sense of meaning in my life—an unmistakable feeling that I was connected to a larger whole. My calling as a writer, I decided, was to literally bring meditation down to earth. I became determined to find an accessible language to communicate the powerful experiences I was having.

But something unexpected happened along the way. To my disappointment and chagrin, I noticed that when I opened my eyes after meditating and returned to everyday life, I often fell right back into my old patterns. I resumed worrying about problems that had seemed trivial from my meditative stance. The chatter of my mind returned. My impatience flared up. I found myself looking outward again for approval and feeling a familiar restlessness. I despaired that while I'd undoubtedly glimpsed a better way to live, embodying it in my everyday life was a whole other story.

Perhaps, I told myself, the problem was that I'd only just begun meditating. It was absurd to expect enduring changes in my life in a matter of months, much less instant enlightenment. But, as I began to spend time with people who'd devoted many years to meditation, people who had built their lives around spiritual practices aimed at transcending the ego, I saw that they had many of the same difficulties I did. Few of them behaved more compassionately, sensitively, or selflessly than the majority of people I knew who didn't meditate at all. However valuable the perspective of the higher meditative states, they didn't seem to provide all of the answers I was seeking. Learning to deeply quiet the mind was plainly one piece of the wisdom puzzle, but it didn't seem sufficient by itself.

The result was that I began to look more widely for wisdom. Only much later did it dawn on me that I was following a tradition that dates back thousands of years: the search for the Holy Grail, for meaning, for the true self—the path that Joseph Campbell called the hero's journey. I also realized that I was seeking a form of wisdom suited to my own life and to the culture I lived in. I wasn't interested in renouncing my material desires, moving to an ashram, or giving up my professional ambitions. I wanted to continue to participate passionately in the world, but I also wanted passionately to connect to something deeper in myself and others.

For four years, I traveled the country, seeking out people who had made the search for meaning primary in their lives. I spent hundreds of hours talking with psychologists, philosophers, physicians, mystics, psychics, teachers, and scientists about their ideas and experiences. I looked carefully at the ways in which discoveries in more traditional fields such as psychology, medicine, and science have contributed hard knowledge to the highly subjective challenge of defining a complete life. And wherever possible, I set out to experiment myself with techniques, technologies, and practices aimed at transformation.

Much of this work was born in the counterculture climate of the 1960s, as a reaction to the elitism, sterility, and pathological focus of psychoanalysis. The people I turned to were concerned at least equally with higher human possibilities. Many of them took their work out of the analyst's office and into the world. They couldn't help but be influenced by Freud's seminal insights about the nature of the unconscious. But they were drawn as well to Carl Jung's focus on the discovery of the true self through the process he named "individuation," and to Wilhelm Reich's theory that neurosis is rooted in people's disconnection from their bodies and the resulting inability to fully experience their feelings. Finally, many of these pioneers became interested in integrating the insights of modern psychology with the wisdom of the Eastern contemplative traditions.

Under the rubrics of the human potential movement, the New Age and the consciousness revolution, a wide array of new approaches to transformation emerged through the 1960s and 1970s. For perhaps the first time in America, concepts such as self-discovery, personal growth, and even self-transcendence became legitimate middle-class aspirations. I was interested not just in the ideas, techniques, and practices of those I met, but in the ways in which their work was related, the lineages from which they drew inspiration, and the degree to which their discoveries had transformed their own lives. I drew hope from the wide evidence that human beings can indeed evolve throughout their lives, both in degree of consciousness and self-knowledge, and in the range and depth of their skills. Long before I experienced any significant changes in my own life. I saw evidence of the vastness of untapped human potential.

The work I explored had taken place in many contexts and guises: the early experiments with psychedelic drugs; the emergence of the fields of humanistic and transpersonal psychology; the advent of biofeedback; the multifaceted study of dreams; the scientific research into the connections between mind and body; the groundbreaking discoveries about the left and right hemispheres of the brain; and the attempt to import Eastern spiritual traditions—most notably the techniques of meditation and yoga—to the West. It also included some surprisingly rigorous and well-documented research into areas long considered the province of occultists: parapsychology, healing at a distance, and even near-death and out-of-body experiences.

My own journey included meditating in settings ranging from a week-long retreat in the mountains of Utah, to a weekend sitting in silence with a hundred other urban seekers in a cramped room above New York's Times Square, to a course in transcendental meditation taught to all the members of my family at our home. I lay alongside two hundred people on the floor of a cavernous meeting room in the desert outside Palm Springs and practiced a powerful breathing technique designed to break through ordinary consciousness and tap deeply repressed emotions and memories, including the experience of birth itself. I traveled to Berkeley, California, to spend five days doing exercises aimed at helping me to become more aware of my body and to recognize how different bodily postures are connected to specific emotions. I was hooked up to biofeedback instruments in New York City, Topeka, Kansas, and Palo Alto, California, which fed back to me the information I needed to voluntarily warm my feet and hands, relax my muscles, alter my heartbeat, slow my brain waves, focus my attention, and even produce dreamlike imagery.

I visited Cambridge, Massachusetts, to learn to draw using

the right side of my brain, and Sarasota, Florida, to practice accessing the ideal performance state while playing tennis. I was read by extraordinary psychics on both coasts, and I got pummeled and kneaded by bodyworkers in cities ranging from Boulder, Colorado, to Amherst, Massachusetts, to Petaluma, California. I was taught by a Unitarian minister in San Rafael, California, and a renegade psychoanalyst in Dobbs Ferry, New York, how to work in a group setting to interpret and make creative use of my dreams. I spent time in large groups in Big Sur, California, and New Rochelle, New York, learning to observe and to let go of the deeply established personality patterns that prompt us to react in habitual, automatic ways. I spent several weekends learning to appreciate the difference between the experience of my personality and my underlying essence.

Different as these practices and practitioners often were, I was struck repeatedly by their interconnectedness. When it came to telling the story of my travels, it seemed natural to begin with the people who pioneered the modern American search for wisdom by attempting to bridge Eastern and Western ideas, techniques, and technologies. From there, I looked at a series of practitioners who have developed especially innovative and accessible ways to tap specific aspects of the human potential. Finally, I focused on a group of people whose work represents the most comprehensive, balanced, and distinctly American approach to wisdom that I came across. I made a constant effort to separate the wheat from the chaff—to make clear, qualitative distinctions among practitioners, theories, and practices. I found no absolute answers to my questions, but to a remarkably satisfying degree, I did emerge with a sense of how to effectively pursue a richer, more authentic, and more complete life.

I never wavered in my belief that most people experience only a fraction of their potential—that there is something deeper and richer waiting to be tapped. But much as I hungered for simple solutions, my search kept leading me to deeper mysteries and more questions. How is it possible to balance personal needs and desires with the more selfless and transcendental orientation that can emerge through meditation? What is the relationship between what Jung called the "persona"—our conscious face to the world—and what he termed the "shadow," the darker impulses and conflicts that remain unacknowledged in our unconscious? How was I to reconcile my hunger for inner exploration and greater self-knowledge with my simultaneous desire to take decisive and effective action in the world? How was I to deal with the conflicts between my head and my heart—between what I deduced rationally and logically and what felt right to me intuitively? And finally, how was it possible to balance my desire to grow and evolve with my equally powerful instinct to protect and defend the status quo, however imperfect and painful it might be?

These very issues arose in the process of reporting this book. As a journalist, I'd been taught to present the facts coolly and objectively, uncolored by my personal feelings. I'd always recognized that this was impossible, except by pretending that I had no subjective experience. Still, for years I tried to carefully reflect at least two sides of every story, only to despair that what I wrote lacked any real honesty and depth. When it came to this book, I had no desire to report from a careful distance. I'd undertaken my search because I was looking to experience a richer and more satisfying life. How was that possible merely by gathering and interpreting facts? If I wasn't willing to let go—to immerse myself in experiences without trying simultaneously to assess their value—how could I truly expect to discover anything meaningful? Conversely, if I simply suspended my critical faculties, could I possibly come to any discriminating and credible conclusions? I made a simple choice: Experience first, and assess later.

I struggled with the same opposing instincts in reporting about the people who form the center of this book. As a journalist, I had found that keeping a certain distance from my subjects was what allowed me to write about them dispassionately. I'd interview a person at great length, evaluate his or her work, ideas, and life, and then one day I'd just move on. Often, however, I did so with a feeling of sadness and loss. I tended to write about people, after all, whose lives had interested and attracted me in the first place. This time out, I felt anything but dispassionate. I was looking for people who embodied wisdom and completeness—role models for my own search. Those I interviewed often shared my deepest concerns and passions. I didn't believe that I could come to know them merely by asking a series of questions. I felt compelled to engage them more deeply, to make more of a personal connection, and I often did. Several became real friends. Still, at a certain point, I had to sit down and write about them and about their work. Was it possible, I wondered, to honestly evaluate their contributions and the degree to which they embodied their insights, knowing that by doing so I might in some cases hurt or offend them? Was it realistic to be both critical and compassionate, friendly and discriminating?

I still don't know the answer, but I made my best effort. I tried to assess each person's work in terms of the complete life I was seeking to define. Did their ideas, techniques, and everyday behavior advance this mission? If not, where did they fall short, and what got left out? I wasn't looking to sort out good guys and bad guys but rather to better define the nature of an authentic search for wisdom. Still, I have no doubt that my own unconscious biases, preferences, and defenses have colored my perceptions. I tried to be especially alert to my automatic tendency to focus more on people's shortcomings than on their strengths. I resisted my inclination to arrive at absolute conclusions and tried instead to appreciate the richness, complexity, and mystery of the people I encountered and the journey I undertook.

I wasn't satisfied merely to sample techniques or to survey various approaches to wisdom. Rather, I was determined to identify a path and a set of practices that truly led to a more satisfying and meaningful life. It became clear to me early on that transforming lifetime beliefs and behaviors requires an ongoing practice—disciplined techniques for breaking through fixed patterns and penetrating to deeper levels of the truth. I began with a conviction that someone—or some way—would finally pull it all together for me. Sure enough, nearly everyone I spent time with had a clearly articulated vision of the wise life and an approach by which best to seek it. Many of them were quite charismatic and persuasive, and my allegiances shifted frequently and intensely.

An unmistakable pattern emerged. Introduced to an impressive teacher, a new system, a novel set of insights, or an interesting technique for tapping the depths of the unconscious, I quickly became enraptured and immersed. Frequently enough that it amused my friends and colleagues, I'd announce that I finally had the answer—or at least the best way to go about seeking it. In time, however, my initial passion gave way to the skepticism that always lurked just beneath the surface. A particular technique, so powerful at first, inevitably began to provide diminishing returns. I would become increasingly aware of the disparity between a given teacher's inspiring message and his everyday behavior.

At first, I found this phenomenon deeply disillusioning. In time, however, I saw that the gulf between the talk and the walk didn't necessarily mean that the teaching lacked any wisdom or that the teacher was fraudulent. Instead, I got better at appreciating what any given person had to offer, even with his or her limitations and blind spots. Still, I was especially drawn to those teachers who openly recognized and grappled with their contradictions. Doing so meant to me that they were still committed to growing, that they were courageous enough to keep seeking more of the truth about themselves, however difficult that might be. Because this willingness was so rare, I found any evidence of it especially inspiring.

On one level, I spent four years looking for answers to two straightforward, age-old questions: Who am I? and Why am I here? The wisest people I met offered very different answers. Some talked about a self defined by the capacity to summon at will the thoughts and emotions necessary to achieve one's aims in the world. Some described a *real* self in psychological terms as a measure of the capacity to connect with one's deepest underlying feelings. Others referred to the *true* self as an expression of inborn essential qualities that the everyday personality or ego tends to mask and that must therefore be rediscovered and cultivated. Still others claimed that the self is ultimately an illusion and that the challenge in life is to transcend the ego and all sense of separateness, to move instead toward an experience of boundless oneness.

In each case, I found that the way people define the nature of the self dictates how they envision the purpose of life. For some, the highest aspiration is self-improvement, for others it is self-discovery, and for others it is self-transcendence and selfless service. By one view, the goal is to achieve our potential through conscious, disciplined action. By another, it is simply to know ourselves better, to be more conscious and more aware, less defensive and automatic in our behaviors. By yet another view, wisdom is derived from moving beyond rational intention and surrendering to an intuitive knowing that arises from within, when the mind and body quiet down. Finding a way to integrate these often contradictory perspectives into everyday life became my own central challenge. The book that follows, the story of my search for wisdom, is a work in progress. So am I.

I

GROUND: THE PIONEERS

1

REDEFINING REALITY

Ram Dass, Psychedelics, and the Journey to the East

*Our normal waking consciousness, rational conscious-
ness, as we call it, is but one special type of consciousness, whilst all about it, parted from it by the filmiest
of screens, there lie potential forms of consciousness
entirely different.*
—WILLIAM JAMES

*It is because we don't know Who we are, because we
are unaware that the Kingdom of Heaven is within us,
that we behave in the generally silly, the often insane,
the sometimes criminal ways that are so characteristically human.*
—ALDOUS HUXLEY

I BEGAN meditating in 1989 for the most practical
of reasons: I wanted a way to slow down the frenzied
activity of my mind. I wasn't interested in gurus or
rituals, spiritual awakening, or higher states of consciousness. All
of that struck me as mystical, and for me, mystical was the
opposite of useful. I wanted meditation with no frills. I read a
couple of books about how to meditate, and I began with a simple
practice—focusing my attention on repeating a single word while
breathing in and out. I wasn't interested in a mantra, so I settled
on the word *one* as the object of my focus and decided to set aside
time to meditate each morning as soon as I woke up. I knew that
if I allowed the day's obligations to pile up, I'd begin finding

excuses not to meditate. The problem, I learned very quickly, was that this apparently simple activity—sitting quietly and repeating a single word—proved to be one of the most difficult challenges I'd ever faced. The sort of conscious discipline that I used to get my writing done, or even to make myself jog in the mornings, proved useless. Telling one's self not to think—or to focus for twenty minutes on a single word—is like telling a small child to sit silently for twenty minutes. It's an exercise in futility. My mind, I discovered very quickly, has a mind of its own.

At first, I found it intolerable to sit in meditation for more than a few minutes. I squirmed. As my mind wandered, I recalled long-forgotten obligations, and couldn't resist running to get a pen and paper to write them down. I daydreamed, chewed over past events, and planned new ventures. If I had an inspired idea or a flash of insight, I grabbed for my pen. Then I berated myself for not being able to follow what seemed to be such simple instructions. Sometimes I became distracted by physical pain. My knee throbbed, my back ached, and my forehead itched. Or I got lost in fantasy or felt drowsy and began to nod off. No sooner would I become alert than I found myself vowing to concentrate better, only to recognize that making vows is itself a distraction. I did everything imaginable but quiet down and focus on the word *one*. Unwittingly, I'd entered a pitched battle with an endlessly resourceful opponent: my own mind.

Curiously, though, I was never tempted to give up. Perhaps it was because I sensed how extraordinary it would be to have more control of my thoughts. Even the brief moments when my mind stopped racing were so quietly exhilarating that it seemed more than worthwhile to keep at the effort. Even when thoughts barraged me nonstop for twenty minutes, I still got a certain satisfaction from the fact that I'd managed to stay at the task. Without any conscious planning, I began to meditate for longer periods. Inevitably, life's business came up in my thoughts, but at some point I realized that I could just let the thoughts go. I didn't have to pay them so much attention or follow up on them. When they came back up, I could let them go again. The less I resisted, the less forcibly they seemed to press themselves on me.

Sometimes distraction or compulsion or preoccupation prevailed, and I felt as wound up when I finished as when I'd begun. But the next morning, I sat right back down again and started over. In a matter of weeks I began to experience some breaks in the battle. I became more easily absorbed in the word *one* and in the rhythmic pattern of my breathing. Occasionally, I moved below—or perhaps beyond—the level of words and conscious thoughts. I'd never experienced this state before. Paradoxically, I found that when I wasn't actively thinking, my awareness became broader and clearer than usual. Rather than flitting chaotically between thoughts, perceptions, and physical sensations, my attention grew more fixed and stable. I could put it where I chose. Rather than being unsettled, distracted, or controlled by the activity of my mind, I felt some detachment—more as if I were its benign observer.

Often I wasn't aware that anything out of the ordinary had occurred until I opened my eyes. Only then did I realize that what had felt like the passage of a few minutes had in fact been twenty minutes or occasionally even thirty. Whenever that happened, I felt lighter, calmer, and even happier. Although meditating didn't prompt any sudden, profound changes in my life, subtle ones became more noticeable. The first was that I gained more resilience. When something upset me, I found I could return to a state of equilibrium more easily, without any conscious effort. Eventually I decided to try sitting and meditating directly after an upsetting event. Sure enough, when I sat for at least ten or fifteen minutes, even the most vexing anger, frustration, or disappointment began to lose its grip on me. At times it simply melted away altogether. On those occasions it was as if I'd found a safe harbor, a place to go that was calm and quiet even as storms raged around it. I was fascinated to find that whenever I was able to mute my tendency to think, analyze, and assess, I felt more control and comfort, not less.

Two events in those first six months brought home for me the unusual practical power and value of meditation. The first occurred one morning as I was waiting to catch a train to attend a meeting in Manhattan. As I boarded the car, I suddenly realized that I had an aura—a woozy form of double vision. It was the unmistakable and unvarying sign of an imminent migraine headache. Starting at the age of seventeen, I'd suffered from occasional migraines—the initial aura followed a short time later by a blinding sledgehammerlike headache that attacked one side of my head. I got them only two or three times a year, but each migraine lasted eight to twelve hours. During those periods, I could do nothing but retreat into a dark room, lie down, close my eyes, gulp down medications that barely helped, and wait. It was hell, pure and simple.

This time, however, there wasn't even a dark room to escape into. I was on a train, headed to an important meeting that had been difficult to arrange. Feeling desperate, I decided to close my eyes and see if meditating—focusing all my attention on something other than the aura and the anticipated pain—might somehow help. When we got to the station, I reluctantly opened my eyes. Thirty minutes had passed. To my astonishment, the double vision was gone, and I felt no pain. It was the first time I'd ever experienced an aura that did not lead directly to a migraine. Later, I discovered that there was a plausible physiological explanation. The migraine aura is the result of a severe constriction of the blood vessels in the head, which impedes blood flow. The pounding headache ensues when the same blood vessels powerfully dilate and trigger enormous pressure in the head. Focusing and quieting my mind through meditation had somehow prompted the blood flow in my head to normalize. In effect, I'd gained control of an involuntary physiological process. I used the same technique the next time that I experienced an aura, and it worked again. It has now been more than five years, and I've been almost completely free of migraines. The couple of exceptions were relatively modest, and even then the pain was ameliorated by meditating.

The second event also occured on a train, in this case on a

warm, fall evening. It was around six o'clock, I was in New York City, and I'd gone to Grand Central Station to catch a train home in time for dinner. As the train pulled out of the station, the lights went off. Perhaps ten minutes later, it stopped. The conductor's voice came over a loudspeaker to announce that there was an electrical problem and that he had no way of knowing how long the repair would take. All that my fellow passengers and I could do was sit and wait in the tunnel—indefinitely. It wasn't the sort of challenge that tended to bring out the best in me. I'd long been the sort of person who considers waiting in traffic jams a personal affront. Great patience was not among my virtues. Add to that the need to sit in total darkness, and I found myself in the sort of scenario that I consider close to torture. Nor did my fellow commuters seem much more sanguine. In their rumbling and sighing, I could sense a rising irritation.

I decided to close my eyes and focus on repeating the word *one* silently, while breathing slowly and rhythmically. Very quickly, I lost track of time and became absorbed instead in the meditative process. The longer we sat, the calmer I felt. When the lights finally came on and the train began to move, I looked at my watch. Nearly ninety minutes had passed. It was far and away the longest I'd ever meditated, but it felt as if I'd been at it no more than twenty or thirty minutes. By the time I stepped off the train at eight-thirty—two full hours late—I was as relaxed as I could ever remember feeling. My wife was incredulous. She'd already warned our kids that I'd be in a bleak mood when I finally got home, and to give me plenty of room. The experience had a profound effect on me. If I moved beyond my thoughts and focused deeply enough, I now realized, there was a state I could access that felt calm and comfortable almost regardless of the external circumstances. It occurred to me that I'd stumbled onto a piece of a much bigger puzzle. Meditation was plainly a powerful technique for relaxation. What began to interest me even more was the unique state of consciousness that it helped access and the possibility that it might have some relationship to my search for wisdom. It was with that in mind that I turned to Richard Alpert, a.k.a. Ram Dass.

Among all the seekers who emerged from the counterculture ferment of the 1960s, perhaps no one more than Richard Alpert so dramatically turned his back on a traditional American success story, embraced such a radically different path, and still managed to make his new perspective seem both accessible and appealing. A Harvard psychology professor on a fast track, Alpert and his colleague Timothy Leary began conducting scientific research into psychedelic drugs in the early 1960s. Experimenting with the drugs reshaped Alpert's views about the nature of reality and dramatically transformed his life. When opposition to the research grew at Harvard, and both Alpert and Leary refused to pull in the reins, they were ultimately fired.

After several years of pursuing psychedelic research independently, Alpert decided to travel to India in the late 1960s. It was there that he met and began studying under his guru, Maharajji. By the time he returned to America a year later, Maharajji had given him the name Baba Ram Dass—Sanskrit for "servant of God"—and Alpert had fully embraced his new identity. He soon began drawing large crowds to the colorful talks he gave about his experiences in India. *Be Here Now*—the loose story of his search for enlightenment as well as a "manual for conscious being"—was published in 1972. The book became a cult best seller and helped introduce hundreds of thousands of young Americans to meditation, yoga, chanting, breathing techniques, spirituality, and the notion that it is possible to achieve higher states of consciousness and a more meaningful life.

I was in college at the time, but what interested me more than mysticism was antiwar politics, finding a girlfriend, and building a career in journalism. The consciousness movement barely flickered on my radar screen. Nearly two decades had passed by the time I sought out Ram Dass in the summer of 1990. During the previous year, I'd become deeply drawn to meditation and to the possibility that I might gain access to a broader reality than I'd experienced in my ordinary life. I went to Ram Dass because he seemed a logical starting place both for my own journey and for the story I wanted to tell.

At the age of sixty, he was living alone in the guest house of a Marin County estate that belonged to two of his close friends. I wasn't prepared for the tanned and clean-shaven man who answered the door. If anything, Ram Dass looked younger than he had in pictures twenty years earlier, when he had returned from India sporting a heavy beard and long white robes. At the time he lived the life of a renunciate. Now, in his white chinos, pullover shirt, trim moustache, and easygoing smile, he had the relaxed, prosperous look of an upper-middle-class businessman just back from a round of golf at the club. His house consisted of four rooms that were modestly but comfortably furnished in postmodern pastel colors. Classical music was playing on his stereo when I arrived, and the shelves were packed with books and cassettes. He couldn't have been a more solicitous host.

From our first meeting, it was plain to me why so many seekers have been drawn to him. Ram Dass speaks about meditation and Eastern spiritual practices in down-to-earth, Western psychological terms. He has an extraordinary gift for storytelling, a stand-up comedian's timing, and an easygoing willingness to laugh at his own shortcomings. For all his experimentation with altered states of consciousness, there was something very grounded and comforting about him. I found Ram Dass both charismatic and vulnerable, straightforward and friendly. For more than twenty-five years he has been working to integrate Eastern thinking into everyday Western life. Today he divides his time between writing books and articles, lecturing to audiences that often exceed a thousand people, leading smaller, more experiential workshops, and devoting a considerable percentage of his time to what he now considers his main spiritual practice: service to others. His activities range from counseling the terminally ill to working on behalf of SEVA, a nonprofit organization that does work with the blind in India and Nepal and development work in

Guatemala. More recently, Ram Dass has begun to focus on an issue that is increasingly close to his heart: aging. In addition, he continues to meditate for at least an hour a day and much longer when he goes on extended retreat himself, at least once a year.

R ichard Alpert's longing for a better way was fueled by a childhood of material privilege and emotional despair. Although he has written about his life in a half-dozen books and talked about it in hundreds of speeches and interviews, he has never said much about his early years. In *Be Here Now*, for example, he dispensed with the first twenty years of his life in a phrase. "Until you know a Jewish middle-class, upwardly mobile, anxiety-ridden neurotic," he wrote with deceptive breeziness, "you haven't met a real achiever." Even now, after years of self-examination, Ram Dass remains reluctant to talk about his relationship to his parents and the role that his childhood played in the choices he's made. "I think it's one of the areas where my consciousness is the least clear," he explained to me. "It hasn't given up its secrets to the kind of spacious awareness that I've cultivated in my spiritual work. I still tend to be judgmental of my parents, and I don't feel that's very conscious."

It doesn't require much probing to discover that Alpert's feelings about his childhood remain powerful, vivid, and often painful. The last of three sons, he was exceptionally close to his mother, but the relationship was difficult. On the face of it, his mother, Gertrude, was a very conventional, energetic Jewish suburban housewife. "She taught me how to be good, and what is appropriate and proper," Alpert told me. At the same time she was deeply insecure. Although she adored babies, who were utterly dependent on her, she had much more difficulty with her children as they grew up and began to have their own needs and desires. "The only relationship I could have with her was as a dependent child," Alpert explained. "Since I was the last child she was going to have, she infantilized me. In turn, I developed a dependency on her, an inordinate love affair with her that I have

26

never fully gotten over. In my teenage years I would eat everything she gave me, trying to get her to love me more. I grew fatter and fatter. On some level, I knew that the minute I became a man, she would reject me in the way she rejected all men. It was a horrendous mixed message I got from her. In one sense, she understood and supported me. But in another, she was very scornful of any aberration from her very conventional beliefs. She was extremely emotionally controlling, and there just wasn't a lot of room left for me."

Alpert's relationship with his father was very different, but it had a similar underlying quality. Orphaned as a young man, George Alpert grew up to become a successful businessman who survived the crash of 1929 in unusually good shape. When Richard was born two years later, the family moved to an affluent suburb of Boston. Although he remembers spending a fair amount of time with his father growing up, Alpert also recalls his father as a man who needed "continuous appreciation from others. We can obviously see the way I'm a chip off the old block." Through his work, George Alpert got a great deal of appreciation. He was eventually named president of the New Haven Railroad, helped found Brandeis University, and won acclaim as a popular public speaker and philanthropist. He also entertained lavishly at the huge New Hampshire farm that he purchased in 1938. He transformed it into an estate, and began transporting corporate titans to his Gatsbyesque parties by private train.

For young Richard, his father was a hard act to follow. It didn't help that both of his older brothers were high achievers themselves—one an excellent athlete, the other a fine artist and musician. Richard loved and admired his father but found his values disorienting from early on. "There was a way in which my father's reverence for people who had power—political or economic—had a very unhealthy influence on my life," he told me. "It made all of those things inordinately important to me. I'm still struggling with that issue to this day. I never got from him, or from my mother, a real love of learning, or any connection to nature, or any reverence for just being." One memory typifies this void for Alpert: "I remember sitting with my father on our golf course one day when I was ten or so, watching an incredibly beautiful sunset. He said to me, 'Isn't that a beautiful sight?' I agreed that it was, this natural thing of God. Then he said to me: 'Just *look* at how close the grass is cut.' *He'd* been referring, of course, to the beauty of the golf course. In a way, his vision never went beyond what he was personally involved in. I needed recognition of my existence as a human being. But he was so busy with himself that as children, we really didn't exist."

Unlike his high-achieving older brothers, Alpert didn't at first live up to his father's expectations. He was overweight, awkward, uncertain in his sexual preferences, and a mediocre student. When it came time for college, he was rejected at his first choice, Harvard. Instead, he attended Tufts University. It was there, on his own for the first time, that he finally carved out an identity. Alpert had a gift, he discovered, for drawing people to him. Before long, he lost weight, began to nurture his talents as a charming raconteur, educated himself about wine and antiques, and became highly sought after socially. One result was that academic work got less priority. By his senior year, he realized that he didn't have the grades to get into a top medical school.

Alpert set his sights instead on graduate school in psychology, but his father refused to pay for anything but medical school. In this case, Alpert's charm served him well. He applied for graduate school at Wesleyan and in the process befriended David McClelland, chairman of the psychology department. Impressed by Alpert's warmth, energy, and ambition more than by his academic achievements, McClelland offered him a research assistantship. Afterward, Alpert went on to get his Ph.D. at Stanford, writing his thesis on a subject with great personal resonance: academic performance anxiety. He still felt a deep sense of inadequacy in the university world. Still, that didn't halt his steady march up the career ladder. In 1958, McClelland—by now a professor at Harvard and the head of its prestigious Center for Research in Personality—once again reached out to Alpert, this time inviting him to join the faculty. It was a sweet moment—an offer to teach at the very institution to which he'd been unable to gain admittance as an undergraduate. He had also been offered a position at Stanford but ultimately he chose Harvard.

Alpert was just twenty-seven years old, but he was soon on a tenure track, with appointments in three separate departments, including social relations, psychology, and education. He wasted no time in building a small empire at Harvard. He served on several prestigious committees, secured a series of research contracts, became a popular lecturer, and commanded a corner office with a full complement of research assistants and secretaries. "I was on a power play track, taking over more and more," he told me the first time we met. "I couldn't get it fast enough. I was drunk for the power and control and the mastery." He was also living high. As he described it much later in *Be Here Now:* "I had an apartment in Cambridge that was filled with antiques and I gave very charming dinner parties. I had a Mercedes-Benz sedan and Triumph 500 CC motorcycle and a Cessna 172 airplane and an MG sports car and a sailboat and a bicycle. . . . I was living the way a successful bachelor professor is supposed to live in the American world of 'he who makes it.' "

Tim Leary and psychedelic drugs prompted the first dramatic shift in Richard Alpert's life. Leary arrived at Harvard in the fall of 1959. Although he'd originally been a respected authority in the field of personality diagnosis and a professor at the University of California at Berkeley, he was recruited by David McClelland explicitly to stir things up in the psychology department at Harvard. Leary, then thirty-nine years old, had just written a manuscript suggesting a blueprint for an alternative vision of therapy. He described it to McClelland when they met for the first time in Florence, Italy, where Leary was living at the time. Leary's theory was based partly on the notion that psychologists should get more personally involved with patients, rather than keeping the safe, emotionally neutral distance that the Freudians favored. Leary's rebellious spirit, his heretical ideas, and his energetic charm attracted McClelland. While McClelland played the academic game by the books, he was eager, he told Leary, to hire someone who might set up "activist research projects which will require the institution to change itself."

No sooner did Leary arrive in Cambridge than he and Alpert became close friends. Alpert was forever on the lookout for mentors who seemed to have better answers, and he felt immediately drawn to Leary's creativity, confidence, and renegade daring. Leary, meanwhile, saw in Alpert a potential Huck Finn to his Tom Sawyer—a willing fellow traveler, a charming sidekick, and a potentially loyal disciple. While Alpert continued to revel in the prestige and power of life at Harvard, he was also vaguely aware of an underlying emptiness and despair. He knew that he was never going to be a scholar, and he felt like something of a fraud. "I began to see my colleagues as less than the wise elders I thought they should be," Alpert told me. "None of us had much understanding of the human condition or how to change it. As psychologists we weren't making people much happier or healthier." Five years of his own psychoanalysis, for example, hadn't eased his anxieties. He was making all the right moves, but they weren't getting him the satisfaction he sought. "The nature of life was a mystery to me," Alpert wrote in *Be Here Now*. "All the stuff I was teaching was just like little molecular bits of stuff, but they didn't add up to a feeling anything like wisdom."

The next stage in Alpert's life began when Leary found his "activist" research project the next summer in Mexico. It was born out of his first experience with the consciousness-altering mushroom *Psilocybe mexicana*. For Leary, it was a challenge to his whole belief system, an awakening to the brain's vast untapped potential. "The journey lasted a little over four hours," he wrote more than twenty years later. "Like almost everyone who has had the veil drawn, I came back a changed man. In four hours by the swimming pool in Cuernevaca I learned more about the mind, the brain, and its structures than I did in the preceding fifteen years as a diligent psychologist. I learned that the brain is an underutilized biocomputer, containing billions of unaccessed neurons. I learned

30

that normal consciousness is one drop in an ocean of intelligence. That consciousness and intelligence can be systematically expanded. That the brain can be reprogrammed. That knowledge of how the brain operates is the most pressing scientific issue of our time. I was beside myself with enthusiasm, convinced that we had found the key we had been looking for."

Very quickly, Leary convinced a reluctant McClelland to let him begin formal study of psychedelic drugs at Harvard. Leary also persuaded McClelland to hire another investigator for the research project—his close friend, Frank Barron, a Stanford psychologist and a leading authority on the psychology of creativity. Meanwhile, the drug company Sandoz had already figured out how to extract the psychoactive ingredient of the Mexican mushroom and had begun marketing it to qualified researchers in synthetic form under the name psilocybin. Psychedelics were not yet illegal, and Sandoz was interested in finding out more about their effects—particularly the degree to which they could mimic the symptoms of schizophrenia.

Leary jumped in headfirst—serving as his own primary experimental subject. During the first three months of that fall, he took psilocybin more than fifty times. He and Barron also began giving it to a wide variety of other people in the first primitive attempts to study its effects. As it happened, Alpert was away that fall, teaching for a semester at Berkeley. It wasn't until he returned to Harvard in the winter that he got his introduction to psychedelics. His first trip took place in Leary's living room in Cambridge, Massachusetts, on a snowy evening in March 1961.

Alpert later recounted this experience in *Be Here Now*—and in countless lectures and workshops since then. His account remains one of the most vivid and accessible descriptions I've found of the way that psychedelic drugs can prompt a shift of consciousness and a radically different view of one's identity. The key part of Alpert's trip took place while he was sitting alone in Leary's living room. As the drug began to take hold, Alpert suddenly became aware of someone across the room. When he looked carefully, he realized that he was viewing himself, in cap and gown, as a professor. "It was as if that part of me, which was Harvard professor, had separated or disassociated itself from me," he wrote. At first, Alpert was worried, but then he thought, "Well, I worked hard to get that status, but I don't really need it." Next, the professor vanished, only to be replaced by a succession of people whom Alpert knew to be aspects of himself: social butterfly, cellist, pilot, lover. Finally, as he looked across the room, he saw a child, the original Richard Alpert, his basic identity. When that too vanished, he became very frightened. How, he wondered, could he do without something so fundamental—his very self? Well, he rationalized, as least I have my body. At that point, however, he looked down at the couch and discovered that his body seemed to have vanished as well.

"Nothing in my philosophical materialism prepared me for that, and I freaked," he told me. "I started to call for Timothy when the thought went through my mind 'Who's freaking out?' If I'm not my body, and I'm not all my social roles, what's left? And then something suddenly connected for me. It was like a figure-ground reversal. I became aware of a part of me, an essence, that had nothing to do with life and death." Although he didn't realize it at the time, Alpert was having the sort of classical transcendental vision that has been described by all of the enduring Eastern meditative traditions. It was an experience of spiritual essence, the true self. Much later, Alpert summed it up this way: "Although everything by which I knew myself, even my body and this life itself, was gone, still I was fully aware! Not only that, but this aware 'I' was watching the entire drama, including the panic, with calm compassion. Instantly with this recognition, I felt a new kind of calmness. I had just found . . . a place where 'I' existed independent of social and physical identity. And something else— that 'I' Knew—it really Knew. It was wise rather than just knowledgeable. It was a voice inside that spoke truth. I recognized it, was one with it, and felt as if my entire life of looking to the outside world for reassurance—David Riesman's 'other-directed being'—was over. Now I need only to look within to that place where I knew." And what place exactly was that? I asked Alpert.

"I felt like I'd come home," he told me. "It was an incredible exhilaration."

My own experience with psychedelic drugs, nearly ten years after Alpert's first trip, was quite different. As a college student in the early 1970s, I experimented perhaps a dozen times with psychedelics. By then, however, they'd long since been made illegal, and people were talking less about their transformative potential than about their recreational value. I never took seriously the possibility that my experiences on these drugs might have any larger meaning or any practical usefulness in my life. In the aftermath of certain psychedelic trips, I could sometimes recall a sense that I'd experienced something more essential in myself—a level of connectedness, fearlessness, and authenticity that was new for me. But by the time I came down each time, I was utterly at a loss to recapture the *felt* experience of these epiphanies. It was not unlike the experience of waking up from a moving and vividly believable dream, only to have it suddenly vanish from consciousness—the sole trace a wistful sense that something meaningful has been lost.

On one occasion in college, I set out to preserve any significant insights I might have during one trip. I hooked up a tape recorder, and once the drug came on, I began recording my thoughts each time something important occurred to me. However, when I listened to the tape the next morning, the words were embarrassing. Some of what I had said was simply incomprehensible, while the rest was full of the sort of oversimplified platitudes that you typically find on greeting cards and in fortune cookies. It didn't occur to me then that my experience might have been ineffable—that language simply couldn't explain the feelings and insights I was having in this altered state. In any event, I lacked the tools to usefully incorporate what I was experiencing into my life. Instead, my friends and I treated tripping as escape, akin to a supercharged day at an amusement park.

Alpert took his psychedelic visions far more seriously. He had turned to this tool for shifting consciousness at a time of intense dissatisfaction with his life, in the explicit hope that the experience

33

on drugs might provide some alternative answers. He and his Harvard colleagues quickly envisioned psychedelics as a way to part the curtain of everyday consciousness, to enter a different, broader, and more satisfying level of reality. They were after nothing less than transformation. Very quickly, Leary and Alpert recognized that two factors—one's initial expectations and the social context in which the drug is taken—had an enormous impact on the outcome. They termed these variables "set," meaning mindset, and "setting," or the particular environment.

The drugs, Alpert soon concluded, served primarily to open a person up, removing the barriers that thinking usually places in the way of direct perception and the deepest emotions. Once this opening occurred, any number of things could happen. The possibilities ranged from the grief of facing new and painful truths about one's life, to the sublime joy of transcending boundaries and feeling deeply connected to others. "If a trip was gently guided, you could get a verification of the deepest parts of your being," Alpert told me. "You would also get a lot of pain and sadness about how far afield you'd gotten from yourself, a deepened appreciation of your predicament. And you would come out with a feeling that you were going to change—with some initial enthusiasm and energy."

Leary, Alpert, Barron, and a rapidly growing cadre of graduate students began spending more of their time together taking psychedelics. At the height of their project, twelve of fifteen new graduate students in the psychology department at Harvard applied to work with them. Increasingly those on the project preferred each other's company, both professionally and personally. "It was as if we'd discovered a new country and evolved not just a new language but a whole new set of beliefs, values, and customs," Alpert explained. What they didn't foresee was how much this work would alienate their nondrug-taking colleagues and friends. "It completely divided the world for us between those who had turned on and those who had not," Alpert told me. "It was impossible to fully appreciate what happened in a shifted state of consciousness without actually entering one. What we were experiencing *began* where Western psychology left off."

The experience of psychedelics, Leary and Alpert believed, pointed to a reality that superseded ordinary experience. While it wasn't clear to them at the time, this view represented a classic choosing up of sides. No sooner had they discovered a more selfless, spiritual perspective than they began to denigrate the insights of Western psychology and the importance of understanding the issues of personality and the unconscious. They also began to debunk the rational mind as a barrier to direct perception. Nor was Leary, for one, much interested in using traditional scientific methods to study psychedelics. What happened on these trips was nearly impossible to quantify, he concluded, and thus there was no reason to even try. Frank Barron disagreed. He was already concerned about how much psilocybin Leary was taking. To assure continued support from Harvard, he insisted, it was important to follow scientific protocols. When he couldn't prevail, Barron began to pull away from the work, and after a year he quit and returned to Stanford. Alpert took over as senior project adviser—less inclined to confront Leary over his excesses and willing instead to support him as a mad genius with a higher vision.

"I became a kind of base camp person keeping the finances and structure and interface with the university together," Alpert told me. "I was willing to define my life entirely in terms of support of Tim's creativity. I didn't believe I was creative at all. I felt I was just a politically shrewd Jewish neurotic achiever. Meanwhile, Tim went further and further out. It wasn't until three years later that I realized I was screwing myself by going along." Sure enough, by allying himself with Leary's extreme views, Alpert hastened their mutual demise at Harvard. In turn, this brought to an early end the promising research that Alpert had been appointed to keep on track.

In early 1961, shortly after Alpert's first trip, the Harvard team began an extraordinary program in which they administered psilocybin to the most hardened criminals in Concord Prison—

among them murderers, armed robbers, and heroin dealers. The historical rate of recidivism for these inmates was over 70 percent. "Our idea was to see if by changing their consciousness, they would view their whole predicament differently," he explained. "Could we get them to see their lives in a broader context that made them want to change?" Standard personality tests were administered to prisoners both before and after their drug experiences. Because Leary believed in the importance of establishing an atmosphere of mutual trust, he and others on the research team took the drugs along with the imprisoned subjects, and they tripped together inside a locked room.

It was a daring, dangerous experiment—and despite the absence of any comparative control group, the early results were intriguing. After just three sessions, the inmates evidenced an unmistakable transformation both in their behavior and in their psychological test scores. They scored lower on depression, hostility, and antisocial tendencies and higher in energy, responsibility, and cooperation. A separate follow-up program for parolees was established. By the second year of the program, only ten percent of those who'd participated in the drug experiments had returned to prison.

Even at that, David McClelland's misgivings about Leary and Alpert's research grew. As he put it in a memo distributed to the faculty meeting in October 1962 and quoted in Jay Stevens's brilliant book about the era, *Storming Heaven:* "The history of the project has been marred by repeated casual ingestion of the drug, group decisions which are not carried out, etc. . . . One can hardly fail to infer that one effect of the drug is to decrease responsibility or increase impulsivity."

During this same period, both Leary and Alpert became increasingly interested in the spiritual dimensions of their consciousness-altering experiments. They were especially fascinated by the parallels between their psychedelic experiences and the descriptions of authentic spiritual realization in the mystical literature. At the initial urging of Frank Barron, Leary, Alpert, and others began reading a syllabus that included William James's

Varieties of Religious Experience, as well as Buddhist, Taoist, and Sufi texts. They also read classic Eastern spiritual teachings including the *Bhagavad Gita,* the *Visuddhi Maga,* and the *Tibetan Book of the Dead.* The latter, in particular, detailed the mystical description of the process of death and rebirth in a way that tracked precisely the changes of consciousness they were all experiencing on psilocybin. Eventually, Alpert, Leary, and a colleague, Ralph Metzner, edited a loose translation of the *Tibetan Book of the Dead* and simply retitled it *The Psychedelic Experience.*

McClelland was equally skeptical about these insights. "It is probably no accident," he wrote in the same memo to the faculty, "that the society which most consistently encouraged the use of these substances, India, produced one of the sickest social orders ever created by mankind, in which thinking men spent their time lost in the Buddha position under the influence of drugs exploring consciousness, while poverty, disease, social discrimination and superstition reached their highest and most organized form in all history."

Alpert heard McClelland's criticisms and set out both to make his team's approach to data collection and research more professional, and to mend fences with Harvard administration officials. At the same time, as word of his and Leary's research spread, two eminent religious scholars were drawn to it. Huston Smith was the forty-three-year-old chairman of the philosophy department at MIT, a comparative religion scholar, and a prolific author. Walter Houston Clark was a sixty-two-year-old professor who taught the psychology of religion both at Harvard and at Andover-Newton Theological Seminary. Both men wanted to know more about the capacity of psychedelics to facilitate transcendental experiences. Smith himself began running psilocybin sessions for students in his MIT seminars on mysticism, while Clark actually joined Alpert and Leary's Harvard project.

So did a young physician named Walter Pahnke, who was in the midst of getting his doctorate at the Harvard Divinity School. After meeting Alpert and Leary, Pahnke decided to base his thesis on a rigorous, clinically controlled study of the capacity of a psychedelic drug to prompt an authentic mystical experience. He set as the date for his experiment Good Friday 1962 and chose as his setting the Marsh Chapel church basement at Boston University. There, while the holiday service in the church was broadcast over speakers, he planned to gather twenty divinity students provided by Walter Clark. Half of them would be given psilocybin, and half a placebo. As the date grew closer, Harvard administrators grew more uneasy. At the last minute the university refused to release any psilocybin for the Good Friday study. Leary and his cohorts wouldn't be deterred. They simply went out and bought the psilocybin that they needed on the street.

The study couldn't have come off better. It was quickly apparent which students had been given the drug. They began wandering around the basement singing and chanting as the service played over the loudspeakers, while the members of the placebo group simply sat quietly. Later, all the subjects were asked to fill out detailed questionnaires describing their experiences. Pahnke then asked theologians unfamiliar with the study to assess the subjects' responses, using a system for rating mystical experiences that had been developed by several Western religion scholars. There were eight characteristics: the experience of unity between the subject and the universe; certainty of the knowledge obtained; transcendence of space and time; a feeling of sacredness; paradoxicality in terms of ordinary thinking; ineffability; transiency; and lasting positive changes in attitude and behavior as a result of the experience.

Nine of the ten students who took the drug were judged to have had authentic mystical experiences. Only one of the ten placebo subjects described anything similar. Twenty years later, a researcher resurveyed most of the members of the original Good Friday group and found that all of those who took the psilocybin believed that the positive effects of that single experience had endured in their lives. Leary and Alpert, for their part, came to believe that psychedelics provided a quick route to the sort of wisdom that practices such as long-term meditation were intended to cultivate.

The novelist, philosopher, and visionary Aldous Huxley wrote the definitive Western text on this subject. Although he is perhaps best known as the author of *Brave New World*, Huxley published *The Perennial Philosophy* in 1948. The book was a scholarly attempt to demonstrate that at the basis of all enduring religious traditions, there lies a single shared view of divine reality. Only when the mind is in a state of detachment, clarity, and humility, Huxley argued, can this reality be apprehended. Huxley, it so happened, was teaching down the street at MIT when Leary and Alpert began their drug research, and he soon became perhaps their most famous supporter. His own interest in psychedelics had preceded theirs, and he described his first such experience in a slim volume entitled *The Doors of Perception*. Published in 1954, the book recounted Huxley's initial trip on mescaline—a synthetic version of the active ingredient in the peyote plant.

Huxley made an elegant case that under the right circumstances, consciousness-altering drugs had the power to enhance perception, broaden awareness, and tap more of our highest possibilities as human beings. The book was especially notable because Huxley himself was such a clear-headed, careful, and provocative thinker. "To be shaken out of the ruts of ordinary perception," he wrote, "to be shown for a few timeless hours the outer and the inner world, not as they appear to an animal obsessed with survival or to a human being obsessed with words and notions, but as they are apprehended, directly and unconditionally . . . this is an experience of inestimable value to everyone. We must intensify our ability to look at the world directly and not through that half opaque medium of concepts, which distorts every given fact into the all too familiar likeness of some generic label or explanatory abstraction."

Much as Huxley believed that serious research into psychedelics was essential, he also recognized that the issue was threatening to the established order and therefore potentially incendiary.

He warned Leary about this frequently, but to no avail. "I am very fond of Tim," he wrote to a friend in 1962, "but why, oh why does he have to be such an ass? I have told him repeatedly that the only attitude for a researcher in this ticklish field is that of an anthropologist living in the midst of a tribe of potentially dangerous savages. Go about your business quietly . . . don't break the taboos or criticize the locally accepted dogmas. Be polite and friendly—and get on with the job."

Leary would have none of it. To the contrary, he was increasingly drawn to what he called "naturalistic research"—which meant giving the drug to people in a variety of settings and asking only that they provide brief written reports on what they'd experienced. Most of his colleagues viewed this approach as slipshod and scientifically useless. Alpert, for his part, made a modest effort to pull together some statistics from their highly informal research, including the fact that 61 of the first 98 subjects who took psilocybin reported "insights that resulted in positive changes in their lives." He then detailed a series of examples from their descriptions. Even so, this was pretty thin evidence, and Alpert delivered it in memo form rather than in any sort of formal paper. The truth was that the scene around Leary and Alpert was more akin to an endless, hip party. People ranging from Allen Ginsberg to Alan Watts, Jack Kerouac to jazzman Maynard Ferguson, all stopped by to offer their minds up to the psilocybin experience.

When it became clear that the growing opposition to their work demanded some sort of dramatic response, Alpert found that he couldn't turn against Leary to save himself. "I felt in my heart that if I negated the truth of what I'd experienced for my social and political benefit," he told me, "it would dishonor the inner truth I'd discovered. My experiences with drugs had made my life so beautiful and rich that I couldn't walk away from that truth." Harvard finally made the choice for Alpert. He was fired in May 1963, on the grounds that he'd violated university policy by giving psilocybin to an undergraudate. It was precisely the unregulated use of these powerful drugs that most frightened

Harvard administrators. That same month, Leary was relieved of his teaching duties, on the technical grounds that he failed to show up for classes.

McClelland was discouraged by the demise of the two men he'd recruited to Harvard. "It tears my heart to see what's happened to them," he said at the time. "They started out as good scientists. They've become cultists." The irony is that by refusing to accept any limits, Leary and Alpert forfeited a unique opportunity—the chance to systematically demonstrate the value of psychedelics within the confines of the country's most prestigious and respected university. Instead, the highly public controversy they created became a factor in the eventual government ban on all psychedelics.

In the meantime, Leary and Alpert set out after leaving Harvard to publicly promote psychedelic research through their own organization, the International Foundation for Internal Freedom (IFIF). After being deported from several countries—among them Mexico, Antigua, and Dominica—they eventually ended up at a huge estate in Millbrook, New York, which belonged to a wealthy friend. For a time, they paid lip service to a loose form of research. In reality, the Millbrook house served as a new place in which artists, intellectuals, and hippies could come on weekends, hang out, and take psychedelics in a hospitable setting. Meanwhile, Leary and Alpert slowly drifted apart. In 1965, while traveling across the border from Texas to Mexico, Leary was arrested for possession of a small vial of marijuana that his daughter had actually been carrying. He might have gotten off with a small penalty had he not insisted on turning the bust into a high-profile constitutional case. After a long fight, he was ultimately sentenced to ten years in prison. He managed to escape after serving less than three months and spent the next several years as a fugitive in Europe. Leary's main claim to fame during the period after he left Harvard was the phrase that he came up with while showering one morning in 1966: "Turn on, tune in, drop out." In retrospect, it was not so much a call to higher consciousness as a plea for regression to the freedom of childhood.

Meanwhile, Alpert's belief in the transformative power of psychedelics was fading. "After six years," he told me, "I realized that no matter how high I got, I came down. It was as if you came into the kingdom of heaven, and you saw how it all was, and you felt these new states of awareness, and then you got cast out again." Alpert had mistaken glimpses of higher possibilities, he came to believe, for enlightenment. "We did cultivate an appreciation of other planes of consciousness through these drugs," he explained. "In addition, a whole range of things were intensified by people's inner experiences on psychedelics. They became more willing to trust their own intuitive sense of justice and freedom as opposed to accepting the social and political structures they were living in. But we didn't integrate these insights, and we didn't have the discipline to use them in our lives. We were also very naive about how fast change could happen in those years. We felt a shift, but it wasn't pure in us."

A small number of researchers persisted in believing that psychedelics had enduring transformative powers. Perhaps the most thoughtful and serious-minded was Stanislav Grof, a Czechoslovakian psychiatrist who first began researching LSD in Prague in the 1950s. In 1967, Grof moved to the United States to continue his work at Johns Hopkins University and the Maryland Psychiatric Research Center—one of the few institutions where such research was still being permitted. He focused on the use of LSD as a psychotherapeutic tool. If Leary and Alpert were quintessential renegades, Grof was the straightest of arrows. Square-jawed, handsome, and powerfully built, his personal style is cool, highly focused, and distant. I found it difficult to make any strong connection with him, but friends invariably describe Grof as kind and generous and attribute his coolness to the instinctive reserve of his Eastern European upbringing.

Born in 1931 to a chemist father and a concert pianist mother, Grof had both scientific and artistic inclinations as a child. He drew and painted but also performed well academically and began medical school at the age of eighteen along with his undergraduate work. He also began reading Freud. "I was enthused by his theory of psychoanalysis," he told me. "In practice, however, I saw that it was painfully ineffective, as well as very time consuming and expensive." Grof was working as a student volunteer in the psychiatric department at Prague's Charles School of Medicine in 1954 when a package arrived from Sandoz Laboratories. It contained a new psychoactive drug, LSD-25, which had first been synthesized by a Swiss chemist named Albert Hoffman in 1938. Sandoz was interested in feedback about LSD's effects, much as it was later about psilocybin.

Ever curious himself, Grof volunteered to be a subject. His first trip included many of the sensations that Huxley, Leary, and Alpert would all describe: heightened perception, intense emotions, and a flood of early memories. At one point, Grof felt himself literally catapulted out of his body, whirling through the cosmos and experiencing a universe far beyond himself. What interested him most, however, was the power of LSD to provide a direct doorway to the recesses of the unconscious. "I felt strongly," he wrote later, "that LSD-assisted analysis could deepen, intensify and accelerate the therapeutic process." Appointed to oversee a clinical study, Grof began running carefully supervised LSD sessions for patients with a variety of psychological disorders. Rather than simply remembering and talking about childhood experiences and traumas, as patients did in traditional psychoanalysis, those on LSD found themselves regressing and vividly reliving their early experiences.

Grof began to see a pattern in LSD sessions. As the sessions continued, patients moved from reexperiencing childhood events to even earlier memories that psychoanalysis couldn't account for. Many subjects literally found themselves reliving the experience of birth—and all of the terrifying trauma often thought to be associated with that process. In addition, a significant percentage of people ultimately broke through into a transpersonal realm, in which they reported the feelings of unity, transcendence of time and space, awe and ecstacy that Leary and Alpert later described.

As a Freudian, Grof had been trained to view these bizarre states as either psychotic or as fantasy. Still, he was astonished by the impact that the LSD trips had on his patients' lives. "Difficult symptoms that had resisted months and even years of conventional treatment often disappeared," he wrote. Eventually, Grof speculated that the emergence of this material under the influence of LSD "may actually be the organism's radical effort to free itself from the effects of various traumas, simplify its functioning and heal itself."

One of the most profound experiences for patients, Grof eventually reported, were the encounters they had with their own death. What actually seemed to die for patients, he discovered, was the ego or the "false" self—"a sense of general inadequacy, a need to be prepared for all possible dangers, a compulsion to be in charge and in control, [and] constant efforts to prove things to oneself and others." In short, what died, as it did in Alpert's first trip, was the self-image that people had nurtured and defended throughout their lives—and wrongly assumed to be their true identities. Grof insisted that these profound changes endured for many of his patients. For those who truly went through the death experience on LSD, he reported, the terror of confronting ego death ultimately gave way to visions of intense white light and a sense of joy and rebirth. In turn, he said, this led many subjects to a more loving and compassionate appreciation of their fellow human beings and of the universe.

"Worldly ambitions, competitive drives, and cravings for status, power, fame, prestige and possessions tend to fade away," Grof wrote. Over a period of twenty years, Grof systematically collected and categorized two thousand clinical accounts of LSD experiences and identified their common themes. Unfortunately, neither Grof nor any other investigator did any clinically controlled research. His description of LSD's positive effects on patients—including positive results based on eighteen-month follow-ups—was fascinating, but it was still ultimately anecdotal and inconclusive. In the end, his work never attracted mainstream scientific attention.

E ager to assess these experiences for myself, I considered taking psychedelics under the supervision of someone like Grof or Ram Dass. Eventually, though, I concluded that neither my mindset nor the atmosphere in the culture made this an attractive option. Psychedelics have long since been made illegal, and taking them illicitly didn't seem the ideal way to make deep forays into my psyche. Even Ram Dass discouraged me. "Ours is not the right kind of cultural set for doing this sort of work," he said. "To do it in a paranoid setting, you're asking for trouble." I also realized that as I'd grown older and taken on more responsibilities, I wasn't so willing to experiment with a powerful drug whose effect couldn't be predicted. It turned out, however, that there was an alternative. After LSD was completely banned by the government even for research purposes in the mid-1970s, Grof himself began searching for ways to prompt dramatic shifts of consciousness without drugs. Together with his wife Christina, he developed a technique that he eventually named holotropic breathing. By the time I signed up for one of his workshops, several thousand people had tried the technique.

The Grofs' method is built around a basic form of intense breathing that has been used in many mystical traditions, from Kundalini yoga to Taoist meditation and most notably as part of the Indian science of breathing known as pranayama. In the west, Wilhelm Reich was among the first to observe that psychological resistance often shows up in the form of restricted breathing—and that faster, deeper breathing often loosens the defenses and provides unusual access to the unconscious. Influenced by all these methods and by a more modern technique called rebirthing that seeks specifically to evoke the birth experience, the Grofs developed an approach that involves increasing the rate, intensity, and duration of breathing.

In October 1990, I traveled to a retreat center called the

Institute for Mentalphysics, near Palm Springs, California, to take the Grofs' workshop. I was joined by more than 150 fellow seekers, each of whom paid $575 for a six-day program. I felt immediately comfortable in the desert setting. The air was crisply clean, the sun was bright and hot, and the vistas were starkly beautiful. A dozen forms of cactus dotted a flat pastel landscape that extended as far as one could see in every direction. The small discussion group to which I was assigned included a social worker, two psychologists, a psychiatrist, a Buddhist monk, and a retired forest ranger. The week was composed of meditation and lectures, but the main attraction for nearly everyone was the breathing sessions.

As preparations began on the first afternoon, the meeting hall in which we gathered took on the atmosphere of an air-raid shelter temporarily housing a crush of people jockeying for a place to sleep. Each of us was paired with a partner. Sessions took place lying down, which meant that some seventy-five people, dressed mostly in sweats and leotards, staked out small areas of the large room. Next, they proceeded to set up small forts composed of pillows, mattresses, blankets, cups of water, Kleenex, and even airline-style plastic bags—just in case the going got tough. Our instructions were notable mostly for their simplicity. The highly accelerated breathing was intended to induce a shift in consciousness. Such breathing has no deleterious physiological consequences, Grof assured us. A carefully chosen program of mostly classical music would play over huge speakers at the front of the room while we did our breathing. The music, he explained, had been chosen to enhance and to pace our experience—starting out with driving, evocative pieces, then quieting in intensity as the hours passed.

The key, we were told, is to be open and nondirective. "Don't do anything until it starts to *do* you," Grof instructed us. "The healing intelligence is part of our own deeper intelligence. The goal of the breathing is to shift attention away from analysis and intellect, to your body and emotions. You have to be adventurous about letting it happen. If you try to think while it's happening, you effectively block the experience." As unconscious material got freed up and came to the surface, Grof explained, we should expect all kinds of seemingly extreme and even bizarre behavior to emerge—tears, rage, physical contortions, age regression, spontaneous dancing, even speaking in tongues. The more we were able to give up conscious control and simply let go, he said, the deeper our experience would be. "This is a technique designed to activate the unconscious and let it take its own course," Grof went on. "Breathing brings repressed emotions to the surface. Our premise is that the only way to resolve these feelings is to fully experience them. Society has a lot of rules about what is acceptable to express, what is civilized, but that just prevents us from owning our own elemental forces. Don't have rules about what is acceptable. Initial turmoil is common. Just continue breathing. It may get worse before it gets better. Let it build up and resolve by itself."

Sometimes, Grof warned, the powerful emotions triggered by the breathing and the music don't fully resolve themselves and instead get stuck in a painful physical form—anything ranging from muscle spasms to headaches. In such cases, he explained, the group of facilitators around the room were all trained in something he termed "focused bodywork." Borrowing again from Reich, this technique involves releasing emotional blocks by focusing on their physical manifestations. Facilitators, Grof later told me, are trained to apply exaggerated physical pressure to the area where the breather is feeling pain, in an effort to help release it—along with the underlying blocked emotion. "Your body decides for itself what is best," Grof said. "There is a deep wisdom operating within you that knows how to get rid of tension and aggression, if you let it."

I decided to ask my more experienced partner to do the first breathing session. Alice (not her real name) was a woman in her fifties who made her living doing a form of hands-on bodywork called "energy balancing." She'd tried a variety of consciousness-altering techniques, including a previous holotrophic breathing workshop, which she attended with her husband. Unlike me, she didn't seem a bit apprehensive. My job, serving as a sitter, was to make sure that Alice kept up an accelerated pattern of breathing and to provide anything that she needed to help make her feel comfortable. If she developed a problem—fear or pain or loss of control—I was free to call over one of the facilitators stationed around the room.

To my astonishment, within minutes after the session began plaintive wails and piercing cries of agony arose from various pockets of the room. When I stood up to get a better look, discreetly trying to appear as if I just needed to stretch, I could see people writhing on the floor in a variety of contorted positions. Over the next several hours, I heard every imaginable sound: screaming, chanting, incomprehensible guttural chatter, and baby talk, as well as delighted laughter and sounds of apparent ecstasy. I saw people shaking, twitching, grimacing, gagging, and rocking from side to side. It was like watching an animated Hieronymus Bosch painting.

At least two breathers got so physically worked up that it took two facilitators to restrain them. Some of the men ripped off their shirts, although I was struck that no women were prompted to similar lack of inhibition. Men and women alike stood up and broke into dance, many with their eyes closed. Others lay in absolute stillness, breathing deeply but barely moving. My partner Alice seemed to shift states, quiet for a time with a blissful look on her face, then suddenly waving her arms and yelling angrily. A couple of times when she seemed to be in some pain, I called over the nearest facilitator, but I was assured that it was best to interfere as little as possible. Alice and most of the others stayed at it for more than four hours. When she finally opened her eyes and told me that she thought she was finished, I felt relieved. Alice seemed exhausted, having obviously ridden an emotional roller coaster. We didn't talk much as we walked out.

That evening, my group sat around with Pat McCallister, our facilitator, who had studied under Grof and had done dozens of breathing sessions herself. Enthusiastic and nurturing, she made me feel immediately comfortable. The tales that members of my group told were almost surreal—trips taken to other galaxies and descents into a hellish underworld. One woman described seeing angels, others experienced moments of joyous transcendence, and still others described feeling a deep meditative serenity. There were also reports of bizarre bodily sensations and long-repressed memories that had come bubbling to the surface. The breathers who had the most unusual experiences seemed the most satisfied. All but one or two felt they'd derived some benefit from the process.

By the next day, when my turn came, I felt the sort of anticipatory anxiety I associated with the locker room before high school basketball games. I made myself comfortable in a pile of pillows, Alice by my side. It didn't take long before breathing intensely became almost automatic for me. A short time into the session, I found myself traveling back to college and unexpectedly reliving the romantic relationship that had ended so unhappily. I thought I'd long since left all that behind me. Instead, a series of images from our time together flashed vividly before my eyes. Some were joyous, but others brought back a searing feeling of loss and abandonment that I sensed immediately was mixed up with similar experiences from my childhood. At this point, I realized that tears were streaming down my face. I was experiencing a level of grief that was rare for me. I also became aware that I usually held feelings like these at a careful distance, precisely to avoid this sort of pain.

Alice didn't say anything, but I was comforted to have her there. I never exhibited any of the extreme behaviors I'd observed in others the previous day. Nor, to my disappointment, did I travel to any higher realms or enjoy any soaring visions. I wasn't even moved to get up and dance. What I did feel was unusually relaxed, at ease, and at home in my own body. For several hours, my ordinary self-consciousness let down, and my relentless internal dialogue ceased. I was able to freely experience the images and sensations that arose. If nothing else, the first session had a loosening effect on me. I felt less standoffish, more open, and warmer.

To some extent, the depth of my feelings also frightened me. In my second session two days later, I found it much harder to let go and permit the experience to unfold on its own. My usual fears and defenses against giving up control reasserted themselves. I wasn't prepared to trust entirely that it was safe to let whatever might come up do so freely. Each time I came near something emotionally charged, I instinctively backed off by breathing less deeply. I was more comfortable with the familiar sensation of holding emotions at a distance than with taking the risk of exploring them. The one feeling I did have, after an extended time breathing, was a vague sense of deprivation. I wasn't even sure what it was that I felt deprived of. When I tried to locate the feeling physically, I became aware that it was in my heart and that it took the form of tightness.

Toward the end of my session, I mentioned this to Alice. She suggested that I try some of the focused bodywork that Grof had spoken about. Alice called over two facilitators, including Pat, who led my small group, and a man named Sheelo Bohm. Together they stood over my chest. As they pushed their hands down on me, I was instructed to breathe out hard into their pressure. Very quickly and to my surprise, the pain shifted into my head, a kind of knot around my temples. Sheelo then began to apply pressure there. As I breathed into his hands—and he exhorted me to push even harder—I felt a totally unexpected surge of emotion. "Why are you doing this?" I heard myself screaming in the plaintive voice of a child. "I'm doing the best I can." Next, I felt a wave of sadness and bewilderment and a sense of being overwhelmed. Sheelo kept up the pressure and encouraged me to keep breathing. Finally, and just as suddenly, I felt yet another intense rush of emotion—this time the helpless feeling that I was being taken advantage of. A fierce anger welled up, and I had an urgent desire to fight back and push him off me. I was so absorbed in the experience that I became convinced Sheelo was literally trying to take advantage of me—to hurt me without cause. I felt like an innocent abused victim. Eventually, I realized, the pressure in my head gave way, and I simply felt spent—and cleansed.

I knew immediately that I had touched some deep, primitive, and early experiences in my life, even though I couldn't locate them specifically. I also knew that I'd discovered a window into emotions—helplessness, dependence, and fear—that I rarely allowed myself to feel. But what I finally got was no more than a glimpse, much the way that Alpert talked about being opened to a new level of awareness by psychedelics, only to be cast back into ordinary reality after the drug wore off. There was no question that the Grof's work had the potential to uncover long-repressed emotions by cutting through the mind's everyday defenses. But the technique did little, I felt, to address the role of the mind in processing any new insights that arose. Only much later, while trying another kind of work aimed at accessing deep emotions, did I began to understand precisely what childhood memories had been triggered by the holotrophic breathing and how to integrate this understanding more usefully into my life.

B y 1967, Richard Alpert was looking for more enduring answers. He had mixed emotions about making his living lecturing on psychedelics, given his own doubts that the higher states of consciousness experienced on drugs endured after the high wore off. When a wealthy friend named David Padwe invited Alpert to take a trip to India, Alpert jumped at the opportunity. Perhaps there, he decided, he might find the answers that still seemed so elusive. Padwe had made his fortune selling his small company to Xerox, and he intended to travel in style. He arranged to have a Land-Rover flown to Tehran, and from there, he and Alpert began a first-class journey through the East. By this stage in his life, Alpert had read much of the classical eastern literature, studied the maps of higher consciousness, and taken countless psychedelic visits to the promised land. Still, he didn't feel particularly wise or enlightened, and he was once again on the lookout for a mentor or a teacher.

It was several months later that Alpert found himself sitting in the Blue Tibetan Restaurant in Katmandu, when a rail-thin, six-foot-seven-inch man with a long blond beard walked in and sat down at his table. The man called himself Bhagwan Das. It later turned out he was a twenty-three-year-old former surfer from Laguna Beach, California, but Alpert instantly felt he was in the presence of someone who knew more than he did. For the next six days, Bhagwan Das joined Alpert and Padwe in their hotel suite, talking to them about esoteric mystical texts and teaching them meditation and yoga. When Padwe announced that he'd decided to make Japan the next stop on his itinerary, Alpert elected instead to join Bhagwan Das on a pilgrimage to Indian temples—by foot. Alpert was compelled to travel light: a shoulder bag of belongings, a bottle of LSD, and a small sum of money.

In the early part of their travels, Alpert would start to recount tales from his past as they walked. Each time, Bhagwan Das gently waved him off. "Don't think about the past," he said. "Be here now." Or: "Don't think about the future. Be here now." It was disorienting. "He had just sort of wiped out my whole game," Alpert told me. "I was, after all, a great storyteller." At the same time, Alpert was awed by how serence and satisfied Bhagwan Das always seemed, how little he needed, and how at home he was wherever they went. After nearly three months of wandering from temple to temple, Bhagwan Das announced one day that he needed to see his own guru. He and Alpert headed back to Bareilly, picked up the Land-Rover that Moore had left behind, and drove a hundred miles to a tiny temple in the Himalayas.

No sooner had they arrived than Bhagwan Das jumped out, tears pouring down his face. He rushed up to a little old man who was sitting cross-legged on the ground, and fell to his knees bowing. The old man was called Maharajji ("Great King"), and at first Alpert simply assumed that he was a clever hustler. They'd barely been introduced when the guru asked sweetly if Alpert might give him the Land-Rover as a present. But when Alpert demurred, Maharajji seemed unperturbed. Instead, he requested that the new arrivals be fed. Later the same day, Alpert was called back to see the guru. Through an interpreter, Maharajji proceeded to describe precisely what Alpert had been doing the previous evening, including the fact that he'd been thinking about his dead mother. Maharajji also noted, accurately, that Alpert's mother had died the previous year from an unusual illness of the spleen—something Alpert had never discussed with anyone in India.

As Maharajji made these revelations, the effect on Alpert was overwhelming. "I felt this extremely violent pain in my chest and a tremendous wrenching feeling, and I started to cry. And I cried and I cried and I cried," he later wrote. "The only thing I could say was it felt like I was home. Like the journey was over. Like I had finished." Much as he had on other occasions, Alpert concluded that he'd found a powerful man who had the answers he'd long been seeking. The morning after their first meeting, Alpert was called back to see Maharajji. The first thing the guru did was ask Alpert to fetch the "medicine." Alpert was baffled until someone suggested that the guru meant the LSD he'd been carrying. When Alpert returned, Maharajji pointed to the LSD and said, "Gives you siddhis?" He was using the Sanskrit word for nonordinary powers that emerge in other states of consciousness, among them the psychic capacity that Maharajji had earlier demonstrated.

To Alpert's amazement, Maharajji proceeded to swallow nearly a thousand milligrams of LSD, twenty times a typical first-time dose. For the next several hours, nothing happened. Whatever higher states of consciousness that LSD opens up, Alpert concluded, they were ones that Maharajji lived in without drugs. The experience confirmed his sense that he was in the presence of someone extraordinary. In fact, nearly all of the Eastern traditions warn against being beguiled by the *siddhis*. There is general consensus that while nonordinary powers frequently arise in the course of spiritual practice, treating them as special only diverts energy from seeking one's essence or true nature. This true nature, in turn, doesn't necessarily have anything to do with the capacity to demonstrate special powers.

Looking back, Ram Dass told me that he was moved not just by Maharajji's demonstration of *siddhis* but by the intensity of love he felt from him and by the guru's apparent nonattachment to worldly needs and desires. Trusting his instincts and setting aside his doubts, Alpert asked no further questions following their first meeting and instead became a faithful disciple. He was given a small room and simple clothing and put under the guidance of a yogi who instructed him daily in meditating, chanting, and hatha yoga—the yoga of physical movement. He was also given spiritual lessons, mostly in the form of pithy aphorisms that his yogi wrote in chalk on a blackboard. Much later, Alpert realized that these were the teachings of raja yoga—a highly detailed system for reaching enlightenment that was first developed by the Indian wise man Patanjali, somewhere between 500 B.C. and A.D. 500. Alpert felt he'd finally discovered the real thing. On one occasion, he asked Maharajji whether taking LSD had any value in the search for wisdom. It could be useful, the guru told him, as a way to strengthen his faith that higher states of consciousness exist. But in the end, the guru told him, drugs were not a route to true enlightenment. "It is better to become Christ than to visit him," he said, "and your medicine won't do that for you."

Alpert was taken to see Maharajji perhaps a half-dozen times in eight months, and the encounters were always brief. Once the guru asked him, "You like to feed children?" Alpert had always loved children and answered yes. Then the guru asked, "You make people laugh?" Alpert nodded. "Good," said Maharajji, who then tapped him on the head three times. Alpert walked out feeling inexplicably ecstatic. These cryptic exchanges he took to be messages about how to live. Another time, Maharajji said, "You know Gandhi?" When Alpert said he did, Maharajji replied: "You be like him." Alpert couldn't help smiling. "I'd like to," he said. On still another occasion, the guru gave Alpert his new Indian name, Baba Ram Dass.

He deduced from these exchanges that his role in the world was to be of service—at least in part by helping to take care of children, and by using his skills of communication to share the wisdom that he was learning at his guru's knee. The message that he eventually brought back to America—and which has remained central for him—focuses on the ways that people deceive and underestimate themselves by identifying too closely with their thoughts and concepts. "The mind is there to protect your sense of who you think you are," he told the audience at one lecture I attended. "It keeps creating models and expectations. 'I know what's happening,' it says. But you may be more than you think you are. The intellect is a subsystem of a bigger game. We're addicted to being connected to each other through thoughts and through our senses. Wisdom recognizes that you can be connected because of that part of you which is not different from others. When you fall into separateness and take that seriously, you lose wisdom. The mind is where knowledge resides, and the heart is where wisdom resides. We are afraid to open our hearts for fear that we'll have to give up our separateness and that in doing so, we'll be overwhelmed."

This vision first took shape for Ram Dass during the months that he spent studying with the yogi that Maharajji had assigned him. It was a very safe and protected world in which he subsisted. He had few responsibilities, and few material needs. His days were spent sitting in a room meditating, doing yoga, and studying. Although he didn't see Maharajji very often, he felt embraced and protected by him. In this simple environment, he felt his heart opening, his fears dropping away, his worldly desires and attachments diminishing, and his sense of separateness giving way to a broader, more connected awareness. It was, he told me, an exceptionally rich and satisfying time in his life.

E arly in my own meditation practice, I had a taste of the experience that Ram Dass described so evocatively. In retrospect, I suspect that my own powerful opening occurred partly because I knew so little about what to expect and brought so few preconceptions to the table. My experience took place in the course of a five-day retreat held in the mountains of Alta, Utah. The retreat was run by a psychologist named Joyce Goodrich, whose primary focus is on psychic healing. Specifically, she is interested whether it is possible, by moving into certain meditative states of consciousness, to affect the course of another person's illness, even from a distance. This is plainly a notion that defies any conventional scientific understanding, and I felt agnostic about it—skeptical, but open to any evidence. My primary reason for taking the seminar was that I wanted to deepen my meditation practice. Goodrich promised to teach a variety of techniques over a period of several days. Less than a year earlier, the notion of meditating for even twenty minutes would have been unthinkable. Now, I found myself exhilarated by the prospect of being able to sit in meditation, freed of other responsibilities, for upward of six or seven hours a day. I was hopeful that meditating for so many concentrated hours would help me to experience more deeply the quiet calmness, ease, and wordless well-being that I'd felt intermittently during my twenty or thirty minutes of daily meditation over the previous year.

I arrived at the Alta Peruvian Lodge on a Thursday evening. The setting, high in the mountains, was beautiful and serene. The Alta Peruvian itself was more like a college dormitory than a hotel. The furnishings in my room consisted solely of a bed and a small desk, but somehow that seemed appropriate. The fewer distractions, the better. The six other people who had come for the retreat fit no particular stereotype. They ranged from Betty, a tall, thin, energetic woman in her fifties who worked at a high-level state government job in Utah but whose primary passion was meditation and consciousness, to Jack, a carefully groomed, buttoned-up man in his early forties who lived in San Francisco, worked with computers, had never meditated, and was attending the retreat only at the urging of his girlfriend.

The first evening, we gathered in a large room and sat in a semicircle of chairs. After introducing ourselves, Goodrich spoke first about the nature of the meditative experience and its relationship to psychic healing. Drawing on the work of psychologist Lawrence Leshan, Goodrich told us how psychic healers describe their work. Healing generally occurs, she said, only when a healer shifts into a meditative state of consciousness and is able to experience humor herself and the patient as a single entity—unseparated by everyday boundaries.

Our meditative work would be aimed at nurturing this state of consciousness. After Goodrich spoke, we did several meditation exercises, each about twenty minutes long. In the first—a concentration technique not unlike the one I'd been doing on my own—we simply counted our breaths, going from one to six and then returning to one. Next, we moved to a contemplative technique: focusing on a single object—in this case, a match—and studying it with as much singular focus as possible. This was difficult, elusive, and even frustrating. I wasn't used to bringing so much attention to something so one-dimensional, and I found it nearly impossible to remain absorbed. By the time I went to bed that first evening, I realized that I'd gotten myself into something more challenging than I'd anticipated.

Beginning the next morning, we worked in three- to four-hour stretches—morning, afternoon, and evening—alternating meditations of twenty minutes to an hour with discussions about our experiences. The meditations took a variety of forms. There was more work in concentration: counting breaths, noting the breath as it entered and left the nostrils, repeating a word or a sound. There was also more contemplation—first of the match, next of our hands, and then of a picture that we looked at from close range and later at a distance. My habit in life, I began to realize, was to look at objects only to the extent necessary—and usually on the way to doing something else. I was amazed by how much more richness and detail I saw when I had no explicit agenda and really took the time to look. There were also visualization exercises. In one, we were asked to imagine a river running from the top of the Himalayas and then to place ourselves in a bank alongside the river. As thoughts and distractions arose, we were instructed to deposit them one at a time inside a log and send them down the river. It was a practice aimed at letting go of attachment, even to one's own thoughts and emotions.

Visualizing proved particularly difficult for me. I was used to thinking in words and concepts. The notion of creating a visual world inside my head was foreign to me. I tried gamely, but what most often came to me was the *concept* of a river, rather than an internal picture of one. Only much later did I learn that the brain simply doesn't produce images in a highly verbal state of mind. Truly visualizing requires a literal shift of consciousness. Sure enough, images came to me only when I managed to let go of the logical, linear world of language. I began to see how I used words and thoughts partly as a form of security and protection. Letting go of this familiar state of mind—the currency of ordinary reality—represented a scary voyage into the unknown.

For all that, the cumulative effect of the meditations began to grow on me. Both the supportive setting and the sheer time devoted to the work helped me to quiet my mind. Some time midmorning during the second full day of the retreat, I realized I was becoming deeply absorbed in certain meditations. I felt free of distraction and unusually clear and serene. I was alert but had no agenda, and I was content just to be sitting quietly. Unfortunately, it didn't last. By that same afternoon, some door inexplicably began to close, and my ordinary thoughts and emotions returned. At one point we were doing a long walking meditation in which we watched each movement we made with deliberately attentive awareness. For the first thirty minutes, it seemed to go fine. After that, however, my mind began to race, my impatience grew, and I became irritated that Goodrich would demand so much of us. It was as if my conscious mind—my personality—had suddenly balked at all this silence and giving up of conscious control.

At the time, I didn't fully realize what was happening. All I knew was that I could feel resentment and irritation kick in. That evening, I became upset after Goodrich gave an instruction for a meditation that I found confusing. I berated myself when I couldn't keep my mind from wandering off. I felt frustrated, defeated, and even angry. I was envious that it appeared to come more easily to the others, particularly Betty, who shifted easily and deeply into a quieter state, and Elaine, another group member who described vivid, detailed images whenever we did visualization exercises.

Even in my discouragement, however, I retained at least some of the more detached awareness that I'd cultivated during the earlier meditations. Much later, I came to understand this experience as the "witness" stance in meditation—the ability to watch thoughts and emotions without reacting to them so instantly and automatically. In this case, I could see that all my resentment was merely my mind's invention. No one had done anything to provoke it. The real cause of my upset was that my deeply satisfying experience earlier in the day hadn't sustained. In truly letting go of thoughts, I'd touched something new and very rewarding. But then the fear of giving up control had returned, and with it my doubts. It was paradoxical: The harder I consciously sought to reconjure the experience of letting go, the more elusive it became.

The next morning, a Sunday, I woke up shortly before seven. It was a crisp, cool, brilliantly blue day in the mountains. As I do nearly every day, I went out jogging. For the first two days in Utah, the limited oxygen at the high altitude had slowed me considerably, and I wasn't looking forward to this run. As I set out, I began to muse about the unexpected surge of anger I'd felt the previous evening. Suddenly, my eyes filled with tears. I had never cried easily or comfortably, and the tears took me by surprise. Instantly, I sensed that they were connected to the experience of letting go. All of this sustained meditation had begun to dissolve my usual ways of coping: relentless activity, constant talk, ruminating, regretting, rationalizing, and planning. As I ran, it became clear to me how much unconscious effort I expended each day just trying to feel safer, less conflicted, and more at home in the world. It's difficult to evoke in words the blend of grief, freedom from fear, and boundless love that I felt during that run. Somehow, with my normal barriers down, I gained access to deep emotions that I was not used to feeling.

The grief was connected to the burgeoning awareness of all that I'd missed by keeping such a careful distance from my feelings. The uncharacteristic fearlessness gave me the soaring, spacious sense that anything was possible. And the boundless love was most powerful of all—a feeling of my heart opening to those around me, a rare instinct to reach out and experience the best in people, to let down my barriers and judgments. By the time I returned for the morning seminar, I was feeling deeply relaxed and very happy to be with the members of our group. It wasn't that my doubts had somehow vanished. Almost immediately, I found myself looking for evidence that I might be inventing these experiences simply because I so much wanted to have them, or because I was being swept along on a wave of the group's collective enthusiasm. But as the day unfolded, there was no doubt that I'd experienced a rare shift—not just out of my mind but into my heart. More vividly than I could ever remember, nonseparateness became not just a concept but something I was experiencing palpably and directly.

The sense of being in my heart more than in my head grew as the days passed. At one point, I mentioned this to Betty, and she suggested a form of meditation that she'd fashioned for herself. Much later, I discovered that her technique was very similar to a traditional Buddhist practice known as "metta"—the Sanskrit word for love. In Betty's version, she first conjured up the image of someone very close to her. Then she imagined herself sending love to that person. Next, she saw herself receiving love from the person, and finally she imagined sending the message "I wish you well." She did this one person at a time, moving from family members, to friends and co-workers, and eventually even to people with whom she was having conflict. Sending waves of love across the landscape was new territory for me, and under ordinary circumstances, I'd have found the notion silly and even awkward. But by now, I was in my fourth day at the retreat. I felt unusually relaxed, far less quick to short-circuit my experience, and eager to cultivate the open-hearted state I'd first touched on my run.

When I thought of people in my life and simply repeated to myself the phrases that Betty suggested, I didn't feel much impact. But then I began connecting the exercise more closely to my deepest feelings. I focused on one of my daughters and tried to imagine a real-life situation in which I'd felt great love for her, and then another in which I'd felt especially loved by her. The more vividly I recalled a scene, the more satisfying the experience. It was harder to send love to some people, or to receive love from them. Often, I discovered, this was because there was some conflict in the relationship that I hadn't articulated to myself before. In some cases, I discovered that I just didn't want to send a person love, or felt it hard to accept love back. This was all occurring in my mind, of course, but it often seemed as if the person were right there with me. When I got in deep enough, the meditation seemed to have a life of its own. I could almost literally feel my heart opening.

After I'd conjured up the people I cared most about in my life and then my closest colleagues, I turned to people with whom I felt active conflict. I thought of one person in particular who had treated me with genuine malice and toward whom I felt a great deal of anger. Love was perhaps the last emotion I associated with this fellow. He'd purposely set out to hurt me—unfairly, I felt—and I'd genuinely suffered from the attack. As I sat trying to imagine a way to experience love toward him, something else came into my mind. I realized how much anger he must feel toward me, or some image he had of me, and what a toll that likely took on him. Since we hardly knew each other, I wondered how much he had projected onto me aspects of himself that he found unacceptable. Experiencing all this from his point of view suddenly made me feel that his hostility was creating more misery for him than it was for me. I didn't get a sudden urge to invite him to dinner, but I did find myself able to feel compassion for him, even to send him love. It shocked me to see that a simple change in my own way of perceiving a situation could prompt such a powerful emotional shift. It also showed me how easy it is to get locked into habitual, defensive patterns that diminished my ability to remain open and compassionate.

When it came time to receive love back from this person, I couldn't kid myself that he felt any love or compassion for me. I opted instead for a slight modification of Betty's instruction. "I accept whatever love you have to give me," I told myself. That, too, seemed to take. At first, I was reluctant even to tell this story to friends, because it seemed so soft-headed and improbable. But in time, I realized that I'd made some sort of powerful and positive connection with my former nemesis. From that day on, I never again felt any significant anger toward him. Although we never spoke about my experience, he stopped lashing out at me. As the years went by and I occasionally heard something about his life, I was always surprised to discover that I bore him no ill will and even felt some inexplicable bond—as if the challenge of successfully making my peace with him had given us common ground.

By the time I left the retreat, I was more relaxed, less defensive, and more open-hearted than I could ever remember feeling. I'd experienced a sustained state of consciousness in which the boundaries that typically separated me from others had largely dissolved. In the days after my return home, even my most hardheaded friends and colleagues sensed a glow in me that they found very inviting. One evening, my wife and I were invited to a dinner party, and I was seated next to the host—an aggressive lawyer disinclined to engage any vulnerable emotion, much less boundless love. I found myself describing my retreat experience to him. I made no particular effort to convince him of its authenticity, but I noticed that as I spoke, his attention grew rapt, his face visibly softened, and eventually he even began nodding his head.

The experience of the retreat stayed with me for several weeks. Over time, however, my ordinary habits and fears began to resurface. Occasionally, I could bring back some of the openness by returning to the metta meditation. Even then, I found a certain resistance to opening my heart so freely. Eventually, the experience in Utah lived on mostly in my memory—a powerful sense of having touched a more essential aspect of myself, inspiring evidence that there is the potential to connect more deeply with others. Nonetheless it remained a way of being that I couldn't yet incorporate enduringly into my everyday life.

Affter a year of meditating in India, Ram Dass experienced a powerful comeuppance when he returned to the United States in 1968. It wasn't a total surprise. Even before he left his guru, he'd felt apprehensive. "I'm too impure. It's like throwing me to the wolves," he told Maharajji. "I don't see any impurities," his guru told him. "I will never let you do anything wrong in America."

But Ram Dass had good reason to be concerned. As he put it in a lecture two years later, "It's very easy to break attachments to worldly games when you're sitting in a cave in the Himalayas. It's quite a different take you do of sex, power, money, fame, and sensual gratification in the middle of New York City in the United States with television and loving people around and great cooks and advertising and total support for all of the attachments." Ram Dass had always been compulsive in his desires, especially about sex. Once he'd returned to the land of temptation, the broader perspective of meditation didn't provide much real relief. His solution was to continue to try to live the renunciate life that he'd adopted in India—to consciously and willfully resist his intense desires. "The essence of civilization consists not in the multiplication of wants," he wrote at the time, "but in their deliberate and voluntary renunciation." The result was something of a double life—a public image at odds with his inner experience and his everyday behavior.

He had returned from India to pursue his *sadhana,* or spiritual life, in part by sharing what he'd learned with others. When *Be Here Now* became a best seller, he found himself invited to speak at universities, communes and at growth centers, in churches and Rotary Clubs, and even to doctors and psychologists at places ranging from the Menninger Foundation to Albert Einstein Medical College, where he was invited to give grand rounds. Ram Dass focused his talks on freedom from attachment—to social roles, to success, to sensual pleasure, and finally even to one's separate sense of self. He spoke about how the mind is forever an obstacle to the highest understanding—that so long as what we think and believe consciously determines our actions, we can never truly grow. "Thoughts keep us separate," he explained in *Be Here Now*. "To break your identification with your own thoughts is to achieve inner freedom." And he mused about the paradox of power: "When you have given up all of your position and power, you end up having all powers."

At the same time, he retained his very human shortcomings and self-deceptions, and he acted on them in subtle and not-so-subtle ways. He returned to his guru in India more than once, hoping to overcome his persistent desires and what he called his "impurity." But by the early 1970s, he was traveling to lectures across America with a road manager and a backup band, netting as much as $10,000 a night. While he gave most of the money away to various causes, he reveled in the attention and power that his fame brought him. David McClelland ran into Ram Dass in robes and a beard shortly after his return from India. McClelland was struck by the fact that his old friend looked and acted so differently but seemed fundamentally driven by the same forces. "He appeared to have changed in almost every way—in his appearance, his attitudes, his career and his purpose in life," McClelland wrote later. "Yet after spending some time with him, I found myself saying over and over again, 'It's the same old Dick.' He is still very much involved in high drama, just as he had always been. He is still very much involved in power games. It is only the nature of the power that has changed—from standard Western symbols of importance and influence to psychic or spiritual siddhis. [And] furthermore he still feels guilty about being so interested in power."

By the mid-1970s', Ram Dass had reached the apotheosis of his popularity. *Be Here Now* had become something of a young seekers' bible. One reason was that it told the paradigmatic story of a spiritual transformation so evocatively. It was also full of pithy stories and aphorisms about the nature of the spiritual journey, and it offered a practical and accessible guide to subjects such as meditation, renunciation, diet, *siddhis*, choosing a guru or a teacher, psychedelics, yoga, chanting, sex, and even dying. In 1974, Ram Dass spent the summer lecturing several nights a week to audiences of more than a thousand people at the Naropa

Institute in Boulder, Colorado. But even as he attracted hordes of followers, he remained filled with self-doubt. His wisdom, he felt, was thin gruel compared with the Tibetan teachings of Naropa's other star teacher, a Buddhist monk named Trungpa Rinpoche. And the renunciate life he'd chosen just wasn't taking.

"I was . . . getting caught in more worldly play," he wrote later in *Grist for the Mill,* "and I felt more and more depressed and hypocritical." Although Maharajji had died the previous year, Ram Dass decided to return to India anyway. He wasn't sure what he'd find this time, but he felt he had more spiritual work to do. When the summer ended, he began driving toward New York, where he intended to catch a plane to India. A few days before he was scheduled to leave, however, his guru came to him in a vision during a meditation in a hotel room in New Jersey. Speaking in uncharacteristically perfect English, Maharajji said, "You don't have to go to India. Your teachings will be right here."

The next day, Ram Dass arrived in New York City and called an old friend to say hello. She told him that she'd become involved with a woman who had extraordinary spiritual powers, and that Ram Dass really ought to meet her. Joya Santayana—born Joyce Green—turned out to be a Jewish housewife from Queens. In her forties, she wore heavy makeup and long false eyelashes and showed off plenty of décolletage. When Ram Dass showed up to see her the first time, Joya was in a rigid trancelike state. He looked more closely, couldn't even detect a pulse, and concluded that she had indeed moved into the spiritual state of unification known as *samadhi.* When Joya finally emerged from trance, her first words were: "What the fuck do you want?" By some odd logic, Ram Dass took this unprovoked hostility as evidence that the woman before him was no fraud. "If she were a charlatan," he explained later to a reporter, "she'd surely have tried to act more holy."

Much as he had been drawn in by Maharajji's psychic powers, Ram Dass was deeply impressed by Joya's apparent capacity to enter samadhilike states. He was also moved by her ability to shift into another voice, in which she appeared to be a channel for ancient teachings and could recite lyrical poetry for hours at a time. Joya even claimed to have the power of stigmata—the mystical capacity to bleed spontaneously in ways that mimic Christ's suffering on the cross. Although Ram Dass was well aware that even the most extraordinary *siddhis* are no evidence of enlightenment, he was seduced by them nonetheless. Over the next fifteen months, he began to study intensively with Joya, remaining by her side for up to twenty hours a day. He also declared publicly that she was an enlightened being. The result was that scores of seekers who considered Ram Dass a source of higher consciousness came to study under Joya. Her real genius, he recognized later, was to hone in on precisely the psychological needs that Ram Dass had never satisfied in himself, while packaging it all as a high spiritual teaching.

With the death of his guru, Ram Dass hungered anew for someone who seemed to have answers. Moreover, even as he lectured about the importance of moving beyond the ego, he was flattered by Joya's insistence that she was preparing him to become a world spiritual leader. In turn, Ram Dass came up with a spiritual explanation for setting aside his powers of logic and discrimination. "Surrender and devotion was a method I had opened my heart to through the teachings of my guru," he wrote later. "So this process was just a deeper letting go, a letting go of even my resistance to much of what seemed to go against common sense." He even found a convoluted way to justify a sexual relationship with Joya, despite the fact that she required all of her students to take a strict vow of celibacy and publicly took one herself. Joya professed no physical desires, and Ram Dass willingly accepted her explanation that by having sex together, she was actually teaching *him* to become just as unattached to physical desire as she claimed she was.

Still, his doubts grew in the face of her outrageous claims, and he finally turned on Joya in March, 1976. She was not an enlightened being after all, he explained in a confessional article titled "Egg on My Beard," but just another person with worldly attachments. Even her alleged powers were a hoax. Her extraordinary energy, for example, came not from her spiritual work, he concluded, but from amphetamines. "An incredible tapestry of half-truths and lies started to unravel," he wrote. "Finally, I had to admit I had conned myself." Ram Dass went on to suggest several other reasons that he'd embraced Joya, including his hunger to believe that someone could magically provide him with answers, his grandiose need to feel powerful, and his reluctance to place any faith in his logical and critical faculties. In the end, he compared his own experience to what invariably occurs in cults. "Once you are in them, they provide a total reality which has no escape clause," he wrote.

For all that, Ram Dass held on to the belief that one of his mistakes was simply choosing the wrong guru. One reason for the Joya fiasco, he concluded, was his "insufficient faith in Maharajji." Even so, the experience with Joya served as another turning point in his life. He continued to believe that the humbling experience had been valuable for him—"grist for the mill of awakening," as he put it—but he also acknowledged that others had suffered in the process. "Some seemed to have been hurt and came away from her teaching with despair, cynicism and paranoia," he said. For Ram Dass himself, the experience marked the end of his ill-fated attempt to renounce worldly desire in the name of wisdom. Over time, he began to cultivate a more balanced and complex view of the complete life. "What happened after Joya is that I finally realized that my incarnation was not an error," he told me. "I became a renunciate because I wanted to get away from my desires. But eventually I realized that I was trapped in aversion. The problem is that every time you struggle against something, you actually reinforce it. To be free, I finally realized, I had to fully participate and delight in life, rather than rejecting it. I couldn't push anything away."

The turning point was an evening Ram Dass spent drinking wine with Alan Watts, the former Episcopalian minister who helped introduce Zen to the West but continued to enjoy the sensual pleasures of a more material life. At one point late in the night, Watts said to him: "Your trouble, Richard, is that you're too attached to emptiness." For much of his life, for example, Ram Dass had searched for a sexual identity, even as he fought against his overwhelming sexual compulsiveness. All this became less preoccupying, he discovered, when he simply acknowledged his desires and finally came to terms with being gay.

Part of Ram Dass's struggle was giving up the belief that he was going to find all the answers. "The spiritual journey is a journey of continually falling on your face," he concluded in 1988, during a public panel titled "Is Enlightenment Good for Your Mental Health?" "You take a step, which you think is wise, and you blow it and you fall on your face. And you get up and brush yourself off. You sheepishly look at God and you take another step. And then you fall on your face. It's like doing prostrations all the way to heaven. . . . When I look at the path, I notice that it has a spiral rather than a circular quality. Each time I got back into meditation, I let go quicker. And each time I come out of meditation, I seem to get stuck a little less thickly, or more subtly."

The challenge, Ram Dass concluded, is less to find the perfect state of consciousness than to recognize that a complete life must be lived on several levels. "The realities which we thought were absolute are really only relative," he wrote in *Grist for the Mill*. "The free being lives within all realities simultaneously." On the one hand, he told me, this includes earning a living, raising children, assuming responsibilities, and participating fully in the world. On the other hand, it means recognizing a level at which one's individual drama is merely part of a much larger tapestry; that life itself is impermanent and forever changing; and that physical death is a passage, not an end.

"I'm in nobody training," Ram Dass told his audience at one of the lectures I attended. "The first part of my life I spent trying to become somebody. Then I turned around and tried to become nobody. Now I'm trying to become nobody being somebody. So long as you think you're somebody, you will be frightened, because somebody ultimately dies. But nobody doesn't die. The trick is to live as if being somebody makes a difference, even when you know it finally doesn't. It's a double track. You live passionately, yet there is this other part of you that is absolutely empty and equanimous. You are in this world but not of it."

It also became clear to Ram Dass that he couldn't simply transcend all of the real-life suffering around him. To the contrary, part of his spiritual path required finding a way to reach out to others in distress—to act selflessly. This seed was first planted in India when he asked Maharajji, "How do I get enlightened?" "Feed people," his guru answered simply. Later, Ram Dass asked the guru, "How do I know God?" and Maharajji said, "Serve people." Learning to deeply quiet his mind in meditation, he discovered, only intensified his awareness of the pain of those around him. Working to reduce his own suffering became inextricably entwined with working to reduce the suffering of others. In a sense, he concluded, they represented the same path.

Over time, Ram Dass has found several ways to serve. In addition to his work for organizations such as SEVA, he travels and speaks to a variety of groups. The range of his activities during one recent week, for example, included meeting with a group called the Temple of Understanding, which focuses on imbuing the United Nations with more spiritual awareness; giving the keynote address at a large conference centered on creating community; spending an evening with a group of wealthy, successful people who are looking for new ways to be of service; exchanging letters with a high-level White House aide on how to bring more reflective consciousness into political decision making; and preparing for an extended trip to Israel prompted by his rediscovery of the role of Judaism in his life. He also now spends considerable time in direct service to others, much of it aimed at helping the terminally ill come to terms with death. He writes letters, speaks by telephone, and visits with people who are suffering from AIDS, cancer, and other life-threatening diseases.

"In trying to become free, the deepest issue is letting go of one's attachment to life in this form," he told me. "To be around the dying is to deal with the most fearful issue in life. It's the ultimate practice of nonattachment—to stay reasonably equanimous in the midst of the very rapid change of consciousness that is part of dying. When people start to lose their control and identity, the impulse is to grab hold and hang on. That's where it pays to have some guides who've learned to flow with change. The art form is to stay aware. You're saying 'Who you thought you were, you aren't, but here we are.' Holding people's hands as they die has been a way to be of service, but it's also been a path of spiritual growth for me."

As he has sought a more balanced pursuit of the truth in his own life—at both the personal and the universal level—Ram Dass has grown less inclined to dismiss the importance of personal psychological work. Over the years, in addition to his spiritual work, he has gone in and out of psychotherapy and has come to see the two approaches as mutually reinforcing. "It keeps going back and forth," he told me. "The witness stance in meditation keeps bringing psychodynamics to the surface. You see your fear, or your greed, or your anger, and then it is more amenable to psychotherapeutic intervention. I've become more impressed by the interplay of these processes than by using either one to the exclusion of the other." The truth remains his touchstone, however elusive it might be. "There are infinite ways you can con yourself," he told me. "My ego still has subtle ways of taking what I've learned and turning it into something that still leaves me trapped. I have to be very quiet inside to hear when I'm going astray, because otherwise I end up just conning myself again."

Ram Dass continues to focus more attention on the practice of meditation and developing a transcendental perspective than he does on exploring his unconscious and seeking to resolve psychological conflict. "I milked that drama," he told me, referring to his years exploring his difficult childhood in psychoanalysis, "and eventually it just began to seem incredibly uninteresting." At some point, he told me, he made a decision that he couldn't wait to be completely uncrippled and unconflicted before moving forward. Where fear persisted, he decided he simply had to walk around it, rather than continue to see himself as a victim. But reasonable and practical as that seems, I somehow sensed that it wasn't the whole story. Had he, I asked, ever simply mourned for the emotional needs that were never met in his childhood and the pain he'd suffered as a result? Had he moved through them, in addition to rising above them? "I would say that I've partially mourned," he told me, "but probably not fully." Was such mourning simply self-indulgent, I asked, or did he feel it might have value? "Mourning is a way of liberation, absolutely," he said without hesitation. "To the extent that I haven't fully mourned, I'm not yet free." Why then, I asked, had he *not* fully mourned, given his lifelong hunger for freedom? "I just don't think it's happened, and I don't know why," he told me. But in the end he was too honest to leave it at that. "It could be," Ram Dass concluded with his usual bluntness and humility, "that it's just been too painful."

2

NURTURING THE HUMAN POTENTIAL

Michael Murphy and the Founding of Esalen

*We stand on an exhilarating and dangerous frontier—
and must answer anew the old questions. "What are the
limits of human ability, the boundaries of the human
experience? What does it mean to be a human being?"*
—INTRODUCTION TO
THE 1965 ESALEN CATALOG

*We fear our highest possibilities (as well as our lowest
ones). We are generally afraid to become that which we
can glimpse in our most perfect moments, under the
most perfect conditions, under conditions of greatest
courage. We enjoy and even thrill to the Godlike possibilities we see in ourselves in such peak moments. And
yet we simultaneously shiver with weakness, awe and
fear before these very same possibilities.*
—ABRAHAM MASLOW

I ARRIVED at the Esalen Institute for the first time
in 1991 unsure what to expect, but full of curiosity
and anticipation. I knew Esalen only by its reputation
from the 1960s and 1970s, when it became celebrated as the red-
hot center of the human potential movement. My image was of a
place where people shed their clothes, shucked their inhibitions,
allowed their most forbidden feelings to surface, and expressed
them with blunt directness—to hell with the consequences. Esalen,

in my mind, was a place of intense encounters, dramatic emotional breakthroughs, and open sexual experimentation. I simply wasn't yet aware that it had also served as a clearinghouse, launching pad, and initial meeting place for an extraordinary array of pioneering thinkers and practitioners who together began to develop a uniquely American approach to the pursuit of wisdom.

No sooner did I turn onto its grounds than I understood a key aspect of Esalen's enduring allure. Its setting in Big Sur—three hours south of San Francisco—could scarcely be more spectacular. Esalen sits on a long, narrow expanse of lushly planted property nestled between mountains to the East and the Pacific Ocean to the West. A large central lodge, with meeting areas and a dining room, dominates the center of the property. The lodge is surrounded by rustic cabins where guests stay and by several other houses. A walk down a steep set of stairs leads to the property's natural hot springs, which feed oversized tubs that are set out directly over the ocean. On a large deck, tables are set up and Esalen's two dozen masseurs and masseuses continue to do a thriving business, seven days a week.

When I walked into the airy, rustic dining room for my first dinner, I felt an immediate buzz, but also a sense of great comfort. Esalen's workshops—offered in weekend and five-day versions year round on dozens of subjects spanning the body, mind, and spirit—are more popular than ever. The dining room was crowded. When I sat down at one of the long wooden tables and began to overhear pieces of the conversations around me, it was clear that the level of intimacy and intensity was unusually high. The legacy of openness and introspection lives on.

Still, if Esalen was once seen as the apotheosis of me-decade narcissism, a very different spirit prevails today—one that I found more communal, low-key, respectful, and reflective than I'd expected. Even today, almost no one wears clothes down at the tubs. Yet once the surprise of seeing so much uncovered flesh had passed, I found evenings at the baths less a charged sexual scene than a surprisingly comfortable way to hang out and talk, sometimes for hours, with people I'd met during the day. I returned to Esalen several times in the course of my travels. In each case, I was drawn not just by the particular teacher or practice I was exploring, but by the prospect of being among others who are genuinely committed to more complete lives. After several days of living in simple circumstances and incredibly beautiful surroundings, I invariably returned home from Esalen not just with more information and experience, but with a sense of renewal and inspiration.

To begin to understand the history of both Esalen and its role in the human potential movement, I turned to Michael Murphy. Like most people who meet him, I felt drawn to Murphy immediately. He was about to turn sixty when we met for the first time, but he looked much younger. A big easy smile dominated his round, open face. When he walked into a restaurant near his home in San Rafael, California, it was with the loose, loping gait of an athlete. Most of all, he radiated exuberance: an infectious laugh, boundless enthusiasm, and an easy charm. At the same time, I was struck by the range and depth of his intellect. Over lunch, he spoke with equal ease and authority about philosophy, mysticism, sports, psychology, religion, politics, and above all, human evolutionary possibility.

More than any single person, Murphy is responsible for the birth of the human potential movement in this country. In 1962, he and a college classmate, Richard Price, co-founded Esalen. Murphy remains chairman of its board and Esalen continues to give a public platform to a broad spectrum of teachers, psychologists, physicians, psychics, philosophers, bodyworkers, mystics, and scientists eager to share unconventional ideas, techniques, and practices for cultivating a more complete life. Gestalt therapy, encounter groups, and body-oriented therapies such as Rolfing, Feldenkris, and the Alexander method all first came to wide attention at Esalen. For better and for worse, Esalen has served for thirty years as the primary experiential testing ground for new approaches to the search for wisdom in America.

Murphy's personal interests remain as eclectic as ever. At the time we first met in the fall of 1989, he had just finished his seventh and most ambitious book, *The Future of the Body: Explorations into the Further Evolution of Human Nature.* For seven years, he spent six days a week, eight hours a day, trying to gather in one place the historical evidence for the higher capacities of the human mind, body, and spirit. Like Esalen, the book grew out of Murphy's conviction that human beings have enormous undeveloped potentials. With growing access to the ideas and techniques of both the Eastern contemplative traditions and modern psychology, Murphy is convinced that our potential for self-discovery and growth has been vastly expanded. Armed with this knowledge, he argues, we stand at the precipice of the next great evolutionary leap—a transformation of consciousness that has the power to change every aspect of our lives.

Murphy brought to his own search for wisdom an unusual blend of qualities. As an undergraduate philosophy major at Stanford, he developed a deep and discriminating understanding of the Eastern wisdom traditions. For most of his twenties, he spent an average of eight hours a day meditating but also retained a passionate interest in how our higher potentials can be embodied in everyday life. Murphy can speak simply and movingly about his own transcendent experiences, for example, but he is equally concerned with how to use meditative skills such as focused attention, broader awareness, and deep physical relaxation in the service of practical goals ranging from physical healing to better athletic performance.

Ironically, the focus at Esalen has often been a direct contrast to Murphy's own instincts and preferences. Esalen began as a place in which people were encouraged to open the floodgates and share even their darkest secrets. Murphy is not the sort of person you'd expect to share intimacies with strangers. An incisive, logical thinker and a voracious reader, Murphy revels in the life of the mind. Esalen for years lacked a library, and its best-known teachers often decried the tendency to use thinking as a way to avoid feeling. Murphy's solitary, long-term meditation practice was aimed at transcending personal desire and attachment. Esalen became known for group techniques that led to powerful emo-

tional catharsis and highly intimate sharing. Murphy lived monk-
ishly in his twenties and remained a virgin until the age of thirty.
Esalen celebrated the body and became widely known as a hotbed
of open sensuality and sexual experimentation. How then, I
wondered, was I to reconcile these very different visions in my
own search for wisdom? It was clear to me that both Murphy and
the institute he founded brought important pieces to the wisdom
puzzle—but neither, I concluded, had all the answers.

T he first part of Murphy's life could scarcely be a more
all-American success story. He was born into one of the
wealthier establishment families in the small California town of
Salinas in 1930. His paternal grandfather, Henry, was the town's
leading doctor and built two hospitals in the area. Henry's wife,
known as Bunny, was a successful businesswoman in her own
right. Together, in 1910, they purchased a huge tract of land
overlooking the Pacific Ocean in Big Sur, two hundred miles south
of San Francisco. It became a family vacation retreat, and for a
time, they considered turning it into a health spa. As a child,
Murphy went with his family to spend weekends relaxing in the
natural hot springs on the property and enjoying its breathtaking
beauty. Much later, this setting would become home to Esalen.

Murphy grew up in a household that reflected his parents'
opposite temperaments. Murphy's father, John, was a successful
lawyer in Salinas. He imparted, both to Michael and to his
younger brother Dennis, his love for sports, including boxing, and
for literature. At the same time, he was strict and had a fiery Irish
temper. By contrast, Murphy's mother, Marie, whose parents
came from the south of France, had the unwavering buoyancy
and ebullience so typical of the Basques. Murphy's temperament
mirrored his mother's. When his father became frustrated or
upset, Michael's instinct was to lie low and later to recast the
events in a positive light. His parents had their share of fights and
arguments. But as he remembers it, even dark storms in the family
household were always followed by bright clearing and good

times. His parents rarely openly discussed feelings, and that was fine with the young Michael. His brother Dennis had a very different and much darker temperament. Rebellious and confrontational, Dennis was forever ready to jump into a battle, and he let nothing slip by.

"One big difference between us was that I got into a dance with my mother where I couldn't do anything wrong," Murphy told me. "To me, she was unconditionally loving, but to Dennis I think not. It must have been an awful burden to my brother, and he became my opposite. He was wild, while I was the ultimate goody-goody." In his last year in high school, Murphy was the valedictorian, the president of his class, and the captain of the golf team. At the same time, he was already experiencing glimmerings of higher potentials that defied rational explanation. There were times playing golf, for example, when Murphy found himself performing at a level far beyond what he consciously believed was possible, and experiencing a feeling of both deep serenity and great joy. Sometimes, he was similarly touched through prayer. Neither of his parents was a churchgoer, but when Murphy was eleven, his grandmother Bunny took her two grandsons to the local Episcopal church. Dennis was bored and never returned, while Michael was so moved by the experience that he began to attend regularly. Although he'd long planned to become a doctor, he started to seriously consider the ministry.

Even as a teenager, Murphy started to evolve a philosophy of life that perfectly reflected his personality. On the one hand, he saw that pain and unhappiness were part of many lives, including his own family's. At the same time, he concluded that joy lay at the core of all human beings and that it was forever seeking to express itself. There was, in short, a way around the darkness—an imperative to seek higher ground. "I had this feeling that we all had access to the ground of being, or God, or light," he told me. "Our job in life was to get in touch with it and to bring it into the world—through meditation, prayer, friendship, music, even sports." Murphy was particularly drawn to any evidence of higher human capacities. Here, he was influenced not just by his own transcendent experiences in prayer and in sports, but by the books he was reading, ranging from Will Durant's *The Story of Philosophy* to Esther Harding's *Psychic Energy,* a text drawing on Jungian psychology. "At fifteen," Murphy told me, "I was already pretty sold on the idea that society's attempt to make people normal was doomed to failure if it didn't provide them with some deeper meaning, or sense of satisfaction."

Still, Murphy remained on a conventional course for the next several years. Accepted to Stanford University, he was promptly elected class representative, where he served with upperclassmen including future Harvard president Derek Bok and Oregon senator Mark Hatfield. He joined Phi Gamma Delta, a leading campus fraternity, wore cashmere sweaters, attended football games, and dutifully worked his way through his pre-med courses, fully expecting to become a doctor. He even went through an atheist phase, reacting strongly against the rigidities and dogma of organized religion and abandoning the idea of pursuing the ministry. The event that dramatically transformed his life occurred one day in January of his junior year. He was searching for a psychology class that he'd signed up for when he wandered accidentally into a lecture on comparative religions. It was being taught by a professor named Frederic Spiegelberg.

A world-famous Asia scholar and an immensely charismatic teacher, Spiegelberg had just returned from sabbatical. In the course of his travels, he'd spent time with two renowned Indian mystics and teachers: Ramana Maharshi, on whom Somerset Maugham based his novel *The Razor's Edge,* and Sri Aurobindo Ghose, a scholar and sage who ran a large ashram in Pondicherry, India. Spiegelberg was openly critical of organized religion, arguing that it divided people far more often than it brought them together. Instead, he believed that the route to higher truth grew out of cultivating the fundamental spiritual principles that lie at the heart of all enduring religions—the perspective that Aldous Huxley termed "the perennial philosophy."

The highest form of religion, Spiegelberg told his students, was to transcend religion. Murphy responded to these ideas instantly. "Hearing Spiegelberg wasn't just a thunderbolt," he told me. "It was more this intuitive knowing, all at once, that what he was saying was right. Here was this guy lecturing to maybe 650 people on the Vedic hymns, on the concept that Atman—the deepest self—is one with Brahman, the essence of all existence. It's one of the purest statements of world mysticism. Atman is Brahman. Tat Twam Asi. Thou art That. We are all one. Hearing it was an electrifying event for me, like getting water in the desert. It still stirs me thinking about it. The fact is that I've spent the rest of my life unpacking and developing what I experienced in that first lecture."

Almost immediately, Murphy determined to build his life around the principles that Spiegelberg had laid out—among them a rejection of any limiting orthodoxies and fixed belief systems. Murphy was a passionate student, and Spiegelberg soon became both his mentor and his friend. During the next year, Murphy pulled back from fraternity life, lost interest in his pre-med studies, and devoted his time instead to meditating and reading intensively, mostly about Eastern religions. He focused much of his attention on Aurobindo. In contrast to many Eastern sages, Aurobindo wasn't interested in pursuing an abstract enlightenment that required withdrawing from the world or transcending the body. Instead, he believed that through systematic practices—meditation and yoga, but also sports, interpersonal relationships, and social action—it was possible to embody one's higher potentials in everyday experience. Like most Eastern teachers, Aurobindo didn't focus much attention on the role of the personal unconscious and wasn't drawn to addressing the neurotic conflicts that emerge in the course of personal development. Murphy had similar inclinations. What captivated him was Aurobindo's forward-looking philosophy and its focus on cultivating higher human possibility. "I was taken most with Aurobindo's idea that by your activity in the world you could realize divinity," he told me. "As I heard it, he was saying that evolution is a reflection of the stupendous drama of divinity unfolding with us."

Aurobindo's own life was especially inspiring to Murphy.

Born in Bengal, India, in 1872 and educated in England, Aurobindo started out as a teacher. He grew increasingly political, and in his late twenties he became the editor of the most influential revolutionary magazine, and the British secret service made him its public enemy number one. Arrested for his alleged role in a bombing that killed an English-woman, he spent a year in jail but was never convicted. It was during this period that he began what he described as a spiritual transformation. He was already interested in Eastern practices, but he cultivated an even more contemplative life, built around a deep practice in meditation and yoga. Upon his release, he turned his attention to reflecting his spiritual concerns in his external actions. Aurobindo founded his ashram in Pondicherry, wrote books, and occasionally attempted to influence political events. As the Nazis came to power in Germany, for example, and Gandhi remained on the sidelines, Aurobindo gave the considerable sum of two thousand pounds to support his former enemies, the British, in their battle against Hitler.

In his junior year in college, Murphy joined a weekly group largely devoted to reading Aurobindo's main work, *The Life Divine*. The group was led by a brilliant, mysterious graduate student named Walt Page. While Murphy was intrigued by Page's eclectic synthesis of Eastern spiritual beliefs and Western psychological insights, he was put off by Page's gurulike demands for unwavering loyalty and subservience. To Murphy's dismay, many of the group members simply went along with anything that Page suggested. Looking back, Murphy saw it as his first direct lesson in the dangers of authoritarianism. The mistake that other members made, he came to believe, was investing faith in a flawed messenger rather than in the message itself. Years later, Murphy wasn't entirely surprised to learn that Page had committed suicide.

Long before that, Murphy began to pull back from Page's group, even as he became more absorbed in his meditation and his reading. Continuing to attend classes and lead a traditional college life grew increasingly unbearable for him. Finally, the dam simply broke. "I was sitting by a statue on the Stanford campus meditating," Murphy told me, "and suddenly the vows just rose up in me—a powerful sense of inner calling. It was like I had to do something to confirm this direction I felt myself heading. I walked straight over to the fraternity and told the student president I was quitting. The next day, I moved out to a room off-campus and dropped out of school. I felt I was running toward something that was enormously exciting and worthwhile, and away from a social role that had largely been imposed on me."

Meditation quickly became the center of Murphy's life—four hours in the early morning and four more in the late afternoon. The rest of the time, he spent reading. This intense discipline came to him easily. He found meditation both exhilarating and joyous, a direct experience of something larger than himself. "If you sit in meditation as much as I did, you could almost say by the law of averages, you're bound to have an epiphany now and then," Murphy told me. "I was living a very simple life, and it was very rewarding. There was a compelling logic to the whole vision, and through the sitting, I found every experience heightened—from serenity to evenness to extreme delight. Sometimes the experiences were absolutely overwhelming. When Jung was asked, 'Do you believe in God?' he responded, 'I don't believe in God, I know.' Well, that was absolutely so for me." At the same time, Murphy found his practice personally liberating. "I'd been almost totally achievement-oriented and other-directed growing up," he told me. "Here in meditation I found this simple essence. The practice suddenly gave me an enormous depth of confidence that didn't depend on anyone else."

His family and friends were less enthralled by Murphy's solitary lifestyle. Conventional wisdom in 1951 held that no one in his right mind dropped out of Stanford to live a life of ascetic contemplation. Murphy's father responded by telling his son not to come home anymore. A short time later, a prominent clinical psychologist showed up at Murphy's door, sent by a family friend, apparently to assess the young man's sanity. The psychologist could find no evidence that Murphy was crazy, and before too long his father decided to make amends. Murphy returned to Stanford the next fall to finish up, but mostly by taking independent directed readings with Spiegelberg.

After graduating, Murphy did a two-year stint in the army, and then returned to Stanford intending to get a Ph.D. in philosophy. Once again, however, he grew restless in school. This time, he began to develop obsessional symptoms, most notably the constant, irrational fear that he was about to have a seizure. Finally, it dawned on him that the fear of seizures was his body's way of telling him that he was suffocating. Fortified by this insight, he quit graduate school and decided to fulfill a longtime dream: to visit the Aurobindo ashram in Pondicherry. Sure enough, the fear of seizures disappeared almost immediately.

Aurobindo himself had died five years earlier, but his work was being carried on by a Frenchwoman in her seventies named Madame Richard and known simply as "the Mother." The ashram, located on the Bay of Bengal, consisted of some two hundred buildings, most with enormous interior gardens. There was also a huge athletic complex, including an Olympic swimming pool, and a large farm that made the ashram virtually self-sufficient. It accommodated up to two thousand people, and while most of the devotees were Indian, there were always a handful of Westerners there.

For Murphy, the ashram was a congenial environment in which to deepen his meditation practice and to read, and to participate in sports, which Aurobindo believed were an ideal vehicle for growth and transcendence. In many ways, it was an idyllic existence—simple, healthy, uplifting, athletically competitive, and free of big responsibilities. The one drawback was what Murphy perceived as the cult atmosphere that had grown up around Aurobindo. Devotion had shifted to the Mother after Aurobindo's death, and many disciples ascribed magical powers to her. They also accepted unquestioningly the demand for acceptance of all her teachings. Much as he admired the Mother,

Murphy felt that her powers were wildly overstated. They were also unsupported by his own observations.

Murphy took all that he could from Aurobindo's teachings, but he was not about to become anyone's disciple. After sixteen months, he decided to return to Palo Alto. He continued his contemplative life, supported himself by working as a bellhop, and mostly felt content. It wasn't until two years later, nearing the age of thirty, that Murphy met Richard Price and began to envision a way to put his unconventional interests to practical use in the world. Price and Murphy, it turned out, had been undergraduates together at Stanford but had never met. Price went on to graduate school in psychology at Harvard, where he had encountered much the same problem that Murphy had at Stanford. At Harvard, the psychology department had shifted from a focus on psychodynamics and subjective, internal experience to a much drier, research-based experimental psychology.

Like Murphy, Price decided to drop out and pursue an interest in meditation and mysticism. In time, however, his life took a far darker turn. The key period is described in Walter Truett Anderson's rich and evocative history of Esalen, titled *The Upstart Spring*. Following weeks of intensive meditation and very little sleep, Price was drinking one night at a bar in San Francisco's North Beach. Suddenly, he experienced what he felt was an ecstatic opening to a much broader sense of himself. The only way that he could find to express it in words was as a repetitive chant—"Light the Fire, Light the Fire," The bartender finally decided to call the police. The next thing Price knew, he'd been taken to a locked psychiatric ward. He never believed that he was crazy, but after three months of hospitalization, he felt calmer, clearer, and more knowledgeable about himself than he ever remembered feeling. When he tried to sign out, however, he discovered that his father had arranged to have him recommitted to another hospital. At this point, Price spiraled downward. After several months, he was moved to a third institution and subjected—over his violent objections—to a nine-month course of electroshock and insulin-shock treatments. By his own account, he emerged from this experience a year later feeling both physically impaired and emotionally battered.

Price had been out of the hospital for two years when he calmly and lucidly recounted this story for Murphy. As a horrified Murphy saw it, Price had suffered at the hands of an authoritarian psychiatry that used allegedly therapeutic tools to force Price to conform to society's prevailing standards of acceptable behavior. Being locked away, Murphy realized with a shudder, could just as easily have happened to him when the psychologist showed up back at Stanford to assess his sanity. Price and Murphy developed an immediate kinship based on their shared experiences and outlook. Nearly everywhere they'd looked for answers, they'd encountered very bright people zealously guarding some narrow set of beliefs—in the graduate schools of prestigious universities, in the psychiatric profession, in spiritual settings, and even within their own families. What they both longed for was a community of active seekers who resisted fixed answers. Wasn't there a way, they began to wonder, to freely explore their shared eclectic interests—East and West, psychology and mysticism, science and religion, mind and body, human possibility and ancient wisdom?

Murphy suggested that his family's property at Big Sur might be an ideal home for their vision. He was eager to share with others what he'd experienced in meditation and to gather in one place a variety of Eastern techniques for accessing other states of consciousness. He was also interested in providing a home for new Western psychotherapies, including disciplines that emphasized working with the body. Inspired by John Dewey, the educator who emphasized the "education of the whole person," Murphy had in mind an institution of learning that simultaneously addressed the mind, the body, and the spirit. Price, meanwhile, had been profoundly moved by a lecture that Aldous Huxley gave at the University of California, Berkeley, in 1960. Titled "Human Potentialities," Huxley's talk was based on the notion that human beings use only a fraction of their brain's capacity. "There are still a great many potentialities—for rationality, for affection and kindliness, for creativity—still lying latent in man," he told his audience. Huxley went on to describe a series of new techniques for growth, mostly focused on helping to expand self-awareness and to experience higher states of mind. He ended his Berkeley lecture by calling for the establishment of some kind of institution where the techniques that he'd been studying and trying out could be more formally tested and studied.

Both Murphy's and Price's parents were enthusiastic about the plan, relieved that their respective sons were finally planning to do something concrete with their lives. Murphy's grandmother Bunny agreed to give him a long-term, low-cost lease on the Big Sur property, while Price's family released money to him from a trust fund. The project quickly took shape. With the help of the caretaker on the property—future gonzo journalist Hunter Thompson—they evicted the young homosexual men and grungy locals who'd been trooping over at night to hang out in the property's natural hot baths overlooking the ocean. By the fall of 1962, operating under the name Big Sur Hot Springs, Murphy and Price had their first programs in place. Murphy assumed the prime organizing role, and his blend of his charm and passion made him successful in attracting prominent thinkers to Bug Sur to give talks.

Before long the seminars were being led by a group of cutting-edge thinkers including Murphy's former teacher Fred Spiegelberg; Alan Watts, by then perhaps the leading Western exponent of Zen Buddhism; behaviorist B. F. Skinner; psychologist Gardner Murphy; James Pike, the radical Episcopalian bishop of California; theologian and writer Norman O. Brown; parapsychologist J. B. Rhine; psychologist and creativity authority Frank Barron of the University of California at Berkeley; anthropologist Gregory Bateson; and linguist S. I. Hayakawa. Many of the early seminar leaders, it turned out, had been motivated to search for deeper answers through their experiences with psychedelics. Indeed, within a year, Richard Alpert and Timothy Leary showed up to give a series of talks on "The Ecstatic Experience." Murphy himself did not simply sit on the sidelines. He attended every one of Big Sur's first two hundred lectures and workshops.

Nsone of Big Sur's early teachers shared Murphy's vision and temperament quite so compatibly as did Abraham Maslow. If Aurobindo was Murphy's chief Eastern influence, Maslow became a Western counterpart, both Murphy's mentor and his close friend. The two men shared a similar vision about human possibility, as well as a disinclination to dwell on its darker side. They came to this similar philosophy from utterly disparate backgrounds. Maslow bluntly characterized his childhood as "miserably unhappy." Born in 1908, he had grown up in Brooklyn, where his father ran a barrel-repair business and worked such long hours that Maslow rarely saw him. Instead, he was left under the nearly exclusive care of his mother, whom he later described as "cruel, ignorant and hostile . . . so unloving as to nearly induce madness in her children." Time failed to heal these wounds and even when his mother died, Maslow refused to attend the funeral. "The whole thrust of my life-philosophy and all my research and theorizing," he wrote many years later, "has its roots in a hatred and revulsion against everything [my mother] stood for." Instead, for most of his life, Maslow focused his energies on the higher side of human nature.

Trained in the 1930s as a behavioral psychologist, Maslow won early recognition for his research into the patterns of dominance and sexual behavior in monkeys. By the end of World War II, psychology was utterly dominated by two schools: behaviorism at the universities, and Freudian psychoanalysis in clinical settings. Maslow was influenced by both but finally felt comfortable with neither. Behaviorism, he concluded, was oversimplified and reductionistic. It used an animal model to understand human beings, and it focused on conditioning—the predictable pattern of response to rewards and punishments—as the explanation for all behavior. Behaviorists such as B. F. Skinner gave insufficient credence, Maslow believed, to the immense complexity of human motivation and the vast inborn capacity for personal growth. Maslow found Freud's psychodynamic approach richer and more complex, particularly in its pioneering recognition of the role of the unconscious and the patterns of childhood development. But Freud's approach, he concluded, was finally limited by the medical model on which it was based. "The psychology of 1949," Maslow said in a speech that year, referring primarily to classical Freudian thinking, "is largely a psychology of cripples and sick people . . . based upon the study of men at their worst. . . . Under such circumstances, how could it possibly be discovered that man had capabilities higher than . . . the neurotic?"

Maslow's strongest early influence was Kurt Goldstein. A German-born psychiatrist, Goldstein refused to assign human beings labels such as "neurotic" and "psychotic." Rather, he believed that each person had to be viewed as a whole, in his environment. In this "gestalt," as he called it, man was more than the sum of his parts. In turn, Goldstein posited that all human beings have an innate instinct to grow and to achieve their potential. He called this the drive for "self-actualization." Maslow ultimately made this broad concept the centerpiece of his work. His belief in an inborn human drive toward health became the basis of *Toward a Psychology of Being,* the book that won him his first broad recognition. It was published in 1962, the same year that Big Sur Hot Springs was founded. The ideas in the book also laid the groundwork for the field of humanistic psychology, the "third force" alternative to behaviorism and Freudianism that he helped found.

"Every age but ours," Maslow wrote in *Toward a Psychology of Being,* "had its model, its ideal. . . . About all we have left is the well-adjusted man without problems, a very pale and doubtful substitute. Perhaps we shall soon be able to use as our guide and model the fully growing and self-fulfilling human being, the one in whom his potentialities are coming to full development, the one whose inner nature expresses itself freely, rather than being warped, repressed or denied." Shortly after the book was published, Maslow paid an unplanned visit to Big Sur Hot Springs, which was soon to be renamed Esalen after a local Indian tribe. The visit represented the sort of meaningful coincidence that Carl

Jung had termed a "synchronicity." In this instance, Maslow and his wife Bertha were vacationing in California and happened to be driving one night along Highway 1, which runs past Esalen. Feeling tired but unable to find an inn, they eventually came upon a light on the road, turned into a driveway, and found themselves on the grounds at Big Sur.

When the Maslows appeared at the main house and inquired about a room, the desk clerk—a colorful martial arts instructor named Gia-fu—treated the strangers curtly. But when Maslow signed the register, Gia-fu recognized his name. Like nearly everyone else at Esalen, he had read *Toward a Psychology of Being*. Suddenly, Gia-fu transformed into a whirling dervish of excitement and reverence. Murphy was away that night, but Gia-fu ran to get Richard Price. Big Sur Hot Springs, Price explained to Maslow, was a new center built around many of the principles of humanistic psychology promulgated in *Toward a Psychology of Being*. Maslow was immediately intrigued. Ultimately, it was Murphy with whom Maslow made the strongest connection. They shared many qualities. Both of them were relentlessly optimistic, polite, kind, and nonconfrontational by nature. They shared a passionate vision of the possibility for transforming society, and both were far more at home discussing ideas than engaging feelings—particularly troubling ones.

Like Murphy, Maslow had a scholar's love for orderliness and logic, and he was determined to systematically delineate the higher states of mental health. Freud had brilliantly evolved such a model for understanding neurotic illness, in large part by looking at the blocks and pathologies that arise at various stages of childhood development. But Freud's model ended at the resolution of neurotic symptoms—what he called the return to ordinary human unhappiness. Maslow believed that human beings had higher possibilities. In "A Theory of Motivation," perhaps his most influential paper, Maslow argued that all human beings operate out of what he termed "an inborn hierarchy of needs."

"The physiological needs, when unsatisfied, dominate the organism," he wrote. "Relative gratification submerges them and allows the next higher set of needs in the hierarchy to emerge, dominate and organize the personality." When basic survival needs have been met, Maslow found that the "belongingness" needs emerge next—for safety, approval, and acceptance. Most people who get their survival needs met, he posited, suffer the symptoms of unfulfilled belongingness needs, including fear, insecurity, selfishness, and anxiety. When these belongingness needs are satisfied, Maslow argued, people have the security and serenity to move to a higher level. This happens only to a small minority of people, but the effects are striking. Instinctively, such people begin to act on a higher, more selfless set of "needs," including generosity, loyalty, empathy, and public-spiritedness—values that Maslow found give real depth and meaning to life. Such people, Maslow said, "may be understood, at least in part [as having been] satisfied in their basic needs throughout their lives, particularly in their early years."

Because these individuals are less preoccupied by inner demons—unresolved angers, anxieties, and stresses—Maslow argued that they are better able to listen and learn, to tap their creativity, and to be productive. These self-actualized people, he concluded, find fulfillment because they are able to function in all areas of their lives—internally and externally, for themselves and for others—near the peak of their potential. The healthiest people, Maslow wrote, "are devoted to some task outside themselves." This sense of mission or "metamotivation," he went on, is "passionate, selfless and profound." For such people, distinctions between "self" and "not self" are transcended, and a broader sense of self emerges that effectively experiences no boundaries.

Even without using the word *spiritual*, Maslow was introducing transcendental concepts into the language of Western psychology. Conversely, he characterized certain "metapathologies"—drug addiction, alcoholism, violent crime, hopelessness—as spiritual illnesses that emerge when people's inborn need to find meaning in their lives is thwarted. The ultimate expression of one's potential, Maslow wrote, comes not from personal achievement but from the capacity to transcend one's self in the service of others. Murphy, not surprisingly, found this theory compelling, particularly its focus on the higher reaches of human possibility. Maslow was not a working therapist, however, and he did not suggest any means by which people with troubling conflicts from childhood—what he called "unmet belongingness needs"—might go about resolving them. Instead, he wrote about soaring human possibilities as a theorist, mostly in dry academic prose.

The limits of this highly intellectual approach were soon apparent in practice at Esalen. The very first set of seminars, inspired by Huxley's speech and Maslow's work, had been entitled "The Human Potentiality." Like most of the early Esalen offerings, these were staid, civilized events that—but for the subject matter—could easily have taken place at a university. Learned men lectured on self-actualization, the human potential, and even transcendence. The audience, seated in hard-backed chairs, listened politely. All this talk about higher possibilities was a far cry, however, from the direct "peak experience" that Maslow described in his work. *Peak experience* was the term he coined to describe breakthrough moments in which, operating close to our potential, we feel an almost overwhelming sense of pleasure or euphoria, a deep sense of wonder, a feeling of harmony with the universe, or even a profound feeling of boundless love. But Maslow himself was something of a stranger to these experiences.

One afternoon in the spring of 1962, shortly after the publication of *Toward a Psychology of Being*, Maslow was standing at the curb at Logan Airport in Boston when his friend Timothy Leary walked by with a female companion and offered him a ride. At the time, Leary was still a renegade Harvard professor doing psychedelic research. As Leary later recounted it, when Maslow got in the car, the young woman turned to him and asked, "What do you do, Abe?" Leary jumped in, "Abe is one of the most important psychologists of our times. [He] introduced the term peak experience, and he's convinced a lot of people that the psyche is filled with wonderful potentials waiting to be awakened and used." The woman pressed on innocently. "What's a peak experience?" she asked Maslow. "I wouldn't know," he replied, "because I never had one. It's the old philosopher's paradox. Those who theorize about it are often the last to do it."

I t soon became clear that the people attending Esalen's early seminars were less interested in intellectual inspiration and theoretical pronouncements than in direct experience. These seminarians, as they were soon called, were nearly all professionals: lawyers and psychologists, clergymen, social workers, and teachers. What they had in common was a reasonable level of conventional success and a hunger for something more in their lives. Many had put in hundreds of hours in traditional Freudian psychoanalysis, but still felt something was missing in their lives. It soon became clear that they were desperate to discard their confining habits, express their pent-up feelings, and get more in touch with their bodies. Both Murphy and Maslow envisioned Esalen as an educational center focused on the top rungs of Maslow's hierarchy of needs: self-actualization, self-transcendence, empathy, and selfless service. Those who came to Esalen had a more primal and compelling agenda. For them, the first order of business was breaking down the conventions and rules they'd lived by. Self-actualization—much less moving beyond the concerns of the self—would have to wait.

Nor was Murphy about to impose his beliefs on anyone. The single quality that he and Price cared most about cultivating at Esalen was an openness to a wide array of ideas and practices. "We didn't want to fall into dogma, fundamentalism, and totalitarianism," Murphy told me. "We wanted to create a place where you could explore ideas and practices in an open system." In turn, Esalen evolved in almost direct reaction to the values of the mainstream culture. If conventional social interaction called for politeness and discretion, the watchwords at Esalen became honesty and openness—saying exactly what you felt to anyone about anything, no holds barred. Many of the first visitors to Esalen, reflecting the puritanical era in which they'd grown up, felt cut off from their bodies and from their feelings. Esalen, in turn, offered myriad ways to increase body awareness and embrace sensuality—languishing in the hot baths, being massaged in the nude on the deck, attending classes on sensory awareness. Neither marijuana nor psychedelic drugs were officially permitted at Esalen, but they were widely used anyway, and the inevitable effect was to make people feel even less inhibited.

Where traditional therapy focused on talk and intellectual insight, Esalen's most popular workshops disparaged thinking and analysis and emphasized getting connected to one's feelings. And if psychoanalysis required years on the couch trying to ferret out deeply buried childhood traumas, Esalen offered powerfully cathartic technologies for releasing emotional blocks, unmasking defenses, and making rapid and dramatic transformations. Whatever else Esalen had to offer, it was a very exciting place to be.

Murphy's and Price's laissez-faire style had another unintended consequence. It created a vacuum that was filled—perhaps inevitably—by the teachers with the most powerful personalities, the most dramatic techniques, and the greatest capacity to meet their students' passionate desire for intense experiences and quick results. No teacher exemplified this better, or caused more grief to Michael Murphy, than Fritz Perls. The contrast between the two men was nearly complete. Murphy was polite, charming, and friendly to a fault. Perls was mercilessly blunt, uninterested in social niceties, and frequently nasty. Murphy was a mystic, and Perls was an atheist—although Murphy typically saw Perls's apparent aversion to Eastern practices in a more positive light. Looking back much later, he described Perls as "a closet mystic"—someone who suffered from "repression of the sublime."

A short, bearded man already in his seventies when he arrived at Esalen, Perls was openly lecherous with younger women, a regular visitor to Esalen's hot baths, and without embarrassment about his aging body. Murphy was tall, young, and handsome but avoided Esalen's baths, and never felt comfortable with the open nudity that characterized the institute he'd founded. Perls demanded center stage, nearly always got it, and was loath to go out of his way for anyone. Murphy was instinctively deferential, an excellent listener, and he had a terrible time saying no to anyone. Perls was sharp, intuitive, and well-educated, but defiantly anti-intellectual. Murphy reveled in ideas. They were opposites who never reconciled—Apollo and Dionysius.

Born in 1893 in Berlin, Perls had been trained in Germany as a classical Freudian psychoanalyst. Like Maslow, he grew disillusioned with analysis, particularly after he was snubbed by Freud in their one face-to-face meeting. Over the years, he became convinced that analysis simply led people to endless insights without ever prompting them to fundamental change. Perls, like Maslow, was influenced by the Gestalt psychiatrist Kurt Goldstein, with whom he worked in Frankfurt in the 1920s. Several years later, Perls moved to Berlin and became a patient of psychiatrist Wilhelm Reich. Like Carl Jung, Reich had been one of Freud's most favored disciples before he broke off to start his own school. Reich grew to believe that all neurotic problems are reflected and expressed in distortions in the body that he called "character armoring." Increasing one's awareness of the body, he believed, was a far more powerful and direct way to uncover and resolve psychological symptoms than simply talking about them.

Specifically, Reich found a strong relationship between patterns of muscular holding and certain personality traits. Unlike Freud, who avoided any direct contact with his patients, Reich believed in hands-on work to help release muscular blocks that masked underlying emotions. He might, for example, apply pressure to a part of the body where he detected intense holding or spasm—say, the jaw, or the neck, or the back, or the eyes. Often, such pressure led not just to physical release but to emotional catharsis that could take the form of rage, or terror, or grief. By bringing these deep emotions to awareness—ones that talk therapy rarely accessed—Reich believed that patients deeply experienced the disowned parts of themselves. In turn, true healing occurred. Among Reich's most controversial views was that the capacity to experience in sex what he called "true orgasm" was the highest measure of mental health—the ultimate creative act of self-expression.

Perls was deeply influenced by Reich, but they lost touch after both men were forced to flee Germany in 1933. Perls moved first to South Africa and eventually to the United States in 1946. As a therapist, he had already begun to shift away from the traditional Freudian style of delving into patients' early memories. Instead, he began focusing on the ways in which they manifested pathology in the present—including through their bodily tensions and distortions. Gestalt therapy won its first broad public recognition when Perls collaborated on a book by the same name, with educator Paul Goodman and psychologist Ralph Hefferline. While Goodman deserved primary credit for writing the book, it was Perls's clinical work that brought Gestalt therapy to life and eventually won him a wide following.

Gestalt therapy was conceived around a simple premise: that people suffer because they have lost touch with their bodies and their feelings—and thus, in the deepest sense, with themselves. Therapy, Perls believed, should consist of an effort to help the patient recover this self-awareness. "We live in patterned behavior," he wrote much later. "We are playing the same roles over and over again. So if you find out how you prevent yourself from growing, from using your potential, you have a way of . . . making life richer. . . . What we are trying to do in therapy is step-by-step to re-own the disowned parts of the personality. . . . The ability to stay with what we are avoiding is not easy, and for this you need somebody else to become aware of what you are avoiding."

Perls was seventy-one years old when he took up residence at Esalen in 1964. Michael Murphy had seen him work at a conference held at Esalen the previous December and agreed to have him come and give three weekend seminars the next spring. Neither Murphy nor Price had much liked Perls personally, but both were impressed by his work. It never occurred to them that Perls would end up staying at Esalen for nearly six years—or that he would come closer than any teacher to remaking Esalen in his own image.

From the start, Esalen gave Perls a forum in which to work before large and appreciative audiences. In return, he invariably provided a show. Typically, he worked in Esalen's main lodge, sitting at the front of the room in a large easy chair, with two smaller chairs placed in front of him, puffing away on a cigarette. He insisted that everyone call him Fritz, although he rarely encouraged any other form of easy familiarity. The client he was working with sat in one of the empty chairs and moved at times to the other chair, under Fritz's direction. This was in order to act out different aspects of himself, or to shift into the role of an important figure from his life—say, a withholding mother or a suffocating spouse.

Most defenses, Perls argued, reflected ways of using the mind to keep feelings at a distance. This occurred in predictable patterns that he described in characteristically blunt language. "Chickenshit," he proclaimed, is the trivial small talk that dominates most people's lives. "Bullshit" refers to the rationalizations that people concoct to justify their often destructive and neurotic behavior. "Elephant shit" is the sort of high-minded talk about change, transformation, and consciousness that he believed pervaded many Esalen workshops. "A little bit of honesty goes a long way," he wrote, "and this is what most of us are afraid of—being honest with ourselves and stopping the idea of self-deception."

In Perls's view, the end—forcing people to reconnect with these underlying feelings—justified very harsh means. "Fritz evolved an approach to working with people that had to do with truly bringing them into the present moment, whatever that required," explained Robert Hall, a psychiatrist who met and began training under Perls at Esalen in 1967. "He did it in a way that allowed them to experience their past suffering in the present, to work through it toward an opening and a letting go. There was something magical about what he did. He went right for the hook, and he didn't fool around." It was just this ability that made Perls's work so popular at Esalen—and such a stark alternative to traditional forms of therapy. His approach was confrontational and emotionally cathartic, and it delivered powerful, immediate results. Richard Price himself set out to study under Perls, and students lined up to have Perls probe their deepest vulnerabilities and expose in public their most carefully guarded defenses and self-deceptions.

But there were costs as well. Justifiably concerned about people's tendency to use thinking to avoid feeling, Perls chose to reject the intellect altogether. "Leave your mind and come to your senses" became his rallying cry. By choosing up sides in this way, he disparaged the very qualities—self-consciousness and the capacity for reflective discrimination—that make human beings unique. Moreover, while Perls was brilliant at helping people to recover often painful repressed feelings, he wasn't much oriented to providing follow-up and support—nor was Esalen generally.

Murphy himself was deeply ambivalent about Perls. On the one hand, he looks back on him now as a clinical genius. "If Joe Montana knew how to win football games, Fritz knew how to push buttons," Murphy told me. "He was very creative and resourceful, and he could get to you and bring the issues in your life to the surface very quickly. I had that experience myself with him." On the other hand, Murphy was troubled by the limits of this singular approach. "Fritz was so focused on breaking loose that he didn't pay much attention to anything else," Murphy explained. "He had this naturalistic belief in the power of awareness but no notion of any ongoing practice aimed at integrating the insights." Robert Hall, who was far closer to Perls than Murphy, saw similar shortcomings in his mentor. "He was wonderful at contact, which can take place in a split second," Hall told me, "but terrible at intimacy, which develops over time. He had a capacity for great love, but he didn't have any long-term relationships that sustained successfully—including with me." Perhaps nowhere was Perls's emphasis on independence and honesty at the expense of intimacy and compassion more plain than in something he called the Gestalt Prayer. "I do my thing and you do your thing," he wrote. "I'm not in this world to live up to your expectations, and you're not in this world to live up to mine. You are you and I am I. And if by chance we find each other, it's beautiful. If not, it can't be helped."

The real issue with Perls, Murphy eventually concluded, was that his worldview was "woefully incomplete." Murphy elaborated this concept in *The Future of the Body,* by drawing on the ancient Greek concept of *antakolouthia,* or what he calls "the mutual entailment of the virtues." No virtue, Murphy argues elegantly and persuasively, is a virtue by itself. True virtue requires the balancing of opposites. In Perls's case, for example, honesty in the absence of compassion often led to cruelty. Murphy detailed numerous such examples. "Helpful understanding of others," he wrote, "requires both empathy and detachment. Meditation requires both concentration and relaxation. Strengthening of will sometimes involves a yielding or ordinary volitions. . . . Arousal is complemented by relaxation in [successful] yoga. Painful recognitions are supported by self-acceptance during [successful] psychotherapy. The release of certain muscles is accompanied by their realignment in [successful] somatic training."

Despite this penetrating insight, Murphy himself emphasized certain virtues over others, particularly in the early years at Esalen. Robert Hall saw this, for example, in Murphy's antipathy to Perls. "I like Michael very much, and I've always thought of him as a visionary," Hall told me. "But I also saw early on that emotion isn't his favorite country. He just wouldn't participate in process work, and that disturbed me. He would try things but never really get involved. I always felt he was particularly antagonistic to Fritz. Looking back now, I can see that there was some justification. Fritz was irresponsible with power, abusive, terribly opinionated, and he did hurt a lot of people. But he was also very skilled, and I felt that Michael didn't fully appreciate the subtlety of Gestalt therapy and Fritz's work—in part because he never truly allowed himself to experience it."

The other teacher who wielded enormous early influence at Esalen was William Schutz. Trained at UCLA as a social psychologist, Schutz went on to teach at the University of

Chicago, Harvard, Berkeley, and the Albert Einstein School of Medicine. Although he didn't invent the concept of the encounter group, Schutz was responsible for bringing it to wide popular attention with his best-selling book *Joy: Expanding Human Awareness.* The book was published in 1967, the same year that Schutz took up residence as a teacher at Esalen at the age of forty. He spent much of that year traveling the talk-show circuit, promoting his book, and talking about Esalen. The result was that encounter groups became almost synonymous with Esalen even before Schutz had a chance to try them out there.

By sheer force of personality, Schutz soon challenged Perls as the dominant teacher at Esalen. He was confident and powerfully built, forceful and straightforward, funny and self-deprecating. Like Perls, he said what he felt, whether you wanted to hear it or not. He wasn't unusually handsome, but women were drawn to his energy, and he pursued them avidly. Schutz also benefited from Murphy's initial enthusiasm and goodwill. In contrast to Perls's focus on unearthing self-deception, Schutz preached an upbeat message that could just as easily have come from Murphy. "If there is one statement true of every living person, it must be this: he hasn't achieved his potential," Schutz wrote in *Joy.* "The latent abilities, hidden talents and undeveloped capacities for excellence are legion. . . . Joy is the feeling that comes from the fulfillment of one's potential."

Schutz's first experience working with groups occurred in the early 1950s, while he was serving in the navy. He was assigned to help select a group of men who might work together well under stressful conditions in the crowded combat room of a ship. This sparked his interest in the way people interact in groups and led to an academic book exploring his theories. In the mid-1950s, Schutz returned to teaching, this time at Harvard. There he decided to turn a standard seminar on group dynamics into what was then called a training group, or T-group. Rather than lecturing, Schutz instead became part of the group. Classes were built around talking together openly about whatever was on their minds. "I discovered something that I hadn't known anything about—my feelings," Schutz told me on one of the first occasions that we spoke. "I got as fascinated with feelings as I had been earlier with thoughts."

Dissatisfied, like Perls, with the slow process of traditional psychoanalysis, Schutz became a sponge for new therapeutic techniques. In the early 1960s, he spent time at the National Training Laboratories in Bethel, Maine. There the formal academic approach to studying group process was giving way to looser, less structured T-groups. But Schutz didn't limit himself to group work. When he returned to New York to teach medical students at Albert Einstein, he spent his free hours combing the city for new therapeutic approaches and techniques. He studied Gestalt therapy under Perls's collaborator Paul Goodman and learned about guided imagery. He was drawn to body-oriented disciplines such as Alexander Lowen's bioenergetics, a technique inspired directly by Wilhelm Reich, under whom Lowen had studied and been a patient. Schutz also studied Rolfing under its namesake, Ida Rolf. A former chemist, Rolf developed a hands-on technique that involved probing deeply and often painfully into one's muscular tissue in an effort to release chronically tense muscles that cause pain and distort movement. When he returned to Einstein, Schutz started experimenting in his own classes with the techniques he'd learned. Reflecting the eclecticism of his approach, he called it open encounter.

The overriding theme in Schutz's groups at Esalen was honesty. He believed that most people don't tell the truth—to themselves or to each other—and as a result lived half-baked, repressed, and inauthentic lives. Much like Perls, Schutz had a homing instinct for the ways in which people hold back or dissemble, and he used his groups to help get at the underlying truth. The rules in Schutz's open encounters were simple and stark. You said what you had on your mind, you described feelings rather than thoughts, and you stayed focused in the present rather than turning to the past or the future.

Schutz's goal was to break through the barriers prompted by

one's fears, whether they had their origins in childhood, specific traumas, inculcated cultural beliefs, or authoritarian religious conditioning. The group served as his laboratory. If there was a tension between two people in a group, Schutz often encouraged them to put words aside and literally wrestle, as one way of bringing underlying emotions to the surface. If a person seemed tense, Schutz might use one form of bodywork or another to release feelings. If someone felt uncomfortable with his body, Schutz would ask him to take off his clothes and deal directly with the vulnerability that doing so prompted. And if still another person felt angry, he was encouraged to express the anger full-blown—pounding pillows, or screaming, or even throwing an object across the room.

Schutz and Perls were competitive for Murphy's approval but also for dominance at Esalen. While Perls was welcoming to Schutz at first, he grew jealous as the newcomer attracted more attention than he did, including both the prettiest women and the visiting journalists who wrote about Esalen. Eventually, Perls derided Schutz as a "Joy boy"—inferring that Schutz was more concerned with having a good time than with prompting people to truly face themselves. Schutz remained generous to Perls, but their rivalry became a regular sideshow at Esalen. The irony was that despite this personal antagonism, the two men shared vast philosophical common ground. No two teachers had more to do with defining the public image of the early Esalen. Both railed against a repressive culture that they felt prevented people from honestly expressing themselves. Both were gifted at spotting resistance and at bringing people's underlying feelings quickly to the surface. Both were influenced by Reich and believed that emotions were invariably reflected in the body. And both felt that too much thinking prevented access to authentic feelings. But it was the charming Schutz more than the cantankerous Perls who won most of the media attention.

In January 1968, *The New York Times Magazine* published an article that gave both Esalen and Schutz's open encounter a new level of establishment credibility and visibility. It was written by Leo Litwak, a veteran journalist who had arrived at Esalen with great skepticism but left feeling emotionally transformed. The seminal event in Litwak's encounter group, which Schutz led, centered on reliving the day during World War II that Litwak had killed a young German soldier. It began one afternoon when Litwak lay down with his eyes closed and the group gathered around him. Schutz asked if Litwak might be willing to imagine himself inside his own body. Soon, Litwak became completely absorbed in his own imagination, discovering at first that he literally could find no heart inside himself. And then suddenly, he came across one "sheathed in slime, hung with blood vessels." The image proved cathartic.

"That heart broke me up," Litwak wrote at the conclusion of his article. "I felt my chest convulse. I exploded. I burst into tears. . . . Now, twenty-three years later, I wailed for that German boy who had never mattered to me, and I heaved up my numbness. . . . And in the course of that trip through my body, I started to feel again and discovered what I'd missed. I felt wide open, lightened, ready to meet others simply and directly. No need for lies, no need to fear humiliation. I was ready to be a fool. I experienced the joy Schutz had promised to deliver. I'm grateful to him. Not even the offer of love could threaten me."

Within Esalen, no one was a more articulate cheerleader for Schutz—and for the cathartic techniques that characterized the early Esalen—than George Leonard. A tall, whippet-thin, super-charged southerner, Leonard became interested in Esalen in 1965 while researching an article about the human potential movement for *Look* magazine, where he was a staff writer. He was forty-two when he met Michael Murphy, and they became instant soul mates. Like Murphy, Leonard was already convinced that human beings had enormous unlocked potential and that a transformation of consciousness was on the horizon. Esalen, Murphy convinced him, could lead the way. "I was enchanted [by Murphy]," Leonard wrote years later. "Beneath the persona of the genial fraternity man was a sort of inner radiance that I had never seen before." Leonard's article never got published, but in a short time he became Murphy's closest friend and then a vice-president of Esalen. He also became a passionate advocate for Schutz and for the most confrontational forms of encounter.

"You have to understand that until the 1960s, everything was still in the closet," Leonard told me when we met for the first time at his home in Mill Valley, California, in 1989. "You didn't speak of homosexuality. There was no talk of battered wives, or date rape, or sexual abuse. You didn't talk about your feelings. Even the word *cancer* was not spoken in polite society. Then along comes a guy like Schutz who throws out all the taboos. It's almost impossible to describe what an extraordinary experience it was to be in one of his groups. Suddenly—with all this confrontation— you're expressing emotions you've never shared before, telling secrets you've kept for years. And what happens? The world doesn't end, which is what you had expected. Instead, it actually looks better. There's a real feeling of ecstasy just from letting go. And then people come up and hug you. Everyone loves you more for what you've done, for your honesty and courage."

For Leonard, the most powerful such experience occurred in 1968 when he and his then-wife, Lilly, decided to attend a Schutz-run encounter group for couples. Forever pushing for more truth, Schutz suggested that each couple begin by thinking of three secrets that they'd never told their spouses—specifically, ones that had the potential to threaten their marriages. Before long, horrible tales—infidelities, abuse, deceits, resentments—were being fessed up like hand grenades. For most of the couples, Leonard told me, the initial impact was an experience of great release and exhilaration. Indeed, by week's end, many of the couples in the group felt closer than ever. What they weren't prepared for were the aftershocks. Back home, a week or two later, the painful secrets that they'd shared resurfaced. Once again, the effect was explosive, only this time no one was around to mediate and offer support. The legacy of all this concentrated truth-telling often proved painful and destructive. It was one thing to help people open up and quite another to leave them without the resources to integrate their new feelings and insights.

While Leonard retained his enthusiasm for Schutz's groundbreaking approach, Murphy's support for encounter diminished steadily over the years. "Schutz was mostly focused on breaking loose," Murphy told me. "He was the caboose on a train that began with Freud and Reich. In the name of openness and honesty, he honored and encouraged integrity and courage in his groups, but there was often a shortage of kindness and empathy." It turned out, for example, that anger was the emotion most commonly elicited in encounter groups. The problem was that ventilating intensely angry feelings didn't mean that they got spent or resolved. As the psychologist Carol Tavris wrote recently in *Anger: The Misunderstood Emotion,* "The people who are most prone to give vent to their rages get angrier, not less angry." In addition, as Tavris and others have noted, the expression of anger often deflects attention from the more vulnerable underlying emotions that anger often serves to mask—among them fear, helplessness, disappointment, sadness, and despair.

"You can't live on encounter," Murphy told writer Calvin Tomkins in 1976. "Encounter is like an initiation ceremony, a way of crossing a boundary and looking at what's on the other side." Even after limited experience in such groups, Murphy concluded that he'd had more than enough. "By the early 1970s," he told me, "I wouldn't go near encounter with a ten-foot pole."

Schutz wasn't entirely surprised that Murphy turned on encounter. "Michael's a meditation man, a quiet man, and he's basically very conservative," Schutz told me in 1991, sounding more disappointed than bitter. "His image of what Esalen should be came from Aurobindo. What he wanted most was an intellectual center, where issues could be discussed. To me, there were all sorts of universities where you could do that—Stanford and Berkeley and Harvard. Exchanging ideas doesn't prompt change. What was unique about Esalen were the experiential practices—the sensory awakening, and Gestalt and bodywork and tai chi and encounter. I went through six hundred hours of psychoanalysis myself, and I found that long-term talk therapy—where patients are mostly taught to be patients—isn't nearly as effective as more confrontational, short-term group work. Michael wasn't ever really comfortable with much of this—especially the things I did in encounter, where you get excited and stir up emotions and get physical. But he has an interesting kind of open-mindedness. He always liked to think of Esalen as an umbrella, and so he continued to sponsor people like me, even when he didn't agree with us. That's his real genius, I think."

Even today, Schutz continues to teach occasional workshops at Esalen—albeit a tamer version than those he ran in the 1960s. Meanwhile, Murphy only became more convinced that cathartic techniques like those used in Schutz's encounter groups and Perls's Gestalt therapy simply were not vehicles for enduring change. "I began to recognize that what we were calling the Big Bang approach didn't work," Murphy told me, echoing Ram Dass's conclusion about psychedelics. "It got people started. What we didn't provide them with was a lasting set of disciplines. We didn't talk about the dark night of the soul—the ups and downs along the path and the fact that it can get worse before it gets better. We didn't say that change has to be reinforced with disciplined practices and that the learning curve has long plateaus. In the end, we were in too much of a hurry."

This was most painfully evident when Esalen tried to launch a residential program in 1967. It was aimed at providing a small number of "psychonauts" with a highly intense and concentrated set of transformative practices ranging from meditation to encounter over an extended number of months. The program was abandoned at the end of the second year. By that time, two of the original members had committed suicide. Murphy once again proved to be his own most cogent critic. "To me, our program didn't have the sense of center—the balance—that you have to have if you're going to go very deeply into personal transformation," he told Tomkins. "It was too wild and chaotic."

L ooking back, Murphy believes that part of the problem in the early years was his own inability to confront and control people like Perls and Schutz. "I just didn't have the available personal power to stand up to Fritz and others," he told me. "I never felt entitled, even though I was the founder, the owner of the property, and I did all the scheduling. Instead, I allowed a certain set of characters to dominate the scene, often against my better judgment." On the other hand, Esalen may never have gotten the attention it did, nor become so popular, had Murphy been able to impose a more intellectual and transcendental vision on his creation. His loftier hopes—that people might use intensive meditation practice to develop higher levels of consciousness, for example—simply didn't resonate with the ambitions of the searchers who came to Esalen. The catalog always included workshop offerings in disciplines such as meditation and yoga. But through the 1960s and 1970s, these difficult solitary practices never prompted nearly the excitement that Gestalt, encounter, and various forms of bodywork did.

Murphy believed that fully expressing one's potential also included some component of social consciousness and service to others—and he always sought to incorporate that ethic into Esalen's mix. Sure enough, several attempts were made. George Leonard, along with a black psychiatrist named Price Cobbs, ran a series of encounter workshops beginning in 1968, aimed at bringing together blacks and whites to confront each other honestly about the explosive issue of race relations. The program blew up two years later in the wake of a racially charged incident among the group leaders. The Esalen Program in Humanistic Medicine set out in the early 1970s to train health professionals to bring a more personal, caring perspective to their patients—long before the recent explosion of interest in mind-body medicine. Esalen and a professor named George Brown got a grant to study something called "confluent education" that paralleled Murphy's early dream of broadening school curricula to address not just the mind but also the body and the spirit. In 1971, Murphy made the first of many visits to Russia, initially to discuss with scientists a mutual interest in parapsychology and later to open up a broader cultural exchange. While all of these programs enjoyed some success and a few served as precursors to far broader movements that emerged later, they attracted only limited attention at Esalen itself.

What Esalen lacked, as Murphy and others came to see, was teachers with broad and embracing visions. Instead, workshop leaders arrived at Esalen having long since chosen up sides. Perhaps never were these opposites so apparent as during a legendary visit that Abraham Maslow made to Esalen in 1966. Maslow came with the ambitious intellectual goal of trying to evolve a new language that might capture more precisely the sort of peak experiences and higher human possibilities that he'd long been studying. Murphy helped put together a group of twenty-five people for the seminar. He was reluctant to invite Fritz Perls, knowing that Perls was likely to be disruptive and confrontational. Still, he couldn't bring himself to openly exclude anyone—even his combative nemesis.

No sooner did Perls arrive at the meeting than he assumed the role of provocateur. He had little tolerance for the sort of high-minded theoretical discussions that he termed elephant shit, and even less patience for a gathering that he perceived as pretentious and pointless. At least equally important, he couldn't bear ceding center stage to Maslow, who was himself accustomed to the deference typically accorded a college professor. When Maslow complimented a suggestion that one participant made, for example, Perls immediately jumped in. "This is just like school," he said derisively. "Here is the teacher, and there is the pupil, giving the right answers." Nonconfrontational by nature, Maslow simply ignored the jab and several that followed. While Perls was undeniably rude and hostile, he was also articulating a feeling that many group members shared. Maslow's safe formal distance, and his dry intellectual approach resulted in an abstract level of discussion that was largely removed from people's real-life experience.

Eventually, Perls decided to step up his challenge. Sliding off his chair onto the floor, he literally crawled over to Maslow, looked up and invited him to come down to his level. Maslow was appalled. When he accused Perls of being childish, Perls only became more so, hugging Maslow's knees. Finally, Maslow turned in disgust to Murphy, who was both amused and mortified by the performance. "This begins to look like sickness," Maslow told Murphy, at which point Maslow ended the session and went off to regather his thoughts—and his equanimity. When he returned to the group the next day, it was with a stern lecture about the perils of rejecting the intellect and of rebellion without a cause.

"I must urge you to meditate on the fact that Esalen, and many of the people at Esalen . . . are fleeing from overinhibition, overintellectualization," he said. " . . . What's self-actualization for anyway? If you don't want to be a selfish person contemplating your navel, you put your shoulder to the wheel. . . . When your brain is free to work spontaneously, it's a very nice feeling. . . . If you don't use your brain, you're not fulfilling your potential. . . . I'm a good worker. I work hard. I try to achieve things, and this is out of ultimate affection for other people. I would like to do good." Murphy wholeheartedly shared these sentiments, but he also appreciated the feeling of some at the seminar that Maslow was too self-serious and condescending, and that inventing an abstract new language wasn't advancing any truly useful cause.

As he moved toward the end of his life, Maslow grew more critical of Esalen—but in some unexpected ways. In the spring of 1970, according to his biographer Edward Hoffman, Maslow sat down to write a detailed critique of Esalen and other growth centers that it had helped spawn around the country. Like other critics of the human potential movement, most notably the writers Christopher Lasch, Peter Marin, and Tom Wolfe, Maslow was particularly bothered by the often-narcissistic focus on personal growth at Esalen, and by the lack of attention to broader social concerns. He was also increasingly galled by its focus on sensory experience and emotions to the exclusion of the intellect. Finally, he scored Esalen for its quick-fix approach to change and its inattention to values such as hard work, discipline, and long-term commitment. All of these criticisms Michael Murphy seconded.

Surprisingly, however, Maslow also questioned the very premise on which Esalen had been founded and which lay at the heart of his own lifelong work: namely, the importance of developing one's highest and healthiest potentials. This, he felt, remained the ultimate goal. But before higher growth is possible, he concluded, it is necessary to resolve one's underlying conflicts and neuroses. By virtue of Esalen's focus on the higher states of health, Maslow said, more traditional psychotherapeutic approaches had been too readily discarded. The irony was that Maslow himself had helped delineate these higher states. "Esalen should not exclude Freud and psychoanalysis," he wrote in a critique that mirrored a change in his own life: At the age of sixty-one, Maslow entered psychoanalysis.

In the process, he discovered for the first time a great well of anger that he began to recognize he had long repressed. His cardiologist had warned him that this anger posed a direct danger to his health, which had been weakened by two heart attacks. Maslow also began to see how much he had shaped his life around avoiding anger and negative emotions more generally. Now, he found himself more interested in the nature of evil in the world and the degree to which it grew out of human ignorance and lack of consciousness. It was as if he finally felt able to face life's dark side. In a sense he'd come full circle. Influenced by Freudian thinking early in his career, he went on to reject that world view as too limited—only to realize, toward the end of his life, that dealing with unresolved conflict was critical to fully realizing one's potential and living a complete life.

As it turned out, Maslow didn't live to finish his critique of Esalen or his own psychoanalysis. On a sunny Saturday in June 1970, he was jogging in place by the pool of his home in Menlo Park, California, when he suffered a massive third heart attack and died instantly. He was just sixty-two years old. Fritz Perls had died several months earlier, having left Esalen in 1969 to set up his own Gestalt center in an abandoned motel in British Columbia. Schutz remained at Esalen for another three years, but when he left, encounter quickly faded from the scene. Murphy himself had ceased living full-time on the grounds at Big Sur in 1967, when he established a branch of Esalen in San Francisco, and spent more and more time there. The year that Perls and Maslow died proved a turning point for him as well.

In the spring of 1970, Murphy and a group of Esalen teachers were invited to England to discuss and demonstrate their work. They gave workshops and met the leading lights of England's human potential movement, most notably the radical psychiatrist R. D. Laing. It was on a side trip to Italy that Murphy's original vision of transformation—the one he had watched take unexpected turns at Esalen—was powerfully reenergized. He traveled to Florence to meet Robert Assagioli, a psychiatrist then in his mid-80s, who had developed a therapy called psychosynthesis. A contemporary of Freud, Assagioli began as a psychoanalyst but eventually came to the conclusion that Jung and Maslow did— namely, that Freud's theories didn't take into account higher human possibility.

Assagioli didn't simply discard Freud. Rather, he hypothesized that finding one's true self requires not just resolving conflicts in what he called "the lower unconscious," but also developing the "higher unconscious," which contain one's highest intuitions and inspirations. "We have first to penetrate courageously into the pit of our lower unconscious in order to discover the dark forces that ensnare and menace us," Assagioli wrote in *Psychosynthesis,* a book that Esalen published. "What (then) has to be achieved is to expand the personal consciousness into that of the Self . . . to unite the lower with the higher Self." Murphy was moved by the breadth of Assagioli's approach. "I was especially attracted to his idea that modern psychology could be integrated with the perennial wisdom," Murphy told me. "He was a far more comprehensive thinker than either Fritz or Schutz, with a more encompassing worldview. It was a reaffirmation for me of the need for comprehensive practices." Psychosynthesis, however, gained no visible champion in the United States and never attracted more than a modest following.

The challenge of developing comprehensive transformational practices became the cornerstone of Murphy's work over the next two decades. When he got back from Europe, he decided that the intensity of the scene at Esalen had pushed his life badly out of balance. A passionate affair that began when he moved to San Francisco had led him into an ill-fated marriage that lasted for less than a year. He longed now for a quieter life, more like the one he'd lived during his years of meditation. When he found an apartment on San Francisco's Telegraph Hill, Murphy turned his attention to meditation and to writing. His first novel— and the one that remains his best known—was built around his two most passionate interests: sports and mysticism. It was titled *Golf and the Kingdom.* His second, *Jacob Atabet,* was a somewhat autobiographical fiction, describing a young San Francisco scholar/mystic interested in transformation and eager to bring higher human possibilities to greater public consciousness. In 1974, Murphy remarried, to Dulce Cottle, who had started out as his assistant and went on to run the Esalen office in San Francisco after Murphy pulled back.

In the early 1980s, Murphy started working with an assistant on a venture he named the Esalen Institute Transformation Project. His goal was to create a vast library of evidence for people's extraordinary mental, physical, and spiritual capacities. To that end, he gathered documentation not just from scientific studies but from fieldwork done by anthropologists as well as eyewitness testimonies. In mid-1984, he decided to devote himself full time to writing a book that amassed and summarized these findings. That December, Dulce gave birth to a son, and Murphy became a father for the first time at the age of fifty-five. The following October, Richard Price died in a freak accident. He had continued to live at Esalen and was out hiking in the mountains of Big Sur one afternoon when a huge boulder broke loose and apparently caught him by surprise. It broke his neck. Murphy was devastated by the loss, but it only redoubled his commitment to capture in writing the life work that he and Price had shared.

Murphy decided to name his book *The Future of the Body,*

drawing on Aurobindo's notion that the work of transformation is finally about the descent of spirit into the flesh—embodiment more than transcendence. An extraordinary intellectual effort in its own right, *The Future of the Body* runs nearly eight hundred pages, draws on more than three thousand sources, and covers a vast terrain, from the history of evolutionary theory to the evidence for life after death; from remarkable incidences of spiritual healing to bodily changes that occur in hypnosis. On one level, the book integrates and elaborates the themes that led Murphy to found Esalen thirty years ago. He still argues passionately that we stand on the precipice of a third great evolutionary leap. "Twice evolution itself has evolved on this planet," Murphy told me, as he was finishing his book. "It happened when inorganic elements gave rise to life, and then when life gave rise to humankind. Now I'm trying to argue that all basic human attributes—everything from communication, vitality, and movement to cognition, volition, and even the capacity to love—have superordinary counterparts. I'm convinced that these higher possibilities can be harnessed through certain transformative practices. Human development is not finished yet."

A year after my first meeting with Murphy, he elaborated on these ideas at an Esalen workshop that he led with George Leonard. It was a wonderful week. We spent the days and early evenings in the workshop. At night I sat with Murphy and others in his room drinking beer and talking, or sitting down at the baths with others in the workshop. We ran along Highway One in the mornings, argued about transformation over long lunches and dinners, and played touch football on the lawn whenever we had a few minutes between meetings. But mostly Murphy shared with us what he'd learned about human possibility. "I'm heavily influenced by the idea that the culture reinforces certain possibilities and ignores or suppresses others," he explained in his introductory remarks. "All life is evolutionary—although not necessarily in positive directions. Evolution meanders more than it advances. Human beings can progress, or we can regress. We don't yet have the structures set up in our fragmented technological culture to cultivate all that we know is possible. What interests me is identifying and supporting those disciplines which lead to positive transformation. Integral practices engage all parts of one's being—physical, emotional, intellectual, volitional, and spiritual."

Murphy is especially persuasive in elucidating the myriad obstacles to the balanced pursuit of a complete life. "There is something built into existence," he told our Esalen group, "that makes life's journey an athletic contest—Christ with the Devil, the Buddha with ignorance, Freud with the unconscious. There is divinity within us, but getting to it isn't easy." Even as a long-term meditator, for example, Murphy remains critical of the many mystical traditions that emphasize the evolution of consciousness through meditation while overlooking or disparaging the role of embodying one's transformation in everyday life. "Consciousness—awareness—is only one aspect of participation in the world," he told us. "I think meditation is fundamental to any integral practice, but I find it hard to believe that the universe labored for thousands of years so that we could all end up in retreats. If it's all about meltdown into nirvana, there's no further adventure and God gave us a bad punchline. To me, the true adventure in life is through our embodiment here.

In *The Future of the Body,* Murphy enumerates the ways in which even well-established practices can subvert the balanced search for wisdom. Any given meditative discipline, he points out, can provide a way to avoid intimate contact with others. Psychotherapeutic insights can be used to rationalize impulsive and harmful behavior as the expression of authentic feelings. Even the cultivation of superordinary skills or *siddhis*—psychic capacities, for instance—can prompt an inflated sense of self-importance, as well as divert attention from more balanced growth. Relying on a single teacher also poses dangers, Murphy believes. "You're assuming that one person can teach you about all the dimensions, and that's an impossible demand," he told me. "The royal road to an integral practice is through a curriculum that no one guru could ever provide." Finally, unconscious resistance to change inevitably counterbalances even the most passionate commitment to transformation. "People are frequently attracted to activities," he concludes, "that preserve and disguise their shortcomings."

Murphy himself is no exception. The practices that interest him have long been less oriented to psychological introspection and self-exploration than to the cultivation of higher states of consciousness through a blend of will, discipline, and surrender. For all of its value, meditation has been as least partly a way for Murphy to avoid the emotional conflict that he finds so difficult to engage. "I've had to do a lot of work on my own psychodynamics, all through my life," he told me. "My original course did not lead in that direction, but I have had to engage fearful dark sides of myself again and again. I keep coming back to certain weaknesses of mine to understand them more deeply, to both modify them and to accept them as part of who I am. It's certainly not in the center of my interests, but I've had to do it just to cope and to be as creative as I want to be. I don't like to confront the messiness at Esalen, but I keep doing it, and it's always been rewarding. I've been willing to go against this tendency in me to escape." At the same time, his inclinations—and disinclinations—remain very powerful. In *The Future of the Body*, for example, Murphy devotes nearly fifty pages to documenting the charisms of Catholic saints and more than thirty pages to exceptional functioning in adventure and sport, reflecting his twin passions for mysticism and sports. By contrast, he devotes less than four pages to the subject of psychotherapy.

In January 1992, Murphy and George Leonard launched an experiment they call "integral transformative practice." Together, they recruited three dozen people, who agreed to meet once a week for a nine month period. In addition, participants committed themselves to engage in a set of daily practices aimed at promoting what Murphy and Leonard called "the positive, healthy transformation of individual body, mind, and spirit." The purpose was to help people systematically nurture more complete lives. Several of the formal practices focused on transforming the body—including a commitment to at least three hours of aerobic exercise each week in thirty-minute increments; a daily set of stretching, strengthening, and balancing exercises; a vow to try to eat a low-fat diet and a recommended three sessions of strength training per week. There was also regular meditation practice. The group's reading assignments—from Murphy's *The Future of the Body* and a book of Leonard's called *Mastery*—focused on the cultivation of a broader range of skills and capacities more than on any systematic self-exploration. Even so, reports from participants suggest that they derived value from the work on all levels—physical, emotional, intellectual, and spiritual. Recently, several members of the group organized a new one, and Murphy and Leonard hope to open a center specifically devoted to integral practices.

Murphy himself underwent an unanticipated emotional upheaval in his own life in the winter of 1993. The catalyst was the unraveling of his marriage of twenty years. "What it led to was a broken heart," Murphy told me. At the age of sixty-one, he found himself dealing with a level of grief and despair that he'd rarely experienced before. He spent several months in therapy, for the first time in his life, and found it illuminating. "I've gotten a deeper appreciation for the value of long-term therapy," he told me. "It's in my temperament to meet the world with humor, distance and deflection. I love freedom and I love to play, and this more intimate level has meant a lot of hard work and drudgery and pain. But it has also been enriching, and illuminating."

Around the same time that his marriage was unraveling, Steve Donovan, a longtime friend and colleague who'd run Esalen day to day, decided to leave. Murphy chose to take over himself, temporarily. In part, his goal was to rethink and to broaden Esalen's mission for the future, even as its workshops continue to fill to capacity. With that in mind, Murphy made it a practice to go down to the dining room at seven each morning to talk with people about what Esalen meant to them. For several hours at a stretch, Murphy engaged seminarians, staff members, and work-scholars who come and stay at Esalen for several months. "It's been a revelation," he told me in the summer of 1993. "What I've gotten is a whole new level of appreciation for how Esalen serves people. I realized that they come here for self-discovery and to heal broken hearts. I've really just caught up with that. I always talked about it conceptually, but I finally felt it, intensely, in part because of what I've been going through personally. I was moved by the bravery of these people who are not settling for where they are. I saw how they come here to try something new, to have someone to weep with and share with, to get insights about themselves, and to gain courage for the next step in their lives."

Murphy concluded that he'd long undervalued these experiences. Nor had he thought before to question critics who referred derisively to Esalen as too "touchy-feely." Perhaps, he now concluded, this orientation was actually a point in Esalen's favor. "What's wrong with touching? What's wrong with feeling?" Murphy said during one recent conversation. "Maybe the real problem in our culture is that we don't do enough of either one. Is self-discovery bad? Is it wrong to move out into new territories? That's the heart of the evolutionary adventure. It connects straight up with my original vision for Esalen."

For all that, Murphy remains passionate in his conviction that beneath even the darkest moments, ecstasy and higher possibilities are always fighting to break through. For sustenance in his own time of need, he renewed his commitment to meditation—focusing particularly on practices of the heart. He began putting in at least several hours of sitting, beginning with two hours from five to seven each morning. "There's been a lot of pain and loneliness but also great joy," he told me in the spring of 1994. "Out of the broken heart comes the love. This joy passes all understanding. I actually see the suffering as grace. I'm more convinced than ever that our founding idea for Esalen—the development of the whole person—was on target. Part of the lesson, I now realize, is that incomplete as we all are, we can nevertheless keep growing."

3

THE YOGA OF THE WEST

Elmer Green, Biofeedback, and Self-Control

*We have been inhibited, repressed and hypnotized by
our cultural conditioning and education to see ourselves
as powerless to control or change events in our bodies
and lives. . . . We have not been informed that our
bodies tend to do what they are told to do if we know
how to tell them. . . . Only when we do not accept this
limiting image of ourselves can we break the thralldom
and begin to operate as free beings, capable of influencing to a significant extent the course of our lives.*
—ELMER GREEN

*Wherever limitations recede, the body becomes more
plastic and responsive and in that measure a more fit
and perfect instrument of the action of the spirit.*
—SRI AUROBINDO

WHERE Ram Dass and Michael Murphy are
both charming, charismatic, and ebullient seekers of wisdom, everything about Elmer Green
bespeaks his more reserved, flintier midwestern roots. Green, in
his mid-70s when we met, is plain-spoken, low-key, and no-
nonsense. In his quietly forceful way, however, he represents a
third passionate and pioneering voice in the emergence of the
consciousness movement in America during the early 1960s.
While Murphy focused on nurturing the human potential and
Ram Dass on routes to transcendence, Green is a scientist who
has sought to quantify the practical value of meditative states; to

prove the inextricable connection between the mind and the body in treating illness; and to provide a measurable technology— biofeedback—for accessing higher states of consciousness. He has also been deeply interested in people's capacity to transform their lives in these states.

Rail-thin, and balding with a wispy goatee, gold wire-rim glasses, lively eyes, and an open face, Green has an unusual blend of inclinations. He is both down-to-earth and mystical; rigorously objective but also guided by a deep faith in his own intuitive wisdom; systematic and painstaking in his research, yet open-minded, and eager to explore phenomena that defy rational understanding. Immensely self-confident, he has rarely sought recognition for his extraordinary body of work. He believes that he has a larger mission and pursues his interests without regard for their conventional acceptability. Green has been content to be a gadfly within the prestigious Menninger Clinic in Topeka, Kansas, where he spent most of his career.

I sought from Green not just his piece of the wisdom puzzle but some grounding in my own search. Ram Dass, Murphy, and others talked a great deal about the broader, more open-hearted and selfless perspective that emerges in meditation and about the unusual powers that can be accessed in these highly focused states. But what exactly is this relaxed, wordless experience, and why is it so elusive? Even after more than a year of daily meditation and several longer retreats, I was unable reliably and predictably to quiet my mind in meditation, or even to know for certain when I was approaching such a state. I felt hungry for more objective markers, for some evidence that I could gain predictable, voluntary access to these experiences.

The vehicle for Green's search was biofeedback—a field that he, his wife Alyce, and their colleague Dale Walters helped to invent in the early 1960s. Biofeedback is neither mystical nor subjective. It refers simply to physiological information—ranging from muscle tension to body temperature, blood pressure to brainwave activity—that can be fed back to a subject in the form of light, sound, or vibration. As one's blood pressure decreases, for example, a light might be programmed to flash more regularly. Biofeedback training is based on the premise that by bringing internal physiological processes to conscious awareness, it becomes possible to get them under some degree of voluntary control.

The principles of learning to regulate one's own physiology were first articulated at least 2,500 years ago in certain Eastern mystical traditions, but the Greens developed biofeedback as a vehicle to understand self-regulation and self-awareness in Western scientific terms. Biofeedback provides what Green ultimately termed "a bridge between the conscious and the unconscious, voluntary and involuntary, cortex and subcortex, and even between reason and intuition." In short, biofeedback became a means to bring to awareness aspects of one's self that remain inaccessible under ordinary circumstances—"a part of our nature," Green explained, "that is normally blocked off." Ultimately, the Greens' goal was to demonstrate, in very measurable ways, at conscious knowledge and understanding represent just one level of intelligence and that a complete life also depends on tapping the nonverbal powers of the mind, body, and the unconscious.

The Greens went on to become biofeedback's unofficial first family. Alyce's daughter from her first marriage, Pat Norris, and her husband, Steve Fahrion, are both psychologists who worked at Menninger in biofeedback for more than a decade as clinicians and researchers. They have each published extensively based on their own research, and they recently opened the Life Sciences Institute of Mind-Body Health in Topeka. Elmer and Alyce's daughter, Judy Green, and her husband, Robert Schellenberger, are both psychologists and professors at Aims Community College in Greeley, Colorado. Together they wrote one of the best books about early biofeedback research, titled *The Ghost in the Box*. Alyce's son from her first marriage, Doug Boyd, is an author who has written widely about consciousness, including a book about one of the Greens' most extraordinary research subjects, Swami Rama.

By the time I met Elmer, Alyce was suffering from a degenerative brain disease, and he spent all but one afternoon a week taking care of her at their home. We did eventually meet and I visited Menninger, but mostly I spoke with Green by telephone. He was unfailingly generous with his time. Sometimes I spent as much as two hours asking questions, and over several years, we spoke perhaps two dozen times. We developed an unusual relationship. Although he spoke with great conviction and passion about his opinions, I never had the feeling that he was looking to convince me of anything. I was interested in what he knew, he respected the seriousness of my search, and he was happy to help in any way he could. He didn't even seem to be looking for anything from me, yet I sensed he was always happy to talk together. More than virtually anyone I met in my search, Green seemed free of any personal agenda.

In both his research and his writing, Green has focused on finding ways to put biofeedback and the capacity for physiological self-regulation to practical clinical use. Beyond that, he is interested in systematically accessing deeper levels of wisdom, developing untapped potentials, and nurturing what he envisions as a higher self that transcends one's ego or everyday personality. In part, this emphasis grew out of that fact that Green himself didn't feel much preoccupied by conflicts from his own childhood. He characterizes his relationship to his parents in warm, positive terms and feels fortunate and grateful to be free of the "guilt, fear, anger, and jealousy that so many people are stuck in."

In the course of three decades, Green's team at Menninger used biofeedback to teach thousands of patients to overcome illnesses ranging from migraine headaches to high blood pressure to Raynaud's disease. They also carefully documented the voluntary control that certain highly trained individuals could achieve over their own bodies in focused states of consciousness. Citing the difficulty of getting research grants from traditional funding sources, the Greens did not undertake the sort of classically controlled studies that might have given their work more credibility in the medical and scientific communities. Nonetheless, their clinical and theoretical work at Menninger has served as an inspiration for a whole new generation of biofeedback researchers who are now undertaking controlled studies of their own. In turn, these researchers are demonstrating that biofeedback—and most notably, brainwave feedback—is a highly effective treatment for a variety of illnesses and disorders in which conventional medical treatment falls short.

Elmer Green learned to juggle his often conflicting impulses early in life. He grew up the elder of two sons in a religious Methodist family in Duluth, Minnesota. Green's father was forced to drop out of college to support his young family by managing a J. C. Penney store. He remained intellectually curious, however, reading widely and directing the church choir. Green's mother was a housewife, and in contrast to her husband's highly rational, linear approach to life, she was more intuitively inclined. "My dad was often wrong about things, but for exactly the right reasons," Green told me. "He had all the logic, but the problem is that logic doesn't explain everything. My mother was often right, but for all the wrong reasons. She'd say, 'You can't trust that guy. Just look at the tie he's wearing.' She'd turn out to be right, but it had nothing to do with the tie. My parents made an interesting pair because they didn't understand each other at all. I understood both of them, and so I became the family mediator." When Elmer was in college, his parents finally divorced. He wasn't deeply affected by the split, he believes, both because he was largely on his own and because he continued to feel loved, appreciated, and respected by both of his parents.

From early childhood, Green was captivated by an intuitive sense that there are powerful unrecognized forces at work in life. He first became interested in psychic phenomena, for example, because his mother so frequently came up with specific information about people or events that she had no conventional way of knowing. Green himself eventually had several psychic experiences. On one occasion as a teenager, for example, he had a vivid dream about the brother of a friend who was then serving in the navy. In the dream, the brother explained to Green that he had suffered for months from a painful infection in his leg but was finally beginning to get better. Weeks later, Green learned that the brother had just sent a letter home describing precisely the events of Green's dream.

In high school, his interest focused increasingly on science— most notably, physics—and he was taken with the rigorousness and logical beauty of the scientific method. At the same time, as a senior, Elmer and his mother together joined a small religious group conducted by a one-time minister named Arthur Green (no relation). By this point, Green, much like Michael Murphy, felt put off by the doctrine and dogma of organized religion. "I was tired," he told me, "of hearing hackneyed platitudes that just didn't fit with my experience of things." Arthur Green, however, had trained in techniques of mind-body coordination that had been handed down from the Sufi tradition. A mystical branch of Islam, Sufism emphasizes the importance of learning to voluntarily control the mind, body, and emotions as part of the path to self-realization and wisdom. Arthur Green acknowledged the value of the scientific materialist view to which Elmer felt so drawn. At the same time, he suggested there are other forces at work in life that defy rational explanation yet still deserve attention.

Arthur Green taught Elmer and his mother several techniques aimed at using the mind to solve problems in nonordinary ways. One involved asking one's unconscious, in the hazy state just before sleep, to provide answers to questions or problems in the form of dream symbols. He also taught them how to interpret the symbolic answers they received. Years later, Elmer used a variation on this technique to solve a mathematical problem that had vexed scholars for one hundred years—and then published his finding in the journal *Science*. Even so, Arthur Green did not advocate blindly trusting one's intuition—or anyone else's absolute authority. "If you feel that you know a truth," he told his students, "you must be able to demonstrate it in your life to some degree. Otherwise you don't really know it. You are only talking."

In 1936, Elmer enrolled at the University of Minnesota to study physics, but he retained his interest in exploring consciousness and soon found a new group to join. Dr. Will J. Erwood had been a minister in the Spiritualist Church but quit after a fight with the Church elders and went on to support himself by traveling the lecture circuit. In 1937, he settled in Minneapolis and began teaching Eastern and Western approaches to enhancing self-awareness. Green was taken both with Erwood's eclectic knowledge and his powers of self-control. Once, for example, Erwood accidentally cut himself quite badly with a kitchen knife. Within several days, he had completely healed and was virtually scar-free. Green sought an explanation. "The body will do what you tell it, if you learn how to tell it," Erwood told Green. "The way of telling it involves [internal] quietness, plus a visualization of what you want the body to do."

As Green continued working with Erwood and reading widely in the metaphysical literature, his interest in college—and in traditional science—diminished. He was especially fascinated by the notion that learning to relax the body, quiet the emotions, and still the mind makes it possible to tap capacities that most people never know are possible. To Green, Erwood's most extraordinary powers occurred when the minister put himself in a trance state and spoke in a wholly different voice—identifying himself only as "the Teacher." Over two years, Green had more than a hundred sessions with Erwood's Teacher. "It turned out that he knew virtually everything that had happened to me, in every year of my life, including my dreams," Green told me.

But the Teacher was also clear—much as Arthur Green had been—that he was only a resource in Green's search for wisdom and that no outside authority could be relied on for all the answers. "When I asked him his name," Green told me, "he said, 'If I give you a name that you recognize as having some historical significance, you may believe the things I tell you, and that would be for the wrong reasons. If I give you a name that you don't recognize, you might disbelieve me, and that too would be for the wrong reasons.' " In time, this became Green's own credo. "One should not believe, but rather should investigate, until experience enables one to know," he later wrote. "Prejudgment blocks learning, because it distorts perception, so the word of authorities should be used only as data." To trust any absolute authority, Green concluded, is counterproductive. "Such compliance [leads] ultimately to surrender of volition and self-awareness," he wrote, "and our goal was the opposite: to increase both."

While exploring consciousness continued to attract him, Green's more practical instincts took over after he married Alyce in 1941. Suddenly, he needed to earn a living. By the time World War II broke out, he was supporting three children—two from Alyce's first marriage—and he received a deferment from the draft. Financial considerations continued to guide his career choices. After the war, Green enrolled briefly as a graduate student in physics at UCLA, but when money got tight, he was forced to go back to work, this time as a physicist with the Naval Ordnance Test Station in China Lake, California. At the same time, he continued in his free time to read books on yoga and the Eastern mystical traditions.

For more than a decade, Green also focused attention on trying to better understand the forces of his personality and to marshal his energies in the service of goals beyond merely enhancing his own power and position. "I came to understand that the ego is composed of a huge number of autonomous entities that were all screaming for my attention," Green told me. "I could easily have become very egotistical. The challenge was to watch my behavior very carefully and even to look at what my dreams were telling me. I also talked with Alyce every day about what I was seeing. You need someone objective to listen to you, because the ego is always finding ways to deceive you. Working through this personality material is the hardest thing in the world. It means learning to let go of all attachments, so you don't get trapped even in things like accomplishment and success."

Green was also inspired by Alyce's strong interest in pursuing a spiritual life. She had grown up on a farm in North Dakota and was interested from early on in the relationship between the mind and the body. As a young mother, she discovered that she seemed to have the power to heal her children when they were ill, simply based on what she thought and felt. "I would sing to them, sing my visualization of light and energy correcting the difficulty or healing the body," she explained much later. "Often it seemed to work, by bringing relief from pain . . . and sometimes the sudden lowering of a high temperature or quick recovery from a childhood disease. Those times when I could achieve a certain feeling of vibrant aliveness . . . seemed to be followed by success."

Interestingly, it was only after Alyce retired and became ill, shortly after she turned eighty, that she began to deal with a level of her own unfinished business. While the illness left her mostly unable to communicate, she continued to have periods of lucidity. "She explained to me that she's finally finding out what she didn't focus attention on before," Elmer told me at one point, shortly before Alyce died in the summer of 1994. "All her life she was very spiritually advanced. My sins were of commission, but hers were of omission. She didn't fight for herself or say what her needs were. She never meditated to explore herself but only to do healing on others. And of course she did have needs like anyone else, and that's what she's finally begun to see."

Although Elmer worked for more than a decade at the Naval Station, he grew increasingly disenchanted with what he perceived as the narrow objective worldview of his fellow physicists. By 1957, Elmer had finally saved up enough money to return to graduate school. He applied and that fall was admitted to the University of Chicago in biological psychology, while Alyce enrolled to study psychology. Elmer also continued to develop his powers of self-regulation. He taught himself, for example, to go for long periods without sleep and to marshal extraordinary focus of attention when necessary. For example, he wrote his 198-page Ph.D. thesis in one extraordinary ten-day period in 1962, during which he slept a total of just twenty hours and twice typed for thirty-six hours at a stretch without getting up—largely by relying on yogic breathing techniques designed to conserve energy.

It was during graduate school that Green was introduced by a fellow student to a book that profoundly influenced the next stage of his career. Titled *Autogenic Training,* it was written by a German neurologist named Johannes Schultz, who had developed the technique beginning in 1910 as a means of inducing deep physical relaxation in patients. He built autogenic training around visualizing a series of sensations while repeating them out loud to oneself. The sensations ranged from "My right arm is heavy," to "My heartbeat is calm and regular," to "My forehead is cool."

The traditional Western view is that it is impossible to gain conscious control over autonomic nervous system functions such as the regulation of body temperature. However, when the graduate student demonstrated Schultz's simple exercises, Green couldn't help but be impressed. "His hand got so warm and swollen that he couldn't remove his ring for several minutes," Green wrote later. By 1959, when Schultz and his colleague Wolfgang Luthe published *Autogenic Training* in an English-language edition, they had gathered six hundred corroborative studies of their work, conducted by physicians and psychologists across Europe. The technique demonstrably helped alleviate symptoms of insomnia, headache, asthma, and chronic constipation.

Green sensed that such powers were not just a means to self-healing but a necessary step on the road to wisdom. "Learning to warm one's hands involves the development of consciousness and volition," he told me, "To warm the hands, you have to find a way to be calm and quiet inside. And when you learn to do that, you're essentially doing what yogis have been talking about for all these thousands of years: quieting the internal machinery so that you can tune in to other, deeper levels of knowing. My goal was always to empower people to develop their own hidden potential and to discover their higher nature." As soon as he got his Ph.D., Green set out to find an institution that might support the sort of self-regulation research he had in mind.

Years earlier, while at the Naval Center, he had tried asking his subconscious for some guidance on what job to do next. "I had seen many times," Green told me, "that in a certain state of consciousness, I could walk through a doorway and gain some access to a library that seemed to comprise all the knowledge, information and wisdom there is in the universe." This library, he discovered, corresponded to what Carl Jung termed the "collective unconscious," what the Sufis named "general mind," and what the yogi Patanjali described as "the field of mind." On this particular occasion, he posed his question, entered a quiet meditative state, and almost immediately saw a detailed visual image. It consisted of grass, a tree-covered hill, and a watchtower in the background. Because he was working in the California desert at the time, he assumed that the image referred to some future point in his career.

In 1963—more than a decade after this experience—Green decided to again ask his subconscious about his future. To his amazement, no sooner had he moved into a quiet meditative state than the watchtower of his earlier image appeared. This time, it had clocks on each of its four sides and a small museum inside that contained Indian artifacts and manuscripts. He also saw an image of a second building filled with electronic machinery, and a middle-age man who seemed to be in charge. Green so trusted the validity of these images that he decided to take a cross-country car trip, stopping at major universities until he came upon the watchtower from his meditation. Just days before he intended to set out, he got an unexpected call from a graduate student whom he'd known at the University of Chicago. The student had gone on to work at the Menninger Foundation. Aware of Green's Navy background in electronics, he explained that he was calling at the request of Gardner Murphy, the head of Menninger's research department and one of the country's most eminent psychologists.

The next day, Green was on a plane to Topeka. The moment he arrived at Menninger, he felt a jolt of recognition and an instant sense that he'd found his home. "The first thing I saw was the watchtower with the four clocks on a grassy hill," Green told me. "Then I went inside the tower and came on a museum filled with Indian artifacts that had been collected by Carl Menninger. And when I finally met Gardner Murphy, I recognized him as the man from my original imagery."

After interviewing Green, Murphy immediately offered him a job, a laboratory, and the right to spend at least one-quarter of his time on any projects he chose. Murphy himself was a man of unusually eclectic interests. While he'd built impeccable establishment credentials, he had also served as president of the American Society for Psychical Research. He was also the first person to get Green thinking about the potential of biofeedback. For years, Murphy had suffered from chronic tension in his neck, and he was convinced that psychological stress was the cause. "He had this idea," Green told me, "that muscle problems were really mental problems—that tension in the mind gets locked into your muscles and that if he could only get the tension out where he could see it, then he might be able to do something about it. I told him that it was certainly possible, since yogis had learned long ago to control all of the autonomic nervous system through awareness training."

Green was already interested in discovering whether autogenic training could be used to teach people to voluntarily control their body temperature. Now Murphy had given him an added inspiration. Might not the capacity for such voluntary control be enhanced, Green wondered, by providing subjects with moment-by-moment feedback on what was happening to their body temperature, as measured in their fingers? It was already well documented that in a hypnotic trance, patients could be successfully instructed to slow their heartbeat, or produce red welts on their arms, or to cease feeling even the sharpest pain. Green was eager to prove that subjects could produce these effects for themselves. "In hypnosis, you are unconscious, and someone else is manipulating your mind," Green told me. "My idea was that people should become their own masters, self-aware and self-reliant, rather than dependent on doctors or therapists."

The Greens did their first experiments combining autogenic training and biofeedback in 1965. They worked with a graduate student named Dale Walters, who soon became their partner and spent almost three decades as part of their team at Menninger. Green began by building a device that could feed information back to subjects about the temperature in their fingers. Subjects were instructed not to use active will to prompt their hands to become warmer or to make their arms feel heavier. Instead, they were told to visualize the intended change, then simply let it happen without conscious effort or interference—a technique that the Greens termed "passive volition." Sure enough, the vast majority of subjects learned to significantly raise the temperature in their fingers. Conversely, when they used conscious willpower rather than passive imagery to try to get their hands warmer, precisely the opposite typically occurred. If subjects ceased actively trying to succeed, the temperature in their hands usually increased.

But why exactly did visualization make it possible to gain control over autonomic body functions such as body temperature and later blood pressure and muscle tension? "The body," Green hypothesized, "responds directly to the mind's instructions whenever it is spoken to in a language the body understands." That language, he speculates, is not conscious intention or verbal command but imagery. A simple and obvious example of the mind's power to influence the body is what happens to a person who visualizes an exciting sexual fantasy. The physiological response is unmistakable and often instantaneous. By contrast, distracting thoughts and physical tensions—all forms of anxiety—only interfere with the capacity to communicate a specific command to the body. This also helped explain for Green the mechanism by which hypnotism works. "What happens in a deep trance," he argued, "is that the hypnotist gets the conscious mind of the patient to drop out so that the hypnotist can speak directly to the body."

While the Greens' initial goal was simply to prove that physiological self-regulation could be achieved, their work had unexpected side effects. The first occurred when a patient who had been suffering from severe migraines all her life came in to learn to warm her hands. As it happened, when her hands got to a certain temperature, the migraines simply disappeared. Green theorized that the deep relaxation prompted by the hand-warming deactivated her highly aroused sympathetic nervous system and thus normalized the blood flow that a migraine typically disrupts. That was likely what had happened to me on the train, when I felt a migraine coming on, began to meditate, moved into a state of deep relaxation, and ultimately averted the headache. By the end of the 1980s, the Greens had treated hundreds of patients for migraines using biofeedback and reported consistent success rates between 70 and 80 percent. They were also successful in treating other illnesses, most notably high blood pressure, Raynaud's disease, asthma, and gastrointestinal disorders.

While this clinical work was useful to patients, Elmer, Alyce, and Dale Walters remained interested in exploring more deeply the capacity for advanced levels of self-regulation. Over the years, they tested many meditators and yogis in their Menninger laboratories. The abilities of two stood out. The less controversial of the two was Jack Schwarz, an easygoing man of slight build and a quick sense of humor who was in his mid-30s when he came to Menninger. Born in Holland, Schwarz had exceptional control over his body, a capacity that had come to him nearly full-blown as a teenager. His initial inspiration came from watching a hypnotist put himself into a trance and then stick pins into his arms without apparent pain. Intrigued, Schwarz began experimenting with shifting into a state of deep relaxation. He soon found that he could match the hypnotist's feat.

Having heard that the Greens scientifically tested subjects, Schwarz showed up at Menninger in the fall of 1971. Once he got into the Greens' lab, he produced two six-inch steel sailmaker's needles, which he promptly pushed through his biceps. When he pulled them out, he bled freely for ten seconds. Then the bleeding stopped and the hole closed completely. When he did it a second time, he did not bleed at all. Later, this performance was recorded on film, and I found it astonishing to watch. On another occasion,

Schwarz sought to demonstrate that he could anesthetize any part of his body at will. To prove this, he calmly held a lighted cigarette to his forearm for a full twenty-five seconds. He gave no indication of pain or suffering, and afterward only a blisterless reddening appeared on the surface of his skin. When Schwarz was asked how he performed these feats, it turned out that he used the same method the Greens did when it came to getting subjects to increase the temperature in their hands. Schwarz never tried consciously to force his body to do anything. Instead, before he began, he focused on quieting his mind, bringing his attention inward, and asking his subconscious to do all the necessary work. When his subconscious answered yes in the form of an image in his mind, he went ahead with the given task. In Schwarz's view, he had no more intrinsic ability to regulate his physiology than anyone else. Through systematic training, he insisted, anyone could learn to do the same things that he had. Indeed, 20 years later, he continues to devote much of his time to teaching students the skills of self-regulation.

Even more extraordinary than Schwarz's demonstrations were those of Swami Rama, a yoga teacher who had originally been trained in the Himalayas in southern India. *Swami* literally means "master of self," and the Greens had heard that Swami Rama could, for example, stop his pulse at will. Referred to the Greens by one of their colleagues, Swami Rama had a broader agenda. He had been sent to America by his own guru, he later told the Greens, to demonstrate in a measurable way that meditative states were a path not just to greater self-control but to higher self-realization and wisdom. A tall, well-built, charismatic whirlwind of energy, enthusiasm, ideas, and opinions, Swami Rama arrived for the first time at the Menninger Foundation in March 1970.

On his first day in the lab, the swami created a nine-degree difference in temperature between two spots on his right hand only two inches apart—an extraordinary feat of self-regulation. The next day, he was able, on command, to get his heart to beat at five times its normal rate—306 beats a minute—with no visible negative effect. When he returned to his resting pulse of 74, he agreed to slow it down, and he brought it to 52 beats a minute almost instantly. After two days, he had to leave, but he agreed to return to Topeka the following September for a more extended visit. Two weeks later, he wrote to Green suggesting several dozen future self-regulation experiments that they might undertake together. "It is most amazing that people do not understand the power of mind over body," he said, adding, "Doctor, meditation alone is real life. There is nothing higher than meditation, that is my experience in life."

True to his promise, Swami Rama exhibited a number of extraordinary abilities in the course of his two-month return visit to Menninger that fall. In one demonstration, he spontaneously produced a large cystlike lump the size of a bird's egg on his buttock, then caused it to disappear just as quickly. On still another occasion, the swami requested that Alyce's daughter, Pat Norris, then working as a psychologist in Topeka, come to see him immediately. When she arrived, Swami Rama insisted that she ask him a question that was important to her, refusing to say why. When she complied, he repeated the request until she'd asked seven questions in all, including whether she should send her son to private school and whether she herself should get a Ph.D. Then Swami Rama produced a piece of paper. It contained a list he'd written of seven questions, each with answers. Five of the questions were precisely the ones that Norris had asked him.

The swami's most extraordinary feat was one of telekinesis—moving an object solely by using his mind. His preparations were built around several days of intense meditation, during which he claimed to have repeated his mantra nearly 150,000 times. The purpose, he explained later, was to intensely focus his attention and thus his energy. In the meantime, Elmer built a device that included a knitting needle poised over a protractor, so that any movement of the needle could be precisely measured. On the day of the demonstration, Swami Rama's face was covered with a mask and his body with a sheet in order to prevent him from using air currents to move the needle. He sat at a distance of five feet from the protractor device. Several physicians were brought in to observe. After sitting for several minutes in silence, Swami Rama softly repeated his mantra for a minute, then gave a sharp command and the needle instantly rotated nearly ten degrees. He then repeated the demonstration. "What we saw in these experiments," Green told me, "is that the mind and body have capacities far beyond what we normally imagine and that there are systematic techniques for developing these abilities."

Just as Green himself believed that the capacity for self-regulation is a critical first step on the path to a more complete life, so Swami Rama believed in such a progression. He himself had spent many years as a young man in India learning highly disciplined techniques to control his mind as well as his body. Even during the time he spent as an experimental subject at Menninger, he gave twice-weekly talks to interested staff members about the relationship between self-regulation and the pursuit of wisdom. "Yoga," he told the group at one of the first meetings, describing the spiritual path that he had been taught, "is the control of the modifications of the mind. [It] is a system of understanding one's own nature, becoming the master of that nature, and using that mastery for higher purposes. But here, discipline is required. No self-mastery can be acquired without discipline. . . . Study without discipline creates a gap between thought and action, between knowledge and behavior." Swami Rama went on to argue that meditation by itself leads ultimately to a wise life. "Meditation," he told the Menninger group, "is the only path to freedom—freedom from anxiety; freedom from pain, anger, distress and depression; freedom from all sorrows, all fears and all bondages. And meditation is the only path to knowledge."

Nonetheless, many who met Swami Rama quickly deduced that neither his years of meditation nor his knowledge of the higher states of consciousness had prompted him to transcend his ego or to get free of his everyday personality conflicts. Indeed, he hinted strongly to Green that he wasn't much interested in exploring those arenas of his life. This became clear after Green set out to measure whether Swami Rama could move at will into certain brainwave states—among them the deeply relaxed theta state, in which unconscious personal material often arises in the form of images. Swami Rama was able to enter the state rather easily, after Green described it. However, he quickly returned to his ordinary consciousness, looking visibly agitated. "That's a horrible pathological state," he announced.

Green asked what he meant. "All of the things that other people wanted me to do, all of the things that I wanted to do, all of the things I should have done but didn't do, came up and began screaming at me at the same time," Swami Rama said. "It is very noisy and very unpleasant. Usually I keep that turned off." In short, Swami Rama was selective about what he chose to allow into his awareness—and committed to suppressing the rest. Green had long recognized the dangers of this approach. "If you pursue the spiritual path, you unleash energy, and Swami Rama did have real powers," Green told me. "The problem is that if your personality isn't relatively cultivated and tuned and understood, the ego can go totally out of control. Swami Rama never integrated that part of his nature. He had some higher teachings to share, but he couldn't bring the pieces of himself under control. He once said to me, 'The main problem in life is ego, and nobody knows it better than I.' "

The publicity that followed his extraordinary feats of self-regulation at Menninger gave Swami Rama wide attention and credibility. In 1971, he founded his first Himalayan Institute, in Illinois. The institute's lofty mission—based on what Swami Rama called a "scientific" approach to yoga—was to promote the "ethical, social, economical and spiritual development of humanity to attain world peace, international integration, understanding, and spiritual awakening of the human race." Almost immediately it attracted a substantial following. Today, there are numerous branches of the Himalayan Institute. Until recently, the headquarters in Honesdale, Pennsylvania, had a hundred full-time residents and attracted as many as a hundred paying visitors to regular weekend classes in yoga, meditation, stress reduction, and diet, as well as to a longer "self-transformation" program.

All this has begun to change, however, as Swami Rama's personal behavior has come under increasing fire in recent years, even from some of his closest followers. While he has always claimed to abide by his tradition's vows of celibacy, allegations that he not only humiliated and tyrannized certain disciples, but also sexually exploited women in his institute began as early as the mid-1970s. A number of women wrote to Elmer Green during those years, each describing how she had been seduced into a sexual relationship with Swami Rama. Two women later described the swami's alleged abuses in statements about their experiences filed with an organization known as the Cult Awareness Network. But the most comprehensive and damning investigation of Swami Rama was undertaken by a journalist named Katherine Webster. "The Case Against Swami Rama of the Himalayas" was published in the magazine *Yoga Journal* in November 1990.

Webster interviewed more than a half-dozen women who said they had been coerced into sexual relationships with Swami Rama—and numerous others who corroborated the accusers' stories. "Most of the women," Webster wrote, "express feelings of fear, frustration and betrayal." One woman described to Webster the way in which the swami at first gave her special attention and privileges. Eventually, she said, he initiated sexual relations with her on the pretext of teaching her important spiritual lessons. Another woman described how the swami showed up at her bedroom late one night, made sexual advances, then forced her to have sex after she resisted him. When the woman complained to a member of the board of the Himalayan Institute, Swami Rama countered by claiming that the woman had seduced him. Yet another woman said she had been pressured to have sex with the swami even after he had arranged her marriage to another man. "Sex with a guru," Webster concluded, "is a form of spiritual incest." Finally, in late 1993, two teenage girls who grew up at the Honesdale ashram filed multiple-count lawsuits alleging that they'd been forced by Swami Rama to have sexual relations with him.

The story of Swami Rama's dark side is far from unique. In 1985, a survey of gurus and spiritual teachers in America found that thirty-four of thirty-nine who were not celibate admitted to at least occasional sexual relationships with one or more students. Nearly half of the students surveyed—most of them female—reported that such relationships had "undermined their practice, their relationship with their teacher, and their feelings of self-worth." Serious allegations of abuse of power—nearly all sexual and financial—have been lodged against the leaders of more than a dozen of the largest spiritual communities in America during the past decade.

They include Bhagwan Shree Rajneesh, who built a huge group of followers in Oregon, was best known for his fondness for Rolls-Royces, and eventually got deported to India; Swami Muktananda, who had a worldwide following up until his death in 1982 but is reported to have had numerous sexual relationships with young female followers; Richard Baker-Roshi, the Harvard-educated leader of the San Francisco Zen Center who was forced to resign after his affair with a married student was revealed; and Trungpa Rinpoche, the Tibetan Buddhist monk who founded the Naropa Institute in Boulder, Colorado, and died as a direct result of alcoholism in 1986. Perhaps most extreme of all were the abuses of Trungpa's chosen successor, Vajra Regent Osel Tendzin—an American-born disciple, married, and father of two children—who was diagnosed with AIDS in 1987. Ultimately, Tendzin admitted to having unprotected sex with several male students even after learning that he had AIDS. "Tendzin emulated in a more extreme and deadly fashion," concluded one of his students, "a pattern of denial and ignorance exemplified by Trungpa Rinpoche's own attitude to alcohol." Tendzin persistently refused to resign his position and died in a hospital in San Francisco in 1991—officially on retreat from his position as head of the Vajradhatu community.

Some disillusioned followers pinned at least part of the responsibility for the abusive patterns on themselves. Stan Trout was one of Swami Muktananda's closest advisers, for example, until he finally resigned in the early 1980s. Subsequently, he accused the guru of regularly molesting young girls on the pretext of checking their virginity. "Out of a love for truth and for those who teach it and appear to embody it, we unwittingly set ourselves up for exploitation and betrayal," Trout wrote in an open letter to the Muktananda community. "Our mistake is to deify another being and attribute perfection to him. From that point on, everything is admissible. . . . There is no absolute assurance that enlightenment necessitates the moral virtue of a person. . . . The enlightened are on an equal footing with the ignorant in the struggle against their own evil—the only difference being that the enlightened person knows the truth, and has no excuse for betraying it." Elmer Green had much the same explanation for Swami Rama's ability to get away with exploitative behavior. "A lot of people have confused the siddhis—the powers to control body, emotions and mind—with spirituality," Green explained. "But the siddhis can be an ego trap. . . . A saint is a person who does what he says."

G reen continued to believe that the powers of self-regulation could be used in the service of higher ends, including reducing psychological stress, accessing the intelligence of the unconscious, and nurturing a higher self. More even than gaining control over blood pressure or muscle tension, he saw his challenge as teaching subjects to cultivate more voluntary control of their minds. The form of feedback that connects most directly to one's state of mind is brainwave activity. By learning to regulate brainwaves, it seemed to Green theoretically possible to access different states of consciousness and capacities of mind at will. The first widely accepted evidence that this sort of control was possible came from an affable, laconic psychologist and researcher named Joe Kamiya.

Although he was trained as a behaviorist, Kamiya developed

an interest in exploring consciousness scientifically. In the mid-1950s, he began working in dream research at the University of Chicago. Initially, Kamiya was interested in studying whether dreaming is associated with certain brainwave patterns that could be detected on an electroencephalogram, or EEG monitor. Put simply, an EEG measures the speed and intensity of electrical activity in the brain at any given point on the scalp where an electrode is attached.

The modern understanding of brain waves began with a German researcher named Hans Berger, who discovered in 1924 that electrical voltages emanate from the brain. Four broad brain-wave patterns were eventually identified. The most common in everyday waking life was named beta, which comprises faster brain waves ranging from 13 to 26 hertz or cycles per second. Beta is associated with active, focused, conscious attention in the world—anything from engaging in conversation, to watching a sporting event, to solving a math problem. In general, the more logical and deductive the task, the more beta tends to predominate. At the opposite end of the scale is delta, the slowest of the brain waves. It ranges from 0.5 to 3 hertz. Most people produce large amounts of delta only when they are asleep or unconscious.

The two midrange brainwave patterns represent subtler, more internally focused waking states of consciousness. Theta runs from 4 to 7 hertz and tends to predominate only in the period when a person is falling asleep or waking up. It is most commonly associated with spontaneous dreamlike or hypnagogic images. Alpha, which runs from 8 to 13 hertz, is a more conscious, aware, and alert state than theta but is less active and more inner focused than beta. Alpha has been referred to as a neutral or idling gear—a state of quiet relaxation. Most people can produce it, at least in short bursts, simply by closing their eyes. Recent research suggests that much finer distinctions can be made about the nature of brainwave states, such that individual hertz—say 10, for instance, or 14—can be correlated with very specific capacities. Still, the broad characteristics of the four patterns continue to prove useful.

Kamiya began his biofeedback experiments in 1962 with a

simple goal. He wanted to see whether it was possible to move voluntarily from one dominant brainwave pattern to another—and in turn, to experience a palpably different state of consciousness. Kamiya chose to train alpha. Beta, he reasoned, was already the dominant brainwave for most people in ordinary waking life. Neither the delta nor the theta state seemed to Kamiya to have much practical use—a notion that the Greens would later prove wrong. At the time, however, there was already evidence correlating alpha with a specific relaxed meditative state of consciousness. In 1961, for example, three Indian researchers published a study based on a half-dozen yogis. It showed that when they entered a deep meditative state, the yogis persistently produced dominant patterns of alpha—especially as they reached the subject state of ecstasy and oneness known as samadhi. In 1966—several years after Kamiya began his work—two Japanese researchers published a study of forty-eight Zen Buddhist priests and disciples. Once again, their alpha levels consistently began to rise within one minute after they began meditating. In these cases, alpha increased steadily as the meditation became deeper until at a certain point, theta began to rise and alpha diminished.

Kamiya began his own research by hooking subjects up to an EEG, ringing a bell intermittently, and then asking the subjects to say whether they felt that alpha rhythms were present. He immediately let them know if they were right or wrong. It was a primitive form of feedback, but it led to some remarkable results. "My first subject was a junior chemistry major unconcerned with consciousness and not very introspective," Kamiya told me when we first met at his home in San Francisco in 1990. "On the very first day, he was correct about half the time, which you could get just by chance. The second day he hit 60 percent, the third day 85 percent, and on the fourth day, he had 400 consecutive runs. He had no idea how he did it, but clearly he had honed in on this dimension and figured out how to control his brain waves. Remembering that experience makes my hair stand on end, even today."

In the next phase of his research, Kamiya introduced a

tone that beeped whenever alpha was present and became more persistent as it rose. The majority of subjects could be trained in a few hours to increase their alpha. Conversely, engaging in activities that require a focused mind—doing arithmetic or thinking in detail about a specific event—turned out to suppress alpha. Between trials, when subjects were told that they could stop trying to produce alpha, Kamiya discovered that it consistently rose, just as Elmer Green had found with subjects who stopped actively trying to increase the temperature in their fingers. Conscious intention—a linear form of thinking—seemed to suppress alpha, while letting go of such effort tended to increase it.

Kamiya first reported his results in an address to the Western Psychological Association Convention in April 1962. His findings generated a sensation and helped launch the modern field of biofeedback. Before long, the excitement spread beyond psychologists. People from a variety of backgrounds flocked to Kamiya's lab after hearing reports that alpha training was a form of "instant Zen"—a Western technology for rapidly accessing deep meditative states of tranquillity and ecstasy that advanced yogis typically experienced only after years of training. It was soon evident that advanced meditators who came through the lab produced alpha more readily than did nonmeditators. "Quieting the mind of verbal thinking and increasing the level of one's internal awareness will generate more alpha," Kamiya concluded. Michael Murphy visited the laboratory in 1965. With his long training in meditation, he proved able to control his brain waves quickly and easily, increasing and decreasing alpha virtually on command.

The Greens, inspired by Kamiya's work began experimenting with brainwave feedback in 1965 and made similar observations about the patterns of increased alpha activity. For example, when Jack Schwarz pushed the needle into his arm—a highly invasive and typically painful event—he might have been expected to evidence the highly focused and conscious beta pattern. Instead, he began producing significantly more alpha as soon as he touched the needle to his bicep. In effect, he managed to counteract the physical pain by relaxing deeply.

In 1973, the Greens spent several months in India, at Swami Rama's invitation, using portable biofeedback instruments to systematically measure the self-regulatory abilities of advanced yogis living isolated meditative lives. In one extraordinary case, they devised an experiment in which a yogi agreed to be sealed in a tiny box underground for a period of 8 hours, with no access to external air. When they studied his EEG record afterward, it turned out that the yogi had produced smooth, almost continuous alpha. He appeared to have survived by putting his mind and body into a state of such deep rest that his physiological needs for oxygen were uncommonly low.

As it turned out, the early enthusiasm for Kamiya's work with alpha training did not sustain. The first reason was that he simply could not rouse himself to write and publish scientific papers based on his research and ended up simply describing his work informally at meetings. At the same time, other researchers proved unable to replicate Kamiya's findings, and many eventually concluded that biofeedback was not a reliable means for increasing alpha. Discouraged at first, Kamiya ultimately found an explanation. "I realized that most of the other researchers failed to appreciate the importance of personal interaction with their subjects," he told me. "These are very relaxed states the subjects are trying to produce, and encouragement and informality make a big difference. Most researchers preferred to hand the subject a file card with instructions and to say nothing more."

To Elmer Green, the explanation for the failure of most biofeedback researchers was even more basic. "Becoming aware of subtle internal processes is a skill that has to be learned, like any other," he explained. "For most people, it doesn't happen instantly, any more than one could be expected to learn to play a musical instrument effectively after a couple of lessons." The Greens found, for example, that while fifteen of the first sixteen studies of temperature biofeedback aiming at control of blood pressure had no measurable success, the subjects in nearly every case received only a handful of training sessions. "Researchers," the Greens later wrote in the journal *Biofeedback and Society,* "often do not pay the price necessary for clinical effectiveness, that of providing enough time for subjects to become aware, internally, of what is happening in the body."

I was eager to see for myself whether brainwave feedback might help me sustain the quiet, highly aware, and deeply relaxed state that I'd found so elusive in meditation. By the time I met him, Kamiya had long since stopped training subjects and conducting brainwave research. He'd grown discouraged about the usefulness of alpha training. However, I did find a commercial brainwave training clinic called the Mindcenter in Palo Alto, California, in which one of the principals was James Hardt, a psychologist and researcher who had previously worked in Kamiya's laboratory. Hardt and Kamiya eventually had a falling out, but in 1988, Hardt teamed up with an entrepreneur named Foster Gamble to open the Mindcenter—an effort to turn alpha training into a viable commercial venture. Their premise was that teaching people to enhance alpha would help them lower their stress levels and in turn increase their productivity, improve their health and self-esteem, and even deepen their self-awareness.

I flew out to California in July 1991 to take what was called the "Alpha 1 Brainwave Training"—an intensive five-day course for beginners. The training was conducted by a soft-spoken man in his early forties named Dave Mulvey. I had three fellow students—Doug, an affable, slightly mystical contractor in his sixties who had spent much of his life studying consciousness; Adam, a clean-cut, ramrod-straight young man around thirty who'd been sent by the midwestern hospital for which he worked to assess the Mindcenter's biofeedback technology and training protocol; and Paul, a mild-mannered executive at a Silicon Valley computer company who was in his early forties and had come at the urging of his wife, from whom he'd recently been separated. She had found the course useful, and he was willing to try anything that might help them get back together.

The feedback training took place in six-by-six-foot individual booths that felt a bit like space capsules. Hardt had designed them with the notion of creating a maximally relaxing environment. The floors and walls were carpeted to make them soundproof. I sat in an upholstered swivel chair with wheels. In front of me were two monitors—a large one for viewing videos and a much smaller one on which I could see my scores as I practiced. To my right was a switch controlling a two-way microphone that allowed me to speak with Dave. He sat in the control room, where he monitored the reams of paper that poured out documenting the brainwave activity of each member of our group. Each morning, while Mulvey briefed us on the day's plans, a technician quietly wired me and the others—lubricating four electrode sites on our scalps, then attaching a helmetlike device on top of our heads. In the booth, I plugged the switch from my helmet into a jack that hooked me and my brain waves directly into the computer. Mulvey told us what to expect. "Once you're in the booth working," he said, "you'll hear a soft intermittent tone feeding back alpha. It will grow gradually louder and steadier whenever you produce more alpha, softer and less frequent as alpha diminishes."

Alpha, Mulvey explained, has a paradoxical quality. "It's a form of relaxed attention or engaged indifference, a sense of being alert and present but nonetheless feeling miles away," he said. Increasing alpha, he went on, often prompts feelings of freedom, floating and ease, even joy and expansiveness. "But don't be surprised," he told us, "if you also experience feelings of fear or sadness or anger." Quieting the mind, he explained, tends to free up whatever feelings lie beneath the relentless mental chatter that characterizes a typical beta-dominated waking life. Our challenge, he said, was to experiment until we discovered what thoughts and feelings seemed to increase our alpha levels. "This is not about analysis or understanding," Mulvey told us. "It's about tuning in to subtle feelings and sensations."

The feedback occurred in "epochs" or segments of two minutes each. In addition to the ongoing feedback from tones, we were given a score at the end of each segment indicating the average level of alpha we'd reached. I felt just a tad cocky as I sat down that first morning and lowered the lights. After all, I'd been meditating every day for more than two years. I knew something about how to quiet my mind, and I had at my disposal no less than a half-dozen meditation techniques I'd learned and practiced. It might be a quiet, detached state we were after, but I still felt a certain competitiveness and a hunger for success. I wanted to prove—to myself and to the others in my group—that my meditative work had yielded some tangible results.

To my chagrin, I found the challenge harder than I expected from the very start. The simplest and most reliable quieting meditations I knew—counting my breaths, for example, or repeating a mantra—increased my alpha only modestly. Before long, I was feeling frustrated, and my back began to hurt. As I became more anxious, my alpha scores went down. Still, I kept experimenting. To my surprise, I got my highest scores when I drifted into sexual fantasy or simply allowed myself to daydream.

It was soon evident that even with all my meditation practice, I had not spent much time in a demonstrably relaxed alpha-dominant state. At the same time, I began to see a clear correlation between the intensity of my feelings—whatever they might be—and increased alpha. It struck me that conscious thinking, the typical beta state, is in some sense the opposite of feeling. Over the next several days, a pattern emerged. Very quickly each morning, I would find myself stuck, unable to increase my alpha no matter what technique I tried. Nor could I find a way to put aside the sense that I was failing. This only made me more frustrated and more self-critical. The issue was control. In the face of feelings of helplessness or inadequacy, I fought harder to succeed at relaxing. But the harder I tried, the tenser and more exasperated I became, and the more my alpha dropped. It was a vicious cycle, and the only plausible way out was to let go of my need to control the outcome. The problem, I realized, was that I found doing so oddly frightening. Who knew what I might discover if I set thinking aside and simply allowed whatever was underneath to come up?

At one point, as I sat in my darkened module, some stray thought—perhaps just my own absurdly grim determination—made me break into a smile. Somehow the smile prompted a very rich, detailed memory of an immensely pleasurable experience I'd had back in college. Suddenly, I found myself reliving a twenty-year-old day in my life, as if it had just happened. My smile got bigger, and then I laughed out loud. I felt light, airy, happy. My usual pattern of thinking had given way to powerful emotions beyond words. A slight physical shift—from a tight-lipped determination to a relaxed smile—had dissolved a barrier, eased my tension, and opened the door to a wholly different state of consciousness. Sure enough, my alpha jumped dramatically.

The next day, when my low scores returned, I found myself feeling frustrated and self-critical all over again. My primary emotion was one of hopelessness. Somehow I'd made myself the victim of my own negative internal dialogue. It occurred to me that this was familiar territory—a way I talked to myself frequently and automatically. Next, a wave of sadness washed over me—something I didn't often feel. Instinctively, I reached up for my shoulders with my arms, the way you might if you felt cold or frightened. The sadness was as intense as the pleasure had been the day before. Once again, my alpha levels went soaring. Before long, my mind jumped back in. Aha, I thought, I've found a technique that works, a surefire way to enhance alpha: Just focus on strong emotions. But no sooner did I consciously put a smile on my face or conjure up a sad image than my scores went back down. Actively *seeking* a feeling, I realized, requires thinking. Analyzing, labeling, rating, explaining, and conceptualizing are the stuff of beta—all highly useful in their own right but not helpful for deeply relaxing and tuning in to subtler internal feelings and sensations.

"People are not very successful at enhancing alpha until they first learn to relax," Foster Gamble told me later in the week. "Relaxing allows them to become clearer about what's going on inside themselves. The next challenge is for people to let their feelings flow more naturally. The common denominator among those who enhance alpha is the quality of being emotionally authentic, the ability to let yourself feel whatever is there at the moment." In Gamble's case, he initially found himself unable to increase his alpha past a certain point, despite numerous feedback sessions. At one point, his trainer simply looked at him and said, "Happiness is okay, you know." Gamble broke up laughing. Instantly, his scores jumped up 25 percent. "What I realized," he told me, "was that I'd made this whole pursuit so grim that I couldn't possibly relax. When this was pointed out to me, I said to myself, 'Okay, now I've got to make sure I'm happy.' Well, my scores went right back down again. I finally realized that I was carrying around a lot of sadness that I'd been avoiding. My father had died three months before, I still missed him a lot, and when I allowed myself to feel that sadness, my scores jumped up again."

Beyond a certain subjective experience of relaxation and better access to one's feelings, it was difficult to specify or quantify the practical value of the alpha state. I wasn't yet entirely sure how one might most effectively incorporate this state into everyday life. Gamble himself struggled with this issue. "I think this sort of training is just a first step in self-mastery," he explained. "The basic techniques of quieting the mind, controlling attention, and simply watching thoughts are very hard to master, but they're absolutely critical to living more fully. Without this level of mastery, it's as if you were trying to play a sonata without having first learned to keep rhythm and read music." Eventually, Gamble began to experiment with using the self-mastery skills of alpha training as building blocks for further classes in improving communication skills and in creating better life balance. But whatever the added value of this further work might have been, it came too late. The alpha feedback training that lay at the heart of the Mindcenter simply didn't generate a large enough following to cover its costs. Gamble reluctantly closed it down in 1991.

In Elmer Green's view, the focus on training alpha was itself a fundamental error, made not only by Gamble and Hardt but by many other biofeedback researchers and clinicians beginning with Joe Kamiya. "Alpha is finally only an idling state," Green told me. "It's ten times better than beta when you're tense, but beyond a certain level of relaxation, it doesn't have that much to offer by itself. If you want to truly grow, the only way you're going to do that is through the deeper state of theta. That's where you can interrogate the unconscious and even gain the ability to reprogram it. The true value of alpha is that it's a necessary bridge between beta and theta."

It was this same insight that launched Green's research into the unique properties of the theta state in the early 1970s. In reading the Japanese study of the brain waves of forty-eight yogis and monks, Green was struck by the fact that as they moved into the deepest levels of meditation, the dominance of alpha eventually gave way to long trains of theta waves. Zen masters themselves have long described this deep state as one of "knowing"—having access to some deeper level of truth. Green soon realized that he was familiar with the experience in his own life. It was precisely the form of meditative reverie that he'd been taught many years earlier by Arthur Green, as a way to get answers from his unconscious in the form of images.

When Green's colleagues wired him up and he allowed himself to slip into his familiar reverie state, he began to produce a high degree of theta. Green next hypothesized that if subjects could be taught to break the typical habit of falling asleep when they moved into theta, they too might gain more direct access to spontaneously arising and highly revealing imagery. "We found theta to be associated with a deeply internalized state," Green later wrote. "The state of deep quietness of body, emotions and mind . . . achieved in theta training seems to build a bridge between conscious and unconscious processes and allows usually 'unheard' things to come to consciousness."

Deep internal quieting, Green concluded, is what makes it possible to tune in to the very subtle internal information that arises in theta. "It's as if you have two radio signals," he told me. "One is loud, the other is very soft and faint. To hear the faint one, you have to turn the loud one down. We go into theta to get this loud noise of normal waking consciousness turned off, so we can hear the softer voice underneath. And we do that because the breadth of our consciousness turns out to extend far beyond what we're usually conscious of."

The Greens began studying theta by recruiting a pilot group of eight people in 1971, all of whom had strong backgrounds in meditation. The group included Elmer, Alyce, Pat Norris, and Dale Walters. The purpose was to develop a methodology for theta training and to test its effectiveness. All eight subjects were given autogenic training exercises and breathing techniques aimed first at relaxing the body—on the grounds that as long as the body remains tense, it is impossible to quiet the mind or let go of emotional tension. Next, the group began receiving thirty-minute feedback sessions in which the tone grew louder anytime theta increased. In the course of a half-dozen sessions, all eight members of the group managed to substantially increase their theta levels, while remaining awake and alert enough to be aware of the imagery that arose. One of the participants was the psychiatrist Stan Grof, who demonstrated the capacity to enter theta at will—and even to talk while in that state.

The following year, the Greens received funding from the National Institute of Mental Health for a more rigorous study of 26 college seniors, each of whom had been trained with the same pilot protocol, supplemented by more feedback—40 fifty-minute sessions over a period of several weeks. The Greens and Dale Walters were interested in classifying the kinds of imagery associated with different brainwave states. Although few of the students had had meditation experience, nearly all of them were eventually able to increase their theta levels without falling asleep. Most were able to recall rich hypnagogic imagery in the process. This imagery included long-forgotten childhood events, reinforcing Green's hypothesis that the theta state provides a direct doorway into a vast storehouse of unconscious memories that aren't easily accessed in traditional talk-oriented psychotherapy. Unexpectedly, a significant percentage of the students reported that a series of positive changes took place in their lives in the wake of the training. These ranged from a sense of greater clarity, to more energy, to an improvement in personal relationships, to a greater ability to concentrate and recall material in school.

Green suspected that the unconscious could literally be reprogrammed in theta to generate psychological and physiological changes. Early on, he had seen the capacity for such self-regulation and self-healing in trained adepts such as Jack Schwarz and Swami Rama. He'd experienced it himself, when he moved into theta and visualized a desired change. At one point, for example, he used the technique to rid himself literally overnight of painful bursitis in his shoulder that hadn't responded to traditional medical treatment. Green speculated that a wide range of illnesses and disorders might be subject to self-healing if the right method for visualizing physiological changes in the theta state could be developed. "Visualization coupled with brainwave training," he wrote recently, "has led to physiologic change, emotional tranquilization and a degree of mental control seldom reached in meditation without long practice." Over the years, however, neither he nor the members of his group developed a research protocol for a specific illness or disorder that was systematically tested and followed up.

Beyond this clinical focus, Green was drawn to the notion that the theta state provides a doorway to the deepest levels of creativity. Artists and scientists, he realized, often instinctively use various forms of reverie as a means to gain new insights and see new associations. In *Beyond Biofeedback*, Green tells the story of the chemist Friedrich Kekule, who developed a pioneering theory of molecular structure in a dreamlike state. "I fell into a reverie, and lo the atoms were gamboling before my eyes," Kekule reported. Green cites numerous other examples of people who used reverie creatively. Among them were the poets William Blake, John Milton, and Samuel Taylor Coleridge, as well as the children's writer Enid Blyton, who described how she would close her eyes, make her mind blank, then suddenly see her story enacted in her mind's eye almost like a film. The mathematician Henri

Poincaré described mathematical equations rising in clouds and dancing before him as he went to sleep. Even Albert Einstein talked about the "combinatory play" of signs and images that are critical to creativity and precede any logical, verbal analysis.

In 1973, while visiting India to study the brainwave patterns of advanced yogis, the Greens chanced upon a strong anecdotal verification of their assumptions about theta. They were in the midst of running tests on Ram Sharma, a professor of biophysics who had long training in meditation. After hooking him up and explaining the nature of the brain waves that they wanted him to produce, he was able to produce nearly pure theta on command, while remaining fully conscious—a feat that few Westerners can match. When Green asked the professor how he did it, Dr. Sharma explained that he simply dropped into a very quiet state of consciousness in which he had long ago learned that he received answers to difficult intellectual questions he posed to himself. It was a level of mind, he explained, that appeared to "know everything." Green was delighted by this independent confirmation and concluded that theta training could benefit nearly anyone. "It meant," he later wrote, "that the average person, without having to subscribe to a religion, or to a dogma, or to a meditation system, could learn to move into the state of consciousness in which the seemingly infallible Source of Creativity could be invoked for the solution of problems."

M y own first experiences learning to enhance theta were aimed not at treating any symptons but simply at gaining more access to my unconscious. The results were modest but revealing. My first effort took place at the Menninger Clinic in 1991, at a theta-training workshop run by Dale Walters. In addition to a series of lectures on the nature of biofeedback generally and theta specifically, each participant undertook three half-hour theta sessions. Because our time was limited, we did none of the preparatory breathing and autogenic exercises that I believe are critical to deep relaxation—particularly for people who are verbally oriented and aren't especially tuned in to subtle sensations in their bodies. With the time constraints, we were simply wired up and given instructions on how to work with our portable feedback machines. Then we were taken to one of two rooms equipped with a half-dozen Barcaloungers. We had the choice of sitting up or lying in a reclining position, as a way to more easily induce the near-sleep state of theta.

I decided to tilt my Barcalounger back into a virtual bed. At the end of thirty minutes of continuous feedback, I looked over at the small machine that gave me a readout on the percentage of theta I'd produced. To my surprise, I'd produced a dominant theta wave for an impressive 40 percent of the session. Still, I had almost no memories of hypnagogic imagery or anything else for that matter. I was puzzled until one of my fellow trainees mentioned that she had been distracted because someone in the room had been snoring loudly. To my chagrin, I realized I'd spent most of my thirty minutes in a light state of sleep. That likely accounted both for my absence of memories and for my high theta percentage. For the second session, I was careful to leave my chair in a more upright position. This time, my theta only reached 25 percent, but I was certain that I hadn't fallen asleep. I was able to recall an array of images that had flitted through my mind, some seemingly out of nowhere, others more directly connected to my life. I felt more like an observer than a participant in the experience—interested in what I was watching but also feeling a certain remove. This was just the detached posture that Green said was characteristic of the theta state.

In one image, I'd seen my dead grandmother climbing upstairs toward some form of heaven. In another, I watched a screenwriter friend conclude a successful meeting by catapulting straight out the window—at which point I was somehow able to freeze the frame as he remained in midair. I also had a series of images of holding on to something, then letting go. When I tried afterward to categorize these images, the phrase that came to mind was "You've got to take the leap in order to reap the benefits." The challenge of truly letting go seemed applicable both to the brainwave training itself and to the rest of my life. At the same time, I remained aware that I never fully gave up trying to stay in control of what was happening.

In the third and final session, my theta remained at about 25 percent, but the sense of being in a distinctively image-laden world diminished. I was more aware of my distraction and of my desire to succeed, and I felt only intermittently relaxed. I had a few images, including one in which a nerdy Woody Allen somehow suddenly transformed into a virile Warren Beatty, but I was harder put this time to make anything of what had happened. I left Topeka feeling I'd gotten a taste of the possibilities of theta, but uncertain about where more training might lead.

My second experience with theta training occurred six months later, on the last of my five days at the Mindcenter. By that point, I'd spent four long days trying with mixed success to enhance my alpha brain waves. On the final morning, we agreed to spend one session getting feedback only for theta. As we sat down in our booths, I had an idea about what might work for me, derived in part from my earlier experience at Menninger. Rather than trying a specific relaxation technique, I slumped down just slightly in my chair, let my body go limp, and allowed myself to move toward sleep, keeping my eyes half-open to avoid actually nodding off. Almost immediately, I heard the tones begin to chime more loudly and persistently. In contrast to my alpha trainings and my earlier experience at Menninger, I felt immediately and instinctively at home in this theta state. When I reflected later on this sensation, it dawned on me that I had a tendency in my everyday life to slip into a mild form of daydreaming akin to theta reverie. In those instances, I often missed a question that someone had asked me or lost track of a conversation and ended up castigating myself. Here, however, I was being rewarded—if only with louder tones—for something that in other circumstances was perceived as useless and even rude.

As we moved through our-two minute segments, I felt unusually relaxed and free of any conscious thoughts. I did see some images passing before my eyes, but I didn't pay much attention to them. I was taken instead with the loose pleasurable feeling that pervaded me and with the evidence from the tones that I was deeply in some other state of consciousness. I could vary the loudness and frequency of the tones almost at will. I wasn't sure how exactly I was doing it, but I felt a quiet exhilaration and an unusual sense that while no thoughts were running through my head, I was fully in charge of my state of mind. I'd experienced twinges of back pain in the midst of my frustrating efforts to raise my alpha levels, but now my whole body now felt relaxed and flexible. Throughout the alpha training, I'd also struggled with the need to maintain control, physically and mentally. Slipping into theta, by contrast, felt instantly safe, relaxed, and at home.

As I intermittently flitted out of the theta state and became more conscious, I was seized with apprehension. How, I wondered, am I going to hold on to this lovely experience I've just had? As it turned out, I retained a strong sense of what I'd done to get there in the first place. It had nothing to do with control or effort. To the contrary, I simply let myself drop toward sleep while remaining alert. It gave me a palpable sense of what it means to truly let go. The experience was brief, but I emerged from it convinced that I'd discovered a wholly new and potentially useful state. Gaining more facility at shifting states of consciousness is not equivalent to finding wisdom, I knew. Still, I saw more clearly than ever how flexibility expands both one's power and one's potential. No brainwave state is useful in all circumstances, but the ability to move freely into alpha and theta, for example, provides a route not just to quieter, more relaxed states of mind but to unconscious material that remains otherwise inaccessible and unknown. In effect, flexibility is a tool for broadening and deepening consciousness and ultimately for experiencing a more complete life.

Today, Green is more taken with theta's potential than ever. It was during a Menninger biofeedback workshop in 1987, for example, that a little-known psychologist from a Veterans Administration hospital in eastern Colorado came up with a protocol for using theta training to successfully treat chronic alcoholics. Two years later Eugene Peniston published a clinically controlled study documenting his findings. Since then, other researchers found that a similar protocol can be used with great success for cases of drug abuse, post-traumatic stress disorder, anorexia, bulimia, and multiple personality disorder. Conversely, using brainwave feedback to suppress *excessive* theta has proved effective in the treatment of head injuries, attention deficit disorder, and depression.

But Green's primary interest is still in the potential to use theta training as a tool for psychological and spiritual development. "Theta provides a way to walk through a doorway and gain access to the files of the unconscious—everything from the basement to the penthouse," he told me. "What you do with what you find there is up to the individual. It's possible to experience deep compassion for others in this state but also to plan the perfect bank robbery." The impetus to act wisely, Green continues to believe, is contingent on dealing in an ongoing way with the issues of personality that arise. "You can't take an end run around the foibles and flaws of personality merely by transcending," he explains. "In the end, you have to deal with every issue that comes up. There can't be a single pocket of the unconscious that you are not conscious of. Until you are a hundred percent aware, you can always backslide all the way down to zero. There are all sorts of subtle little ego traps along the road, including self-righteousness and a lack of humility. To be fully conscious means watching yourself all the time. You have to get your personality together before you can truly get on to your cosmic role."

It is accessing a dimension beyond personal desires and preferences—a higher self—that is Green's highest goal. The real value of theta training, he wrote recently, "is the relatively rapid development of a skill in shifting, without years of trial-and-error meditation, into a state of consciousness in which one comes face to face with one's Self. This transcendent Being . . . is above, below, behind, within, or hidden by the Freudian ego. The True Self . . . can be quickly approached if the personality is made silent through theta EEG feedback and at the same time we focus detached attention 'upward.' The Self is always willing to help us, it seems, if we approach it in the right way and make ourselves open to it."

And what exactly is the everyday value of nurturing this transcendent perspective, I asked Green during a recent phone conversation. "What the work gives you is an incredible awareness and objectivity," he told me. "You can feel all the mental, physical, and emotional things going on around you and in you and yet not be identified with the individual pieces. The transpersonal point of view literally allows you to become chairman of the board—a position that is necessary to bring together the separate autonomous parts of yourself harmoniously. When that happens, you can turn your attention further inward and become conscious of the higher levels of your own nature—how you fit into the whole spiritual cosmos. We may think we are born to save ourselves. In truth, we are here to transform our nature in order to save the planet."

II

PATH:
MIND-BODY
POTENTIALS

4

SEEING THE BIG PICTURE
Betty Edwards and the Right Side of the Brain

> *Clarity, insight or understanding are only possible when thought is in abeyance, when the mind is still. Then only can you see very clearly, then you can say you have really understood....*
> —*KRISHNAMURTI*

> *At these moments, which are characterized by the sudden lifting of the burden of anxiety and fear which presses upon our daily life so steadily that we are unaware of it, what happens is something negative. That is to say, not "inspiration" as we commonly think of it, but the breaking down of strong habitual barriers—which tend to re-form very quickly. Some obstruction is momentarily whisked away.*
> —*T. S. ELIOT*

BETTY Edwards came to her own search for truth in a roundabout way. She wasn't motivated at first by a desire for a more complete life or by an interest in cultivating higher states of consciousness. An art teacher by training, she was simply looking for a way to teach her students to draw realistically, by seeing more clearly. Through drawing, she unexpectedly found a window into the way that the brain processes information—and why most people fall so short of using its full potential. Since then, she has devoted her career to vividly demonstrating that our logical, analytic, verbal mode of thinking often masks a wholly different level of intelligence that is

159

more visual, imaginative, metaphoric, and nonverbal. This insight not only made it possible to teach people to draw realistically but helped affirm modern scientific discoveries about the distinctive capacities of the left and right hemispheres of the brain. Edwards, in turn, became the first of several people I turned to who have focused with great success on training powerful yet often unrecognized or undervalued mind-body capacities. These capacities, I concluded, are critical tools in any search for wisdom.

Edwards came to believe, for example, that the ability to reconcile and move freely between brain's apparently opposite ways of thinking is essential to using the mind to optimal effect— and to living fully. Edwards was sixty-four when we first met in 1989 at one of her drawing workshops held at Harvard University. I felt drawn to her immediately. Tall and thin, conservative in dress, and gracious, even proper, in her manner, she exuded a sense of comfort with herself that made me feel instantly comfortable. In her own life, Edwards gracefully balances disparate instincts. Gentle, open-hearted, self-effacing, and intuitive on the one hand, she is also logical, articulate, highly discriminating, and tough-minded on the other. She speaks in a soft languid voice that is invariably understated but still manages to communicate an unmistakable passion for her work. In the course of the time we spent together, I came both to love and to admire her.

Edwards has staked out distinctive ground in the ongoing right and left hemisphere research. Among scientists, attention has focused on a narrow debate about the precise role that each hemisphere plays in various tasks. At the opposite extreme, many popularizers have trivialized the complex relationship between the two sides of the brain by promoting the right hemisphere as the source of all creativity, intuition, emotional depth, and even higher consciousness. Edwards argues persuasively that the right hemisphere's strengths have been undervalued and undertrained in our schools and in the culture at large. At the same time, she has set out to establish—particularly with her work on creativity—that the highest level of functioning comes from learning how to use the strengths of each hemisphere appropriately and flexibly, according to the demands of a given task.

On the most practical level, Edwards has used techniques that tap the right hemisphere to rapidly teach students how to draw realistically, even if they begin with primitive skills. At the same time, her techniques prompt students to move into a timeless, wordless, deeply absorbed level of awareness that is most commonly associated with intensive work in meditation. In this state of consciousness, I discovered, one not only sees more deeply and richly but experiences directly how language and thinking can interfere with direct perception. The experience of learning to draw with Edwards was exceptionally satisfying for me and for nearly all of my fellow students. Beyond that, Edwards's approach opens a doorway into dimensions of the mind—including the unconscious and the transpersonal states beyond one's self—that may be uniquely accessible through the right hemisphere.

From an early age, Edwards was gifted both visually and verbally, and she got encouragement and rewards for her strengths in both. She grew up in a poor working-class family in Long Beach, California. Economic circumstances compelled her to develop the visual skills that many other children did not. "There was no television yet, and we were too poor to afford to go to the movies," Edwards told me when we sat down at her home in Santa Monica. "About all we had for entertainment was the radio, which requires a visual imagination. I had a whole menagerie of characters that I could conjure up in my mind each time I turned on the radio. Today, images are fed from the outside, not generated from within. There is no need to imagine anymore, because all you have to do is turn on the TV, and there everything is."

Edwards also attributes her visual orientation to a troubled relationship with her mother. Chronically depressed and preoccupied, her mother paid little attention to Betty, prompting the young child to spend long hours in vivid daydreams. One of the few things that did give her mother pleasure was her visual surroundings. If she was walking to a store and nine-year-old

Betty was tagging along, her mother would exclaim regularly over the shape of geraniums hanging over a wall, or the play of sunlight on the hair of a passerby, or the color of a certain flower. Edwards still remembers being fascinated by what it was about these objects that gave her mother such uncommon pleasure. Eager to solve this mystery as a means of commanding more of her mother's attention, Edwards learned to look very closely at her surroundings. In the process she fell into an experience that she would later describe as a "cognitive shift"—a move into a wholly different state of consciousness. "From an early age . . . I was able to draw fairly well," she explained later. "I think I was one of those few children who stumbles upon a way of seeing that enables one to draw well. I can still remember saying to myself, even as a young child, that if I wanted to draw something, I had to do 'that.' I never defined 'that' but I was aware of having to gaze at whatever I wanted to draw for a time until 'that' occurred. Then I could draw with a fairly high degree of skill for a child."

When Edwards did begin to draw, her mother wasn't much interested, but her father was so proud of his daughter's talent that he often stood at her side and sharpened pencils for her while she worked. This attention gave Edwards the enormous pleasure of being loved and deeply seen, and it fueled her desire to keep drawing. Mostly, however, her father worked long hours away from home, and her mother was off in her own world. Edwards's primary refuge became books and ideas. Her best friend's older sister was a librarian who became something of a surrogate mother to Betty. The sister gave the girls weekly reading assignments and then engaged them in discussions about what they had read. The joy in books gave Edwards a connection to another intellectual dimension. Neither of her parents had graduated from high school, and when she was eventually admitted to UCLA, she became the first person in her family to attend college.

Shortly after graduating, Edwards married and had two children in quick succession, both of whom eventually chose art careers of their own. Anne is a museum director, and Brian is a painter. Like most women of her generation, Edwards never considered that she might have a career of her own. However, when her marriage began to founder, she returned to painting and began exhibiting her work. Pressed for money after her divorce, Edwards opened an art studio on Wilshire Boulevard in West Hollywood. When that proved too uncertain a source of income, she decided to get her teaching certificate. Her first job was in the art department at Venice High School, beginning in 1965. Edwards loved teaching, but it soon frustrated her that no matter what words she used, few students were able to draw realistically. "Why don't you just draw what you see?" she would ask in exasperation. On a whim one day, Edwards suggested that the students try turning upside down a drawing that they'd been assigned to copy. Within minutes a group of fidgety, talkative, easily distracted adolescents had fallen into dead silence, all of them deeply absorbed in the assignment before them. More striking still were the drawings they produced. Their accuracy left Edwards dumbfounded.

The mystery continued to gnaw at her. Then one day in 1968, Edwards came across an article in the *Los Angeles Times* describing split-brain research that was being conducted by the neurosurgeon Roger Sperry at the California Institute of Technology. The work, establishing for the first time the unique capacities of the right hemisphere, eventually won the Nobel Prize. As Edwards read about Sperry's research, she suddenly understood what had happened the day she had students turn their drawings upside down. The verbal left hemisphere, she saw all at once, is ill-suited to drawing, while the strengths of the right hemisphere are exactly those required to see and to draw accurately. In addition, she began to suspect that ordinary thinking and preconceived ideas literally get in the way of simply seeing, deeply and richly. The following year, Edwards began to teach at a trade college in downtown Los Angeles, while taking classes toward a Ph.D. at night at UCLA. In 1976, she got her degree. Her thesis was based on a study of the effects of upside-down drawing. Put simply, she made the case that when the left hemisphere is deprived of its ability to recognize and name objects, it tends to drop out of a task, turning it over instead to the right hemisphere.

Based on her thesis, Edwards landed a teaching job at the University of California at Long Beach. After an editor at Prentice-Hall, a textbook publisher, expressed some interest in having Edwards turn her thesis into a book, she sat down and wrote six sample chapters. In response, she received a curt letter of rejection. Attached was the comment of a scholarly reader who'd been asked to review the chapters. "Well, I read the whole manuscript," the note said, "but I needn't have." Fortunately, her closest friend, a professor of mathematics named William Bergquist, blithely dismissed the rejection. "He had absolutely complete confidence in me," Edwards explained. "He told me, 'Forget it. Just go ahead and finish the book. You can do it.' Without him, I would have stopped." In 1978, Edwards's manuscript came to the attention of a small California publisher named Jeremy Tarcher, who offered her a $6,000 advance for the book. She quickly accepted it. Two weeks after *Drawing on the Right Side of the Brain* reached the bookstores in the winter of 1979, the book landed on the *New York Times* paperback best-seller list. It has now sold more than 1.5 million copies and continues to sell steadily. Her second book, *Drawing on the Artist Within*, which focuses on the right and left hemisphere roles in creativity, has sold more than 500,000 copies.

Although it was Roger Sperry's work that first inspired Edwards, the research that led to his discoveries dates back to the early nineteenth century. In 1836, a French country doctor named Marc Dax made a presentation to a medical meeting in Montpellier, France, suggesting that speech seemed to be associated overwhelmingly with the left hemisphere of the brain. Dax based his conclusion on clinical experience with forty patients who had suffered brain damage. In each case, damage to the left side of the brain had caused a loss of speech, while damage to the right had had no such effect. These sorts of anecdotal clinical observations don't command much respect from scientists, and when Dax died the following year, none of his colleagues chose to follow up his work. It wasn't for nearly thirty years, in 1864, that a British neurologist named John Hughlings Jackson reasserted Dax's observation that speech is most often located on the left side of the brain. Jackson went on to speculate that the right side of the brain might have its own special function. "If it should be proven by wider evidence that the faculty of expression resides in one hemisphere," he wrote prophetically, "there is no absurdity in raising the question as to whether perception—its corresponding opposite—may be seated in the other."

Jackson's ideas were widely discounted by his colleagues. With few exceptions during the next hundred years, little consideration was given to the possibility that the right hemisphere was anything more than a mute inferior companion to the left hemisphere. As scientific method took firmer hold in the West, rationality and logic—the calling cards of the left hemisphere—were increasingly exalted. By contrast, intuitive and impressionistic thinking were disparaged as primitive, magical, and unverifiable. In 1926, a review of the scientific literature concluded, "In every case, the right hemisphere shows a manifest inferiority as compared with the left." As late as 1943, two prominent researchers concluded, "In man, the higher control functions are vested principally in one cerebral hemisphere"—namely, the left. Scientists agreed that the only comparability between the two hemispheres was that the left had apparent control over the physical functions of the right side of the body, while the right had control over the functions of the left side of the body.

Roger Sperry launched his research in the early 1950s. Through experiments on cats, Sperry was able to show that the corpus callosum, connecting the two hemispheres, serves as a conduit for information sent between them. Even then, however, the reason for having two sides of the brain remained something of a mystery. In the early 1960s, Sperry and several of his students began studying patients disabled by severe epileptic seizures. Desperate to gain relief from their disabling symptoms, these patients agreed to undergo a radical surgical procedure known as a commisorotomy, in which the corpus callosum connecting the two hemispheres is severed. The operation diminished the patients' seizures to some extent. The two hemispheres could no longer communicate with each other, but researchers were surprised to find that this had no obvious effect on the everyday functioning of most of the patients.

Sperry's next move was to devise a series of ingenious experiments aimed at exploring the possibility that each of the two hemispheres did indeed have unique capacities. In one experiment, for example, two different pictures were simultaneously flashed on a screen, one to the left hemisphere, the other to the right. This was done in such a way that it was impossible for the patient to scan both images at the same time. Thus, the image of a spoon, flashed on the left side of the screen, was read solely by the right hemisphere. The image of a knife, flashed on the right side of the screen, was read solely by the left hemisphere. When patients were questioned about what they'd seen, they invariably reported that the object was a knife. But if they were then asked to reach behind the screen and pick out what they'd seen, they chose the spoon. In short, the left hemisphere had language to describe what it had observed. The right hemisphere did not but could nonetheless identify the object it had seen by shape and feel. When patients who had chosen the spoon were asked to describe what they were holding, the response was typically a few moments of confusion, then the incorrect answer "knife." This suggested not only the physiological fact that the two hemispheres weren't communicating but something subtler about their respective roles. The verbal left hemisphere, it seemed, had an inclination to jump in and provide an answer to a question, even when it lacked accurate information.

Sperry and his student Jerry Levy were eventually able to declare authoritatively that the two hemispheres had fundamentally different ways of processing information. "By 1970," Levy wrote, "the reign of the left brain was essentially ended. The large majority of researchers concluded that each side of the brain was a highly specialized organ of thought, with the right hemisphere predominant in a set of functions that complemented those of the left." The left, Sperry concluded, was predominantly involved with analysis, especially the production and understanding of language. It appeared to operate, he said, in a sequential, step-by-step, time-conscious manner, making rational statements based on logical deductions and working toward conclusions. In addition to its superiority at verbal tasks, the left hemisphere seemed to be better at skills such as balancing a checkbook, planning a schedule, or getting to an appointment at a prescribed hour.

Much of this had long been known. The breakthrough was Sperry's evidence for the sophisticated capacities of the right hemisphere. In addition to being more visually and spatially adept than the left hemisphere—far better able to recognize faces, for example—the right hemisphere had a greater ability to see things all at once and to relate the parts to the whole. Thus the right hemisphere had an advantage in interpreting inflections in voice, in understanding metaphors, and even in creating new combinations of ideas. Finally, because the right hemisphere was less concerned than the left with fitting into time frames or approaching challenges in a logical, linear way, it was more inclined to solve problems by grand intuitive leaps and sudden insights. For all that, Sperry concluded that hemispheric specialization was not "an all or none phenomenon." Rather, he said, it takes place along a continuum. Certain tasks are better suited to the primary involvement of one hemisphere, while the highest and most complex challenges seem to require the cooperation of both hemispheres.

The intuitive recognition of these two ways of knowing dates back several thousand years in the Eastern mystical literature. The Chinese concept of yin and yang, for example, corresponds closely with Sperry's discoveries about the scientifically verifiable qualities of the left and right hemispheres. Yin refers, among other things, to the left side of the body (and thus the right hemisphere), to the unconscious and to intuition; yang, to the right side of the body (left hemisphere) and to conscious thought and reason. In 1930, Sri Aurobindo, the Western-educated Indian yogi whom Michael

Murphy so admired, characterized two entirely different ways of knowing. "The intellect is an organ . . . divisible into two important classes," Aurobindo wrote. "The faculties of the [right hemisphere] are comprehensive, creative and synthetic; the faculties of the [left hemisphere] are critical and analytic. . . . The left limits itself to ascertained truth, the right grasps that which is still elusive or unascertained. Both are essential to the completeness of human reason. These important functions of the machine have all to be raised to the highest and finest working power if the education of the child is not to be imperfect and one-sided."

Sperry himself came to believe that an imbalance had developed in the West. "The main theme to emerge," he wrote in 1973, "is that there appear to be two modes of thinking, verbal and nonverbal, represented rather separately in left and right hemispheres respectively, and that our educational system, as well as science in general, tends to neglect the nonverbal form of intellect. What it comes down to is that modern society discriminates against the right hemisphere."

I met Betty Edwards early in my research. Fascinated by the ideas I'd come across in *Drawing on the Right Side of the Brain,* I called her at her office at Cal State–Long Beach to see if I could arrange to see her. Her assistant gave me a number in Cambridge, Massachusetts, and I reached her at a hotel there. "I'm happy to talk more with you," she told me graciously after we'd chatted for a few minutes. "But if you really want to understand what I'm doing, I'm going to begin teaching a five-day drawing course at Harvard tomorrow. Why don't you come up and take it?"

It was as if she'd asked me to take off all of my clothes and join her nude encounter group. "I can't draw at all," I demurred.

"That's perfect," she replied, laughing.

"How so?" I asked.

"We love students like you," she explained. "You're the most satisfying ones to work with. The improvements are so dramatic."

"No, you don't understand," I said. "I'm the exception. I *really* can't draw."

"I've heard that before," Edwards replied in a voice so confident and reassuring that it completely disarmed me. "I hope you'll be able to make it." Within an hour, I'd decided to go. My four-year-old daughter drew better than I did, and I suspected that nothing was going to change that. At a minimum, however, I figured I'd learn a lot about what Edwards calls "powerful brain functions often obscured by language."

I arrived at Harvard just as her class was getting under way the next morning. My forty-odd fellow students included a doctor, a real estate broker, and a restaurateur, as well as several art teachers and painters. Drawing realistically, Edwards began by telling us, depends primarily on mastering the skill of direct perception. "The left hemisphere's inclination is to name and categorize, which means by definition to reduce and simplify," she explained. "That gets in the way of seeing what's truly there, in all of its complexity. For most of us, the brain is largely out of our control. It seems to have a life of its own. The paradox is that when it comes to seeing—and drawing—letting go of what we know can ultimately be a source of greater control."

The first problem, Edwards said, is that most people don't draw what's in front of them but rather reproduce what they already know. Since childhood, we have stored in memory hundreds of symbols for objects—primitive representations of a mouth, a nose, a tree, a cat, a chair, a house. When asked to draw, we tend not to look closely at the unique qualities of the object before us. Instead, we automatically recreate some oversimplified version of the object, based on our childhood symbols and concepts. "To see what is really there," Edwards said in her soft melodic voice, "requires shifting into a different level of awareness. Words drop out and thinking gives way to direct perception."

This nonverbal state of consciousness, Edwards told us, is the artist's way of seeing. By letting go of what we consciously "know," we free ourselves to see the world as it actually is—and, in turn, to depict what we have seen. "We already have the skills necessary to draw," Edwards explained. "The trick is putting aside the knowledge that stands in our way." It was by observing her own experience in drawing and by listening to the comments of her students, Edwards said, that she first began to identify the characteristics of the state in which one sees more accurately. When the shift occurs, she found, the internal chatter that most of us hear constantly in our brain quiets down. So, in turn, does the desire to engage in conversation. Instead, one becomes deeply absorbed in the task, often losing track of time entirely.

"In the deepest shifts," Edwards told us, "what I experience is a feeling of oneness. The pencil, the paper, the object being drawn, all of these become one. You lose the sense of your self as separate from the process itself." While Edwards has never studied the Eastern mystical literature or sat in meditation, her description of the ideal drawing state is remarkably parallel to the mystical experience of unity consciousness. In both cases, the active chatter of the verbal mind gives way to a quieter inner experience, while awareness grows broader and sharper. It reminded me of something that Ram Dass had told me. "Thoughts," he said, "feed our sense of separateness and prevent access to our deepest level of connectedness."

Nearly everyone, Edwards told us, has felt some version of what she calls a "cognitive shift." This shift can occur when one becomes deeply immersed in listening to a piece of music, or begins to play "out of one's mind" during competition in sports, or loses one's self in the course of an afternoon of gardening. The latter experience is especially common for Edwards, who happily spends long hours working in the spectacular terraced flower garden that climbs up a steep hill directly behind her home in the Santa Monica Canyon in Los Angeles. "I've had some fantastic experiences gardening—the same kind you have drawing or painting," she told me one day when we were sitting in her garden. "Everything opens up momentarily, and you have an entry into some deep connected state of being that you find yourself wanting to hang on to forever."

After she'd finished her introductory remarks, Edwards turned next to assessing our initial skill levels. She asked each of us to do three "preinstruction" drawings: one of a model seated at the front of the room, another of a person drawn from memory, and the last of one of our own hands. The purpose of the drawings was to form a basis of comparison with what we produced at the end of the course. Most students, Edwards said, find it hard to believe that they have come so far in just five days. This is the case, she has found, no matter what the level at which they begin. Edwards is no longer surprised to find that many of the working artists and art teachers who attend her classes have never learned how to draw realistically and don't even believe that they're capable of acquiring such skills.

For me, the prospect of accurately rendering the model sitting at the front of the room, much less attempting to draw a face from memory, was nothing short of preposterous. Still, I gamely plunged in. Over the next forty-five minutes most of my classmates produced passable drawings, neither spectacular nor embarrassing. When I brought my drawings up to Edwards, she smiled. I smiled back. After all, I'd told her so. "Right," she said in the gentle, affirmative way that I soon learned she began all her critiques. "Well, Tony, it looks to me as if you stopped drawing at about the age of six." She did not mean this as an insult. Edwards is convinced that preinstruction drawings are less a measure of one's talent than an indication of the point in life at which the development of one's drawing skills simply ceased. In most cases, she said, this occurs at an early age, because schools rarely see drawing as an important skill. Only those people like Edwards herself, who happen to discover the cognitive shift in which skilled drawing becomes relatively easy, continue to receive encouragement. Most children simply give up drawing altogether before they become teenagers.

During this same period, Edwards pointed out, education becomes more and more verbal, linear, and numerical, and success is measured largely by performance in these arenas. Artistic, visual, and even imaginative skills are increasingly glossed over or are neglected completely. Drawing classes are almost never required, nor are courses devoted to cultivating perceptual skills, or creativity, or even to understanding how the brain learns. "The result," Edwards explained, "is that a key aspect of the brain's potential—the right hemisphere—is vastly underutilized." Even so, Edwards acknowledged, when I pushed her, that she'd rarely come across someone whose visual development seemed to have stopped dead as early as mine had. That appeared only to fire her enthusiasm. "This is great, Tony," she said. "We're going to have fun with you."

Her next order of business was to demystify drawing. "The assumption that these skills are magical or God-given is a myth," she told us. "It has evolved because so few people learn how to draw realistically, while even those who can draw are rarely able to explain how they do it." Because drawing is primarily a nonverbal right hemisphere skill, Edwards said, it is especially difficult to translate into words one's experiences in this state. Most artists and art teachers are uncertain themselves how exactly they shift into the mode that makes drawing possible. In addition, many of them are protective of the mystique of drawing. Like magicians, they are reluctant to share the knowledge that makes their tricks possible—and sets them apart. "The result is bizarre," Edwards said. "People who cannot draw tend to avoid taking drawing classes. This is like choosing not to take a French class because you don't know how to speak French. The truth is that anyone who is capable of legibly signing his name can be taught to draw realistically."

The key challenge in realistic drawing, Edwards went on, is to find a way around the left hemisphere. "In order to gain access to the subdominant, visual, perceptual R-mode of the brain," she theorized in her first book, "it is necessary to present the brain with a job that the verbal, analytic L-mode will turn down." Put more simply, the right hemisphere can be more readily accessed by choosing a job that only it can do. The sort of tasks that the left hemisphere dislikes, resists, or is incapable of doing, Edwards explained, includes any that require rote repetition, close attention to complex visual details, and open-ended time commitment. The left hemisphere's inclination, she said, is to simplify and summarize, often based on what it already knows. Too impatient to see each strand of hair in all its subtle complexity, for example, the left hemisphere prefers to symbolize hair with a few quick marks. By contrast, the right hemisphere, at home with visual complexity and unimpeded by previous symbols and preconceptions, is comfortable immersing itself in whatever it sees—and in carefully reproducing it.

My first chance to try out Edwards's approach came late in the first day at Harvard, when she handed us a copy of Pablo Picasso's wonderfully evocative line drawing of Igor Stravinsky. Our instructions were simple. We were to copy the picture but only after turning it upside down. Edwards told us to ignore anything recognizable and nameable (mouth, nose, leg, button on a shirt) and to draw instead just the lines and shapes exactly as we saw them. In the process, she said, we'd be learning something about the first skill of drawing: the perception of edges, or lines.

Within moments, I found myself absorbed in the task. I was aware that the experience was enjoyable in some relaxed, wordless way, but that was the extent of my conscious thinking. Although I meditated every day, it was rare for me to become as quiet inside or to so completely lose track of time as I did while copying this drawing. A half-hour or so later, when I finally turned my collection of lines right side up, I was astonished at how accurately I'd rendered the image. I had to look at the two pictures a second time before I could even detect the differences between them. I felt certain that if I'd set out to copy the Picasso drawing right-side up, I'd have scarcely known where to start. At best, I would have produced some primitive caricature of Stravinsky. By simply asking me to copy an unrecognizable set of lines and shapes, Edwards had freed me of the inevitable anxiety of trying to accurately reproduce a complex image.

S perry himself was enthusiastic about Edwards's practical use of his work. He called her book "splendid" and wrote that "her application of the brain research findings to drawing conforms well with the available evidence and in many places advances the right hemisphere story." Some of Sperry's original collaborators have been more critical of Edwards, in part because neurological research has yet to document how exactly shifts from left to right hemisphere dominance take place. For example, Jerry Levy, now a biopsychologist at the University of Chicago, says that the interactions between the two hemispheres are far more complicated than Edwards implies.

"When Betty's book first came out, I said to myself, 'Yes, that's reasonable,' " Levy explained. "But she is not a neurologist, and data subsequently came out which contradicted her assumptions. It is simply neurologically wrong, for example, to suggest that the left hemisphere can be set aside in drawing or any other activity." In a textbook titled *Left Brain, Right Brain,* psychologist Sally Springer and neurologist George Deutsch took similar exception to Edwards's approach. "At this point," they argued, "there is no way of knowing if her methods work for the reasons she indicates." For example, the two authors wrote, there is no evidence to confirm that in a normal brain, "the left hemisphere interferes with the expression of right-hemisphere artistic ability."

Edwards herself sought to transcend the technical aspects of this narrow scientific debate by focusing on the bigger picture. "Since the late 1970s," she wrote, "I have used the terms L-mode and R-mode to try to avoid the location controversy. . . . Explanation of the two cognitive modes . . . have empirically proven successful with students at all levels. In short, the method works, regardless of the extent to which future science may eventually determine exact location and confirm the degree of separation of brain functions in the two hemispheres." This was powerfully confirmed by my own experience. From the first exercise, I felt a palpable cognitive shift. There was no question that my ordinary everyday thinking processes simply ceased as I became absorbed in drawing.

"The neuroscientists and the neurosurgeons are the naysayers," Edwards told me, "and in most cases they haven't even read my work. Almost certainly they are right that it is not a simple thing going on when a cognitive shift takes place in the brain. It is not like turning out one light and turning on another. But never mind. It's still a very useful metaphor for what experience tells you is actually happening." Even Edwards's critics acknowledge that she is effective. Levy calls her a "superb teacher," while Springer and Deutsch go one step further. "The fact is that Edwards' method appears to work," they acknowledged. "It will remain for future research to demonstrate why."

Edwards has been criticized on just the opposite grounds by some colleagues in her own field and at Cal State, where she taught until her retirement in 1993. They complain that her systematic techniques for teaching realistic drawing have no relationship to art or to creativity. Indeed, they argue that focusing on the technical skills of reproducing images may actually undermine artistic expression. "When I hear that, I say, 'Yes, we realize that this isn't about art,' Edwards told me with a certain exasperation. "We are simply building skills among people who didn't previously have them. I believe there's a basic vocabulary to be learned in any field. Would you try to write novels without first learning grammar and sentence construction? Would people suggest that you shouldn't learn to add or subtract because it might spoil you for creative math? Every major artist until this century learned to draw realistically, and it didn't seem to damage their creativity. Even today, the kids who are selected out as being artistically gifted are invariably the kids who start out able to draw realistically. The real point is that education never hurts. Knowledge is a resource. Once you have it, you can always choose to set it aside. My point is to give students the tools to make these choices. That is real freedom."

Because she believes that the left hemisphere mode of verbal, analytic thinking so dominates our culture, Edwards has focused most of her attention on developing the capacities of the right hemisphere. In her own life, however, she purposefully continues to nurture both modes. In addition to immersing herself in long hours of gardening, Edwards continues to draw. "If I find myself in an airport waiting area with an hour before a plane," she told me, "I'll take out my drawing pad and sketch the scenes around me. It's a wonderful way of recording my experiences deeply in memory, and of relaxing by letting go of active thinking." She also enjoys driving long distances on the freeway when there are no time pressures, precisely because this allows her to move out of focused thinking and into a more imaginative right hemisphere realm.

At the same time, Edwards remains a voracious reader and a crisp, clear, and evocative writer. Her two books are testimony to her capacity to use language and logic in the service of selectively setting language and logic aside—to enlist the skills of her left hemisphere to explain ways of accessing those of the right hemisphere. Because she's exceptionally fluent in both languages, the verbal and the visual, Edwards moves easily between the two. Rather than disparage the importance of language, she acknowledges both its value and its limits. "My strong suit," she told me, "is that I enjoy approaching art—which comes from a place that is neither linear nor rational—in a logical, analytic way. Drawing is full of ambiguity and paradox. Most people don't like that. I think it's where the fun is."

Our next assignment in class—the use of negative space— focused on just such a paradox. Negative space, Edwards told us, simply refers to the empty spaces between the lines or the shape of an object. Imagine the hole in a doughnut, and you've understood the essence of negative space. In the left hemisphere mode, it's hard to conjure up much interest in empty spaces. In the right mode, Edwards told us, negative space and positive space—the doughnut itself—command equal interest. Our assignment was to use negative space to draw a picture of a moderately complicated chair. Typically, the problem that most of us have in drawing an object such as a chair, Edwards explained, is that we already "know" so much about how they look—including the ninety-degree angle created by the back and the seat, the fact that the seat is flat, and the knowledge that the legs are all the same length. However, if you draw with that information in mind, you won't produce an object that looks much like a chair. "The paradox," Edwards said, "is that only by drawing unchairlike shapes—what's really out there when you look—is it possible to produce a chairlike image. Knowing the chair's actual shape will only get in the way of your being able to represent it accurately on paper."

The value of focusing on negative space, Edwards said, is that it provides another way of bypassing verbal knowledge. The left hemisphere has no symbols or words for empty spaces, nor any preconceived ideas about them. The only choice I had was to draw the negative spaces just as I saw them, not worrying about what might result or whether I had it "right." By doing this exercise meticulously, Edwards told us, the positive shape of the chair—which the negative space "surrounds"—would emerge as if by magic. "By making the negative spaces as important as the positive shapes," she explained, "you'll also be unifying the composition of your pictures. Defined in terms of language, negative space is the equivalent of context." Put another way, the awareness of negative space makes a given drawing more complete.

At first, I found it very difficult to see the negative spaces in the chair in front of me. I was confused about the difference between the actual shapes and the empty spaces. Not seeing them provoked my anxiety, which made seeing clearly even more difficult. It was a vivid example for me of how fear *literally* narrows one's vision. But sure enough, when I forced myself simply to keep looking, the spaces began to pop suddenly into focus, just as Edwards had assured us they would. Drawing them became surprisingly simple. I felt myself relax, and my focus grew sharper. I wasn't trying to create a likeness or make one shape match another. I was just drawing what I saw. I had no idea where all this was heading, but in this word-free state, I became happily absorbed in the task for its own sake.

When I finished and sat back to look at the result—a surprisingly good representation of a chair—I had an odd experience. I was thrilled, but I wasn't sure how I'd done it. It seemed just to have happened. As a writer, I was used to laboring endlessly and painfully over each sentence. Clear, evocative writing was the reward for hard, conscious work and a fair amount of suffering. I earned the good sentences I wrote. In the case of my chair, I couldn't recall any experience of effort, or even much conscious intention. Nor was I accustomed to remaining happily absorbed for so long, with so little focus on the end result. More typically, I felt antsy and easily distracted when I took on a challenging piece of work. In this case, my attention barely wavered, and time passed so quickly that I was startled to find out how long I'd been at the task. The effect seemed to carry over after class. I felt less preoccupied and more focused in the present. The process of drawing freed me for extended periods from the relentless chatter of my own thinking. It even had an effect on my relationships. I was staying at my brother's house during Edwards's seminar, and while we'd long been strongly drawn to each other, there was always an unspoken competitiveness that became particularly pronounced when we got together. In this instance, the tension evaporated, at least temporarily. Each night, after we'd shared a leisurely, relaxed dinner together I settled easily into the drawing assignments Edwards had given us.

On the third day, we turned our attention to linear perspective, or sighting. In Edwards's view, this is the most difficult skill of all to learn but also the most exciting. To master it, as artists did for the first time during the Renaissance, is to gain power over space—the ability to represent three-dimensionality with correct proportion and perspective on a two-dimensional surface. Part of the challenge, she told us, is that more than any skill in drawing, perspective requires not only the right hemisphere's capacity to see the often-paradoxical relationship between the parts and the whole, but also left hemisphere skills such as measuring, counting, and calculating. To facilitate a process that Edwards told us would eventually become instinctive and automatic, she began by showing us how to measure sizes and angles of objects in relation to one another. All of sighting, she said, involves comparison: how wide is this angle compared to that; how big is this object compared to that. At the same time, one must deal with a level of paradox that defies the left hemisphere's sense of logic. In order to represent a certain angle three-dimensionally, for example, it is often necessary to draw the angle in a way that defies what you believe is accurate. "We must overcome false interpretations which are often based on what we think must be out there," Edwards has written. "You must believe what you see, and draw your perceptions without changing or revising them to fit your verbal knowledge."

By the time we got to the fourth day and the chance to confront our biggest challenge yet—drawing a portrait of a fellow student—my confidence had grown. To my amazement, I now found I could draw the weird converging angles of the corner of a room in such a way that they appeared in near-perfect perspective and proportion. Along with what I had learned from upside-down drawing and the use of negative space, I had found that I could circumvent the preconceptions that had previously limited me to sticklike two-dimensional drawings.

To help us out on our first portrait, Edwards spent a couple of hours clearing up what she told us were common left hemisphere misperceptions about the shape of the head and the placement of individual features. For example, she told us that eyes are often drawn far too high on the face, severely shortening and thus distorting the forehead. This occurs, Edwards speculated, because the dominant left hemisphere, given to naming and categorizing, finds body parts such as the eyes, nose, and mouth more interesting than the forehead. In turn, it "sees" these expressive parts of the face as taking up more space than they actually do. It's as if the left hemisphere automatically diminishes or even eliminates information that it doesn't find compelling.

I chose to draw Audrey, an attractive young art teacher. For the first time all week, I found myself consciously struggling. I wanted the picture to turn out well not just to impress Edwards and my classmates and to do my subject justice, but also to confirm in a visible way how far I'd come. I also felt slightly rushed. Since Audrey wasn't a professional model, she couldn't be expected to sit still indefinitely, and to accommodate her, I hurried to finish. Finally, because I was consciously thinking—mostly in the form of worrying about how the picture would turn out—I was less fully absorbed in simply seeing. The cognitive shift that I'd made easily the previous several days now occurred only intermittently at best. The portrait that I eventually produced was certainly better than my preinstruction drawings, but it didn't make me very happy. It had a labored, somewhat awkward-looking quality, and it bore only a modest resemblance to Audrey. It also lacked a true sense of three-dimensionality. Given my limited expectations for the week, I had reason to feel pleased with my progress. But I also knew that I hadn't yet experienced a real breakthrough.

On the final morning of the course, Edwards introduced a fourth skill of drawing: the perception of light and shadow, or shading. The fifth and final skill—perception of the whole or the gestalt—is the only one that Edwards does not teach explicitly. It emerges, she says, from the successful integration of the first four skills. "Drawing is like riding a bicycle," she explained. "You begin by learning individual skills, including how to steer, pedal, brake, and shift gears. At first, it all seems awkward, confusing, and even frightening. But eventually the skills begin to blend together, until one day you can suddenly ride smoothly and effortlessly, and you do so without any conscious thinking." The result, she told us, is that bicycle riding has become a "global skill." By mastering the individual skills of drawing, Edwards assured us, they too would eventually become global. When that happened, she said, we would be effortlessly fluent in a second language. No longer would we have to think about making the cognitive shift necessary to draw.

We had only a couple of hours to spend on light and shadow. Still, that was enough for me to understand a key aspect of what was missing in my drawing of Audrey. It is through shading,

Edwards explained, that objects are made to appear three-dimensional. "Your job," she said, "is to learn to perceive the different gradations of light and shadow that fall on an object. Just as most people don't see negative space at first, so they don't really notice the subtle 'values' of light and shadow that fall on an object or a form." Once again, we were up against the left mode's inclination to reduce and simplify—to literally see things in black and white, rather than in their true shaded complexity. The solution, Edwards told us, is to look closely at the object or form until a shadow or an area of light comes into focus as a discrete shape, then to draw that shape without trying to name it. To do this, she explained, we needed to make distinctions between degrees of shading, so that we reflected not just black and white but also the gradations in between. In much the way that positive forms emerge out of negative spaces, Edwards said, so three-dimensionality grows out of the accurate depiction of light and shadow shapes.

Our final assignment was to use all of this knowledge in the service of a self-portrait, to be drawn in three-quarter view while we looked in a mirror. In order to help us incorporate light and shadow, Edwards told us to draw a rectangular frame on a piece of paper, then to take the side of a pencil and fill in the frame completely. This ground, she explained, would automatically give us a "middle tone," which is the value that beginning students struggle most to see. In order to represent the darker shapes, she instructed us to draw them in, using a dark pencil. To get the lighter tones, she told us just to erase out parts of the ground. As usual, I couldn't imagine how I could possibly succeed. By this stage, however, inexperience and even doubt didn't faze me. In contrast to the day before, I was now so focused on understanding our directions that I never stopped to think how it might all turn out. As my own model, I was prepared to sit for as long as it took to get down on paper what I was seeing. Very quickly, I became focused on seeing the shapes of shadows, assessing angles, looking at negative spaces, and honing in on each component of the task while remaining only vaguely aware of the whole. Within a short time, I was oblivious to everything around me. I had absolutely no idea how much time was passing.

At some point, it dawned on me that I had drawn all the shapes, shadows, and spaces that I could pick out in the face staring at me from the mirror. I checked my watch, and more than two hours had passed. When I stood up and looked at the drawing, viewing it for the first time as a whole, I was shocked. The face before me—reproduced on the jacket of this book—was unmistakably mine. Even the mood that the picture conveyed was one I instantly recognized. I was utterly thrilled. Suddenly, I realized how much I'd always wanted to draw and how powerful it felt to see so deeply and accurately. My drawing was far from the most skilled or sophisticated self-portrait in the class, but Edwards was nonetheless effusive. The pure technical leap I'd made in the five days was extraordinary by itself, she said. Beyond that, she was taken with how evocatively I'd managed to capture my personality in the picture. I've gone on to draw several other self-portraits during the past several years, including one when I took Edwards's class for a second time. While each drawing is more technically sophisticated than those before it, the first self-portrait I did remains the most viscerally powerful and real. Never since then have I gotten quite as absorbed in drawing for its own sake.

As she stood by my side on that final afternoon, I suddenly understood the powerful impact of Edwards's continuing encouragement. She creates a nurturing, nonjudgmental environment in which the expectation of success is high and the possibility of failure never enters the picture. That makes it easier to let go of fears and insecurities, negative past experiences, and any pressure to meet a certain standard—all aspects of ordinary left hemisphere thinking that interfere with seeing freely and truly. Put another way, the right hemisphere mode is a fragile and elusive state that can easily be overridden by the left hemisphere's rush to judgment. At the same time, when the left hemisphere faces a challenge that it is ill equipped to meet, Edwards believes that it often simply gives up instead of turning the job over to the right hemisphere.

"We work very hard to thwart that inclination to quit," Edwards told me several weeks after the course had ended. "We exhort our students, we show them the evidence that these techniques have worked with other students and we try to create an emotionally supportive atmosphere. I think of the left hemisphere as the gatekeeper of the ego. One of its functions is to protect us from being made a fool of. In order to let the right hemisphere come forward and take over, the left hemisphere needs to be reassured that things will turn out okay. That's what we try to do with our cheerleading. We're creating a safe environment in which to let go of conscious control."

I had no illusion that the realistic drawings I'd produced had much to do with art, or that they reflected the sort of originality and imagination that lie at the heart of true creativity. Still, like Edwards, it struck me that accessing the right hemisphere mode in which realistic drawing becomes possible is essential to creativity and original thinking. Inspiration, I sensed, takes place less in the rational, analytic L-mode, than in the quieter, less structured R-mode. Only in the latter, I suspected, is there expansive space for new ideas and fresh connections to rise up spontaneously. As it turned out, Edwards devoted her second book to precisely this subject. *Drawing on the Artist Within* begins with a wonderful left hemisphere insight. Nearly all of the words associated with creativity, Edwards observed, center on seeing—among them insight, foresight, hindsight, vision, and even illumination, which is defined as throwing light on a subject in order to see it better. Creativity itself, she said, is often characterized as the capacity to *see* problems in a new way. In turn, creative breakthroughs are frequently described with phrases such as "I see it" or "I see the light."

Edwards went on to theorize that the capacity for direct perception—for seeing clearly—is integrally related to creativity. For example, she noted that intuition, a key component of creativity, is typically defined as "the power or faculty of attaining direct knowledge or cognition without rational thought and interference." Both creativity and realistic drawing, she concluded, require the capacity to shift from the verbal thinking mode of the left hemisphere to the right hemisphere's more visual, holistic way of processing information. "The left hemisphere focuses on details rather than larger issues, it tends not to make intuitive leaps based on partial information, and it wants to get to the finish line and come to a conclusion as fast as it can," Edwards told me. "That sort of premature closure is one of the great roadblocks both to drawing and to creativity."

The next task Edwards set for herself was to break down systematically the components of the creative process. Her aim was to better understand the relationship between the left and right hemispheres as any creative process unfolds. She began by combing the voluminous literature on creativity, and discovered a surprising consensus on the basic stages of the process. In the nineteenth century, for example, the German physiologist and physicist Hermann Helmholtz became the first person to categorize his own creative breakthroughs in terms of specific stages. The first, he said, is "saturation," or the gathering of information. The second is "incubation," which involves a period of mulling over the information. The third is "illumination," in which an apparently sudden and spontaneous solution or breakthrough occurs. Nearly a hundred years later, all three of these basic stages remain widely accepted by psychologists who study creativity.

In 1908, the French mathematician Henri Poincaré added a fourth stage of creativity. Verification, he said, is the process by which the illumination is framed in concrete terms and tested for accuracy. Finally, in the 1960s, an American psychologist named Jacob Getzels added a stage preceding the four others—the discovery or formulation of the problem to be solved. This is the sort of "aha" experience that sets the creative process in motion. Another American psychologist, George Kneller, subsequently named this preliminary stage "first insight." Numerous writers and psychologists have tinkered with descriptions of these five stages. The writer Joseph Chilton Pearce wrote a paper titled "Breakthrough into Insight," in which he described the five stages of creativity as "commitment," "service," "gestation," "breakthrough," and "translation." In his book *The Creative Spirit*, writer and psychologist Daniel Goleman described four stages as "preparation," "incubation," "illumination," and "translation."

Edwards set out to characterize the hemisphere of the brain best suited to each stage of the creative process. Two of them, she concluded, clearly depend more on left hemisphere skills. Saturation is the methodical, often step-by-step gathering of existing information before moving to a new level of insight. "One of the paradoxes of creativity," she quoted psychologist George Kneller, echoing her own view about why artists must learn to draw realistically, "[is] that in order to think originally, we must familiarize ourselves with the ideas of others. Information, in short, represents the raw material from which original thinking emerges—and the more knowledge one has, the better the base." Verification, the final stage of the creative process, often demands even more precise left hemisphere skills: analyzing, codifying, and translating the breakthrough into accessible language.

The other three stages of creativity—first insight, incubation, and illumination—have long been considered more elusive, mysterious, and difficult to teach systematically or sequentially. All three, Edwards suggested, depend preeminently on right hemisphere skills, among them a tolerance for ambiguity, complexity, and paradox; a reliance on nonverbal imagery and intuition; and a gestaltlike capacity to see both the whole and the parts. "In each of these stages," she told me, "the creative work occurs largely at an unconscious level—and often after the left hemisphere's conscious, rational search for a solution has been exhausted."

Edwards set out to demystify these stages of creativity, just as she had the components of drawing. The first insight that prompts creative exploration, she found, is frequently described as an intuitive leap beyond the realm of words. The incubation stage begins after sufficient information has been gathered but the left hemisphere has failed to find an answer to the problem using its logical, analytic skills. At this point, often out of frustration and a sense of failure, the problem is simply set aside. Sometimes this is done with conscious intention. An artist or a scientist, for example, familiar with nonanalytic ways of gaining answers to creative problems, might decide to take a walk, or daydream, or literally to "sleep on it." Elmer Green's method, for example, is to interrogate his own unconscious by moving into a waking reverie state, and then to find the answers in the spontaneous images that arise.

"The deliberate giving over of the problem puts it out of conscious control," Edwards explained, "thus enabling . . . R-mode, which is capable of dealing with enormous complexity, to think aside." In effect, the right hemisphere seeks to see the whole picture and not just the component parts. As Green and others have found, answers are often derived in the form of complex images rather than words. The actual moment of creative breakthrough—illumination—typically occurs unbidden and spontaneously. "The pieces literally fall into place," Edwards told me, "and you see the whole picture."

Edwards's next important contribution was to recognize that creativity often depends on finding specific techniques to mute the left hemisphere's inclination to maintain control. For the right hemisphere to do its job—say, in the incubation phase—a certain amount of open-ended quiet time is required. If the left hemisphere remains too outer-focused, judgmental, and dominant, the necessary cognitive shift may be thwarted. I have experienced this phenomenon in my own work many times. Getting started each day and becoming deeply absorbed remains a remarkably persistent challenge, even after twenty years as a writer. When I look at a blank screen, I still frequently confront myriad fears characteristic of the left hemisphere: the uncertainty that I'll produce any original insights; the difficulty of wrestling complex ideas into clear, comprehensible language; the powerful hunger to find simple solutions and quickly arrive at closure; and the chilling specter of failure in the end.

Instinctively, Edwards says, the left hemisphere tries to avoid these anxieties by looking instead for challenges it can readily meet. It dawned on me that my own methods of avoidance are nearly automatic. Rather than write when I first sit down, I rearrange papers on my desk, make lists, catch up on phone calls, run downstairs for coffee. I'm increasingly convinced that writer's block—and perhaps all creative blocks—are in large part the failure to permit the right hemisphere to take a more dominant role in creative tasks for which the left hemisphere is less well-suited. To subjectively test this theory, I decided to see if it was possible, in the course of writing this chapter, to get my left hemisphere to cede some ground to my right. I chose a technique that Edwards herself employs when she writes. Rather than simply sitting down before a blank page—which invariably arouses a feeling of anxiety and frustration—I decided to begin each day by going back and editing the previous day's work. Because the basic ideas were already in place and the editing work had mostly to do with rearranging words, the task was well-suited to the left hemisphere.

As I became more immersed in the work, I felt myself relaxing and shifting into the more absorbed right hemisphere mode that I recognized from drawing. In this frame of mind, conceiving and writing new material became less daunting. Rarely, however, did my left hemisphere venture far afield. Instead, it lurked at the periphery, a voice forever urging me to divert my energies, to take on something simpler and less open-ended, or at the very least to take a break. Allowing myself to fall into the absorbed right hemisphere mode invariably proved pleasurable and productive, but it also meant letting go of conscious control. I rarely find that easy. What it requires, I eventually realized, is a genuine leap of faith—the willingness to trust one's deepest unconscious potentials. As Edwards put it, "One becomes more creative not by trying to be more creative, but rather by further developing that part of the mind . . . which is so deeply involved in creative thinking. It seems only logical that adding visual skills to already existing language capabilities stands a very good chance of increasing the overall power of the brain."

Bⁿⁿⁿ ut is the right hemisphere truly the seat of creative inspiration, as Edwards came to suspect? Elmer Green— the only researcher I found who has studied the relationship between brainwave activity and the two hemispheres of the brain—had a more complex explanation. To Green, understanding creativity requires differentiating not just between the roles of the right and left hemispheres but between the upper and lower cortexes of the brain. In teaching patients to voluntarily produce slower, theta brain waves as a means of retrieving information from the unconscious, for example, Green focused first on quieting the left hemisphere. Specifically, he attached electrodes to the scalp above the left cortex, or outer layer of the brain.

"Our goal is to gain access to what's going on in the lower brain centers, where the deeper levels of consciousness reside," Green told me. "The problem is that if you don't train the left cortex to quiet down by moving into theta, it will keep acting like a supercharged coach, instructing and yelling orders and creating distraction. It takes a long time for people to become aware that the most profound intelligence isn't in the rational left cortex. Rather, it comes up from the lower brain centers by way of the right cortex—in the form of gestalts, and pictures, and feelings. Only the right cortex can truly see the whole picture. First, though, you have to get the loud noise of waking consciousness turned off, because the information that comes up from the lower brain centers is as delicate and subtle as the draft of a butterfly's wing. The instant you turn too much left cortex attention to it, the information tends to slip away."

Green has often seen this conflict play out in his own experience, most especially during his years in graduate school. Whenever he found himself unable to solve a problem through deductive reasoning and rational analysis, he would turn to interrogating his unconscious, using the methods he'd learned as a teenager. "It didn't work until my left hemisphere had literally run out of ideas," he told me. "Then I'd let my mind get totally still, and I'd assume that the next impression or idea that came up would be the answer to my problem. Soon, I'd get a little flash, or a picture, just above the eye level. Then I'd look at this answer rationally, with my left cortex, and invariably I'd find myself saying, 'That's a stupid idea.' So I'd dismiss it, just the way the left cortex dismisses anything that doesn't fit its worldview. After a while, if I couldn't come up with a better answer, I'd finally go back to my unconscious and my right cortex. Sure enough, I'd get the same image, and it would turn out to be the right answer. After this happened about twenty-five times, I began to believe it."

Edwards eventually developed her own technique for accessing the intelligence of the unconscious. Her goal, she told me, was to "dredge up the inner life of the mind" by using the visual language of something she calls "analog drawings." Over a period of years, she asked hundreds of students to draw pictures of specific emotions, or of problems they were facing, without using any recognizable symbols at all. She permitted the use only of the language of lines and shapes. In time, Edwards discovered remarkably consistent patterns in the way that certain emotions are depicted symbolically. Joy, for example, mostly shows up as light, curving, circular forms that reach upward, while anger is typically jagged, dark, and pointed. Peacefulness or tranquillity is almost invariably expressed in horizontal lines or gentle waves, while depression is reflected not just by darkness but by forms that are literally drawn low on the page. In effect, Edwards found that students could learn a great deal about powerful underlying feelings simply by expressing themselves visually. "By means of drawing," Edwards concluded, "we can unlock a door not otherwise open to consciousness."

At the deepest level, Edwards recognized that using these techniques to gain access to the unconscious has the potential to unlock a more authentic self. Still, she has resisted undertaking this sort of self-exploration. "In some sense, I think I've avoided the aspect of the work that bears on the self," she told me. "Perhaps it's a reverberation of my upbringing, in which I was never permitted to be self-involved. The purpose of my being was to make my mother happy. My attention was always directed outward. I've been healed by giving, not by looking within. I don't think I have a desperate need to find out what my problems are because I have a feeling that I can always cope when the crunch comes down. Neurotic as I am, I'll be okay."

But was this, I found myself wondering, the rationalization of her left hemisphere? To what extent, I asked her one day, was she simply fearful of the suffering entailed in probing more deeply within? "Yes, that's there, I can feel my right hemisphere agreeing," Edwards told me, laughing gently. "I have let myself be a victim of my mother—this person who canceled me out, who forced herself on me. Even now—and she's almost ninety—I can't let go. I still feel responsibility for her, even though it's at great cost to myself. At bottom, I don't believe I can ever change it. That *is* my left hemisphere talking. It just keeps saying, 'Don't make waves.' "

Edwards is convinced that the right hemisphere provides a route to a deeper level of truth and depth than does the left hemisphere. "What if it turns out we put our eggs in the wrong basket?" she has taken to asking students at the end of her five-day classes. "What if, by spending all these centuries cultivating language, mathematics, and technological skills, we put in abeyance another system—visual and nonverbal—that is ultimately more powerful and better suited to our survival? What if language seduced us, by its power and dominance, into a tradeoff in which we have limited ourselves and lost the capacity to see the real complexity and the larger connections in the world we live in?" Edwards elaborates this insight at the end of *Drawing on the Artist Within*. "Drawing gives one a feeling of power—not power over things or people but some strange power of understanding or knowing or insight," she explained. "Through drawing, one becomes more connected to things and people outside oneself. . . . By looking outward and seeing the world around you in the artist's mode of seeing, you gain insight into yourself. Conversely, by looking inward to find the artist within, you gain insight into the world outside yourself."

Despite her strong intuitive preference for the right hemisphere's mode of perception, Edwards remains convinced that the left hemisphere does have a critical role to play in the complete life. As Elmer Green put it, "The power of the left cortex is that it keeps us rational, helps us discard superstitions, and gives us a way to analyze and sort through information. Without it, we'd be back in the dark ages." For Edwards, the biggest challenge has been to strike a balance between the strengths of the two hemispheres. "The ideal role of the right hemisphere," she told me, "is to provide access to the deepest levels of one's true experience and to serve as a reality check against the left hemisphere's tendency to make up stories when it doesn't really know the answers. The ideal role for the left hemisphere is to be an articulate spokesperson for all the information that comes up from the right and to discriminate between what's important and what is merely trivial. Each mode of thinking is incomplete without the other. You need access to both hemispheres to be whole."

5

CONNECTING THE MIND
AND BODY

Can We Make Ourselves Sick—and Well?

*The great majority of us are required to live a life of
constant systematic duplicity. Your health is bound to
be affected if, day after day, you say the opposite of
what you feel, if you grovel before what you dislike and
rejoice at what brings you nothing but misfortune. Our
nervous system isn't just a fiction; it's a part of our
physical body, and our soul exists in space and is inside
us, like the teeth in our mouth. It can't be forever
violated with impunity.*
—BORIS PASTERNAK

*The witch doctor succeeds for the same reason all the
rest of us succeed. Each patient carries his own doctor
inside him. . . . We are at our best when we give the
doctor who resides within each patient a chance to go
to work.*
—ALBERT SCHWEITZER

IT seemed obvious that the pressures in my life had
something to do with my back pain. When it first
began in 1985, Deborah was pregnant with our second
child, and she was in bed herself with what appeared to be a
herniated disk. We had just moved into a new apartment to
accommodate our growing family, and we faced far bigger ex-
penses. I was working madly to keep us afloat. But eventually our

second child was born healthy and adorable, Deborah's pain disappeared, and I signed a book contract. Our burdens lifted, yet my back pain only got worse. Eventually, it became the central focus of my life. I visited orthopedists and neurologists, got adjusted by a chiropractor and readjusted by an osteopath. I stretched with a physical therapist, endured the needles of an acupuncturist, and spent two weeks at a pain clinic in Florida. I took classes in yoga and tried to build more relaxation into my life. I straightened my posture, strengthened my abdominals, spread lumbar cushions around the house, filled my freezer with ice packs, and stashed a heating pad under my bed. Nothing helped.

Finally, I went to see a physician named John Sarno at New York University's Rusk Institute of Rehabilitation Medicine. By that point, I'd been in nearly continuous pain for eighteen months. Sarno is a short, robustly healthy-looking man in his sixties with a passionate belief in his work and limited patience for skeptics. I was open to any approach that might lead to relief from my suffering. In a matter of hours, Sarno convinced me that there was nothing structurally wrong with my back. My physical symptoms, he explained, were actually serving to mask unconscious emotions that I resisted acknowledging, and fear itself played a key role in perpetuating my chronic cycle of pain.

At its heart, Sarno's treatment aims at helping patients become more aware of the effect that specific thoughts and emotions have on their bodies. What remains unconscious, he argues, may prompt not just psychological suffering but physical pain. More effectively and consistently than any practitioner I met, Sarno demonstrated that simply bringing unconscious thoughts and emotions to awareness can have a powerful healing effect. Three weeks and two long classroom lectures after I first saw him, my back stopped hurting. With very minor and short-lived exceptions, it hasn't troubled me since.

Sarno provided my first direct experience of the connection between the mind and the body. In time, I began to see that this relationship is critical to any search for a more complete life.

When the mind and body begin to work together in harmony, the healing effects often defy conventional medical and scientific understanding. Sarno believes, for example, that in more than 95 percent of the patients he sees, no structural abnormality can account for their pain. This includes patients with symptoms long thought to be associated with back pain—including herniated disk and scoliosis.

Most people, Sarno argues, suffer from what he calls tension myositis syndrome, or TMS. By this, he simply means that the physical pain is attributable to underlying emotional factors—including anxiety, fear, and anger. Telltale TMS symptoms, he told me, include tenderness and pain in disparate and unrelated areas of the back; a highly driven and demanding personality; and a history of other conditions associated with stress—among them migraine headaches, heartburn, stomach ulcer, colitis, spastic colon, asthma, and allergies. More recently, Sarno has concluded that TMS is the primary factor in several other syndromes for which there is no clear physical explanation: certain kinds of knee and shoulder pain, tennis elbow, shin splints, pain in the ankles and Achilles tendon, and many forms of foot pain, including bone spurs, flat feet, and even foot drop. The implications of this theory are enormous. Back pain, for example, is the second most common reason—after the common cold—that Americans visit doctors. The annual cost of treating people with back pain is more than $8 billion, and the number of spinal operations in the United States is nearly ten times that of any other Western country.

Although he has never conducted a controlled study, Sarno does track his results. Over the past twenty years, he has treated more than ten thousand back sufferers. In 1982, he conducted a random follow-up survey of 177 patients whom he had treated during the previous three years. Seventy-six percent were experiencing little or no pain and had resumed all normal activities. Eight percent were improved, and only 16 percent were unchanged. In 1987, Sarno did a similar random survey focusing on patients he'd treated who had been diagnosed on CT scans and MRI's as having herniated disks. An astonishing 88 percent—96 patients—reported that in the wake of Sarno's lecture-based treatment, they were experiencing little or no pain. Ten percent cited improvement, and only two percent were unchanged. While these statistics don't constitute scientific proof, they mirror my own experience in referring patients to Sarno over the past seven years. I have sent him more than 50 people—a dozen of them friends and neighbors—and followed up with nearly all of them. Although many were initially skeptical that Sarno's approach would help, all but a handful are pain-free today. Given the limited effectiveness of nearly all treatments for back pain, including surgery, this rate of success is extraordinary.

Even so, the medical establishment has viewed skeptically Sarno's contention that back pain rarely has any structural basis. In July 1994, however, *The New England Journal of Medicine* published an extraordinary study in which 98 men and women with *no* back pain underwent magnetic resonance imaging tests, or MRI's. The researchers, led by Dr. Michael Brant-Zawadzki, found that nearly two-thirds of the subjects evidenced spinal abnormalities, including bulging or protruding disks, herniated disks, and degenerated disks. The study's authors concluded—as Sarno first did more than twenty years ago—that an abnormal disk has no apparent relationship to pain. "Certain physicians like to be able to explain to their patients why they're feeling what they're feeling," Dr. Brant-Zawadzki explained. "The temptation is there for doctors who are not sophisticated to be glib about disk abnormalities and patient symptoms." While the study made it clear that a great deal of unnecessary back surgery is performed, it did not point to any more effective ways to treat the symptoms.

The main part of Sarno's treatment consists of attending two, two-hour lectures that he offers—to as many as forty patients at a time—on the emotional genesis of back pain. In all but a small number of cases, he argues, the pain itself derives from the soft tissues, namely muscles, nerves, tendons, and ligaments. The precipitating event may be an injury. But Sarno theorizes that various forms of tension—whether conscious or unconscious— then cause constriction of the blood vessels that lead to the muscles and nerves in the back and often in the shoulders and neck. The deprivation of blood and of the oxygen it carries ultimately leads, he says, to painful muscle spasms and nerve pain. Under ordinary circumstances, this could be expected to quickly resolve itself, much the way one sometimes briefly experiences a case of leg cramps after running long distance or sitting too long in one position. When it comes to backs, however, the pain itself often prompts fear of more serious injury and suffering. This creates more tension, says Sarno, and leads to further constriction of the blood vessels. The result can be a chronic cycle of pain that interferes with the body's otherwise natural ability to heal itself.

In effect, Sarno uses a talking cure. In part, this is built around making a logically convincing case that there is no structural basis for most back pain. He has long pointed out, as *The New England Journal of Medicine* now confirms, that a substantial percentage of all adults show evidence of herniated disks on MRI and CT scans, but only a very small number report any pain. He explains that nearly all of his patients feel pain and tenderness in various parts of the back, neck, and shoulders that have no relation to one another. He points out that even in the case of major physical injuries, the body's ordinary self-healing mechanisms are characteristically powerful, predictable, and finite. Finally, he argues that there is no reasonable structural explanation for the fact that people's back pain often comes and goes; that it moves from one part of the back to another; and that it typically becomes more intense under psychologically stressful circumstances.

The origin of the tension that leads to muscle spasms and nerve pain, Sarno believes, is repressed emotion. Back pain, he explains in his book *Healing Back Pain,* "is a command decision by the mind to produce a physical reaction rather than . . . experience a painful emotion." Based on his clinical experience, Sarno is increasingly convinced that anger is the emotion that is most often responsible for back pain. His challenge, he says, is to make patients aware that repressed anger—or fear—ultimately shows up disguised in the form of physical symptoms. By exposing this charade, Sarno says, the physical pain can no longer serve its diversionary purpose. "It's a bit like blowing the cover on a covert operation," he has written. "As long as the person remains unaware that the pain is serving as a distraction, it will continue to do so, undisturbed. But the moment the realization sinks in . . . then the deception doesn't work anymore; pain stops, for there is no further need for the pain. And it's the information that gets the job done." In a small minority of cases, patients appear to accept his TMS diagnosis but still fail to get better. At that point Sarno prescribes follow-up psychotherapy, specifically aimed at uncovering the link between the physical pain and the psychological factors. Almost invariably, he says, these patients uncover deeper levels of underlying emotional conflict.

The second key to treatment, Sarno has found, is convincing patients that their ingrained fears about their backs are unwarranted. The concern that certain activities will somehow further damage the back simply leads to more anxiety, he argues, and thus reinforces the pain cycle. In effect, the mind sends a message of anxiety to the body, and the prophecy becomes *physiologically* self-fulfilling. In one recent controlled study of back patients, for example, electrodes were placed on their backs, and they were asked to talk about their pain. The level of electrical activity in the monitored muscles—a measure often associated with spasm— rose as much as seven times while they spoke. "That tells you that just thinking can affect your physiology and your pain," reported Dr. Dennis Turk, the University of Pittsburgh psychologist who conducted the study. Even now, as I myself sit writing about this once painful subject, I can feel a slight tightening in my back—a vestige, I'm convinced, of my old fear and apprehension. The difference is that I now have confidence that the pain will quickly pass—and a deeper belief that I've gained a remarkable capacity to directly influence my body.

I t was not long after my experience with Sarno that I set out on my search for wisdom. From early on, the mind-body connection struck me as an important piece of the puzzle.

Was there, I wondered, any measurable scientific evidence that thoughts and emotions affect physical health? I was especially interested in evidence that what we think and feel may influence not just mild conditions such as back pain but life-threatening illnesses including cancer and heart disease. Research in the field known as behavioral medicine—or psychoneuroimmunology—remains inconclusive and sometimes conflicting. Still, I was struck by at least one unmistakable pattern. Put simply, what is healthy for the mind, emotions, and spirit consistently appears to promote physical health. Conversely, what's unhealthy for the mind, emotions, and spirit tends to make one more vulnerable to disease and less able to recover from it successfully.

The two emotions most consistently correlated with illness are depression, which leads to hopelessness and isolation; and chronic anger, which is stressful and alienating. The two emotions most associated with physical health are the capacity for love, which prompts feelings of security and intimacy; and hope or faith, which leads to a sense of meaning and resilience. In effect, emotions that encourage more connectedness and awareness appear to be healthy, while those that prompt separation and alienation are unhealthy. At a slightly more metaphorical level, the research into the mind-body connection suggests that the fewer the barriers we erect—between conscious and unconscious, between ourselves and others, and between personal and universal concerns—the healthier we're likely to be. Conversely, the more narrowly we define ourselves, the more separate we feel from others, and the more disconnected we get from our own deepest needs, the more vulnerable we become to disease.

There is also increasing evidence that the mind can be enlisted to instruct the body to heal itself. The key seems to be to speak to the body in the language it appears to understand best: images. Through imagery, it appears possible to communicate directly with one's unconscious and to affect physiological processes long thought to be involuntary. The capacity to conjure up and send such images depends, in turn, on learning first to quiet the mind, calm the emotions, and physically relax. Finally, optimal health has less to do with finding some perfect state of physiological balance than with nurturing the body's capacity to respond flexibly to the varied challenges that we each face regularly. This means having the ability to recover quickly from all forms of stress. Whatever promotes such resiliency appears to serve health—emotionally, intellectually, spiritually and physically.

The modern mind-body movement has many fathers. Back in the 1880s, the French neurologist Jean-Martin Charcot dazzled students and colleagues with his capacity to take patients suffering from something called "hysterical paralysis" and demonstrate that under hypnotic trance, they became perfectly capable of walking. Freud himself studied what he called "hysterical conversion" symptoms—physical ailments that he theorized were veiled expressions of repressed emotional conflict. In the 1930s, the Harvard physiologist Walter Cannon introduced the concept of "homeostasis"—the process by which the body instinctively maintains a healthy state. Cannon went on to suggest that many factors can interfere with homeostasis—including fatigue, physical stress, and everyday anxiety. These, in turn, lead to illness, he said.

In the 1940s, the psychiatrist Franz Alexander pioneered the field of psychosomatic medicine—suggesting that ailments such as ulcers, colitis, hypertension, headaches, and asthma are a function more of psychological stress than any of specific physical cause. And in the 1950s, the endocrinologist Hans Selye began conducting research at McGill University in Montreal into the pernicious physiological effects of stress. Selye defined stress as "the nonspecific response of the body to any demand made upon it." In practical terms, stress refers to people's perception that their life circumstances have exceeded their capacity to cope. Specifically, Selye demonstrated that the stress hormones we all produce as a means of responding efficiently to danger—along with reactions such as increased heart rate and blood pressure—can become poisonous to the body if they remain at elevated levels. In short, Selye showed that chronic stress takes a measurable toll on the body.

Among all of the pioneers of mind-body medicine, I was

especially drawn to Larry LeShan. Now in his early seventies, LeShan was recovering from a serious heart attack when we first met, but he still radiated vitality. A tall man with piercing eyes, an imposing girth, and a hawkish nose, he has a full head of white hair and thick black glasses that give him a professorial air. LeShan speaks in the blunt, aggressive no-nonsense style of a native New Yorker. Although this belies a sweeter and gentler side, he takes a certain pugilistic pride in his lifelong role as a renegade and an outsider.

LeShan has spent his career as a psychologist tackling problems that few others were inclined to engage or take seriously until long after he did. He has followed this pattern with subjects ranging from the relationship between physics and mysticism, to the historical evidence for psychic phenomena, to the varied Eastern and Western approaches to meditation. Typically, he has been at least a decade ahead of other researchers. The result is that despite highly original work in several arenas, LeShan has never received nearly as much public recognition as those who have built on his work. Only one of his twelve books—*How to Meditate*—has sold more than a modest number of copies.

LeShan began thinking about the relationship between the mind and body in the early 1950s, while he was an army psychologist stationed in Fort Smith, Arkansas. He had just received his Ph.D. from the University of Chicago when the Korean War broke out, and he was recalled by the army. His job was to help select from new soldiers those whose personalities made them more likely to be killed in combat—and then assign them other duties. Eager for an intellectual diversion from this dispiriting work, LeShan became intrigued when a fellow psychologist suggested that he look into the possibility of a correlation between personality and cancer.

LeShan went off to the local county medical society library and uncovered a raft of statistics that had been gathered back in the nineteenth century—and then left to gather dust. Typical of the conclusions was one from Sir James Paget, author of the classic textbook *Surgical Pathology:* "The cases are so frequent in which deep anxiety, deferred hope and disappointment are quickly followed by the growth of and increase in cancer, that we can hardly doubt that mental depression is a weighty additive to the other influences favoring the development of the cancerous constitution." LeShan also discovered statistical evidence. The mortality rate among widowed and divorced men and women, for example, was dramatically higher than for any other group of cancer patients. He later reaffirmed these findings by looking at more modern epidemiological studies, which showed that divorced and widowed women have higher mortality rates from cancer than married women of comparable age.

As soon as he was discharged from the army in 1952, LeShan applied for a grant to investigate his theory that emotional life is correlated with the likelihood of developing cancer. He got his funding, but even then he was turned down by fifteen hospitals before the Institute for Applied Biology in New York City, and the now defunct Trafalagar Hospital, agreed to let him explore his controversial thesis with its patients. LeShan's first protocol was to give three types of standardized personality tests to nearly five hundred cancer patients, as part of an effort to unearth any obvious patterns. Over the next decade, he selected 250 of these patients to interview in more depth—anywhere from two to eight hours each.

The first pattern LeShan unearthed was that the overwhelming majority of cancer patients had suffered a devastating personal loss in the year before being diagnosed with cancer. These losses ranged from the death of a spouse, to losing a job, to having a child leave home for college. Whatever form the loss took, the result was that the patients uniformly felt they'd been robbed of their central reason for living. This led, in turn, to feelings of isolation, worthlessness, despair, and a deep sense of hopelessness about ever again leading a satisfying life. More than three-quarters of the cancer patients whom LeShan studied had suffered this pattern of loss, versus just 12 percent of a healthy control group.

The second pattern that LeShan observed in cancer patients was a lifelong difficulty in openly expressing their needs and a tendency to repress strong negative feelings such as anger. Instead, such patients tended to be cooperative and seemingly easygoing, deferring automatically to others even when doing so meant setting aside their own needs. Nearly 50 percent of the cancer patients whom LeShan interviewed evidenced this pattern, compared with 25 percent of those in the control group. Later, when LeShan was given the personality tests of 28 people—without being told which among them had cancer—he correctly guessed the diagnosis in 24 cases. Three of those that he wrongly guessed had cancer turned out to be suffering from other serious illnesses. Beginning in the late 1950s, LeShan began to publish his research findings in mainstream psychology journals. In 1959, when he undertook a review of the literature for the *Journal of the National Cancer Institute,* LeShan was able to cite dozens of studies corroborating his observation that the nature of a person's emotional life is often closely correlated with the onset and course of cancer.

"If responsibility and self-control are rigidly maintained at the expense of the expression of genuine feelings," LeShan wrote later, "a part of the self is denied. When tensions are not released, when anger is repressed, it can begin to feed upon itself. We know that this happens in the development of ulcers. Can we deny the possibility that it also occurs in the development of cancers?" LeShan is not a physician, and he did not focus on the physiological process by which this might occur. However, considerable evidence has since emerged confirming that immune functioning can be profoundly affected by one's emotions. These findings have begun to suggest that psychological stress may contribute to cancer both by causing abnormal cell development and by suppressing immune cell activity.

LeShan focused on treating the emotional crisis that his patients were facing. What would happen, he wondered, if he could help cancer patients identify, express, and fill their deepest needs? What if he could help despairing patients who had lost the will to live regain the desire and determination to fight for their lives? From the outset he rejected the traditional psychodynamic approach of working with patients to uncover the origins of their underlying conflicts and then seeking to resolve them. Effective as he believed that this could be for many people, he concluded that it wasn't appropriate for those facing an urgent and life-threatening illness.

Influenced by humanistic psychologists such as Abraham Maslow, Carl Rogers, and Victor Frankl, LeShan directed his "crisis therapy" to helping his patients identify what was right about their lives rather than what was wrong. "To fight for your life, you must have the resources of self-acceptance and self-approval," he explained. He took the position that most of his patients had given up the battle for authentic expression of their own being, and that their most urgent need was to reembrace life. Specifically, he encouraged patients to explore any action that had the potential to reignite their will to live and to pursue this goal with total commitment—even if it meant changing careers, ending a marriage, or moving to a new city. If patients could be helped to discover passion and even joy, LeShan speculated, it might reawaken their physical healing mechanisms—and specifically their immune systems. "Nothing can be more important for them," he wrote much later, "than to discover their own particular song and [to] learn to project it loudly and clearly."

Over a period of nearly twenty years, until the late 1970s, LeShan saw approximately 70 cancer patients in extended therapy. All of them had been diagnosed as terminally ill, and all had had limited life expectancies. Although he never published his results in a conventional scientific journal, LeShan reported in his book *You Can Fight for Your Life* that fully half of his patients eventually went into full remissions and were still alive twenty years later. Many others, he said, substantially outlived their medical prognosis. Nearly all reported a significant improvement in the quality of their lives during whatever period they remained alive. Even anecdotally, these are powerful statistics.

On another level, precise statistics are beside the point. To *whatever* degree his psychotherapeutic intervention had an impact on the course of any patient's cancer and life expectancy, LeShan was demonstrating a powerful connection between mind and body. In addition, his meticulous compilation of cancer mortality rates clearly established that certain emotional life circumstances are closely associated with the onset of cancer—most especially, social isolation and depression. Ultimately, LeShan's work set the stage for a host of other researchers to deepen and further verify this mind-body connection.

M eyer Friedman and Ray Rosenman set out in the late 1950s to demonstrate the impact of certain emotions and behaviors on the incidence of heart disease. Both cardiologists, they chose to look at potential psychological factors simply because they couldn't explain why certain patients were developing heart disease. Many of these patients evidenced none of the traditional risk factors—smoking, elevated cholesterol, high blood pressure, obesity, and failure to exercise—and yet they still became sick. When the two physicians investigated more closely, they discovered a set of traits common to the vast majority of their patients, regardless of whether they had any traditional risk factors. These included a relentless drive for external achievement; an underlying sense of insecurity; a perpetual sense of being rushed; chronic impatience; an intensely aggressive competitiveness; and a pervasive free-floating hostility. Friedman and Rosenman named this pattern "Type A behavior" and hypothesized that it was a major risk factor in heart disease. They also characterized a second group as Type B's—more easygoing, relaxed, friendlier, less status conscious, more inner directed—and conjectured that such people were far less likely to get heart disease.

Hans Selye's pioneering work had already demonstrated that any form of chronic stress can wreak havoc on the body—particularly through long-term increases in heart rate and blood pressure. Friedman and Rosenman confirmed this effect for the first time in research published in 1957. When they studied the blood cholesterol levels of a group of 40 accountants, they discovered that as April 15 grew closer—and their level of psychological stress increased—the accountants' blood cholesterol levels rose dramatically. It was the first scientific demonstration that thoughts and emotions can directly influence cholesterol levels. In 1960, the two researchers reported that Type A's produce highly elevated levels of the stress hormones that have been directly implicated in the development of coronary heart disease: norepinephrine and ACTH.

Supported by a large grant from the National Institutes of Health in the early 1960s, Friedman and Rosenman recruited 3,000 middle-aged men who had no prior evidence of coronary heart disease. These men were subjected to carefully structured interviews aimed at identifying Type A's and Type B's. In addition to looking at the behavior of their subjects, the researchers assessed their physical habits and facial expressions, looking for Type A patterns. For the next nine years, the subjects were followed. Predictably, all those with traditional risk factors— smoking or high blood pressure, for instance—proved more likely to develop heart disease. The extraordinary finding was that all else being equal, men designated as Type A's were twice as likely as Type B's to develop heart disease over the course of the study.

Type A behavior, the researchers concluded dramatically, was more insidious than *any* other single risk factor, including smoking. Many physicians remained highly skeptical that emotional factors could be so powerful, but Friedman and Rosenman's research met the most rigorous scientific standards. Meanwhile, the public embraced their findings. When the book *Type A Behavior and Your Heart* was first published in 1974 it became a huge best seller. Rosenman eventually went off to do other work. Friedman, now in his mid-eighties, has continued related research ever since.

Over the years, however, their original Type A hypothesis came under considerable attack. In 1985, for example, a nine-year study of 12,000 men with multiple risks for coronary disease found no significant relationship between Type A behavior and heart disease. Eight of ten other studies failed to confirm the connection. One explanation, quickly seized upon by many traditional physicians, was that emotional and behavioral factors do not play a role in heart disease after all. Another, less dismissive hypothesis was that the definition of Type A had been too broad and that to truly identify risk factors for heart disease, it was necessary to tease out more precisely the behaviors that are harmful.

Redford Williams, a psychiatrist at Duke University who was inspired by the initial Type A findings, decided to look at them more closely. He hypothesized that many of the qualities initially identified as Type A weren't necessarily toxic to the heart. For some people, Williams suggested, intense competitiveness, or rushing, or doing several things at once may not be experienced as stressful and can even be energizing and exhilarating. But at least one Type A factor struck Williams as harmful by nearly any measure: the experience of chronic hostility. This broad term encompassed anger, cynicism, suspicion, and hyperaggressiveness. Behavior that is plainly harmful to oneself and others in everyday life, Williams hypothesized, is also most likely to be harmful to one's physical health. "There is some utility in some aspects of Type A behavior, like time urgency and ambition," he wrote. "It [is] far more difficult to find redeeming virtues in hostility."

Beginning in 1980, Williams reported that patients with higher hostility scores on personality tests were significantly more likely to develop heart disease than the more broadly defined Type A patients and than Type B's. In one study of nearly 2,000 men, Williams found that those with the highest hostility levels were 1.5 times more likely to die from heart disease than those with lower levels. A second study of 255 doctors found that those with high hostility levels were 4 or 5 times more likely to develop heart disease than their friendlier counterparts. In all, more than a half-dozen studies corroborated these findings. "Hostility predicts mortality better than any other specific cause," Williams concluded.

But how, then, to reconcile LeShan's conclusion that cancer is associated with the *repression* of emotions such as anger, and Friedman and William's evidence that the *expression* of anger promotes heart disease? As in so much mind-body research, I was struck by one common denominator: the role of connectedness versus the experience of alienation. For the cancer patients who chronically suppress negative emotions, the cost is both to diminish the authenticity of their relationships to others and to prompt a sense of alienation from their own deepest feelings and needs. As for the angry Type A's, by constantly expressing their hostility—and by typically blaming it on others—they tend to push people away and isolate themselves. In addition, by failing to acknowledge the underlying feelings that prompt them to lash out so frequently—most notably their sense of vulnerability and insecurity—they too become alienated from their truest selves. In one instance, the cost derives from failing to acknowledge upsetting and powerful feelings; in the other from the inability to take responsibility for such feelings and to exercise some degree of self-control over them. In both cases, the disconnection from a deeper emotional truth appears to increase the risk of physical illness.

More recently, however, even the role of hostility has come under fire as a risk factor in heart disease. At least two large studies have found that subjects with high hostility scores evidenced no more heart disease than their friendlier counterparts. The explanation, Williams believes, is that the current methods for measuring hostility remain crude and need to be further refined. Specifically, these conflicting studies rely on subjects to rate their own levels of hostility rather than have an outside investigator make the assessment based on behavioral observations. Williams argues that hostility—a trait that most people find undesirable—is not typically acknowledged. In short, many of those who develop heart disease may be far more hostile than their scores on self-report tests indicate.

Meyer Friedman has much the same explanation for the fact that numerous studies have failed to support his original findings. The techniques for identifying Type A's in studies subsequent to his, Friedman told me when I visited his institute in San Francisco, have been consistently inadequate. In nearly all cases, researchers have relied primarily on written questionnaires rather than clinically examining patients for telltale physical manifestations of

Type A behavior. These include chronic narrowing of the eyelids, facial tics, rapid and grating speech patterns, and contraction of the muscles around the mouth—all of which are very difficult to mask in an interview. "Questionnaires won't do," Friedman told me, "because many people won't answer them honestly, or simply don't know they are aggressive or impatient or hostile." Friedman also took issue with the attempt to isolate hostility from the broader range of original Type A factors. Hostility, he argues, is part of a constellation of inextricably related Type A emotions. Time urgency, for example, directly feeds impatience, and being rushed and impatient makes hostility more likely. I certainly saw these patterns in my own life.

Friedman's approach to *treating* Type A behavior still strikes me as more comprehensive than that of any subsequent researcher. Williams, for example, explicitly resists exploring the root causes of hostility, focusing instead on behavioral strategies for dealing with it. "It may be just as well not to go digging too deeply," he told me. "Doing so is just not that efficient." Friedman, by contrast, argues that consciously modifying Type A behavior and exploring its childhood origins must occur simultaneously. The fundamental issue for Type A's, he argues, is the failure to receive sufficient unconditional love as children and the toll this takes on their self-esteem as they grow up. Just as animals often exhibit violent aggressive tendencies when deprived of maternal care, Friedman says, Type A's respond to a lack of sufficient parental love by turning into defensively angry adults. "The true 'toxic' factor in Type A behavior," Friedman has written, "is the inadequate security and self-esteem that initiates and fuels the emergence of impatience and hostility." While this is somewhat oversimplified, it is a valuable insight.

Friedman's most compelling study was designed with much the same therapeutic aims as LeShan's work with cancer patients. In 1978, Friedman and his team began studying 1,000 men who had suffered previous heart attacks and were later diagnosed as Type A personalities. These men were randomly placed in three groups. One group got no special therapeutic intervention at all, while a second received traditional advice about eating and exercise habits as well as medication. The third got traditional help but also met regularly in a group run by a counselor who was trained to help them modify all aspects of their Type A behavior. Like LeShan, Friedman set out to see what might happen if patients transformed their lives—both by changing specific behaviors and by cultivating more positive emotions.

The varied techniques in the group meetings ranged from seeking to understand better the origins of certain destructive behaviors to challenging patients' fixed beliefs, as well as their habitual and self-destructive behaviors. Members of the group also worked on issues such as rearranging their daily schedules to reduce chronic sources of stress and to provide for more down time; finding new ways to give and receive love; learning to be more accepting of other people's shortcomings; practicing speaking less harshly, loudly, and quickly; developing the capacity to observe their impulses without reacting to them so precipitously; and looking for ways to get beyond their immediate concerns and to be of service to others. Broadly speaking, the group work focused on helping members to let down the barriers that distanced them from their underlying emotions and needs, as well as from other people in their lives.

Within one year, the group in the behavior modification program had shown a 30 percent reduction in the intensity of their Type A behavior. Over three years, this group suffered only half as many heart attacks as each of the other two groups. During the fifth and final year of the program, the men who got no special help from their Type A behavior suffered five times the number of heart attacks as those in the group receiving Type A behavioral counseling. "No drug, food, or exercise program ever devised," wrote Friedman and his collaborator, Diane Ulmer, "could match [this] protection."

While modifying behavior remains the central focus of Friedman's Type A groups, there is growing scientific evidence that merely being part of a group of people with shared concerns protects against disease. More broadly, the healthy effects of love, intimacy, and social support have been corroborated in a range of studies. This is true even at the earliest stages of life. For example, Tiffany Field, a scientist at the University of Miami, showed that premature infants who were regularly physically touched rather than left alone in incubators tended to gain weight 50 percent faster than those who were more isolated. A long-term study of 7,000 adult citizens of Alameda County, California found that those with strong social ties—whether through marriage, close friends, church, or other activities—were between two and three times less likely to die from *any* cause than those who lived more isolated lives.

Social support may even have an impact on immune functioning. At Ohio State University, immunologist Ronald Glaser and his wife, psychologist Janice Kiecolt-Glaser, conducted a series of studies aimed at examining this connection. In one experiment, they found that the loneliest among a group of students on a college campus showed the greatest impairment in immune activity. In another study, recently divorced women evidenced poorer immune functioning than their married counterparts, while among married women, the happier they described themselves with their relationships, the more robust their immune activity. In 1992, Redford Williams published a study in *The Journal of the American Medical Association* showing that among a large sample of patients with advanced coronary heart disease, 82 percent of those with strong social connections survived at least five years, compared with only 50 percent of those who were most socially alienated and isolated.

Perhaps the most dramatic study of how social support affects mortality rates—in this case for women with breast cancer—was conducted by David Spiegel, a psychiatrist at Stanford University. Spiegel had a built-in population to investigate. In the late 1970s, he and his colleague Irving Yalom, one of the pioneers of group therapy, launched several support groups for female patients suffering from metastatic breast cancer. While continuing conventional medical treatment, 50 women were invited to attend weekly groups led by Spiegel and Yalom. All of the patients had a fatal prognosis, and influencing the course of their illness was not the goal. Instead, the experiment was aimed at helping the women to deal better with their fears about death, communicate more effectively with their doctors and families, and live more fully and freely in face of highly stressful circumstances. Thirty-six women with similar diagnoses served as controls and got no special intervention. At the end of a year, Spiegel and Yalom discovered that the women who attended the weekly group therapy sessions demonstrated significantly less anxiety, confusion, fatigue, and emotional disturbance than the controls. "They were also denying less, were able to face their problems more directly, and were less frightened," Spiegel wrote. Spiegel and Yalom judged the experiment a success, published their results, and moved on.

Ten years later Spiegel decided to revisit his own study. He had his eye especially on the claims of people such as Bernie Siegel, a former surgeon who wrote the best-selling book *Love, Medicine and Miracles*. In his book, and in lectures and workshops across the country, Siegel has argued that patients can improve their chances of recovery from life-threatening illnesses by nurturing qualities such as hope, will, optimism, and love. Siegel also founded a group called Exceptional Cancer Patients (ECAP), in an effort to provide an emotionally supportive environment for patients seeking to participate in their own treatment. "Peace of mind sends the body a 'live' message," he wrote, "while depression, fear and unresolved conflict give it a 'die' message." This was precisely the sort of grand and nonspecific language that aroused David Spiegel's ire.

I myself felt some ambivalence about Bernie Siegel's message, even after hearing him speak before appreciative audiences and interviewing him at some length. I shared his conviction that one's state of mind directly affects physical health; that hope and love can be powerful healing agents; that there is value in accessing deeper feelings in the unconscious through meditation, dreams, and even drawings; and that far too many physicians treat diseases mechanically and without regard to the whole person. But I also found his message oversimplified and potentially misleading. For example, when Siegel encourages patients to ask themselves, "Why did you need this illness?"—as he does in both of his books—I came to believe that he did them a disservice.

The first risk is that patients who believe that they brought an illness on themselves may also believe that they can heal it by themselves. In turn, they may be prompted to shun traditional medical care altogether. Beyond that, by putting so much emphasis on the role that one's own emotions and behavior play in disease, Siegel vastly understates the powerful factors beyond one's control—most of all, genetics and the environment. How does his question apply, for example, to a two-year-old with leukemia, or to an adult who gets cancer after inadvertent exposure to massive asbestos poisoning? Why not consider instead a more open-ended and nonjudgmental question: "Is there anything that I can learn about myself from this illness, and does it provide any inspiration to change the priorities in my life?"

David Spiegel took an even more hardheaded view. By returning to the mortality records of his own group therapy patients, he fully expected to demonstrate that neither social support nor emotional factors had *any* impact on the length of survival from metastasized cancer. To his astonishment, however, Spiegel discovered that the women who participated in his weekly group sessions turned out to have lived an average of *twice* as long as the controls—36.6 months for the treatment group, versus 18 months for those who did not attend therapy. Only three of the 86 women were still alive, but all of them had attended the therapy groups. "I sent twenty colleagues an advance copy of our findings and did everything I could to get them to find fault with our methodology, but no one did," Spiegel told me.

Spiegel reported that the difference in survival rates between the two groups of women began to emerge about eight months after the weekly therapy sessions had ended. This led him to speculate that the effect of the groups was slow and cumulative. Indeed, the more sessions a woman attended, the longer her average survival. Those who attended one to ten sessions lived 36.5 months, for example, while those who went to more than ten sessions lived an average of 41.5 months. "Social support may be an important factor in survival," Spiegel concluded, directly contradicting his own initial assumption. "Involvement in the group may have allowed patients to mobilize their resources better. . . . Neuroendocrine and immune systems may be a major link between emotional processes and cancer course." He has since written a book based on his findings, *Living Beyond Limits*.

Especially striking in Spiegel's study is the fact such a modest and short-term intervention was correlated with such powerful results. The women met together just once a week, for only a year, and were never given any reason to believe that this intervention might lengthen their lives. Spiegel's study suggests that even a moderate increase in the experience of connectedness—to others, in the form of love and mutual support, and to one's own deepest emotions—can affect the course of a life-threatening disease. How much more might be achieved, it seems reasonable to ask, with a more sustained, multilevel intervention?

At the same time, there is evidence that the nature of the group process itself has an impact on the disease. A follow-up study was conducted, for example, of 34 breast cancer patients who attended Bernie Siegel's Exceptional Cancer Patients Program in New Haven, Connecticut. On average, the women did not survive any longer than 102 other people who had similar types of cancer but attended no weekly group sessions. At the same time, there were clear differences between the Siegel and Spiegel groups. Neither Bernie Siegel nor the leaders of his groups had any specific psychotherapeutic training. Spiegel, and especially Yalom, both psychiatrists, brought to the women they worked with substantial experience as group leaders. The focus of their groups was not on healing or on positive thinking—as it was in Siegel's groups—but rather on addressing deeply and honestly whatever issues arose in the course of dealing with the disease. In effect, the emphasis was on becoming more conscious and more connected to the truth. "If you're always expected to be positive and optimistic and other feelings aren't as acceptable in the group," Spiegel told me, "then that isolates you from yourself and from an authentic connection with others. The key, we've found, is to allow people to ventilate and deal with strong emotions, whatever they are, and to experience strong social support in the process."

When he was first approached by several practitioners of transcendental meditation in 1968, Herbert Benson was a young researcher at Harvard studying how certain behaviors among monkeys affected their blood pressure. The young TM practitioners offered themselves to Benson as experimental subjects, claiming that through meditation they could lower their own blood pressure—long thought to be an involuntary process. This had powerful implications, since elevated blood pressure has been clearly correlated with heart disease and other illnesses. Researchers such as LeShan and Friedman had already demonstrated that emotional factors can play a significant role in illness. But except for the work of Elmer and Alyce Green in biofeedback, relatively little had been published about the role that the *mind* plays in influencing the body. Benson was a Harvard physician and scientist with an establishment reputation to protect, but he was also very curious. When the TM practitioners persisted, he finally agreed to take a closer look. In part, he was attracted to studying TM because the technique was taught uniformly, with a minimum of frills, and could be easily replicated.

Benson began his research by comparing a variety of measures of physiological stress before and after the young practitioners meditated. During this same period, Keith Wallace, a doctoral candidate at the University of California–Los Angeles, undertook research similar to Benson's. Wallace first published findings in the journal *Science* in 1970. The following year, he joined Benson's team at Harvard. Together they went on to publish several papers in which they characterized meditation as a uniquely relaxing physiological state—distinct both from everyday wakefulness and from sleep. Benson and Wallace reported that meditation had just the opposite effect that stress did. During meditation, oxygen consumption decreases, heart rate comes down, hormonal balance returns, and alpha brain waves associated with relaxation increase. Ironically, the TM practitioners who approached Benson proved unable to lower their blood pressure. The reason, Benson speculated, was that they already enjoyed normal blood pressure—and that others with high blood pressure might indeed benefit from trying meditation.

He and Wallace soon confirmed this hypothesis. After several weeks of daily meditation, 36 research subjects who began with an average systolic blood pressure of 146 dropped to 137—or from borderline into the normal range. Their diastolic blood pressure dropped from 93.5 to 88.9, once again a move into the normal range. Despite this notable success, Benson and Wallace parted ways acrimoniously in 1973. By then, Wallace was deeply involved in the TM movement, and convinced that the healing powers of TM were unique. Benson took a very different view. While he declined to try any form of meditation himself—claiming inexplicably that to do so might compromise his scientific objectivity—his research convinced him that the positive physiological effects of meditation were "in no way unique to Transcendental Meditation." These effects could be achieved not just by meditating with a TM mantra, Benson asserted, but by using virtually any word, phrase, or sound that served as an ongoing focus of concentration.

In effect, Benson took meditation entirely out of any spiritual or mystical context and used it instead simply as a technique for treating chronic stress. He called this effect the *Relaxation Response,* and his book by the same name became a best seller in 1975, just one year after *Type A Behavior and Your Heart* was published. As it turned out, Benson's findings about blood pressure proved to be his most notable. He has published many papers since then, but neither he nor any other researchers have been able to demonstrate that meditation has a substantial and sustained healing effect on other chronic diseases. Keith Wallace has continued his research into the effects of TM, and he has made a variety of claims about its value, but he and his TM colleagues have only rarely published findings in scientific journals—and none of their studies employ traditional controls.

On a broad scale, meditation has proved most effective with stress-related symptoms such as headaches, gastrointestinal disorders, and irritable bowel-syndrome. Benson's Mind/Body program, located at Deaconness Hospital in Boston, is specifically aimed at patients with medical problems complicated by stress. Indeed, one outgrowth of Benson's work was the establishment of a mind-body clinic at the hospital, specifically designed to incorporate meditation as a central mode of treatment for stress-related disorders. The co-founder was Joan Borysenko, a cell biologist turned psychologist, who went on to write the best-selling book *Minding the Body, Mending the Mind,* which described not just meditation as an intervention, but also breathing techniques, yoga, visualization, and a series of exercises aimed at dealing with underlying emotional conflict.

The most well-documented and sustained clinical use of meditation—as a treatment for chronic pain—was pioneered by psychologist Jon Kabat-Zinn. Kabat-Zinn brought to his work a deep personal background in meditation practice. In his early twenties, he studied the Buddhist practice of mindfulness—in which one learns to observe without attachment whatever arises and passes in the field of awareness. In 1981, at the age of thirty-five, Kabat-Zinn founded a stress reduction program at the University of Massachusetts Medical Center in Worcester. His eight-week course is aimed at patients suffering from various forms of chronic pain that have proved impervious to traditional medical intervention—most commonly, back and neck pain, hypertension, headaches, and GI disorders.

Developing the capacity to simply witness thoughts, emotions, and physical sensations, Kabat-Zinn found, gave patients a way out of the vicious cycle of pain and anxiety that feeds and exacerbates their suffering. In a series of studies over the past decade, Kabat-Zinn has consistently reported positive and enduring results. Chronic pain patients followed up as much as four years later, for example, showed significant long-term decreases in pain. More than a third rated it "greatly improved." Kabat-Zinn's patients also reported less need for pain-killing drugs, less depression and anxiety, more physical mobility, and even some improvement in self-esteem.

This last finding suggests that the experience of mindfulness meditation not only affects one's perspective on pain but may also nourish some deeper sense of well-being. The practice of letting go of expectations and accepting what arises with equanimity, Kabat-Zinn argues, lies at the heart of both health *and* wisdom. "When we learn to calm down enough to enter and dwell in states of deep relaxation, this nourishes and restores body and mind," he wrote in his first book, *Full Catastrophe Living*. To that end, he makes unusual demands of his patients: a minimum of forty-five minutes a day of meditation and yoga, six days a week for all eight weeks. In addition, they attend one full-day meditation retreat at the end of the course.

Kabat-Zinn's patients are referred to him primarily after conventional treatments have failed, and most have never been introduced to meditation before. Nonetheless, they respond to his enormous passion with a high degree of commitment. Even four years after attending the program, more than a third of the patients report that they continue to meditate at least three times a week. One reason, Kabat-Zinn believes, is that mindfulness practice offers not just a method for patients to relax but a broader spiritual perspective. "The calmness you develop in concentration meditation will only take you so far," he told me when I came to Worcester to observe his program. "Through mindfulness you are introduced to a higher level of awareness, a taste of what it feels like to be lighter, less fragmented, more balanced, and more whole—and no longer the prisoner of your own thoughts."

As rich and useful a contribution as he has made, Kabat-Zinn's intervention remains limited as a technique for physical healing. By relying on a classic meditation model, for example, he consciously chooses not to deal directly with the emotional factors that other researchers have shown play such a significant role in health. "We don't see it as group psychotherapy at all," he says. "We're not aiming at developing profound emotional bonds between people, or having people tell each other about their feelings or their personal history or their current dilemmas. . . . We simply try to help people develop the capacity to go into deep states of relaxation, calmness, stability of mind and mindfulness, and we let what's wrong with them take care of itself."

Unfortunately, what's wrong at an emotional level rarely does take care of itself. Take just the example of chronic back and neck pain patients, who represent a significant percentage of those who attend Kabat-Zinn's program. While most of them experience measurable relief through mindfulness meditation— including the capacity to view their pain with a greater degree of detachment—Kabat-Zinn himself acknowledges that only a minority become pain-free. The explanation, I believe, is that meditation by itself fails to sufficiently address what John Sarno has identified as the underlying cause of many pain syndromes— namely, unacknowledged emotional conflict, most often anger. Mindfulness meditation doesn't seek to work through such feelings. Sarno addresses them head on, and that may help explain why his approach so regularly prompts a full resolution of symptoms, while Kabat-Zinn's often does not.

E lmer and Alyce Green were among the first mind-body researchers to suggest that the mind has the potential to communicate healing instructions directly to the body through imagery. The Greens experimented with asking patients to passively visualize a desired result, such as increasing the temperature in their hands. By providing positive feedback whenever they succeeded, the patients began to learn which images and associated sensations produced the desired results. In the deeply relaxed brainwave state that the Greens identified as theta, they theorized, imagery becomes an effective language by which to communicate with the body. In turn, perhaps no researcher has done more to explain the mechanism by which imagery affects physiological processes—and its history as a technique of healing—than Jeanne Achterberg.

Trained as a research psychologist, Achterberg grew interested in the power of imagery after meeting an oncologist named Carl Simonton, who was teaching patients to visualize bullets of energy attacking their cancer cells—in the hope of sending that message to the body. Unconventional as this approach seemed, Achterberg was impressed both by Simonton's passion and by the positive results he appeared to be getting. Achterberg soon became interested in the special state of consciousness in which patients become able to produce vivid imagery. Accessing this state dates all the way back, she discovered, to the ancient healers known as shamans, who cultivated altered states of consciousness to do their healing work. Achterberg describes the state that they entered as "dreamlike . . . somewhere between sleep and wakefulness, where vivid imagery and experiences are possible." The verbal mind, she argued, is one step removed from the body's physiological processes. "I submit that messages have to undergo translation by the right hemisphere into nonverbal or imagerial terminology before they can be understood by the involuntary or autonomic nervous system," she wrote in *Imagery and Healing*. "The imagery of the right side of the brain is the medium of communication between consciousness and the internal environment of our bodies."

Achterberg went on to demonstrate that imagery arising from the unconscious can be a highly reliable indicator of one's state of health. In one fascinating study, she had cancer patients lie down, relax, and respond to tape-recorded instructions such as "Describe how your cancer cells look in your mind's eye" and "How do you imagine your white blood cells fight disease?" Patients were also asked to imagine how their treatment was proceeding and what sort of prognosis they envisioned for themselves. Nearly 100 patients in two separate hospitals were studied. Achterberg sought to quantify their imagery in a variety of ways, including the vividness and strength of the cancer cells and white cells that patients described, and the frequency with which patients imagined a positive or a negative outcome for their treatment. These images, she found, predicted with more than 90 percent certainty which patients would either die or show evidence of significant deterioration during a subsequent two-month period, and which would be in remission. "The symptoms were symbols, the symbols symptoms," Achterberg concluded. "The immune system was synonymous with the patients' own self-concept. When it was imaged as strong and pure, it overcame disease."

The most compelling and well-documented evidence suggesting that imagery can be enlisted to change the course of a chronic illness—specifically by reprogramming the mind and body—grew out of clinical research beginning in 1988 by a psychologist named Eugene Peniston. At the time, Peniston was working in a small Veterans Administration hospital in rural Fort Lyon, Colorado. Over the course of his career, he'd grown increasingly skeptical about the power of traditional talk therapy to prompt substantial changes in people's lives. After reading Elmer Green's work on biofeedback, Peniston began to wonder whether learning to voluntarily control internal processes might ultimately be a more effective tool than talk therapy for prompting behavioral changes. In particular, he was searching for more effective ways to treat the chronic alcoholics who regularly showed up for the thirty-day detoxification program at his VA, only to resume drinking soon after they were discharged.

At Green's suggestion, Peniston flew to the Menninger Institute in 1987 to take a three-day training in the uses of theta biofeedback. Peniston quickly proved able to access the theta state himself. In the course of four sessions, he experienced a series of images that proved unexpectedly revelatory. The first time he entered theta, he saw the human brain as well as images of alpha brain waves. Eventually, he interpreted this as a hint that one key to treating addiction was to raise his subjects' alpha wave amplitudes. Alcoholics, he later learned, classically evidence very little alpha activity. In his second theta session, Peniston saw himself inside the brain, watching people in masks working with microscopes. In his third session, he had the imagery of the alpha brain waves again, but this time they were interspersed with bursts of theta waves. And in his fourth and final set of images, he saw an actual brainwave training session taking place, along with the alpha and theta brain waves he'd seen previously, and the flashing number 30.

Although Peniston felt confused by this welter of images, he couldn't get them out of his mind. "They just kept gnawing at me," he told me, when I visited him at the VA hospital in Fort Lyon. "Eventually, I began to see that a whole treatment protocol had been laid out." As Peniston interpreted it, his challenge was first to introduce his patients to alpha and then help them move further down into theta, where Green had earlier speculated that it was possible to reprogram the unconscious. The number 30, Peniston decided, referred to the ideal number of training sessions for patients. Encouraged by the Menninger group, Peniston returned to his VA hospital and began experimenting with the chronic alcoholics on his in-patient wards.

He started by using temperature biofeedback to teach his patients to warm their hands, thus assuring that they had the capacity to become deeply physically relaxed—a prerequisite to entering theta. Next, Peniston instructed his patients to rehearse specific visualizations, on the premise that the body is capable of responding directly to the mind's images. For the first visualization, he told patients to imagine increasing the amplitude of their alpha brain waves. Next, he asked them to envision a scene in which they explicitly rejected alcohol. Finally, he encouraged them to visualize "normalization" of their personalities. Once they'd practiced creating these images, Peniston hooked his patients up to biofeedback machines. Initially, he told them, they'd receive feedback whenever they produced more alpha waves. When they relaxed more deeply and began producing more theta waves, he told them, they would hear a different set of tones. As they entered this nonverbal theta state, armed with the visualizations they'd practiced, Peniston instructed his patients to initiate the reprogramming with the simple command "Do it." The notion was to have the images literally tell the body what to do.

The first changes that Peniston began to see were behavioral. "I couldn't believe it," he told me. "These patients became calmer and friendlier and more relaxed. At first, I didn't say anything to anyone. But eventually the other nurses and psychiatrists started to notice." Partly to fend off criticism of his unorthodox approach, Peniston decided to undertake a clinically controlled, randomized study of alcoholics using his alpha-theta brainwave training protocol. From the hospital's in-patient population, he recruited 30 patients. Twenty were chronic alcoholics, defined as those who'd been drinking for twenty years or more and had at least four previous hospitalizations. Ten of the patients were randomly assigned to an experimental brainwave training group, while the other 10 simply continued to receive standard VA hospital counseling for their alcoholism, including the twelve-step program and individual and group counseling. The third group, identified as nonalcoholics, served as controls.

Using the protocol that came out of his own theta experience, Peniston provided his experimental group with temperature training, then helped them construct specific imagery, and finally gave them thirty daily sessions of brainwave training, each one lasting thirty minutes. The sheer intensity of this training set Peniston's experiment apart from nearly all those done by previous biofeedback researchers. Typically, researchers trained subjects for only a half-dozen sessions at most and rarely for as long as half an hour. Offering more and longer sessions proved critical. Often, Peniston didn't see the first changes in patients until the fifteenth session.

His initial observation was that the alcoholics receiving biofeedback training showed a steady rise in alpha and theta brainwave activity and that their alpha levels eventually almost tripled those of subjects in the traditional treatment group. This was impressive, but it was the other results that truly shocked Peniston. First, based on standardized psychological tests that he administered before and after imagery-based brainwave training, the experimental group showed statistically significant personality changes. These included substantial decreases in aggression, anxiety, and depression and increases in warmth, stability, imagination, and self-control. No similar positive changes occurred among the alcoholics receiving standard hospital treatment or among the nonalcoholics.

More extraordinary still was the effect of the training on alcohol use itself. In 1989, Peniston published these findings in the journal *Alcoholism: Clinical and Experimental Research*. All 20 alcoholic patients were followed up thirteen months after the training—and ultimately four years later, with similar results. Eight of the 10 brainwave training subjects maintained total abstinence, and reported that they no longer had any desire to drink. Two had suffered relapses, but in both cases, they became violently physically ill soon after they drank. This suggested that as a direct function of the training, they could no longer physiologically tolerate alcohol. Among the group of alcoholics who received no brainwave training—but continued in standard treatment—8 of 10 had relapsed within a year to the point of being rehospitalized. Both of the other two had experienced at least one period of uncontrolled drinking. It is rare to find any treatment program for chronic alcoholics with a success rate much above 30 percent.

These results seemed so extraordinary and so unprecedented that I flew out to Colorado myself to interview the subjects who had gone through the brainwave training. I met with a half-dozen, and each of them confirmed for me that they had simply lost the desire to drink and had remained abstinent ever since the training—one of them even while working as a bartender. The men also described to me a range of positive changes in their lives, most notably better relationships with family members and friends and the ability to hold on to a job.

By the time Peniston left Fort Lyon in 1991 for a new job as chief of psychology at the VA hospital in Bonham, Texas, he had administered his brainwave training to more than 150 chronic alcoholics and achieved results comparable to those in his first study. Approximately 80 percent had stopped drinking altogether. Nearly all those who tried to drink became physically ill. At least seven other independent studies—one on a Navaho reservation—

have since corroborated Peniston's findings, and other studies are in process. In a state-funded study at Riverside Hospital in Houston, Texas, for example, Peniston's protocol was used with a group of patients addicted to crack and cocaine, and similar rates of success were achieved.

In time, Peniston became curious about how else his protocol might be applied. Nearly all of the addicts with whom he worked at the VA, for example, turned out to be veterans of the war in Vietnam. In the course of treating them, Peniston discovered that many had suffered for years from the sort of recurrent nightmares and flashbacks symptomatic of post-traumatic stress disorder (PTSD). Even very high levels of anti-anxiety drugs had proved to be of no help to these patients. Peniston decided to see if brain-wave training might prove to be an effective treatment. In this case, rather than telling his subjects to create specific images as they entered theta, he asked them instead to instruct their unconscious to go back to the time of the traumatic events and then to resolve the conflict. As the patients moved into theta, many of them reported abreactive imagery, in which they found themselves vividly reliving long-repressed Vietnam memories. Because the theta state is so relaxed, they were able to do so without the terror that characteristically accompanies such flashbacks and nightmares. By the time the training was finished, the vast majority of patients were no longer suffering the PTSD symptoms that had plagued most of them for more than two decades.

In 1991, Peniston published these findings in the journal *Medical Psychotherapy*. The fourteen PTSD patients who had undergone brainwave training all demonstrated positive changes on personality tests, including decreased depression, hysteria, paranoia, and psychopathic behaviors. They also all reduced their dosages of psychotropic medicines after treatment. The control group evidenced no similar personality changes, and only one of them reduced medication during the same time frame. Moreover, thirty months later, all fourteen controls had suffered recurrences of PTSD symptoms, compared with just three of those who had undergone the brainwave training. Peniston now believes that entering the theta state may trigger the hippocampus portion of the brain, where repressed material is stored. "I believe we've shown these patients a safe way into the subconscious, and a safe way out," he told me.

Inspired by Peniston's results, several dozen clinicians around the country have begun to use variations on his protocols to treat not just alcoholism, drug addiction, and PTSD but disorders including multiple personality, clinical depression, chronic fatigue syndrome, and bulimia. In Columbus, Ohio, for example, psychologist Carol Manchester has helped more than a dozen multiple personality patients to become fully integrated in a single core personality. In most cases, she has found, this process involves reexperiencing, in the theta state, early memories of childhood abuse.

At the same time, it has become clear that certain disorders and illnesses are characterized by *excessive* production of theta brain waves. In such cases, patients must be trained to produce more beta and to suppress theta. This protocol has proven particularly effective, for example, in treating attention deficit disorder—which is characterized by difficulty in the sort of focused, task-oriented attention that requires high beta wave activity. Margaret Ayers, a psychologist who practices in Beverly Hills, has had extraordinary success treating patients suffering from closed head injuries, by teaching them to inhibit the overproduction of theta—and decrease its voltage. Ayers reported on a controlled study of such patients in a paper delivered at the National Head Injury Foundation Annual in 1991. All six patients receiving feedback therapy, she found, experienced diminished mood swings, less explosive anger outbursts, and fewer anxiety attacks. None of the controls—all of whom continued in standard psychotherapy—showed evidence of similar improvement.

N o scientifically verifiable mind-body approach has addressed disease more comprehensively than the one pioneered by internist Dean Ornish. In 1988, Ornish, then thirty-seven, launched a study aimed at assessing whether a broad program of behavioral and lifestyle changes could prompt reversal of the sort of advanced heart disease typically treated with drugs or surgery. Conventional medical wisdom holds that *reversing* heart disease is not possible by any means—and certainly not merely by changing one's behavior. Nonetheless, two years later, Ornish reported in the journal *Lancet* that 18 of his first 22 subjects showed significant evidence of both increased blood flow to the heart and reversal of blockage in the arteries. These results were unprecedented. Moreover, the majority of patients in a control group got worse on both counts.

Ornish's study received wide attention, much of it focused on the low-fat diet that participants were required to follow. In fact, the program intervened at all levels: body (through diet *and* required daily exercise); mind (by seeking to change people's beliefs about themselves and their own self-healing capacities); emotions (through twice-weekly group sessions run by a psycho-therapist); and spirit (through the daily practice of meditation and yoga). Although Ornish was trained as a traditional physician, he brought to his study the radical hypothesis that the root cause of heart disease is not primarily physical but rather psychological and spiritual.

Ornish evolved this orientation through his own experience growing up. Raised in a family that valued external achievements and awards, he suffered a crisis of faith soon after he entered Rice University. Overwhelmed by the pressures, he became convinced that he couldn't possibly fulfill his lifelong ambition of becoming a doctor and that even if he did, it wouldn't bring him any enduring happiness. Caught in a downward spiral of worry, insomnia, and depression that led him to seriously contemplate suicide, he finally decided to withdraw from school. It was at that point, in 1969, that his sister took him to hear a lecture by one of the best-known gurus of that era, Swami Satchidinanda. Inspired to try meditation, Ornish found that it gave him at least fleeting experiences of peacefulness and well-being as well as a sense of connectedness to something larger than himself. He continued to meditate and also entered psychotherapy. "The more inwardly defined I became, the less I needed to succeed and the less stressed I felt," he later wrote. "The less I needed success, the easier it came. The less I had to get, the more I got."

Ornish remains an exceptionally driven and ambitious man, but he has channeled his enormous energy and focus toward goals that not only advance his own cause but serve the greater good. These inclinations took shape soon after he returned to college. After graduation, he was accepted at Baylor College of Medicine. In 1977, following his sophomore year, he took time off to run his first experiment aimed at altering the course of heart disease through lifestyle changes. Ornish managed to raise the money to study 10 patients with serious heart disease, housing them in a Houston hotel where the rooms had been donated. He put his experimental group on a strict regimen of meditation, moderate exercise, and a vegetarian diet.

At the end of thirty days, the patients uniformly experienced major improvements, including diminished chest pain, significant reductions in their cholesterol levels, more energy, less depression, and most notably, a substantial increase in coronary blood flow. Three years later, before beginning his residency at Massachusetts General Hospital, Ornish undertook a larger study. This one had 48 patients, half of them in a control group. The experimental group experienced a 90 percent decrease in chest pain after twenty-four days; a 55 percent increase in exercise capability; and a 20 percent drop in cholesterol levels. Ornish published these results in *The Journal of the American Medical Association* in 1981, and then in a more expanded version the following year, in his first book, *Stress, Diet and Your Heart.*

"My idea was never just to offer people a set of stress management techniques," Ornish told me, when we met for the first time at his office in Sausalito, California. "The techniques were also designed to help people identify and transcend their sense of isolation—whether that meant isolation from their own bodies, their feelings, other people, or from a spiritual connection beyond themselves." Ornish hypothesized that alienation in all its forms is physically unhealthy. "Anything that promotes a sense of isolation leads to chronic stress and, often, to illnesses like heart disease," he wrote in the wake of his findings. "Conversely, anything that leads to real intimacy and feelings of connection can be healing."

On the most practical level, Ornish found that people who feel isolated and depressed simply are less motivated to take disciplined action to protect their health—whether by eating a lower-fat diet, or by exercising, or by setting aside time for relaxation. "It's very hard to motivate people to change their diet if they're feeling depressed, and if there isn't any meaning in their life," Ornish told me. "Before you can take other actions, you have to address that underlying emotional pain. In the same way, telling someone to meditate as a technique for lowering blood pressure may have some physical benefits, but if that's all you do, it's almost like prescribing a nonpharmacological drug. The real value of meditation comes from using it the way it was designed—as a tool for increasing awareness and touching something beyond ourselves with which we've lost touch. My emphasis has been on improving people's quality of life by focusing first on the root causes of their isolation—going back as far as we can in the causal chain."

Some critics have suggested that the key element in Ornish's program is the low-fat diet and that it is unrealistic to expect the average person to follow such a strict regimen. I've observed contrary evidence. Shortly after I met Ornish, my own father, then in his early seventies, was diagnosed with very severe blockages in several arteries leading to his heart. For months, he'd been suffering from angina that made it nearly impossible to walk even a city block without severe pain. A physician himself, my father sought opinions from several leading cardiologists and was told unequivocally that he should undergo immediate coronary bypass surgery. He was reluctant to take such a radical step, and I arranged for him to meet Ornish. If my father was willing to make the lifestyle changes that other patients in the program had made, Ornish told him, doing so was a reasonable alternative to surgery. My father went on the diet immediately and began an exercise regimen of walking each day, for the first time in his adult life. The angina began to diminish within weeks. Four years later—still on the diet and still walking every day—he is in stable health and rarely feels pain. He has also lost thirty pounds, and his cholesterol level has dropped more than 40 points to around 170.

When Ornish tried to tease out which of the interventions in his program was most responsible for reversing the course of heart disease, he found that each one of them correlated strongly. Adherence to the diet was important, as well as regular exercise. But so was the meditation and attendance at the twice-weekly group meetings (neither of which my father has done). Subjectively, however, Ornish has come to believe that the single most important factor in "opening" the heart—physiologically and otherwise—is the degree to which people are able to find a greater sense of meaning, contentment, and connectedness in their lives.

W hat, if anything, do these varied mind-body approaches ultimately have in common? The most convincing explanation I got came from an unlikely source. Irving Dardik is a former surgeon who went on to serve for seven years as chairman of the U.S. Olympic Committee's Sports Medicine Council. He has spent most of the past decade developing a theory about the nature of health and illness and applying it clinically to a small number of patients with chronic illnesses. These range from multiple sclerosis to anorexia, from cancer to chronic fatigue syndrome.

Dardik's theory grew out of observing that patients with chronic diseases and healthy world-class athletes represent two sides of the same coin. Athletes, he saw, typically train to progressively increase their work load, while minimizing the time allotted to rest and recovery. By contrast, patients with chronic diseases are often encouraged to avoid stress and to spend as much time as possible resting and recovering. Dardik's initial hypothesis was that neither of these extremes is healthy. Stress without sufficient recovery may lead to illness, he hypothesized, but so can rest without stress, for sick patients and healthy athletes alike. "Health," he concluded, "depends on a balanced relationship between stress and recovery, a recurring, rhythmic wave of energy expenditure and energy recovery." Dardik theorized that when one's wave patterns become too linear and unvarying—the chronic stress of relentless energy expenditure or the relative depression of too little—performance is compromised and disease becomes more likely.

The most powerful way to consciously prompt a physical wave, Dardik reasoned, is through rhythmic exercise and recovery—arousing the physiology, then permitting it to relax fully. He chose to use the heart rate as a window to the overall physiology, both because the heart is connected to so many bodily functions and because it is simple to measure continuously. After equipping his patients with heart-rate monitors, Dardik began giving them exercises designed to raise their heart rates. As soon as they reached a target rate, he had them immediately sit down and recover. Sure enough, the sickest patients turned out to have the hardest time making large rhythmic waves.

Some simply couldn't push their heart rates up to high levels. Other patients overresponded to exercise, their heart rates continuing to climb even after they sat down. Still other patients proved able to push their heart rates up reasonably high, but then dropped back to very low resting numbers the moment that they stopped exercising. Dardik found that the healthiest subjects produced large rhythmic waves—pushing up to high heart rates, then recovering gradually to low resting rates. By training patients with chronic illnesses to produce these "healthy" wave patterns, Dardik felt convinced that their symptoms would begin to ameliorate. In at least a half-dozen cases I observed directly, that is precisely what happened. Because he did not conduct follow-up studies, it is not clear whether these improvements were sustained over time.

On a more theoretical level, Dardik observed that a wide variety of everyday behaviors reflect a similar stress-recovery pattern. The most obvious is the balance between sleep and waking. Too little sleep has been shown to result in a variety of illnesses, while too much sleep often reflects depression, which has likewise been correlated with sickness. Eating represents a means of recovering energy; not eating or eating fewer calories than one burns is a form of energy expenditure. One extreme leads to obesity; the other to anorexia. Both are unhealthy. While Dardik did not focus nearly so much attention on emotions, it struck me that they too have varied wave patterns. Friedman and others have demonstrated, for example, that hostility tends to prompt chronic physiological arousal—a waveless, linear form of stress. The same is true, at the opposite extreme, of chronic depression and hopelessness, which LeShan found so often characterizes cancer patients.

The capacity to respond flexibly and resiliently to stress— what Dardik calls a healthy wave pattern—is plainly compromised when one becomes stuck in chronic anger or fear or depression. "I began to realize," Dardik told me, "that all of these behaviors have a common language—energy—and that they can be worked together to create a large wave of expenditure and recovery. Health is not just about exercise or relaxation or what you eat or how much you sleep, or even what you feel. It's a function of the way that they're all integrated."

Dardik has never conducted a controlled study. I was drawn to him purely because what he said made such enormous common sense. Midway through my research, I spent several months talking with him nearly every day and watching him work with patients. I was drawn to his passionate conviction that he had a cure for chronic illness. I even found it difficult to dismiss his extravagant claim that this same theory explains, more broadly, how the universe works at every level—what physicists call a "theory of everything." Skeptical and questioning as I am, I was seduced by the intoxicating possibility that there might be a single answer in life after all—and that Dardik had found it.

In response, I made precisely the misstep that so many hungry seekers do when they embrace a teacher who claims to have it all figured out. I willingly overlooked his myriad contradictions—

including the fact that Dardik lived his own life chaotically, that many of his patients claimed he failed to follow-up with them, and that he was steadfastly unwilling to consider any viewpoint but his own. All of this dawned on me in time, and my earlier unequivocal testimonials on his behalf became a source of embarrassment and discomfort. Eventually, I fell out of touch with Dardik. Still, the simplicity, logic, and power of his most basic insight about balancing stress and recovery in all aspects of life has stayed with me—a vivid reminder that even a flawed messenger can deliver a valuable message.

The most effective mind-body interventions may be those that cultivate a balance between behaviors designed to increase stress, or energy expenditure, and those that encourage relaxation, or energy recovery. Ornish's program, for example, addresses this balance at several levels. Moderate daily exercise, yoga, and a low-fat diet promote healthy energy expenditure. Meditation represents a healthy means of recovering energy—physically, emotionally, and perhaps even spiritually. Weekly group meetings prompt a greater sense of trust, goodwill, love, and hope—all emotions that make it easier to respond flexibly rather than rigidly to everyday challenges and stresses. Wisdom, by this model, reflects not so much the effort to transcend what is difficult—including pain, conflict, and grief—but instead the capacity to ride these inevitable waves with grace and resilience. Doing so appears to lie at the heart of a balanced life—and good health.

6

THE IDEAL
PERFORMANCE STATE

*Flow, Learned Optimism, and
the Toughness Model*

*Nothing clutters the soul more than remorse, resent-
ment, recrimination. Negative feelings occupy a fear-
some amount of space in the mind, block our
perceptions, our prospects, our pleasures.*
—NORMAN COUSINS

*In every contest, there comes a moment that defines
winning from losing. The true warrior understands and
seizes that moment by giving an effort so intensive
and so intuitive that it could only be called one from
the heart.*
—PAT RILEY

FOR all my focus on deepening self-awareness, I
had spent relatively little time considering the role
of performance in the search for a complete life—
translating understanding into action, insight into desired behavior. Sports seemed an ideal metaphor for this exploration.
Performance can be measured precisely on the playing field, and it
so happened that tennis has been a primary passion in my life for
more than twenty years. At its best, I got from tennis an experience
of relaxed absorption, strength, and ineffable joy. But all too
often, playing prompted just the opposite emotions: anxiety, fear,

envy, anger, and intense frustration. My mind and body became my opponents more often than they did my allies. What was it exactly that stood in my way? And what, if anything, did evincing grace under pressure—and playing closer to my potential—have to do with wisdom?

The notion that there is something more to tennis than strokes and strategy first dawned on me shortly before graduating from college in 1974, when I picked up a book by Timothy Gallwey titled *The Inner Game of Tennis.* Gallwey had very little to say about strokes but a great deal to say about the role of the mind in tennis. The "inner game," he wrote, "takes place in the mind of the player, and it is played against such obstacles as lapses in concentration, nervousness, self-doubt and self-condemnation. In short, it is played to overcome all habits of mind which inhibit excellence in performance."

Two things happened in the months after I read Gallwey's book and began experimenting with his techniques for taking the conscious mind out of the game. I played far better than I ever had before—and I enjoyed the experience immensely. I became so immersed in playing for its own sake that I stopped worrying constantly about the outcome. Even in highly competitive matches, I was uncommonly relaxed. I'd rarely experienced such pleasure doing anything, and for a brief period, I flirted with the idea of taking a year off just to play tennis. But then, just as suddenly and mysteriously as my game had improved, it fell back. I began hearing a familiar self-critical voice in my head, but the harder I tried to stop thinking, the worse I got and the more my enjoyment diminished. Finally, I set Gallwey's ideas aside and went back to working on my strokes. My game remained as erratic as ever. Soon after graduating from college, I went to work for a small magazine. It was there that I got the idea to write an article about Gallwey. His book had become a big best seller, and I was looking for ways to make a mark at the magazine. More important, I saw a chance to recapture the magic I'd once felt—this time by going directly to the source.

I caught up with Gallwey for the first time at a tennis club in

Chicago, where he was giving a two-day clinic in the "inner game" to approximately a hundred people—most of them club-level players like me. Slight in build and soft-spoken, Gallwey cut an elegant preppy figure in his white duck pants and white Lacoste shirt. "Reflect on the moments when you've played best," he began his presentation that first morning. "Ask successful Olympic athletes what they were thinking during a performance, and to a one, they'll say: 'I wasn't thinking. I was totally involved.' That's what the inner game is all about. The greatest enemy you face is mistrust. I'm trying to undermine your faith in this guy inside who tells you *how* to do things, and to increase your faith in your body. Judgment just gets in the way of awareness. A ball can't be hit by a racket that *should be* somewhere. It can only be hit by a racket that *is* somewhere. Some people lead 'should' lives. They always know what they *should* be doing, but they never know what they *are* doing. If your racket is exactly where it should be but you don't know where it actually is, you're going to miss the ball. On the other hand, if you know where your racket is, even if it's behind your ear, you have a much better chance of bringing it to where it can hit the ball."

At the heart of Gallwey's approach was his supposition that there are two "selves" at work each time we walk onto a tennis court. Self 1, the conscious judging mind, gives instructions about how to play, while Self 2, the unconscious automatic doer, carries them out. I now suspect that what Gallwey calls Self 1 is closely correlated with left hemisphere dominance and fast brainwave activity, while Self 2 is correlated with the right hemisphere and more slow brainwave dominance. Playing at the peak of one's potential, Gallwey postulated, requires getting the intrusive, highly verbal Self 1 to quiet down, thus freeing Self 2 to express its intrinsic potential. This approach parallels Betty Edwards's technique of teaching students to set aside the verbal left hemisphere in order to access the visual right hemisphere skills that make realistic drawing possible. In Gallwey's case, he suggested that when the body is unfettered by conscious interference, it instinctively makes the best choice about how and where to hit the ball.

It's no coincidence, he told us, that a player at the top of his game often talks about playing "out of his mind" or "in the zone."

Mihaly Csikszentmihalyi, a professor of psychology at the University of Chicago, has spent more than twenty-five years systematically studying the components of similar peak experiences in tens of thousands of people around the world, ranging from mountain climbers to painters to business executives to chess players. Csikszentmihalyi coined the term *flow* to describe an optimal state of inner harmony in which one's "thoughts, intentions, feelings and all the senses are focused on the same goal." Flow, he concluded, is the state in which people become so involved in what they are doing that the activity feels spontaneous and automatic and the process becomes more important than the outcome. This, he went on, depends on the capacity to keep one's attention focused on the task at hand—and to screen out the external pressures that so often undermine the flow experience. "In a threatening situation, it is natural to mobilize psychic energy, draw it inward and use it as a defense against the threat," Csikszentmihalyi has written. "But this innate reaction more often than not compromises the ability to cope, exacerbates the experience of inner turmoil [and] reduces the flexibility of response."

Gallwey's techniques were all designed to short-circuit the kind of conscious thinking that gets in the way of flow. He asked us, for example, to focus close attention on the seams of the ball as it came toward us; to notice the ball's trajectory as it passed over the net; to say "hit" at precisely the moment that we stroked each ball; and even to see in our mind's eye the path made by the racket during a stroke. "To still the mind, one must learn to put it somewhere," he explained in *The Inner Game of Tennis*. "It cannot just be let go. It must be 'parked.' . . . To the extent that the mind is [occupied] . . . it tends not to interfere with the natural movements of the body." This instinctive mode of play, he concluded, lies at the heart of the inner game. "When the player is in this state of concentration, he is really into the game,"

Gallwey wrote. "He is at one with the racket, ball and stroke; he discovers his true potential."

In Gallwey's view, detailed formal instruction is secondary to removing the blocks to expressing instinctive knowledge. "For the first thirty-three years of my life," he told our group, "I went on the assumption that I was ignorant and had to become smart, that I was uncoordinated and had to become coordinated. I decided how I *should* be and tried hard to fit the concept. The second way of learning, which I've used for the last five years, is to assume that I already am what I am, and that my goal is self-discovery, not self-improvement. I believe that you learn more if you pay attention to what you *do* than if you think about what you do *not* do."

Gallwey spent his own youth responding not just to his parents' high expectations but to an intense self-critical voice that forever exhorted him to achieve. He did so academically, socially, and in tennis, to which he devoted long hours of practice. By the time he was fifteen, Gallwey had reached the National Junior Championships in Kalamazoo, Michigan. It was the first turning point in his life. He wasn't one of the top-ranked players in the tournament, and he expected to lose in the first round. This didn't worry him much, however, because he was in a deeply religious phase of his life and felt that he could put his fate entirely in God's hands. "I'd simply express his will," Gallwey told me when we sat down after the Chicago workshop. "It took the pressure off me because I couldn't control the outcome."

Three of his first four matches were on the center court before large crowds, and Gallwey won each one. His fifth match was against a top-seeded player who went on to win the tournament the next year. The match was hard-fought, but in the third set Gallwey ran off a string of five games and found himself at 5–3, 40–15, a single point from victory. Years later, he still remembered what he told himself at that moment. "Thank you very much, God, for your help," he said. "I can take it from here." Then he promptly double-faulted and missed an easy volley. Before he knew it, he'd lost the match. "It was when I tried to take control instead of letting it happen that I lost," he explained. "Eventually, that became the basis for the inner game."

Gallwey went on to college at Harvard, captained its tennis team, served in the navy, then worked at an experimental college until it folded in 1969. In August 1971, Gallwey met the Maharajji, then a teenage Indian guru who had attracted a large following of Americans. Gallwey became a disciple and eventually spent some time in an ashram in India. The experience of learning to deeply quiet his mind through meditation introduced him to an entirely new level of inner experience. When Gallwey returned to America, he started applying his insights—and the specific skills of meditation—to performing more effectively in sports. He tried out his techniques first in workshops at Esalen and later at the John Gardiner Tennis Ranch in Carmel, California, where he named it "yoga tennis." It was when he sat down to write a book that he renamed his approach "the inner game." The book's runaway success made it clear that tens of thousands of tennis players suffered from anxiety and self-doubt on the court and were hungry for answers that no formal instruction seemed to provide.

At the end of my second day with Gallwey in Chicago, I got a chance to play tennis with him. I already felt reinspired by our time together. The test now was whether I could keep my mind quiet and my attention focused in the present moment under the pressure of match play. With that in mind, I arranged a doubles game that pitted me and the host club's teaching pro against Gallwey and a young woman tournament player who'd also attended his workshop. Among the four of us, my game was the least polished, and Gallwey's was clearly the strongest. In particular, he hit the sort of big, high bouncing top-spin serves that typically gave me fits. From the start, however, I felt more relaxed than usual and played better than I had in a long time. Gallwey and his partner still managed to win the first set 6–4, and the score eventually went to 5–4 theirs in the second set, with Gallwey serving for the match. He quickly reached match point at 40–30.

I was playing the ad court, and so that left it up to me to save the day.

This was just the sort of high-pressure situation in which I usually became anxious, even fatalistic, and ended up making silly unforced errors. By this stage in the match, however, I was feeling unusually serene and highly focused. There wasn't a thought in my head. When Gallwey hit a huge serve wide to my backhand, I reached out and managed to gently angle the ball by him at net. One save. We lost the next point, and Gallwey served a second time for the match. Again, I stretched wide and smoothly flicked a return by him at net. Two saves. When it happened for a third time, Gallwey stopped briefly in midcourt, and I thought I saw the slight flicker of a smile pass over his mostly impassive face. Finally, we got an advantage, and this time Gallwey served to me right down the middle. I'd anticipated it all the way. I watched my racket reach out and hit a fourth straight passing shot between our two opponents. I was awed. It was as if another player had temporarily inhabited my body.

It seemed almost anticlimactic that Gallwey's resolve stiffened, and they ran out the match 7–5. Afterward, I headed with him to the locker room, my pleasure so intense that I could barely contain it. Because Gallwey had so downplayed the importance of the outcome, it somehow felt inappropriate to tell him that I'd just played the best tennis of my life. But I couldn't resist. "I've never played tennis like that before," I said as calmly as possible. Gallwey nodded pensively. "It was good," he replied laconically. "All you need now is a little more toss awareness on your serve."

It wasn't much in the way of encouragement, but I left Chicago certain that I had rediscovered the secret to the inner game. I was also convinced that I understood what had undermined me the first time around. I'd simply tried too hard *not* to try hard. Now I had tools that I knew worked when it came to setting my conscious mind aside. Sadly, the tools didn't work. Within weeks, the magic was gone again. In time, the inner game techniques faded from my consciousness and I returned to meticulously criticizing my every shortcoming. Fifteen years went by, and but for an occasional spontaneous breakthrough, I never again experienced in tennis the extraordinary state of grace I'd enjoyed that day in Chicago.

I first met Jerry Alleyne in the fall of 1987. Only then did I begin to understand more clearly why Gallwey's insights were initially so powerful but ultimately so insufficient. Alleyne was sixty-seven years old when we met, but he looked nearly two decades younger. Of modest height and powerfully built, he'd been teaching tennis full time for more than thirty years. I'd long since given up on the inner game and was merely looking for a traditional teacher who could hit me a lot of balls and help me improve my strokes. It took just a few minutes on the court for me to realize that Alleyne was anything but traditional. Still, I sensed that he was someone who had a lot to teach me. I'd never met anyone with such intense focus and passion for the game.

In contrast to Gallwey, Alleyne didn't believe that quieting the mind and relaxing the body necessarily unlock one's potential. To the contrary, he told me, tennis is a difficult and complex game that draws on the full resources of the mind and the body. The first challenge is to learn how to hit a series of unnatural strokes so well that it eventually becomes possible to produce them without thinking. It's also necessary, he said, to learn court tactics—to know automatically where to hit the ball in any given situation. Mastering both of these skills, Alleyne explained, requires conscious hard work, and he himself taught them methodically and precisely. In turn, he told me, there comes a time when thinking gets in the way, and the challenge becomes to use discipline and will in the service of letting go. At the highest level, strokes have to be produced, as he put it, "from the nervous system." Even then, he said, there are appropriate times to use the mind to critique one's play. Knowing when to think and when to let go, Alleyne concluded, is the key to playing tennis at the peak of one's potential. His mission, he told me, is to help students learn to play tennis with the same relaxed ease, focus, and joy that he does. This he calls being "totally connected, totally alive, and operating on all cylinders."

At first, we spent a great deal of time on the nuances of each stroke. I was surprised by the tiny distortions that Alleyne was able to detect, even though I'd played tennis for many years and had taken countless lessons. He'd suggest a microscopic shift, and the result would be a dramatic improvement in my shotmaking. Only when he felt that I truly understood the concepts and that there were no longer significant technical problems in my strokes did he turn to the challenge of getting me to produce them automatically. To do so, he told me, requires understanding the three central paradoxes of tennis. The first is that you must always have a target, but you must never try to hit it. Consciously aiming, Alleyne explained, prompts distortion. The second is that you produce speed not by exerting force but by releasing energy. The harder you try to get speed, he told me, the more the muscles constrict and the less able you are to fully let go. The third is that you must always play to win, but you can never make winning important. To set winning as a goal, he told me, provides structure and focus, but to worry about the result only induces tension and distraction. The common denominator in all of tennis, he explained, is using discipline and focus to stay in the moment.

Alleyne had used this same quality to overcome considerable obstacles in his own life. He grew up poor in Brooklyn, the son of a black man and a white woman. Before he turned ten, he was working long hours alongside his demanding and hard-driving father, who was the janitor at a local private school and worked seven days a week. Alleyne respected his father's work ethic and commitment to provide for his family, but he resented how mercilessly his father pushed him as a child, and how little appreciation he got for his efforts. He was angered, too, by the dismissive way his father treated his mother, a gentle, open-hearted woman whom Alleyne adored. One of the turning points in his life occurred around the age of ten. He had painstakingly saved his money from odd jobs to buy a box of chocolates as a present for his father's birthday. When he handed it over, full of pride and excitement, his father gruffly tossed it aside and failed even to say thank you. The wound was so deep that Alleyne began to cry. He was mortified. "Afterward," he told me, "I said to myself, 'I'll never cry for him again.' From that day forward, I never let myself want anything from my father."

Instead, he became fiercely self-reliant and successful on his own terms. An extraordinary athlete from a very early age, Alleyne excelled first in boxing and track and then in tennis. He won a full scholarship to Temple University, worked full time on the side, graduated in 1939, and served a tour in the army. By his mid-twenties, he was playing tennis at a world-class level, but blacks were still barred from entering the major U.S. tournaments. Alleyne beat several of the world's top players in exhibitions, but he could play tournaments only by traveling to places like South America. It wasn't until 1959 that he finally got accepted into the draw for the U.S. championships at Forest Hills. Although at thirty-eight he was long past his playing prime, he still managed to reach the third round before losing a close match to Barry McCay, then ranked among the top ten in the world.

Eager for the sort of job security that eluded most blacks in that era, Alleyne decided to become a cop. He served more than twenty years in the New York City Police Department, before retiring on disability after a serious accident that he suffered while on motorcycle patrol. Told that he would never walk again without a limp, Alleyne refused to accept the verdict and worked relentlessly at physically rehabilitating himself. Sure enough, he recovered almost all of his mobility and eventually began to teach tennis at the courts in New York City's Central Park. Later, he was hired to teach and manage an indoor club in a small suburb of the city. Students flocked to him, and much like his father, Alleyne began putting in twelve-hour days, seven days a week. Finally, in the early 1970s, he decided to build a tennis club of his own.

Alleyne succeeded, I came to believe, because he focused so unswervingly on his goals and because whatever challenge he faced, he gave himself to completely. During four years of lessons,

I almost never saw his attention waver on the court, and he brought his passion to every moment. When he finally cut back a few hours from twelve-hour teaching days in his mid-sixties, Alleyne began swimming two miles a day and took up the piano. Often, he told me, he'd practice for hours at a stretch, so immersed in his playing that he utterly lost track of time. Needing very little sleep, he spent his nighttime hours methodically making his way through books about psychology, philosophy, and science, savoring each word, determined to understand every concept. He listened in much the same way—with rapt attentiveness. Children, in particular, lit up in his presence, sensing immediately his genuine interest in what they had to say.

Such focus extends to every area of Alleyne's life. When his night workman didn't show up one evening, Alleyne set to work cleaning the club himself, including the toilets and the bathrooms. Before he noticed the time, ten hours had passed. "It's not what I'd choose to do, but if I have to, I get totally involved and I do it right," he told me later. On another day, a young man he'd recently hired spent two days spreading new gravel on the club parking lot but barely made a dent in the job. At the age of seventy, Alleyne decided to teach the young man a lesson—by example. "I just looked at that big mound of stones," he told me, laughing at the memory, "and I started repeating to myself, 'When Jerry shovels, the mountain falls.' " By the time he stopped, he'd shoveled out two tons of gravel. Far from exhausted, he felt exhilarated.

"The more you stay in the moment, the more alive you become and the more anything you do is enjoyable," Alleyne told me. "The key is to make everything important. I don't care what it is, if you're not doing it to its fullest, you're partly dead." The chief obstacle to being in the moment, he told me, is fear. "You can't be totally present if you have any fear. That's what keeps you from really letting go, and letting go is where the real pleasure comes from. The biggest fear of all is death. Once you're not afraid to die, then you can truly let go." Alleyne himself has suffered two heart attacks, and several years ago, his cardiologist gave him an angiogram and recommended bypass surgery. Alleyne declined. "I'm not afraid of dying," he told me, "but I'm not about to let anyone cut into my body." Three years have passed and Alleyne is still teaching tennis every day.

There were many days when I arrived for a lesson feeling distracted or anxious or angry. In addition to the considerable power of his own example, Alleyne had a wide array of exercises designed to help me get connected. He prodded me to slow down enough to feel my body; to be aware, in my mind's eye, of my racket in relation to the ball; and to *really* see the ball—its spin, its speed, and its trajectory both coming toward me and leaving my racket. Even the sound I made when I stroked the ball he deemed important. When I began to get anxious and out of rhythm, Alleyne had me count each stroke precisely as I made contact with the ball—forcing me out of conscious thinking and into perfect rhythm. "As you begin to get connected," he told me, "the interference drops out and all the senses you had as a child begin to return. You see better, you hear better, you feel more." Sure enough, on most days, I'd eventually find myself absorbed in the lesson and enjoying it immensely. In turn, the level of my game rose dramatically. I played far better with Alleyne than I did with anyone else. Moreover, my sense of relaxation, well-being, and even joy often carried over from the court into the beginning of my work day.

Frustratingly, however, this experience rarely endured for more than an hour or two. Nor could I recreate it reliably in my matches with other players. There was no doubt that my strokes had improved, my anxiety had diminished, and my knowledge of the game—both its technical and its psychological components— had grown dramatically. There were wonderful days when it all came together. On those occasions, I'd somehow fall into a state of deeply relaxed concentration, and suddenly I'd play with a sense of passion and abandon. It was clear that I had the necessary tools. But no sooner did I find myself saying, "I wish it could be this way forever," than the spell was broken. My joy and ease one day gave way on the next to a wandering attention and a familiar critical voice in my head.

When I described to Alleyne how I got nervous about winning points in high-pressure situations, he had a simple explanation. I was too invested in the results. "Wanting," he told me, "is a cancer." For him, wanting implied external dependence—the need for approval from parents or authorities. I had no doubt there was truth in his explanation. I worried about losing because I feared that it would diminish me in my opponent's eyes and in my own. I also worried about winning, fearful that it invited envy, anger, and even punishment. All this and more ran through my head when I played. To Alleyne it was all nonsense, useless baggage from my past that merely created interference.

I saw how this played out in my life as well. Ruminating about the past and worrying about the future often prevented me from totally immersing myself in whatever I was doing—being with my children, working on this book, even listening to a piece of music. It baffled Alleyne that I saw so clearly how pleasurable and productive it is to set my distractions aside but still couldn't do so reliably. Alleyne believed that I was taking something very simple—being in the moment—and making it overly complicated. If I could simply let go, he insisted, it would transform not just my tennis but my whole life. When it came to performing on the tennis court, I concluded that he was right, even though a breakthrough continued to elude me.

At a broader level, however, I came to believe that as valuable as Alleyne's insights were, there was more to a complete life than he acknowledged. At times, I felt he took something quite complex and made it overly simple. Eventually, this created a tension between us. As Alleyne saw it, he had made himself utterly self-sufficient by learning to derive pleasure solely from his own resources. He refused to dwell on past pain or deprivation, preferring to focus his enormous energy in the present and to rely entirely on himself rather than on others. He gave generously of himself but said he neither wanted, needed, nor expected anything in return. For example, he is married and clearly loves his wife.

But if the relationship were to end, he often told me, he would neither feel pain nor look back. Even at the funeral of his mother, whom he deeply loved, he never shed a tear. "I loved her totally when she was here, and so I could let her go when she was gone," he explained. This philosophy provided Alleyne some relief from ordinary suffering, particularly the experience of vulnerability. He simply refused to entertain for very long emotions such as pain, sadness, and fear.

I admired all this, and Alleyne's lessons were exceptionally valuable, but I envisioned yet another dimension to a complete life. Where Alleyne chose consciously to set aside underlying conflict, my growing inclination was to move toward it. Doing so didn't help my tennis, where emotions such as fear and anger only get in the way of focused attention in the present. But acknowledging and engaging the early experience of vulnerability, grief and unmet desire had helped me begin to recover some part of my heart—a tenderness and warmth that for years I'd simply been afraid to feel. I also had a different perspective from Alleyne when it came to anger. We both had plenty of it. In his case, he felt that the anger was justified on the grounds that so many people act in hurtful ways, much as his own father had.

Certain slights could provoke in Alleyne an anger so fierce that it literally took control of him. He referred to this violent tendency as "the monkey on my back," and his solution was to use his immense discipline to keep it under wraps. The vast majority of the time, Alleyne was gentle, good-hearted, and sensitive in his dealings with people. But occasionally he exploded. Because I was the subject of his rage several times, I knew how frightening and upsetting it could be. In each instance, the force of his anger seemed far out of proportion to the provocation. He was disinclined to look at the unconscious sources of his anger—among them the possibility that it masked more vulnerable underlying feelings or that it had its origins in his childhood. Alleyne hungered to love more freely and deeply, he told me, but he didn't see value in exploring what might be standing in his way. I continued to love and admire him, but at another level, we were like trains passing in the night.

In my case, it was when I allowed myself to feel my anger more fully—watching it without acting on it—that I learned more about the feelings that lay beneath it and their origins. I was left trying to balance two very different challenges. I'd seen the value of turning attention inward to engage the pain and conflict that continued to stand in my way. But the question remained of how to balance that inclination with the approach that Alleyne had so plainly demonstrated best serves external performance: setting aside conflict, doubt, and even conscious thinking, and living more fully in each moment.

I was drawn to Jim Loehr's work because he operates on so many levels—as a sports psychologist, an athlete himself, a careful researcher, and a genuine seeker. No one I met has evolved a more comprehensive understanding of what he terms "the ideal performance state," while simultaneously recognizing its limits. Tall and large-limbed, with an easy smile and all-American good looks, Loehr was a very fit and youthful forty-seven when we met in 1990. For two decades now, Loehr has been trying to define in specific, measurable terms the mental, physical, and emotional factors that help athletes perform at their best, even in the most stressful of circumstances.

Like Gallwey and Alleyne, Loehr has found that quieting the mind and body, staying focused in the present, and letting go of conscious thinking are all key ingredients of peak performance. To these, Loehr added the importance of cultivating a very specific, positive state of mind in competition and a matching physical posture. Then he went still a step further in his inquiry. Why, he wondered, is such a state of mind typical in some athletes and rare for most others? And what exactly makes it possible to access and sustain this ideal performance state? As our discussions evolved, Loehr began to make a clear distinction between the persona that one must consciously adopt to perform effectively in sports, and a more authentic underlying self that retains access to a complete range of thoughts and emotions.

Like the mind-body researchers, Loehr discovered that whatever goes on in the mind has a direct effect on the body—and vice versa. An athlete's thoughts prompt certain emotions, and those emotions have physiological consequences. Thoughts about losing, for example, may lead to fear and anxiety. In turn, those feelings prompt an array of physiological responses including increased heart rate, muscle tightness, shortness of breath, reduced blood flow to the hands and feet, and even narrowing of vision. Each of these reactions undermines performance, much the way that despair and anger have been shown to adversely affect one's physical health. For a tennis player, for example, tighter muscles lead to distorted strokes; reduced blood flow prompts leadenness in the feet and a lack of feeling in the hands; and shortness of breath leads to diminished endurance. This negative cycle is self-reinforcing. Anxiety and fear compromise the physiology, leading to poorer performance, and poor performance in turn prompts more anxiety and fear. Negative thinking, in short, can have devastating consequences, both physiologically and psychologically.

But it is also possible, Loehr discovered, to consciously cultivate a positively reinforcing cycle. "Positive thoughts," he told me when I visited him at his headquarters in Florida, "lead to feelings of relaxed alertness, enthusiasm, and determination." These emotions produce positive physiological responses ranging from more flexibility in the muscles to better feel and increased endurance. Loehr found that this more positive cycle can be prompted through the body. Techniques that help one to physically relax—assuming a confident posture, for example—tend to lead to more positive thoughts and emotions. The natural by-product is strong, focused concentration. "No one I've ever worked with has trouble concentrating when they're having fun," Loehr told me. "It's abnormal to be able to trigger positive emotions in the face of crisis, but the best athletes all develop the capacity to be challenged by stress. They become masters of mind control. What I've tried to do is demystify that process. It's not magical. You can be taught how to think and act positively, just the way you can be taught to stroke a ball correctly."

Loehr's decision to become a psychologist marked him as an apostate in his highly religious family. He grew up in central Colorado, where his father was a civil engineer and his mother a homemaker. Family life revolved around the Catholic Church. Loehr's brother trained to be a Jesuit priest, his sister is a nun, and Loehr himself attended Jesuit schools through college. "All questions were answered in one way as I grew up," he told me. "We were taught to embrace certain higher values in church, but then people would go out and do terrible things in their lives all week long. This background eventually caused me to reexamine everything." The other important value in his family was achievement, and Loehr responded to that challenge more readily. He got his doctorate in psychology in 1969 and soon became director of a community mental health center in Colorado. By then, he had begun to develop deep misgivings about the effectiveness of traditional psychotherapy, which focused on the unresolved conflicts of early childhood. "I just didn't see it working," he told me. "I'd watch people go into therapy, get lost in their own conflicts, and come out no better than when they started and often worse."

Loehr grew more intrigued by the emerging humanistic techniques aimed at developing one's potential in the present. It was during this period that he began working out at a local college. There he got to know a man named Joe Vigil, who coached the school's track-and-field team. Vigil told Loehr that in order to be a great coach, it was necessary to be a first-rate psychologist, too. Loehr was immediately intrigued. He'd been a good athlete himself in his youth but an erratic competitor. The problems began when he played baseball on a Little League team coached by his demanding father. Feeling special pressure to perform, he had developed a reputation as a choker—a talented player who could never produce when it really counted. Later, he took up tennis to gain some independence from his father, and sure enough he performed better. But even as a member of his college tennis team, he found it difficult to control his anger on the court. After meeting Vigil, Loehr started to dream about developing a systematic approach to training not just the body in sports but also the mind.

He quit his job in 1976 and moved to Denver to set up a practice in sports psychology. He was entering uncharted territory. A few university professors were calling themselves sports psychologists, but Loehr may have been the first one to try to make his living by working directly with athletes. For five years, he existed in a twilight world, barely scraping by. Two professional teams and several world-class athletes consulted with him, but in each case he had to agree not to discuss the work publicly. Most athletes, he found, believed that seeing any kind of psychologist conveyed a message of weakness and emotional instability. Loehr's turning point came in 1982, when a tennis player named Tom Gullikson was encouraged by a friend to consult Loehr. At the time, Gullikson was ranked around one hundredth in the world and had just come off one of his worst years on the professional tour. Discouraged and figuring he had nothing to lose, Gullikson agreed to have dinner with Loehr. After a four-hour conversation, Loehr suggested a deal. He'd work with Gullikson at no cost. If the suggestions proved useful, Gullikson agreed that he would simply say so publicly—to journalists, coaches, and other players. Gullikson willingly accepted the terms.

Leaving aside his strokes, which were sound, Loehr worked on every other aspect of Gullikson's game—how he prepared for matches, his diet, his attitude while he was playing, even the role that his marriage played in his tennis. Over the next year, Gullikson's performance turned around. He reached number twenty-five in the world, his highest ranking ever. "The change was largely in my attitude and my approach to the game," he told me. "I give Jim a lot of credit for that." At the end of that same year—1982—Loehr decided to move to Florida in order to be closer to more top players.

Increasingly, he felt convinced that high-level performance is closely linked to one's emotional state. In the face of great external pressure, top athletes consistently told Loehr, they felt both calm and peaceful but also highly energized, positive, and enthusiastic. Most of them had discovered this state intuitively, without any guidance or training. For Loehr, the challenge became to find a way to understand better what these athletes were doing, so that it could be taught systematically and broadly. In search of ways to induce this ideal state that players reported, Loehr experimented with a variety of techniques, from biofeedback training, to hooking players up with Walkmans playing different kinds of music, to teaching them how to meditate. But most athletes, he found, are impatient for quick, tangible results, and none of these approaches had much immediate impact.

The turning point came when Loehr got a call from Irv Dardik, the former surgeon whose belief that health is a function of balanced stress and recovery had struck me as so compelling. Loehr knew Dardik through Dardik's work with the United States Olympic Committee. "I think I've found something that will really work for you," Dardik told Loehr during a phone call in 1986. He was referring to the heart-rate monitor that he'd begun using to work with chronically ill patients. "What it helped me to do," Loehr explained, "was finally get a reliable window into the physiology, through the heart rate. If I had a player wear the watch, I could tell exactly what happened to him physiologically when he got angry or upset or when he gave up. Then I could look at the relationship between those physiological measurements and the player's performance."

The best and most consistent play, Loehr found, took place when players' heart rates rose and fell within a certain range. During the effort of playing a point, the heart rate nearly always increases. The problem for most players begins, Loehr found, when they fail to recover sufficiently between points—a fact made clear by whether their heart rates drop. Loehr also monitored the impact that negative emotions had on his players' heart rates, by outfitting them with tiny remote microphones so that he could listen to the ways that they were talking to themselves between points. Sure enough, any expression of negative emotion tended to push their heart rates out of normal range and, in turn, quickly affected the quality of their play. Anger, for example, tended to keep their heart rates high. So did anxiety and nervousness. Getting discouraged or giving up—"tanking"—tended to drive their heart rates down. Loehr also found that positive emotions such as confidence, enjoyment, and high energy prompted the heart rate to recover from the stress of hard-fought points much more quickly.

The microphones provided one more piece of unexpected information. The best players, Loehr discovered, consistently exhaled deeply and rhythmically as they hit the ball, making an "aaaaahhhh" sound. Weaker players, particularly when under pressure, tended not to breathe audibly at all. Breathing deeply, Loehr came to realize, is an aspect of recovery—a wavelike way to release tension, loosen muscles, and fully relax. Choking, a reaction of fear and nervousness in competition, occurs quite literally on the physiological level in the form of jerky, shallow, and irregular breathing.

Eager to develop techniques for prompting specific thoughts and emotions, Loehr began to investigate how the best athletes maintain the ideal performance state during competition. To find out, he studied hundreds of hours of tapes of top players in matches. To his surprise, he could barely detect differences between them. They all had near-perfect strokes, yet certain players won far more consistently than others. It finally occurred to Loehr to start looking at what the players did *between* points. As much as 50 percent of the time during a tennis match is spent between points, yet this aspect of the game had long been treated as irrelevant. Very quickly, Loehr recognized a pattern unique to the top competitors. Intuitively and often unconsciously, these players adopted a uniform and highly specific ritual between points. By breaking it down, Loehr was able to evolve a step-by-step understanding of how top performers stay relaxed, focused, and positive during competition, despite innumerable potential distractions. At a broader level, he recognized that how a person prepares and recovers—both in sports and in other arenas in life—may be as critical to the outcome as what happens during competition itself.

Loehr was able to delineate four separate stages of recovery in tennis. He named stage one "the positive physical response." When a point ends, he found that top players turn immediately away from the net and shift the racket to the nondominant hand. They do so, he concluded, to minimize tension in the playing hand. Next, these players walk toward the backcourt with their shoulders back and their heads up, projecting energy and confidence. Loehr named this "the matador walk." While traveling in Spain one winter several years ago, he was able to interview a top-level sixty-nine-year-old matador named Manolo Martin-Vasquez who had been badly gored some fifteen times in the course of his career and twice had nearly died. How, Loehr asked him, did he deal with his fear when he went into the ring? "The most important lesson in courage is physical, not mental," Martin-Vasquez replied. "From the age of twelve, I was taught to walk in a way that *produces* courage. The mental part comes later."

Sure enough, Loehr found that the best tennis players respond positively and confidently even after making an error. What they've learned, he concluded, is that any negative reaction depletes energy, increases tension, and compromises recovery. One day, Loehr got an emergency call from Ray Mancini, the middle-weight boxer with whom he'd been working. "I'm really concerned," Mancini told him. "I had a negative thought in the ring today." Loehr was startled. "You're worried about one negative thought?" he asked. "You don't understand," Mancini said. "A single negative thought is what gets you hit in the face." For Loehr, it was an epiphany. "It taught me," he explained, "how devastating negative thoughts and emotions can be in performance."

Eventually, it occurred to Loehr that top athletes have a great deal in common with professional actors. "The mark of a great actor," Loehr concluded, "is the capacity to bring to life whatever emotions the script calls for—joy, sadness, aliveness, anger, weakness. In sports, the script doesn't change so much: the athlete must always bring to life powerful *positive* emotions, regardless of what he may actually be feeling. In a way, I serve as a method acting coach. Anytime I can get an athlete to produce the right feelings, he's going to perform in the upper range of his potential. By learning to control his thoughts and emotions, he gains control of his physiology."

The focus of Loehr's stage two is relaxation. The player continues walking until he moves across the baseline. The sole goal is physical recovery. It's akin to a minimeditation—inhaling and exhaling deeply; contracting and relaxing muscles to keep them loose; and keeping the eyes focused on the strings of the racket to minimize distraction and maintain control of attention. Loehr was fascinated to discover that during the first two stages—a total of anywhere from ten to twenty seconds—the top players all reported having an utter absence of thoughts. While no technology yet exists for monitoring the brainwave activity of tennis players *during* competition, their self-reports suggest that slow-wave alpha activity becomes more dominant, and so, too, does the right hemisphere. It is only in stage three—what Loehr calls the "preparation response"—that players report any verbal left-hemisphere-style thinking. This stage begins when the player steps up a couple of feet behind the baseline, registers the score, and gives himself one or two easily digestible bullets of advice or strategy such as "Remember to bend," "Serve wide and come in," or "Watch the ball."

In the fourth and final stage, Loehr discovered, the mode of thinking shifts again from verbal and analytic to more visual. The top players told Loehr that they do not think in words, but instead visualize hitting the ball to a specific target. Like the mind-body researchers, Loehr came to understand that images are far more effective than words in giving the body complex commands. He also observed that in this final stage, each player has his own predictable set of rituals—twirling the racket, tugging at a shirt, wiping sweat off the brow, bouncing the ball a fixed number of times before serving, and rocking back and forth while waiting to return. These rituals, Loehr concluded, help players to avoid distracting thoughts and reconnect them with a familiar positive frame of mind and a certain habituated set of physical movements. In effect, the best players are using the between-point stages to rest and reprogram their computers. Once the actual point begins, they simply let go of all thinking, permitting their bodies to execute automatically. Peak performance, Loehr concluded, requires a delicate balance between disciplined movement and flexibility, willful effort and letting go, conscious thinking and instinctive execution.

L oehr's insights into the stages between points are part of a much broader approach that he developed to teaching peak performance. The key, he came to believe, is actively cultivating a balanced pattern of stress and recovery at all levels: physical, mental, and emotional. He calls this "toughness training," referring less to sheer will and brute force than to the relaxed, highly focused positive energy that he believes prompts the ideal performance state. The real challenge in maximizing performance, Loehr concluded, is not to avoid stress—which is inevitable—but rather to respond to any given challenge with strength, flexibility and resilience. "Toughness is the ability to consistently perform toward the upper range of your talent and skill regardless of competitive circumstances," he has written. Tough competitors, he has found, "exhibit a highly refined and precise system of trained recovery." By contrast, he said, poor competitors "are less disciplined, less exact, less ritualistic and more varied in their actions . . . [and] much more likely to express a negative emotion each time they make a mistake."

Drawing on Maslow's hierarchy of needs, Loehr argued that the need for a balance between stress and recovery operates at every level. The most basic needs, for example, are physical—for food, drink, and sleep. Failure to meet these bodily requirements, Loehr found, undermines a performer's physical capacities in competition and interferes with their mental and emotional capacities. "Poor nutrition, thirst or inadequate sleep beats down our ability to expend energy or cope with even moderate stress," he explained. "Under these conditions our mental and physical toughness—our fight, passion and endurance—erode. When the physical needs of players [are] no longer being met during match play, even the toughest players [are] likely to collapse."

Eliciting the ideal performance state depends next on nurturing what Loehr calls "mental toughness." Negative thoughts, in Loehr's model, represent a form of stress. That's because they tend to prompt negative emotions such as anger, fear, and frustration, which in turn compromise the person's physiological capacities. Positive thoughts, by contrast, lead to a wave of recovery by prompting the emotions that best serve performance—including calmness, joy, fun, and confidence. The challenge, Loehr concluded, is to learn how to systematically let go of negative thoughts and emotions and to consciously cultivate positive ones. "How you really feel is your Real Self," Loehr has written. "How you need to feel to perform at your peak is called your Performer Self. The ability to move from the Real Self to the Performer Self on demand calls for precision thinking and acting skills."

Peak performance, Loehr believes, depends not just on a disciplined physical training regimen but on training one's thoughts and emotions. "Emotions respond much like muscles do," he has written. "The ones you stimulate the most become the strongest and most accessible." Just as it requires hundreds of repetitions for a complex motor skill to hold up under the pressure of competition, so this is true for mental skills. "Converting bad habits of thinking to good habits—and turning good habits into strong beliefs," Loehr explains, "takes time and lots of targeted energy expenditure." Ultimately, he believes, the goal is to literally reprogram the mind and body. "When you move from how you really feel, to how you *need* to feel to be at your best," he told me, "you are literally changing your underlying physiology. In effect, you're learning how to generate the chemistry of confidence. That's what makes peak performance possible."

Loehr sees a clear illustration of this approach in the rigorous basic training given to new soldiers. "[C]ould the military succeed so well," he asks rhetorically, "without using highly skilled and deliberately obnoxious drill instructors to dish out large and carefully orchestrated doses of mental, emotional and physical stress to recruits? Absolutely not. . . . Reaching over fear into effective performance demands mental and emotional toughness. The necessary level of toughness can only be achieved by training for it systematically." Even the practice of endless drill-formation marching serves this purpose, Loehr concluded. In effect, soldiers are being trained to adopt the matador walk as preparation for battle conditions.

"You never see any visible sign of weakness whatsoever," he said of soldiers in formation. "No visible fatigue, no sagging shoulders, no negativism, no fear. What you see is total focus, confidence, positive energy and precision. . . . [Marching] trains discipline, sustained concentration, decisiveness, and poise, all of which are essential elements in conquering fear." Overcoming fear is likewise critical, Loehr concluded, for athletes seeking to perform at their potential. As Mihalyi Csikszentmihaly put it, "Of all the virtues we can learn, no trait is more useful, more essential for survival and more likely to improve the quality of life than the ability to transform adversity into an enjoyable challenge."

I saw vividly the power of a highly disciplined and balanced approach to training when I spent time traveling with Ivan Lendl in 1990. At the time, Lendl was in his fourth consecutive year as the top-ranked tennis player in the world. Between matches, he spent long hours on the court grooving his strokes, and he adopted a fierce physical conditioning regimen. But he also spent nearly as much time training control of his mind. He regularly practiced observing his thoughts and emotions the way that a meditator might, for example, simply noting their arising and passing without reacting to them. He also did mental-focus exercises in order to strengthen the sharpness of his awareness and his capacity to be absorbed in one thing at a time. Before matches, he sat down and briefly reviewed his goals—"Be strong, confident, eager, quick," he might write—in order to program his mind more

positively. Finally, he closed his eyes and imagined himself execut-
ing the goals on the court—sometimes taking himself through
entire games.

Lendl also adopted a long series of between-point rituals that
helped him maintain his focus and rhythm—among them wiping
his brow with his wristband, knocking his racket against his heels,
drying his hands with sawdust from his pocket, and bouncing the
ball four times before his first serve, three before his second. In
both cases, he visualized his serving target as well as where he
intended to hit his second shot. At the same time, he was highly
attentive to recovery between matches. When I traveled with him,
he napped every afternoon at the same hour, slept essentially the
same hours at night, and ate a carefully circumscribed diet. He
instructed those around him not to bring any potentially disquiet-
ing events to his attention during tournaments lest they undermine
his focused, positive state of mind. Even after a difficult loss, I
was astonished at how quickly he put it behind him and turned
his attention to the next challenge. It was no accident that while
other players were considered more physically talented, Lendl
managed to remain the number-one player in the world for
so long.

Loehr himself has worked with top tennis players ranging
from Jim Courier to Martina Navratilova, as well as with boxer
Mancini, Olympic gold medal skater Dan Jansen, and numerous
professional golfers. One of his most striking successes grew out
of an intensive period of work with Gabriela Sabatini in 1990.
When Loehr first met with the young Argentine tennis player in
April of that year, she was in a deep slump. Feeling lost and
confused, Sabatini eventually acknowledged to Loehr that she was
suffering from a lack of motivation and feelings of confusion and
anxiety on the court. With the rise of young players such as
Monica Seles and Jennifer Capriati (who both later suffered their
own crises of confidence and motivation), Sabatini worried that
her best days might be behind her, even though she was only
nineteen years old. Her strokes required no work. Instead, Loehr
focused on her state of mind. "My challenge," he concluded after

watching Sabatini play listlessly in practice, "was to help her reenergize her game by discovering the sense of fun, excitement and intensity that she'd so obviously lost."

Loehr encouraged the young player to be more expressive on the court—to give a pump of her fist following a great shot, to smile, even to scream, anything to fuel her enthusiasm and bring her alive again. He told Sabatini that even if she didn't feel strong positive emotions, she should act as if she did, on the grounds that the body responds physiologically to a convincing performance much the way it does to authentic feelings. "I asked her to see how often she could *look* like she wanted to *feel*," Loehr explained. "The more she did it—the more gestures, intensity, movement—the better. Eventually, she started to feel the way that she was acting."

When Loehr asked Sabatini how she'd most like to be playing, she told him that she dreamed of being more aggressive, taking short balls, coming to net, and knifing away volleys. But she also admitted that she utterly lacked the confidence to do that, which was why she'd been parking herself at the baseline in matches and hitting looping top-spin moonballs. Loehr decided to put together a video of Sabatini's best moments playing aggressively over the years and set it to her favorite music. Then he bought her a tiny portable television and VCR so that she could watch the tape over and over on the road. Loehr's goal was to visually reprogram Sabatini's self-image by reacquainting her with a pumped-up, enthusiastic version of herself.

The results were astonishing. Four months after he began working with her, Sabatini won the first grand slam title of her career, defeating the highly favored Steffi Graf in the finals of the U.S. Open. But at least equally interesting was the aftermath. It became public after the Open that Loehr had been working with Sabatini. Sensitive to any public impression that their daughter needed the services of a psychologist, her parents immediately canceled the arrangement. Under a new coach whom Loehr had helped her find, Sabatini continued to play well for the next several months. But slowly and inexorably, her play fell off. Three years and several coaches later, she has never come close to winning another grand-slam title and remains mired in the worst slump of her career. Remarkably, Loehr took on a similar challenge with Arantxa Sanchez-Vicario in the winter of 1994, and that August she, too, won her first U.S. Open, defeating a favored Steffi Graf.

The results of my own first experience working with Loehr were scarcely as dazzling as Sabatini's and Sanchez-Vicario's, but they were still exhilarating. The first time I traveled down to see Loehr at the Nick Bollitieri Tennis Academy—he has since opened the LGE Sports Science Center located at Lake Nona in Orlando, Florida—he worked with me on and off for four days in between his other appointments. Loehr began by giving me a heart-rate monitor to wear. In this way, I could see for myself how I responded physiologically in a variety of playing situations and what effect my thoughts and emotions had on my heart rate. We also worked at a series of exercises designed to promote the ideal performance state. For example, we played out points. At the end of each one, my challenge was to pump my fist enthusiastically into the air, even if I'd just hit the ball a foot wide of the court. I had a hard time summoning up much enthusiasm after such mistakes, but Loehr pushed me to act the part anyway.

When I began playing sets, it surprised me to discover how difficult it was to take any significant time between points. My instinct at the end of a point—particularly when I'd made an error—was to step right back up to the line and get on with the match. Recovery and relaxation simply weren't in my repertoire, even though there were many times when I finished a point feeling winded or frustrated or simply nervous. Rushing, it dawned on me, was a way to keep myself from thinking and worrying. When a point ended and I no longer had an obvious focus of attention, my thoughts often tended to be negative—regretting the previous point or worrying about the next one. My instinctive solution was to give myself no time to think—and therefore none to recover.

What Loehr offered me with his four-stage process was a very disciplined program for recovery.

I soon discovered that when I followed Loehr's recovery stages carefully, my heart rate dropped down after each point in a smooth, predictable pattern—from a high around 155 to near 125 by the time I was ready to play the next point. In this range, I felt both relaxed and energetic. Following the detailed stages of recovery left me little time for distracting thoughts. When I did notice a negative emotion arising, I was instructed to treat it the way I would a stray thought in meditation—by turning my attention back to my main focus. To the extent that I talked to myself at all between points, I now tried to keep the messages brief and positive: "Stay relaxed," "Keep the intensity up," "You can do it."

On the last day of my visit with Loehr, he arranged for me to play a match against one of the sixteen-year-old hotshots at the academy—a ranked player who had reached the semifinals of a state tournament just the past week. This was silly, I told Loehr. I could play at the peak of my potential, and I would still be utterly outgunned. "That's not the point," he told me. My job, he explained, was simply to go through the stages between points in perfect sequence, monitor my heart rate, and let the outcome take care of itself. He'd videotape the match, and afterward we'd look together at how I'd done. Unconvinced, I started out nervously. My opponent had a huge serve and powerful groundstrokes, and I felt handcuffed. Still, I dutifully played the confident role. With the tape rolling, I made sure to exaggerate my matador walk and to smile often, even as balls went whizzing by me at net. I kept my eyes on my racket strings between points, resisting the urge to look at my opponent.

I also took my time, despite an intense desire to speed things up. I was losing, but after a few games, I realized that I still felt surprisingly loose and positive. On a couple of occasions when I checked my watch, my heart rate had dropped below 120, evidence that I'd let myself get *too* relaxed. This was a competitive first for me. Time began to slow down. The ball looked unusually big. I couldn't quite believe that I was feeling so chipper. My routines between points were starting to take on an easygoing rhythm. I was down 3–1 when I managed to get my racket on one of my opponent's huge first serves. I stroked the ball back with authority, catching him by surprise. I glanced up and saw a wave of consternation cloud his face as my return sailed by his outstretched racket. I'd done something similar years earlier with Gallwey in Chicago. The difference was that back then, it seemed to happen out of the blue. This time I was aware that I'd methodically worked my way into a groove and that the recovery process was helping me to voluntarily sustain it. The more loosely I played, the more frustrated my opponent became, until it was clear that he'd simply begun to crack. I resisted offering advice or solace and ended up winning the set 7–5. When I went inside and looked at the tape with Loehr, I saw myself hitting winning shots that I literally couldn't believe had come off my racket.

While I did not return home miraculously transformed as a player, I understood more clearly than ever what stood in my way. On the most basic level, I'd simply never devoted the hundreds of hours of disciplined practice, drilling and physical conditioning necessary to make my strokes so automatic that they'd cease breaking down under match pressure. Beyond that, my habits of thinking and feeling remained deeply negative on the court. The two most insidious emotions when it comes to performance are fear and anger, and I experienced more than my share of both. Still, Loehr had no doubt that he could turn me into a consistent peak performer on the tennis court if I were willing to devote a sustained period of time and effort to the task. It was no coincidence, he said, that I'd played so well that day in Florida. After four intensive days of practice, my mental habits had begun to change. "If you get angry and frustrated on the court," he told me, "all that says to me is that you've consistently accessed those emotions in the past, and so they're the ones most readily available to you. What's not so available are positive emotions, simply because you haven't spent much time stimulating them. These performer skills don't just appear spontaneously."

At the same time, Loehr increasingly came to believe—as I did—that the skills of peak performance are often overvalued and misused. "You don't have to be a great human being to compete at the highest levels in sports," he told me. "What you get with most great athletes are marginally well adjusted people with exceptional performer skills. Often they don't even know how they do it. Through a blend of instinct and experience, they become highly skillful at triggering emotions that are essential to achieving their performance goals. The reward is not just winning and fame and money. The ideal performance state—making powerful waves of stress and recovery in competition—is highly pleasurable, even thrilling, and it can be almost literally addictive. In the end, however, it's just a high. The real risk for these athletes is that they can so easily lose a connection to what they really feel. They get to the point where if they don't like the emotional state they're in, they use their performance skills to switch to feelings that they like better. A lot of them end up with no idea of who they really are."

In a similar sense, Csikszentmihalyi found that the capacity to experience flow is not necessarily a measure of wisdom or even a guarantee of good conduct in everyday life. A skilled bank robber or compulsive gambler can experience flow, for example. Even those who cultivate flow to highly productive and positive ends in one sphere often act far more chaotically and destructively in other parts of their lives. Csikszentmihalyi cites Pablo Picasso and Bobby Fisher as just two examples of this phenomenon. "Optimal experience is a form of energy," he concluded. "Energy is power, but power is only a means. . . . The flow experience is not 'good' in an absolute sense. The goals to which it is applied can make life either richer or more painful."

Yet another expert on cultivating positive thoughts and emotions eventually came to the same conclusion. Martin Seligman, a professor of psychology at the University of Pennsylvania, helped pioneer the field of cognitive psychology, which posits that how we feel and perform is largely a function of how we think. In his best-selling book *Learned Optimism,* Seligman makes the case that people can be systematically taught to think more positively, even about events that they've habitually found upsetting and stressful. But effective as he believes his techniques are, Seligman recognizes a cost to the positive thinking that characterizes many of the people he's spent years studying—most notably life insurance agents. "What they gain they also pay for," he told me over lunch one afternoon in Philadelphia. "They sacrifice wisdom for likability and cheerfulness. Who wants to spend an evening with people who tell you the upside of everything? It makes me very uneasy and arouses a lot of negative emotion in me. When I'm around people like that, I find I just want to get out of there."

Indeed, while he's spent much of his professional life promoting the virtues of optimism, Seligman sees an increasingly complex picture. "There's a trade-off between the virtues of optimism and its costs," he told me. "If you decide you're going to be successful and not depressed and your immune system is going to be perky, optimism is a virtue. But it may also require blissful ignorance and even denial. It may even be that optimism and a deeper level of wisdom are antagonistic. Given a choice, I myself choose wisdom." The best balance, Seligman now believes, is something he calls "flexible optimism." In this state, he has written, "you can choose to use optimism when you judge that less depression, or more achievement, or better health is the issue. . . . [But] we must have the courage to endure pessimism when its perspective is valuable. What we want is not blind optimism . . . but optimism with its eyes opened."

Loehr has experienced precisely this conflict in his own life. Valued for his achievements from an early age, he learned over time to trigger powerfully the positive thoughts and emotions that best serve performance. He has written some ten books on performance and has emerged as one of the country's leading sports psychologists. As an athlete, he won a national singles championship for professional tennis teachers and the doubles title five consecutive years. Along the way, he's become adept at keeping painful and troubling feelings at bay. "I've done whatever it's taken to be a success, and in the process I've pushed away uncomfortable feelings that didn't fit the script," he told me. "What I've sacrificed is evolving into a fully integrated person comfortable with all of my feelings. I just don't have access to certain emotions. There's something still missing in my life."

Loehr now believes that the ultimate challenge is to find a balance between an internal and an external focus. "If you don't develop and utilize your performer skills you probably won't accomplish much. Your talent and skill will remain largely untapped," he explained recently. "On the other hand, if your Performer Self dominates your personality, important needs of the Real Self often get suppressed and therefore remain unmet. . . . A sense of alienation sets in, values break down and things suddenly stop making sense." Often, Loehr has seen, the motivation for prompting certain positive emotions is simply to avoid suffering. "Although somewhat effective in reducing pain," he concluded, "the problem with blunting personal awareness is that you progressively lose contact with the truth."

After spending most of his own career promoting the virtues of the ideal performance state, Loehr, too, has found himself seeking a richer blend of capacities. "The most exciting part of learning to access this ideal performance state is that it empowers people," he told me. "When you understand how you can control your chemistry on the tennis court, that's going to help you perform close to your potential. You can also bring those skills to other areas to serve your deepest values." Nonetheless, Loehr says, performance is only part of the story. "In the end, the truth is the one thing that frees you and gives you comfort," he told me. "If you constantly try to defend against it in order to avoid pain, you'll eventually find yourself walking around with a smile on the outside, and a fanatical sense of emptiness on the inside. It's only when you embrace the truth—including the pain—that the real healing begins."

7

WAKING UP

Montague Ullman, Jeremy Taylor, and
the Wisdom of Dreams

*It is certainly true that there are dreams that embody
suppressed wishes and fears, but what is there that the
dream cannot, on occasion, embody? Dreams may give
expression to ineluctable truths, to philosophical pro-
nouncement, illusions, wild fantasies, memories, plans,
anticipations, irrational experiences, even telepathic visions and heavens knows what besides.*
—CARL JUNG

*From the standpoint of spiritual growth, the purpose of
dreamwork . . . is to tap into the deepest resources of
your self in order to bring up hidden potentials and
integrate them into your working life.*
—LOUIS SAVARY

I WAS drawn by the alluring mystery of dreams: the
many levels on which they operate and the window
they provide into what we've not yet seen in waking
life. Where optimal performance depends on the capacity for
willful action in the world, dreams arise unbidden from the
unconscious. While performing calls for narrow, highly focused
attention, working with dreams requires an open receptivity to
messages that frequently seem unfathomable at first, and even
alien. More than anything else I came across, dreams provided
regular access to an uncensored and unvarnished level of truth

about my inner experience. Above all, I was drawn to the modern dreamworkers who have moved dreams out of the confines of the analyst's office and into everyday group settings. The result is that nearly anyone seeking access to the wisdom of the unconscious can now learn to work productively with dreams.

It was Sigmund Freud, of course, who established the modern framework for understanding dreams, largely in the context of psychoanalysis. Freud published *The Interpretation of Dreams* in 1900 and asserted that "dreams [are] the royal road to a knowledge of the unconscious activities of the mind." In simple terms, Freud saw dreams as highly veiled expressions of repressed sexual and aggressive wishes dating to early childhood. Dreaming, he said, represents the satisfaction of these forbidden impulses. Freud believed that dreams express themselves in symbols in order to disguise from dreamers their consciously unacceptable urges. A trained analyst is challenged, he said, not just to decode dream symbols but to help patients to acknowledge the unpleasant truths about the meaning of their dreams. Doing so, he concluded, is a powerful tool for resolving the deepest neurotic conflicts.

Any modern practitioner who works with dreams owes an enormous debt to Freud. He established ingeniously that dreams have a meaning, usefulness, and deep intelligence that isn't readily apparent from their often bizarre, often nonsensical manifest content. In turn, it was Freud's onetime disciple Carl Jung who developed the theory of dreams that helped to spawn the modern dreamwork movement. Jung, who broke with Freud in 1914, came to view dreams not as repressed wishes but as reflections of the drive for growth and wholeness, or what he called individuation. For example, Jung saw in the characters in people's dreams rich evidence of the "shadow." The shadow, in Jung's terms, is composed of the parts of oneself that are deemed unacceptable and thus get denied or projected onto others. In the end, Jung said, this shadow material must be reowned if one is to be whole. Jung also observed in dreams an archetypal imagery that transcends individual concerns and reflects recurring universal conflicts—themes that dominate mythology. He even found that dreams may have a psychically predictive function—accurately pointing toward future possibilities as well as potential pitfalls.

Above all, Jung focused on the everyday role that dreams can play in restoring psychological equilibrium, by bringing to conscious attention feelings that have been shunted aside. "Dream symbols," he wrote, "are the essential message carriers from the instinctive to the rational parts of the human mind, and their interpretation enriches the poverty of consciousness so that it learns to understand again the forgotten language of the instincts." Jung argued that a dream may be interpreted on many levels simultaneously. "No dream symbol," he wrote, "can be separated from the individual who dreams it, and there is no definite or straightforward interpretation of any dream." In effect, Jung returned to dreamers the authority to conjure with their own dreams, rather than claiming, as Freud did, that dream interpretation be left solely to highly trained psychoanalysts. "It ought not matter to me whether the result of my musings on the dream is scientifically verifiable or tenable," Jung wrote. "I may allow myself only one criterion for the result of my labors: Does it work?"

Theorists have since suggested more than a dozen levels of potential significance in any given dream. There is relatively broad agreement, for example, that all dreams address the dreamer's current circumstances. Beyond that, dreams regularly make reference to specific unresolved conflicts and issues from the dreamer's past, much as Freud originally suggested. Some theorists believe that it is possible to glean from dreams information about the state of one's physical health. In addition, dreams can comment on broader social issues connected to the dreamer's life and on his or her religious or spiritual growth. Finally, several modern theorists share Jung's controversial claim that dreams can be specifically predictive of future events—long a tenet of certain ancient wisdom traditions. At one time or another, I have discovered each of these levels in my own dreams.

The modern era in dreamwork began in the early 1950s with two events. The first grew out of research by two University of Chicago researchers—Nathan Kleitman and Eugene Aserinsky—into the phenomenon called rapid eye movement sleep. It is in this less deep stage of sleep, the two researchers discovered, that people dream. They do so in each REM cycle, at least four or five times in an average night, whether they remember their dreams or not. Around the same time, a psychologist and academic researcher named Calvin Hall founded the Institute of Dream Research at the University of California at Santa Cruz. Trained as a Freudian but dissatisfied with highly subjective psychoanalytic interpretations based on a limited population of patients, Hall set out to study the dreams of a wider cross-section of average people. He published *The Meaning of Dreams* in 1953.

Building on Jung's quarrel with Freud, Hall began by contending that dreams have no intent to mislead the dreamer. To the contrary, he concluded that a picture is literally worth a thousand words. The language of visual image and metaphor, he argued, "reveals in the clearest, most economical way possible the *present* state of the dreamer's life." Only much later did neurological evidence emerge suggesting that the right hemisphere serves as the brain's primary link to the unconscious, from which dreams spring, and that the left hemisphere's job is to make sense of these images. But even in the 1950s, Hall intuitively recognized that such a process occurred. "The goal of dream interpretation," he wrote, "is to discover the meaning of a dream by translating images into ideas."

Hall called his method "content analysis," and his goal was to assess the meaning of dreams objectively and scientifically. An analysis of some ten thousand dreams led him to conclude that they serve as an extension and amplification of the dreamer's everyday experience. "On the whole," he found, "the dreamer is concerned with himself, his relationships with those close to him, and his conflicts and anxieties." Hall went on to assert that dreams persistently deal with the attempt to resolve five basic human conflicts: freedom and security; right and wrong; masculinity and femininity; life and death; and love and hate in the parent-child relationship. Sure enough, my own dreams and those I listened to in groups focused overwhelmingly on these conflicts. I came to believe, however, that Hall left out at least one key conflict—between one's personal concerns and those that transcend the self. Hall himself simply never acknowledged any spiritual dimension in the thousands of dreams he analyzed. "Dreams are not mysterious, supernatural, or esoteric phenomena," he insisted, taking a view I came to see as too narrow. "They are not messages from the gods nor are they prophecies of the future. The meaning of a dream will not be found in some theory about dreams; it is right there in the dream itself. . . . Any clear-headed person should be able to interpret dreams."

Hall's work was primarily theoretical. Perhaps the first well-known psychiatrist to bring dreams out of the analyst's office and into a more public setting was Fritz Perls. At Esalen in the late 1960s, Perls began working with one person at a time before a large group of onlookers. His main prop was the empty chair he called the "hot seat." A volunteer sat in a chair alongside Perls, then moved in and out of this chair in order to play the role of individual characters and objects from the dream. The Gestalt technique was to treat everything in a dream as an aspect of the dreamer's own personality—and to prompt dialogues with these different parts of the self. Doing so, Perls said, invariably revealed what he referred to as a "topdog" and an "underdog."

The topdog generally served as the punishing boss—roughly analogous to Freud's superego—while the underdog represented the aspect of one's personality that had been denied or projected onto others—akin to Jung's shadow. Splitting off this underdog, Perls concluded, created a "hole" in the personality. This might take the form of an absence of self-confidence, for example, or a lost capacity for assertion. This hole has to be acknowledged, accepted, and integrated, Perls said, in order for the person to become more truly whole. Because dreams provide uncensored access to the underdog, he found, they served as an ideal vehicle through which to conduct the therapeutic process. While Perls helped guide the dialogues that dreamers had with the characters in their dreams, his clients finally produced their own insights.

Dreamwork first reached a mass audience in 1972 when Ann Faraday, an Australian-born psychologist, wrote *Dream Power,* the first best-selling book about dreams. Her goal was to begin integrating the work of disparate dream theorists in order to produce a more comprehensive and accessible method of dream interpretation. As different as Jung, Hall, and Perls were in their ideas, for example, Faraday argued that they shared certain fundamental ideas. The first was that dreams address one's present life situation and feelings, even as they simultaneously shed light on unresolved childhood conflicts. Second, they all agreed that dreams are best interpreted at whatever level the dreamer himself finds most useful and significant—even when that simply means taking dream images, or the manifest content, at face value. A dream about anger toward another person, for example, might simply be a way of focusing more of one's attention on precisely that conflict. Finally, Jung, Hall, and Perls agreed that working with dreams can be useful not only to those actively engaged in psychotherapy but to people trying to deal with the ordinary issues of everyday life. Faraday herself went on to posit that dreams provide three kinds of insight: into real-life events that have yet to be fully understood; into the dreamer's subjective and often distorted way of perceiving real-life events; and finally into the dreamer's deepest inner self.

An organized dreamwork movement began to emerge in 1982, with the founding of a newsletter called *Dream Network Bulletin.* The following year, the Association for the Study of Dreams (ASD) was launched by a group of dreamworkers in northern California. Its stated purpose was to "promote a greater professional and public appreciation of the dreaming process, and to provide a forum for eclectic interdisciplinary communication among those studying and working with dreams." Rather than treating dreams as the exclusive province of psychotherapists, the association opened itself to scientists, philosophers, religious leaders, and even to lay people with a special interest in dreams.

It also took an interest in more unusual forms of dreamwork such as lucid dreaming—the capacity to become fully conscious while dreaming and to voluntarily affect the content of the dream. I myself was most drawn to ordinary dreams and the rich trove of unconscious material they provide each night. Above all, I was attracted to the group dreamwork done by two practitioners: Jeremy Taylor, a writer and Unitarian minister from San Rafael, California, and Montague Ullman, a self-described "recovering psychoanalyst" from Ardsley, New York.

When I met Jeremy Taylor in 1989, he was forty-six years old and had already spent more than twenty years working with thousands of people's dreams in varied settings—schools, hospitals, prisons, and even a home for schizophrenic adolescents. Early in his work, Taylor became convinced that dreams are best shared in a group setting. Doing so, he found, permits the dreamer to benefit from multiple points of view. Group work showed him that dreams carry many layers of meaning simultaneously. In addition, it takes advantage of the power of dreams to cut past everyday pretense, artifice, and posturing and thus connect people at a very intimate level. Beyond that, Taylor came to believe that however bizarre, conflict-ridden, and upsetting dreams may seem to be, they ultimately serve what he calls "wholeness." Dreams, he determined, can be a source not just of self-discovery but of shared concerns, common goals, and even spiritual awakening. "Over time, a reliable perception builds up in people who share dreams that life makes sense, that it is a purposeful enterprise," Taylor told me. "You begin to see that it is possible through the open-hearted practice of dreamwork to align oneself with the larger purposes of the cosmos."

A bearish man with a salt-and-pepper beard, a warm smile, and a gentle manner, Taylor grew up in difficult circumstances. His father left for World War II just after he was born, didn't return to the family for four years, and even then stayed only several months before leaving for good. He was raised by his mother, who earned a living by teaching English in prep schools around Buffalo. Because she was working, Taylor was forced to fend for himself from an early age. Even so, the experience of his father's brief return ultimately proved more traumatic to Taylor than his later absence or his mother's problems. It was in the course of working with his dreams during his early forties that Taylor began to vividly recall having been sexually assaulted as a four-year-old by his father. When he told his mother what he'd remembered, she simply denied that it could be true. Suddenly, however, much of the mystery about his life became clear to Taylor: the origins of his pervasive mistrust of all adult authority, his deep sense of loneliness and isolation, and the free-floating anxiety he'd been plagued by for so many years.

As a teenager, Taylor channeled antiauthoritarian energies into organizing against the war in Vietnam. "I encouraged my contemporaries to apply for conscientious-objector status, on the grounds that the adult male authority system perpetuating the war was not to be trusted," he told me. "It wasn't for many years that I began to see why the issue of abusive authority had such a special charge for me." A good student, Taylor won a scholarship to the State University of New York at Buffalo. Afterwards, he sought and won conscientious-objector status. One of the requirements was that he undertake some form of alternative service.

In 1969, Taylor moved to Oakland, California, to work at a local community action organization. To his surprise, he turned out to be the only white employee on an otherwise all-black staff. The Black Power movement was in its heyday and he was not warmly welcomed. Other whites—most of them highly educated and upper-middle class—had worked as volunteers in the organization, only to be forced out when they were accused by people in the community of being condescending and unconsciously racist. The residue was a great deal of acrimony and tension on all sides. Taylor himself was given clerical tasks such as filing, making coffee, and answering phones.

Eager for something more productive to do, Taylor came up

with the notion of a weekly training seminar titled "Overcoming Racism." He invited as participants all of the white volunteers who had been thrown out earlier. More than a dozen showed up, but the sessions soon degenerated into acrimony. Desperate to change the tenor of the group, Taylor suggested one day that they try sharing their dreams—particularly those with any apparent racial content. The idea occurred to him because it had proved unexpectedly useful in his own life. In the course of arguing bitterly over issues of male-female roles and sexism, he and his wife had spontaneously begun relating dreams to each other that bore on their conflicts. Their dreams revealed to them unconscious fears that each brought to the relationship but hadn't previously recognized. Buttressed by this new level of mutual understanding, the tensions between them ameliorated.

Very quickly, the atmosphere at Taylor's seminar changed in a similar way. As dreams were shared, the tone of blame and confrontation diminished. It soon became obvious that many in this all-white group shared nightmarish dreams of being menaced, attacked, and demeaned, often by people of other races. Grim as these emotions were, it dawned on several group members that their most frightening images had less to do with other people than with their own underlying fears and inner demons. Beneath their carefully cultivated personas, the participants discovered, lay more vulnerable emotions. These ranged from insecurity to a simple hunger for love and connection.

What resulted from sharing dreams, Taylor told me, was "a greater sense of compassion—for themselves and for one another—and a renewed sense of hope." Nearly all the volunteers eventually went back to working with the mostly black community residents. "Within a few weeks our organization was getting unsolicited testimonials from people in the community about the quality of the volunteers' work and their sensitivity," Taylor told me. "I figured I'd just keep doing this dreamwork until I decided what I really wanted to do. A couple of years down the road, I realized that I'd found what I wanted to do with my life."

Taylor accepted work in any setting where he found an

interest in dreams. His groups at the local Unitarian church in Berkeley were so well received, for example, that the congregation eventually decided to ordain him as a teaching minister. Taylor developed a group approach that ran completely counter to traditional psychoanalytic method. No one in his groups served as an authority. In Taylor's view, only the dreamer could say for certain what his dream finally meant. The touchstone for such understanding is what he calls the "aha experience"—a felt shift that occurs in one's body when an evocative insight about a dream truly hits home. Even the most brilliant interpretation offered by an outsider doesn't amount to much, Taylor concluded, if it doesn't resonate emotionally for the dreamer.

For me, this felt experience became a reliable way to sort through the invariably contradictory interpretations of a dream that any given person might have to offer. By seeing that the experience of a dream is highly subjective, Taylor came to believe that no single self-limited approach can do a dream justice. Each of the major schools of thought regarding dreams are right, he argued, but only so far as they go. "Do we throw away an orange because it isn't an apple or a peach?" he asked in his most recent book, *Where People Fly and Water Runs Uphill.* "All these theories are quite useful and none need to be excluded from our investigations."

Taylor's personal approach is relatively unstructured. He begins his groups with what he calls a "touch in"—inviting everyone to say at least something about what's been going on in their lives. This helps to relax everyday barriers and to build the atmosphere of intimacy and honesty in which dreamwork thrives. Taylor also does a brief centering exercise—a meditative technique aimed at quieting the mind so that it becomes easier to connect to unconscious feelings and intuitions. Finally, he asks each person to briefly share a recent dream. This process reinforces trust, he says, by putting everyone on the same self-revelatory ground. After one person in a group agrees to work on a dream, Taylor permits the process to unfold spontaneously—with one central caveat. Concerned about protecting the dreamer's sense of safety, he asks that all group members begin their comments with the phrase "If it were my dream . . ." In this way, Taylor has found, the inevitable tendency for people to project their own prejudices is acknowledged up front. The dreamer is then free to make use of interpretations that he finds useful and to discard those he does not.

This group process can be remarkably powerful even when the dreamer offers only fragmentary memories. Perhaps the most extraordinary example of such an experience occurred during a dream group that Taylor was teaching at a theological seminary in Berkeley in the late 1980s. One participant—call him Mike—regularly reported to the group that he never remembered even the smallest fragment of a dream and therefore had nothing to share. Increasingly frustrated, Taylor decided to push Mike harder for memories. When this failed, Taylor tried another way to jog the student's unconscious. "What would your dream have been like this morning if you *had* been able to remember one?" he asked. Mike still had no response, but moments later, he suddenly offered a tiny memory. "Maybe there were some pastel colors in my dream last night," he said. Taylor decided to let the group take a stab at this fragment. Dutifully they offered their associations to the notion of pastel colors, but none prompted a response from Mike. Finally, one group member had an idea. "Is there any association in your mind," he asked, "between the word *pastel* and the word *pastoral*?"

Sure enough, Mike had an immediate aha. It struck him, he said, that his commitment to the pastoral life—he was then studying to be a minister—was "distinctly pastel." This prompted a rush of associations from other members of the group and from Mike himself. Very quickly, it emerged that Mike had been pursuing seminary training to please his parents, that it didn't truly interest him, and that his studies hadn't touched his deepest spiritual longings. As he began to express these feelings, the frustration and anger beneath Mike's gentle facade came pouring out. Condensed into this lone bland image was a welter of powerful emotions that he had completely suppressed.

Taylor, meanwhile, had one other strong association to Mike's dream fragment. One of the pastel colors that he wasn't remembering, Taylor thought, might be lavender. If the dream were his, Taylor concluded, it might be about being gay. As it happened, Taylor chose to keep the thought to himself. It was quite a leap to make, Mike had already contended with a lot that night, and the issue of sexual orientation was not something that Taylor felt comfortable introducing in a group setting. He decided that he'd mention the association to Mike privately. As it turned out, he never got the chance. In the weeks that followed, Mike increasingly withdrew from his classmates, stopped doing his work, and quit attending his classes—including the dream group. At the end of the semester, he decided to drop out of the seminary. He moved into nearby San Francisco and took a job at a bank, where he eventually became quite successful. Eventually, Taylor learned that Mike not only came out of the closet but became a prominent gay activist.

For Taylor, it was a powerful lesson in the value of engaging the shadow. In Mike's case, his shadow took the form of a pastel color—a side of himself he feared and had disowned but at a considerable cost. "These ugly, scary, dark, powerful, sexy, violent, irresponsible, dangerous dream figures are vitally alive parts of [our] own authentic being," Taylor has written. "By increasing [our] self-acceptance . . . repressions are released, projections withdrawn and even the most fundamental, ingrained and habitual patterns of self-deception and destructive behavior are transformed." The irony, Taylor concluded, is that these darker aspects of ourselves retain power in our lives only so long as we resist them. "When we admit to ourselves that we are evil as well as good," he explained, "the energy previously wasted in repetitive, unconscious neurotic behavior is released and made available . . . for conscious, choiceful, creative use."

I eventually participated in several of Taylor's workshops, and I saw his process vividly at work one afternoon when we worked on the dream of a shy, prim, soft-spoken woman in her fifties whom I'll call Ann. At first, she was reluctant even to tell a dream that she considered so seamy and repulsive. Finally, though, Ann's hunger to understand the dream's bizarre and vivid images compelled her to share it. The dream was built around a visit that she made to two highly religious friends in her life. At one point in the dream, Ann rose from a couch in the living room to go to the bathroom, only to discover that the toilet on the second floor was overflowing. "Something is really wrong with your plumbing," she told her friends. Feces—a word she had to struggle to say out loud—were coming through the ceiling and staining a pale-color rug in the living room. Agitated and eager to escape, Ann began a steady retreat toward the door as the puddles of sewage kept rising. Meanwhile, her friend simply refused to acknowledge what was happening. Ann herself never did walk out the door. That was as much of the dream as she remembered.

When the group began to work with these images, we were as surprised as Ann was to discover that her associations were actually quite positive and hopeful. Ann connected the overflowing feces to a capacity to express freely feelings that she'd long held in. She recognized in her friend's lack of concern about the rising mess on the carpet a side of herself that transcended attachment to image and material concerns. Finally, Ann's willingness in the dream to endure deep discomfort without finally fleeing—to stand her ground in the face of this mess—struck her as evidence of an emerging willingness to hold true to her convictions. She'd been taking a great deal of flak from her own family for straying from their fundamentalist religious beliefs, and Ann took the dream as evidence that she was making the right choice for herself. The fact that she was able to describe this disturbing dream to a group of strangers was an act of both assertiveness and liberation. As I watched Ann work with her dream images in our group, I could see how emboldened she felt by what she'd unexpectedly discovered. Just as Taylor had suggested, acknowledging and even embracing a dark and messy side of her self had served to defuse its imagined power.

Perhaps no one is as responsible for establishing a systematic approach to modern dreamwork as Montague Ullman. Trained first as a physician, Ullman went on to become a psychoanalyst, where he began working with dreams. Eventually, he grew disenchanted with the limits of the Freudian perspective and developed a passion for less doctrinaire dreamwork done in groups. Even there, however, his approach reflects his scientific training. I was drawn to him by the clarity and open-mindedness of his work. A gentle, diminutive, and self-effacing man, Ullman is now in his seventies and spends most of his time writing and running dream groups. He brings to this work a rich and eclectic background.

Raised in Manhattan, Ullman was the son of Jewish parents who deeply valued education and traditional achievement. From early in his life, he felt ambivalent about his parents' bourgeois materialistic values. But even as he dabbled in interests ranging from dreams to psychic phenomena, Ullman continued to excel academically. He entered City College shortly before his fifteenth birthday and was admitted to medical school at New York University just three years later. Although he felt far less worldly than his older classmates, Ullman was excited by the prospect of becoming a doctor.

In time, his interests focused on the mind, and he studied both neurology and psychiatry. Within several years, however, he gave up neurology to enter psychoanalytic training. His studies were interrupted in 1942 by the war, but after he returned, Ullman spent more than a decade seeing patients in a psychoanalytic practice and working with their dreams. To his surprise, he found that several of his patients appeared to have had psychic or telepathic experiences in their dreams. "They were picking up things about my life that they couldn't have inferred or known about in any ordinary way," Ullman told me. "It left me with a deep conviction that there was more to the nature of reality than we'd thought."

It wasn't until 1961, after he was hired to create a department of psychiatry at Maimonides Hospital in Brooklyn, that Ullman had the time and resources to explore scientifically some of these clinical observations. Eager to look more into both dreams and psychic phenomena, he devised a series of fascinating, carefully controlled experiments. Ullman's goal was to see whether a sleeping subject might be able to produce telepathic dreams under laboratory conditions. The protocol was to have a waking subject look at a free-hand drawing or a striking photograph, then attempt to "send" it telepathically to a sleeping subject in another room. As soon as the subject had finished a stage of REM sleep, he was awakened and asked to describe what he had been dreaming. Independent evaluators were then asked to compare the images in the dream with the drawing or photograph that the first subject had tried to send telepathically.

In nine of twelve studies that Ullman conducted, the similarities were judged to be statistically significant—meaning that chance alone could not explain the results. Ullman and his colleagues published a series of papers about their findings. In an altered state of consciousness such as dreaming, they concluded, telepathic events occur regularly, and so do precognitive ones in which people accurately predict future events. Beyond demonstrating for Ullman the reality of psychic phenomena, these experiments had another impact on him. "They led me to believe that dreams are concerned with our connectedness to one another," he told me, "and that the psychic mechanism can be called on to maintain that connectedness."

By day, Ullman spent his time launching and overseeing a community mental health center. In the course of devising ways to deliver psychological services to large numbers of people, he began to focus on how he might take dreamwork out of the narrow world of individual psychotherapy into a broader group setting. As it turned out, he didn't find an opportunity until he left Maimonides in 1974 and accepted an invitation to teach mental health workers and psychology graduate students in Gothenburg, Sweden. The students were studying to become psychoanalysts, and when it came time to talk about dreams, he decided to experiment by bringing his first fifteen young students together and seeing if they might learn more by working together on their own dreams.

The work in Sweden helped Ullman to crystallize several basic observations. He began with the view that dreams always have current value and significance. Beyond that, he came to believe that all dreams are connected in some way to the unfinished emotional business of the previous day, as well as to memories from the past that one might not ordinarily remember in waking life. And finally, he observed that dreams are always profoundly honest—reflecting not how we might like to be seen but how we truly see ourselves.

When Ullman returned to the United States, he began introducing his group techniques to lay people who had expressed an interest in working on their dreams. "I became convinced," he told me, "that the best environment for dreamwork is not the therapeutic hour but a small supportive group. That's where you get the time and the many points of view that a dream deserves." The group, in turn, takes over the therapist's primary function. "In a dream, you are involuntarily presented with an honest picture of who you are," he explained. "Awake, we are not as honest with ourselves. The social facade takes over. We don't want intimate things to be seen, and so we rationalize, deny, suppress, distance, and detach ourselves. The group process helps us cut through all of this."

Like Taylor, Ullman begins by creating an environment conducive to the sharing of dreams. "If you're going to undress psychically, you have to feel safe," he explained by way of introduction to the first dreamwork seminar I attended at his home. The members of our group included two artists, a meditation teacher, and several psychotherapists. Sure enough, as they introduced themselves, several expressed apprehension about sharing highly personal dreams with a group of strangers. I had just the opposite feeling. Revealing myself to people I'd never met and probably wouldn't see again didn't seem so difficult. Later, when I launched a dream group of my own that included people I knew but wasn't used to speaking with intimately, I found it much more daunting to share my dreams. Even then, however, adopting Ullman's techniques made it easier. No one is ever compelled to share a dream in his groups, and the dreamer always controls the process—free to reveal only as much as he chooses to, and to stop at any point. Like Taylor, Ullman is careful to protect the dreamer by encouraging group members to describe only their own experience of a given dream—and not to assume that their interpretation is "right."

Ullman's step-by-step approach provides a way for the dreamer to explore with increasing depth the imagery, metaphors, and real-life context of the dream and to make use of any associations that come up along the way. Typically, Ullman spends an hour and a half on a single dream—about double Taylor's average. He prefers to work with a dream that occurred the previous night, on the grounds that any recent events which may have triggered the dream are more likely to remain vivid. Once a volunteer agrees to work on a dream, he shares it with the group but without offering any associations. Each member of the group writes the dream down exactly as it was dictated. In the second stage, the group is asked to think of the dream as their own and, in turn, to offer associations to its imagery, as well as to describe any emotions that the dream brings up for them.

Because the dreamer hasn't yet offered any real-life context for the dream, the group members are offering interpretations that represent pure projections. What they say may or may not trigger connections and insights for the dreamer. Almost invariably, however, this process helps members of the group connect more deeply and personally to the dream. "We all swim in the same metaphorical sea," Ullman told us. "Even if the projections aren't always right on target, my experience has been that having other people share their feelings about the dream helps loosen up the dreamer's own defensiveness. And that sets the stage for the rest of the process."

Trying to imagine another person's dream as my own proved very revealing. I began to see how automatically I projected my own prejudices, opinions, hopes, and fears onto another person's images and by extension how I bring these subjective feelings to interactions in all my relationships. I soon realized that it is impossible to provide an objective interpretation of another person's dream. Nor is there any guarantee that even the most brilliant insight will prove helpful to the dreamer. Rather, I found that I could be far more helpful by simply describing as honestly and searchingly as possible what the dream brought up for me by association. In the process, I often revealed as much about myself as I did about the dreamer.

In the course of this first workshop, a woman my age—call her Rebecca—described a dream that dealt with the fact that she'd been consciously keeping her distance from men for several years. This decision, she told us, followed a series of painful relationships, and she felt very happy, she said, to be on her own. For me, several images in her dream suggested just the opposite: that for all her hurt and fear, she retained a passionate desire to truly let go and open herself up to a more intimate relationship. At one point, marshaling all the evidence I could gather and feeling full of enthusiasm about my penetrating analysis of her images, I offered up an interpretation. Rebecca had virtually no response. What I said seemed to waft over her like a cool breeze. Only later did it occur to me that the conflict I'd been describing was fundamentally my own—fear and desire deeply intertwined—and that I'd experienced it precisely by embracing her dream as if it were mine. It was possible that what I had deduced simply wasn't true for Rebecca, or perhaps she simply wasn't prepared to accept it. I never found out the answer, but the experience was valuable. I saw not just how easy it is to project one's feelings onto others but how group dreamwork can be useful even when one's own dream isn't up for discussion.

In Ullman's third stage, the dreamer takes over. Using any of the group projections that he finds useful, as well as his own associations, the dreamer begins to develop his own thoughts and feelings about the dream. Then, the group gets involved again by trying to help the dreamer clarify the recent context that led to the dream. This includes recalling real-life events, people, or emotions that connect to the dream, particularly anything that occurred during the previous evening. If the dreamer wants to go still further, group members take turns reading the dream aloud in segments as a way of bringing the dreamer's attention to any images that remain unexplored. Ullman calls the concluding stage "orchestration." Here the group attempts a more informed version of projection, drawing not just on the dream images but on all of the detailed associations that the dreamer has now shared. The goal is to come up with some broad conclusions about what the dream is trying to say.

The first challenge of dreamwork is simply to remember dreams. At first, I found that I couldn't do so with any regularity. Taylor suggested several techniques that proved useful. The first was not to drink any alcohol (or take any mood-altering drug) before going to sleep, since intoxicants tend to obscure memory. Next, he suggested starting a dream journal—a book in which I would regularly record my dreams, my associations, and any initial interpretations that I might have. Next, Taylor suggested developing a ritual of placing this journal next to my bed and writing the date at the top of a given page. As I drifted off to sleep, he suggested that I try to focus my thoughts exclusively on the desire to recall a dream. The unconscious, Taylor and others believe, is more receptive in a sleepy state and can be seeded with specific intentions.

Taylor suggested that I keep a pen with its own light by my bed, so that if I awoke during the night, I could write down dreams without having to turn on an overhead light. I prefer not to rouse myself at four or five o'clock, so I devised an alternative technique that worked for me. When I did remember a dream in a half-sleep in the middle of the night, I learned to tell it back to myself and then give it a title. The title by itself almost always helped to trigger the rest of the dream when I awoke the next morning. At that point, I was careful not to get up too abruptly, since this shift of consciousness usually caused me to lose any dream memories. Instead, I learned to lie quietly and wait to see if any dreams seeped back into my memory. As I followed this routine conscientiously, I started to remember dreams virtually every night—sometimes as many as three or four of them.

It is also possible, I learned, to "incubate" a dream. This technique was first used thousands of years ago as a means of tapping deeper wisdom and eliciting guidance. Taylor and other modern dreamworkers now teach it as a way of eliciting specific information of all kinds from the unconscious. "If we simply focus attention on the desire to remember dreams as our last intentional act before drifting off to sleep," he has written, "and combine that with a gentle focusing on specific issues, problems and situations that we wish to dream about, the dreams will usually oblige."

Rather than simply telling myself to remember a dream, Taylor suggested that I pose to myself a short, simple, and specific question. One night, for example, I asked whether a certain psychological technique that I found intriguing would be likely to help me overcome some of my underlying fear. I went to sleep hoping the answer would be a resounding yes. The next morning, I remembered five short, connected dream images. When I thought about the different male characters in each one, they had something unmistakable in common. All five were engaged in some sort of external action in their lives that was failing to yield the result they desired. The dreams, I eventually concluded, were clearly and repeatedly telling me that the technique I had in mind wasn't going to get me what I wanted. While this message disappointed me at the time, I eventually saw that it served me well. Exploring this technique would simply have diverted me from a very positive and productive course I was already on. In effect, I'd been barking up the wrong tree—and the dream told me so.

My wife, Deborah, had two experiences that demonstrated even more clearly the value of incubating dreams. In the first instance, she'd been suffering for several weeks from a painfully stiff neck. She was inclined to believe that the pain was related to certain stresses in her life, but this broad insight hadn't led to any physical relief. One night before bed, when Deborah was feeling particularly uncomfortable, I suggested that she ask herself to dream about why she was feeling so much pain in her neck. The next morning, she woke up with a dream in which a harsh older woman was criticizing her for being neglectful of our younger daughter, Emily. In real life, we'd recently returned from a week away, during which Emily had missed us a great deal. Later in the dream, the older woman brings Emily to Deborah. At that point, Emily climbs into Deborah's lap, gives her a huge hug, and starts chatting happily about what an adventure she's just had. On waking up, it hit Deborah immediately that she'd been carrying a terrible unconscious burden of guilt about leaving Emily. The pain in her neck was effectively serving as a punishment. The dream suggested that Emily hadn't truly suffered and that Deborah needn't feel guilty. Sure enough, within several hours the neck pain she'd been enduring for weeks completely disappeared.

More recently, Deborah was spending considerable time considering whether to leave her twenty-year career as a successful magazine editor, in order to return to graduate school in social work. Plainly, this represented a dramatic midlife career change, and she was struggling with the decision. In this instance, she asked herself to dream an answer to the question "What should I do with my career?" The next morning, Deborah woke up with a dream in which she was standing in a room that contained a big tank full of tropical fish. When she noticed that one of the fish was on the floor, flopping around, she threw it back into the tank, and the fish happily swam away. At that moment, the owner of the tank walked in. "I can't believe you did that," he told Deborah. "Someone was coming to get that fish." But Deborah was unrepentant. "I had to save it," she told the owner. "If I'd waited any longer, the fish would have died." As Deborah saw it, this dream was a powerful confirmation of her instinct to shift careers. She was, she believed, a fish out of water in her magazine career. Either she found a new place to swim, or she was going to shrivel up and die. It took Deborah another six months before she finally decided to make the change. Within a month after starting school, she had no doubt she'd made the right decision—and that she had found her calling. She hasn't looked back since.

A s I set out on this chapter, I realized that it would be useful to work on a dream of my own in a group setting and then to write about the experience. I decided to try a variation on the incubation technique. One night, as I was falling asleep, I asked myself to have a dream that might be appropriate to write about. I wasn't seeking any specific information. I simply hoped I'd get a dream interesting enough that it might give me an opportunity to demonstrate the value of dreamwork in a group. I got all that I asked for and considerably more: a richly evocative, multilayered dream that shed considerable light on my past, on my current circumstances, and even on my future. It was, in Jung's terms, a "big dream—the sort that is, he said, "often remembered for a lifetime, and not infrequently prove[s] to be the richest jewel in the treasure-house of psychic experience."

I also benefited from a wide range of responses to the dream. The first came in an established weekly dream group that Ullman had been leading for many years and that I joined for a short period. On the night that the group took up my dream, there were six people present. In addition to Ullman and myself, they included a businesswoman studying to be a psychoanalyst, a photographer, a schoolteacher, and a retired housewife. They ranged in age from early thirties to mid-seventies, and they were all experienced at working with dreams. What follows is the dream sequence I told them. Nearly all of the characters, it so happened, were real people from my life.

I am in my maternal grandmother's former apartment on Fifth Avenue, in New York City. She has died, and I'm wondering whether I might buy the apartment myself for a low price. I'm attracted because it has a view of Central Park, but I'm concerned that it's very small and it is only on the third floor. I'm also convinced that no amount of renovation will give it a nice kitchen.

Then I discover that Lisa, a wealthy woman I've known since childhood, has actually just bought the apartment for herself. Indeed, she's bought a total of five apartments on the same floor, intending to put them together. I learn that it wasn't her first choice to buy in this building, but she looked for a long time, couldn't find anything better, and finally settled. Lisa's black housekeeper is in the apartment, and she turns out to be an irascible woman with whom I somehow have to contend. I wonder if Lisa will permit me to stay in one of the bedrooms when I'm visiting New York City. I conclude that with her kids and her live-in housekeeper, there probably won't be room for me.

In the second sequence, I'm still in my grandmother's apartment, only this time I live there. I discover that my children have brought home a puppy. They're assuming that we'll keep it. Then I realize it's actually a kitten. I say to my wife, "No way—I hate cats." She says that our kids will take care of the kitten. I say, "You know there's no chance they'll do that." I also wonder if our dog will eat the kitten. Eventually, I realize that I'm powerless to overrule my wife and children and that we will indeed keep the kitten.

In the dream's final image my paternal grandfather is dying. Just before he does, I realize that he wants to punish someone— perhaps me—for a misdeed, by taking the person out to a woodshed and administering an old-fashioned paddling. I think it is weird that my grandfather's last act before dying is going to be to hurt someone. His explanation is that he's the only one who knows how to do this right, and I conclude that he must get pleasure from abuse.

Bizarre and disconnected as all these images seemed at first, I felt from the moment I awoke that the dream addressed many of the central issues in my life. By the time I shared it with Ullman's group, I'd given it considerable thought. It was certainly possible, I realized, to interpret the dream in classical Freudian terms—the expression of forbidden sexual and aggressive impulses. To the degree that I identify with my abusive grandfather in the dream, I can be seen as expressing a disguised impulse to kill my father or at least to push him off the stage. To the degree that I want to be back inside my grandmother's apartment—and my mother's, by association—I'm trying, in a veiled way, to consummate the Oedipal drama. But to work on the dream solely at that level seemed to me far too narrow and one-dimensional.

Instead, I offered up the dream to Ullman's group. Before they began throwing out their associations and projections, I clarified a few factual issues. The apartment in the dream had truly been my grandmother's. She has been dead for nearly a decade. The grandfather in the dream was truly my father's father, but in real life he died before I was born. The black housekeeper was not someone I specifically knew. The only strong emotion I connected to the dream sequence was bewilderment at my grandfather's actions.

Once I'd shared these facts, the group members were asked to take the dream as their own. While none of their initial projections provoked any powerful aha's for me, several touched on areas of the dream that felt significant. I agreed with the suggestion that the dream had something to do with my sense of not having enough space and struggling over how to be more comfortable. I also agreed that it addressed a conflict I had between the prestige and desirability of a Fifth Avenue apartment, set against the failure of even a luxurious home to fill my deeper needs. Finally, I agreed that my grandfather was trying to deliver some sort of message to me through his last act and that it had something to do with being a man.

In the next stage, I began to talk about my own associations. I mentioned that my grandmother had been a highly critical, unhappy, and difficult woman. I talked about her influence on my mother and the ways in which they were similar and troubling for me. I realized that Lisa, my high school friend, reminded me both of my mother and my grandmother. I was particularly moved by the dream image that no amount of money could make my grandmother's apartment's kitchen desirable. On a broader level, it struck me that no intervention could make the apartment itself a nourishing place to live. I was also struck that while Lisa only had use in the dream for four of the five bedrooms—her own, one for each of her two children, and one for the housekeeper—I didn't feel that she'd want me to use the free room. It occurred to me that there had been five people in my own family growing up and that we too had lived in an apartment on Fifth Avenue. Although the "fifth" bedroom in this apartment in the dream was unoccupied, somehow I could no longer go back to it. In short, the dream suggested that while I still hungered to find some comfort in this unhappy place from my childhood, I also recognized that it wasn't a welcoming environment anymore.

As for the dream's second sequence, I explained to the group that I've never liked cats, who seem to me cool, distant, and beyond control. By contrast, I find dogs more loving but also more dependent. Both dogs and cats require care and attention that I had long felt reluctant to provide. This part of the dream, I speculated, pointed up another way of looking at my conflict between the relative merits of dependence and independence. A pet provides companionship but makes demands. Independence is a form of freedom but sometimes at the expense of intimate connection with others. The dog-cat sequence also captured my ambivalence about being overruled by my wife and children. On the one hand, my authority is reduced in the dream, yet this turns out not to make me entirely unhappy. In spite of my instinctive resistance to adding another member to our household, my wife and children prevail because having a kitten matters to them so much. Heart triumphs over head, instinct over logic. This struck me as a message about the direction in which I needed to move in my own life.

The image of the punishing grandfather seemed to me most important of all. Although my grandfather died before I was born, the dream image reminded me of stories I'd heard over the years about his tyrannical style. It also happened to be the second time in several weeks that I'd depicted my grandfather in a dream as a strong but abusive man. My own father rarely exhibited anger or exercised any authority as I grew up. The apparent power in our family resided almost entirely with my mother. The dream hinted,

I told the group, at why my father had become the man he had—the feelings of anger and aggressiveness that he'd been forced to repress in order to survive his domineering father. It also suggested why he might have chosen to marry a critical and controlling woman—out of an unconscious need to perpetuate a familiar relationship from his childhood.

I've spent much of my own life mimicking my mother's style. Like her, I have sought control, asserted power through anger, and pushed hard to achieve. Like her, I have found it difficult and frightening to open my heart. In this sense, the dream image further amplified my conflict between wanting to build close and intimate relationships and fearing the threat to my sense of power and security. I felt certain, I told the group, that the impending death of my grandfather—and of the values he embodied—was significant, even though I wasn't yet quite sure how.

As the group drew me out about how the events of the previous day might have helped prompt the dream, I had a strong association to the black housekeeper. The previous evening, I'd seen the movie *Passion Fish,* in which the black actress Alfre Woodard plays the role of housekeeper to a white woman who has recently suffered an accident that leaves her paraplegic. The movie was slow, and I actually walked out before it ended. Nonetheless, I was drawn to the Woodard character. Unusually self-possessed, she demanded respect and was clearly independent, but she was also capable of expressing love. This was a balance, it occurred to me, that I longed to strike in my own life. One other association I had to recent events turned out to address this same issue. During the previous week, my wife had been away, and I'd been fully in charge of my children—literally, the housekeeper. By the night of the dream, I was feeling very happy that I'd been able to truly take care of my kids. This also made it possible for my wife to focus on work related to her impending new career, without having to worry about me or the children. Once again, the dream captured my struggle to redefine my role—in this case, within my own family.

By the time we reached the final stage that Ullman calls the orchestration, I'd shared a wide array of my own associations to the dream. Now, the group's challenge was to help me come to more specific conclusions. Nearly everyone had an overall take on what the dream was trying to say. This time, I felt a strong visceral response to much of what they offered up. One group member suggested that I seemed to be engaged in a conflict about whether the costs of seeking a certain level of material comfort—represented by the apartment on Fifth Avenue—might in the end outweigh the advantages. This was literally on the money. I'd been giving a great deal of thought to the question of moving to a less expensive house. I was eager to ease the financial pressure prompted by my having taken so long to write this book, and I also wanted to make it easier for Deborah to leave her job and return to school. The dream suggested this might be the right decision—even though doing so ultimately proved unnecessary. One of the men in the group picked up on the dog-cat themes in the second part of my dream. Noting that I'd referred to cats as less controllable than dogs and that the controlling grandfather in my dream was on the verge of death, he suggested that my own need for control and dominance might be giving way to a more nurturing style represented by the way I'd taken care of my children during my wife's absence.

At the end of the evening, Ullman himself sought to pull together what he saw as the central themes of my dream. He suggested that the movie *Passion Fish*—which, it so happened, he'd seen himself—had been a powerful factor in triggering the dream. The main character in the movie, he pointed out, is a woman of enormous drive. Despite a horrible accident, she retains her energy yet finds herself expressing it only in frustration and anger. What she learns, largely from the no-nonsense black house-keeper, is how to redirect this energy—to use it positively and usefully rather than abusively and hurtfully. This, Ullman suggested, was exactly the challenge that the dream posed to me. The powerful and abusive grandfather in my dream is dying. If I could take his energy and rechannel it, Ullman hypothesized, then I might have a whole new way to use power and strength—not to exercise control over other people but rather to work in their service.

"The dream is about an ongoing inner struggle," Ullman concluded. "For me, you're trying to transform a destructive, reactive energy into a loving, positive energy. A lot of your humanity was paralyzed by the circumstances under which you describe being brought up. You were subjected to the misuse of aggression, and now you're concerned about how to better use your aggression. The dream suggests that you can't simply eliminate the scar tissue and that you may even need to hold on to it for a little bit, just as you are trying to hold on to the old apartment. But it doesn't really suit you anymore. As you establish a new foundation, you can accept the scars and let your humanity blossom. Understandably, this is a painful process, and I think maybe that's why you walked out of the movie before it was over. But in effect, you finished the movie with your dream."

R ich as this work was, I remained eager to work on my dream in one of Taylor's groups—partly because I wondered if it could be seen from yet another perspective and partly because Taylor has an explicit interest in exploring the spiritual dimension of dreams. Ullman treads only tentatively in this territory—in part, through his work on telepathic dreams. "Our dream self has never lost sight of a basic truth," he has written. "Despite the manifold ways in which the human race has fragmented itself in the course of history, we are, nevertheless, all members of a single species." Taylor goes a step further. "I believe that everyone 'goes back to God' every night," he has written, "dissolving away the boundaries of our ordinary ego personalities, our worries about the passage of time and the inevitable approach of death, and the sense of anxious separateness from our deeper unconscious selves, each other and the Divine." Dreams begin, Taylor contends, wherever one's connection to a transcendent presence—a higher power—has been injured or broken. "All dreams, particularly the dreams of sincere seekers of spiritual experience," he has written, "will guide them directly to the roadblocks—to their histories of childhood injury, their current self-deceptions, and their repressed 'secret' desires and opinions—in short, to all the things that block the way and separate them from the felt sense of transcendent meaning in their lives."

When timing and geography made it impossible for me to attend one of Taylor's groups, he agreed to work with me directly on the dream. I began by sending it to him in written form, along with some of the initial associations that I'd shared with Ullman's group. Then we spent more than an hour talking about it by telephone. His first set of associations were intriguing, but several times he seemed to veer far off track. When that happened, I jumped in and told him so. He wasn't offended. Taylor believes that even a negative aha—the clear, felt experience that a certain association *isn't* what the dream is about—can point back toward its deeper significance. Indeed, the more we talked, the more I responded to Taylor's ideas.

On a broad level, he felt that my dream reflected a persistent effort to deal with a sense of limitation and frustration—about buying my grandmother's apartment, whether to get the kitten, and how to deal with my grandfather's abuse. This sense of limitation, Taylor suggested, seemed to originate in my grandparents' generation. "If it were my dream," he said, adopting his own technique, "the central issue would be about reconciling with my feminine energies. Because my father played a passive role, it predisposed me to see the feminine as the only legitimate mode of being. But at the same time, I received so much injury from the feminine—my mother—that I don't easily reach out and embrace this side of myself. What I'm left with is a sense of isolation. My difficulty engaging and connecting with the female figures in the dream—the grandmother, Lisa, the kitten, and the black housekeeper—helps explain my feeling of powerlessness and frustration. Just as Lisa settles for an apartment she doesn't really want, I believe that I've settled for less than the best with respect to my own emotional life."

I felt an even stronger connection to Taylor's insights when he linked them to the part of the dream that dealt with my grandfather. Here he saw certain universal themes at play—what Jung called "archetypal" issues. The dream begins, Taylor noted, in the exclusively feminine world of my mother, grandmother, and Lisa, but it ends up in the highly masculine world of my grandfather. Taylor thought it highly significant that I'd never met this man. The issue in the dream, he speculated, is less my relationship with my grandfather than the legacy he's leaving me—and what inheritance I'll choose to take from him. The issues in my own family, Taylor speculated, connect up with universal themes—the struggle over masculine and feminine principles and the relationship between death and rebirth. "In dreams, no matter how it appears," Taylor has argued, "death is always associated with the growth and development of personality and character." When one accepts and fully experiences death in a dream, Taylor says, it inevitably leads to an equally powerful experience of rebirth.

"It seems clear," he told me, "that the grandfather isn't going to die until he delivers his punishment to you. He's a powerful man who can stand up to the woman you've always feared in your life. At some level, this dream represents a transfer of energy, a passing on of the crown. He is about to die, and you are going to live. What seems to be the nastiest image in the dream—his abuse—also carries the greatest transformative potential for the future." Like Ullman, Taylor cited as a key issue my choice of whether to put my grandfather's abusive energy to more positive use. "In order for the personality . . . to evolve and mature," he has written, "the old self must die and make way for the new. This is a psychological and spiritual death we fearfully equate with physical death." In fact, Taylor told me, the real issue is rebirth. "Your dream suggests explicitly," he said, "that you want to use your energies differently—that the old apartment won't do, that you want to meet the needs of your own children in better ways than yours were met, and that it's critical to incorporate both masculine and feminine energies into your life. What you're searching for in the dream is new ground—not your grandmother's or your grandfather's, or your mother's or your father's, but a nourishing home of your own, with plenty of room and a better view of things."

It struck me, after talking with Taylor, that it may be nearly impossible to exhaust the meanings of a dream. Later, for example, I realized that even my relatively compact dream addressed all of the five fundamental issues that Calvin Hall concluded people dream about. It took up security and freedom through the issue of whether I could still be comfortable in my childhood apartment. It engaged questions of masculinity and femininity by way of my conflicted relationships with each of the dream's main characters. It addressed life and death through my grandfather's impending demise and its impact on me. By way of my many associations, the dream engaged the issue of love and hate in my relationship to my parents. Finally, it dealt with issues of right and wrong, through the dilemma of how to deal with my grandfather's threatened punishment.

The dream has continued to reverberate in my life for more than a year now. On one level, it gave me a unique glimpse into the forces that shaped my parents. For the first time, it led me to my grandfather—a man I had heard about only sparingly through my life. The more I thought about his paradoxical role in my dream, the more I believed I'd tapped into a new source of male energy—one that simply hadn't been available to me before. When I questioned my father after the dream, it became clear that he had indeed suffered from his grandfather's tyrannical style. In the dream, my grandfather rises up from his deathbed to teach me a lesson that I believe I have long needed to learn. I am put off by his style, but not by his intention. It has to do with the straightforward exercise of power. Someone in my dream has committed a misdeed, and a punishment is called for. No one else, my grandfather concludes, is willing to take on this responsibility. Even close to his own death, he will. And once he's finished in the woodshed, that will be the end of the incident. As I came to see it, he is exercising power justifiably and directly.

What he lacks is heart. The Alfre Woodard character—his female counterpart—is likewise tough-minded and direct, but she is also compassionate. I had something to learn from both of them.

Dreams, I came to believe, come not to tell us what we already know but to bring to awareness information that we're not yet conscious of in waking life. Dreams give lie to the facile notion that it is possible simply to transcend conflict. Personal issues are forever alive and kicking, whether or not we choose to engage them. By showing us so directly how we deceive ourselves, dreams are invariably humbling, but they also point us toward a more complete life. Ultimately, it dawned on me that my own dream reflected—for better and for worse and with uncensored precision—where I find myself at this point in the journey. "When read correctly [dream] images tell us who we are instead of who we *think* we are," Ullman says. "They speak to us about our actual impact on others, not about what we would like that impact to be. In short, they are honest, no-nonsense assessments of the immediate predicament . . . we are [in] at the time of the dreaming."

My own dream captured the distance I'd traveled, the unfinished business I still face, and the possibilities that lie ahead. It showed vividly the pain that persists in my life and revealed how much of my energy is still consumed by these conflicts. But the dream was also full of hope and promise. I had begun my search for wisdom consumed by external ambitions, disconnected from the most tender feelings in my heart, and distressed that outer achievement and the exercise of power hadn't given me the sense of inner strength and happiness that I'd long assumed they would. The dream provided some explanations. My old approach, it said, no longer worked, even if I sometimes still wished that it did. Embracing a new way required that I stop seeking sustenance from childhood wells long since run dry; that I find it instead by opening my heart to others in spite of my fears; and that I gather the courage to act more positively in the world by embracing a source of masculine power that the dream made me appreciate for

the first time in my life. If I were to sum up the dream's message—
and the state of my unfinished search for wisdom—it would be
this: My challenge is to love without fear and to freely embrace
my strength. It's possible, the dream told me, to do both.

III

FRUITION: THE INTEGRATORS

8

SEEKING THE HEART
OF WISDOM

Where Jack Kornfield and Joseph Goldstein
Parted Ways

Many people have taken action, but if their state of
being is not peaceful or happy, the actions they under-
take only sow more troubles and anger and make the
situation worse. So instead of saying "Don't just sit
there; do something," we should say the opposite,
"Don't just do something; sit there."
—THICH NHAT HANH

Look at every path closely and deliberately. Try it as
many times as you think necessary. Then ask yourself
and yourself alone one question. This question is one
that only a very old man asks. My benefactor told me
about it once when I was young and my blood was too
vigorous for me to understand it. Now I do understand
it. I will tell you what it is: Does this path have a heart?
If it does, the path is good. If it doesn't it is of no use.
—CARLOS CASTANEDA

UNTIL well into their thirties, Joseph Goldstein
and Jack Kornfield lived remarkably parallel lives.
Both of them were brought up in liberal, Jewish,
East Coast families in the 1950s. Both did well in school, went on
to Ivy League colleges, and seemed headed toward conventional
careers—Kornfield as a doctor, Goldstein as an academic. Both

became interested in Eastern religion during college, joined the Peace Corps after graduation, and sought assignment in Asia. Both ended up studying Theravada Buddhism and the classical meditation practice known as vipassana—Kornfield in Thailand, Goldstein in India. They met for the first time in 1974, shortly after returning to the United States, when each had been invited to teach meditation classes at the Naropa institute in Boulder, Colorado. There they became close friends. That fall, Kornfield and Goldstein decided to teach the first of a series of longer meditation retreats. Two years later, they helped to found the Insight Meditation Society (IMS), a retreat center in central Massachusetts. For nearly a decade, they taught together, attracting a large and loyal group of students to mostly silent meditation courses that ranged from several days to three months in length.

After exploring a variety of approaches to tapping aspects of the human potential—pieces of a larger puzzle—I grew increasingly interested in more integrated and comprehensive approaches. In particular, I was eager to find practices that included attention to both the personal and the transpersonal realms—to the mind, body, and emotions as well as the soul and spirit. I began by looking at the attempts of these two teachers to adapt a classical Eastern spiritual tradition in the West. The form of Buddhism that Kornfield and Goldstein brought back to America was remarkably free of dogma, doctrine, rituals, ceremonies, hierarchies, and any requirement to pledge allegiance to any higher authority. "There was no incense, no chanting, no God, no guru," explains Eric Lerner, one of the founders of IMS. "Instead, it was about sitting and closing your eyes and figuring out the truth for yourself."

I myself was drawn to vipassana by its intellectual clarity, psychological sophistication, and elegant simplicity. In contrast to practices that focus on quieting the mind of all thought, vipassana emphasizes awareness—or "mindfulness." As thoughts, emotions, and sensations arise in consciousness, one is instructed to gently note them, one at a time, then let them go. The goal is to be fully aware of whatever arises in a given moment, but not to identify with it, or get attached to it, or dwell on it, or become lost in it.

The premise of vipassana practice, and of Buddhism more generally, is that all phenomena—including life itself—are ultimately transitory and impermanent. Through the practice of vipassana, one begins to dismantle the illusion of a fixed and permanent self. Life, in turn, becomes seen as a dance of consciousness, a constantly changing process in which all boundaries ultimately dissolve—and with them the sense of separateness and alienation that characterize ordinary life. Developing the witness or inner observer—the capacity to be mindful—allows one to stand back from the fleeting drama of everyday thoughts, emotions, and events and view them with more detachment and equanimity. This can be useful, I discovered, both in developing a broader spiritual perspective and as a tool of greater psychological well-being. As Robert Assagioli, the founder of Psychosynthesis, put it: "We are dominated by everything with which our self becomes identified. We can dominate and control everything from which we disidentify ourselves."

Both Goldstein and Kornfield remain unwaveringly committed to cultivating awareness—increasing consciousness—as a primary tool in the search for wisdom. Along the way, however, their paths have sharply diverged. Goldstein continues to passionately champion what he calls the classical Buddhist teachings. "What we want to do is let go of everything," he has explained, "not to identify with any state whatsoever." This challenge entails bringing an even-handed attention to all that arises and passes, including desires and aversions, pleasures and pains. Kornfield, who was ordained as a Buddhist monk but went on to get a Ph.D. in psychology, grew to believe that directly engaging and resolving the issues of personality—often through psychotherapy—is at least as critical as meditation in the quest for a more complete life. Goldstein views personal concerns in the context of a larger picture. For Kornfield, the personal and universal levels are inextricably intertwined and equally important Goldstein believes that the route to freedom is through transforming the habits of the mind and transcending worldly desires. Kornfield feels that the more difficult challenge is to live fully in one's body and to open one's heart.

Their differences are mirrored on a personal level. Goldstein, a tall, thin balding man with delicate features, is gentle, polite, and fastidious in manner. He speaks carefully and precisely but with an occasional nervous laugh. Kind and solicitous, he is an attentive listener, more cerebral than he is emotionally demonstrative. It's as if he floats just above the fray. In fact, he lives next door to IMS in a simple, tastefully designed, and impeccably furnished house with two living spaces—one for him and the other for his longtime fellow teacher, Sharon Salzberg. The house was paid for by one of their students. At forty-nine, Goldstein is single and childless and expects to remain so. "Marriage has never been a strong desire," he told me when I first visited him at his home. "I'm with people all day long, and I have a nice connection with them. The kind of work I do—my writing, my teaching, and my meditation practice—becomes very intimate and fills that part of myself quite fully."

Kornfield—also slight of build and balding—seems at first glance a shorter version of Goldstein. But the differences are soon apparent. Kornfield's face is more animated and expressive, his gestures more dramatic. Despite his soft way of speaking, he is edgier than Goldstein, balancing more agendas and a wider range of emotions. He has an easy wit, a sharp tongue, and a restless, eclectic mind. Voluble and passionate, Kornfield is both more charismatic and more mercurial than Goldstein. He can tune in deeply and insightfully on one occasion, then be preoccupied and impatient on another. In 1984, Kornfield moved from his home at IMS to northern California in order to begin a family. He and his wife now have a ten-year-old daughter and live in a modest house in Woodacre, a middle-class community thirty miles north of San Francisco. The house, like Goldstein's, was bought partly with a gift from a student. In 1990, Kornfield founded a retreat center called Spirit Rock, which is located just five minutes from his home. The center offers meditation retreats, as well as workshops focused on psychological issues and the challenge of embodying spiritual insights in everyday life. In his own life, Kornfield juggles disparate responsibilities—as a husband and father, an administrator of Spirit Rock, a teacher of classes and retreats, a writer, and a therapist in private practice.

For all the differences that have emerged between them, Kornfield and Goldstein remain bound by shared beliefs that developed early in their lives—most notably, that traditional Western definitions of success and happiness simply are not adequate. Goldstein's search for answers was shaped by the often-confusing emotional turbulence of his childhood. The younger of two brothers, he grew up in upstate New York's Catskill Mountains, where his parents ran a bungalow colony. Both his mother and father worked hard, but Goldstein doesn't remember feeling deprived or mistreated. Nonetheless, as a young boy, he found himself subject to powerful temper tantrums that he could neither control nor understand. "Suddenly I'd feel invaded," he told me. "Some sensitivity was touched, and there would be this explosion. It caused a lot of suffering for me and for everyone else." He saw a psychologist briefly, but it didn't prove very helpful. Goldstein was left to solve the problem for himself.

"At a certain point, there was this realization that I really didn't have to explode, that I had a choice," he told me. "I was eleven or twelve, and that was a major turning point. I didn't know anything about meditation then, but I framed my realization in a way that was suitable to my age. When the angry feelings came up, I'd just count to ten. It was a rudimentary way to observe my feelings instead of being carried away by them, and it changed my behavior. After a while the explosiveness stopped." When Goldstein was twelve, his father died suddenly and unexpectedly. Over the next several years, the youngster also endured the death of a grandfather who had lived with the family, as well as that of a nineteen-year-old cousin killed in a car accident. In each case, Goldstein found a way to modify his reaction by shifting his perspective. Rather than experiencing deep grief and mourning or viewing the deaths as a cruel tragedy, he framed the events in philosophical terms. "People were there in my life, and then suddenly they weren't there anymore," he told me. "These deaths had a profound influence on my understanding that this is the nature of things. Two of these deaths could be considered untimely, but I came to realize that death is not an accident. It's part of the picture. If we have that understanding, then it becomes not such a tragic affair." Goldstein literally taught himself how to gain some distance from troubling emotions. Nearly a decade passed, for example, before he discovered—and began to deal with—his underlying sense of loss and sadness about his father's death.

It was at Columbia, where he majored in philosophy, that Goldstein was first attracted to Eastern religion. He read the *Bhagavad Gita*—the classic poem written around 500 B.C. that describes the spiritual struggle of the human soul to let go of desire and transcend the self. "It rang bells for me all over the place," Goldstein told me. "When I look back at my marked-up college copy, I see that I was drawn to all the elements of nonattachment." At the same time, Goldstein felt frustrated that his professors were teaching philosophy as "an academic discipline and not as a way to live." By his senior year, he no longer felt much interest in going to graduate school.

Instead, he decided to join the Peace Corps, which had been founded just a few years before. He applied to go to eastern Africa but was assigned instead to Thailand. Several months after he arrived, a friend invited him to visit a Buddhist temple. Goldstein accepted and felt an immediate connection to the teachings. He began by asking the monks a lot of questions, but only when he sat in meditation did he feel something stir deeply inside him. "It wasn't that I achieved anything great by sitting," he told me. "It was just seeing profoundly that there was a way to look *in* as well as to look out—to turn your awareness on the mind itself. It was what I'd been looking for."

Goldstein was especially fascinated by the nonconceptual

approach of meditation. "I'd done a lot of thinking in my life, and I knew its limitations," he said. "This was opening to a whole other world." Nonetheless, it was an experience with a book—hearing someone read from a Tibetan Buddhist text—that prompted the major turning point in Goldstein's life. He was still living in Thailand, toward the end of his Peace Corps tour of duty. "My mind was unusually concentrated and clear on this particular day," he remembers. "In some fundamental way, the words of the text I was reading liberated a kind of understanding that wasn't intellectual. It was an opening, a transformative experience of selflessness. Everything I knew was turned inside out. From that point, the course of my life was set."

A short time later, Goldstein moved to Bodh-Gaya, India, where the Buddha himself is said to have been enlightened. Goldstein began to practice vipassana under a respected Bengali teacher named Anagarika Munindra. Before long, Goldstein's discipline became legendary, even among his fellow practitioners. Rick Fields describes it evocatively in his history of Buddhism in America, *How the Swans Came to the Lake:* "Joseph [was] famous in India for sitting patiently . . . sticking with it—watching, watching, watching, as was the way in vipassana meditation; watching his mind, watching his breath, watching his feelings, watching his pain, his pleasure, his hope, his bliss, his hunger, watching whatever rose into the field of his consciousness—while everyone else passed through, sat for a day, a week, a month, maybe, and then went on."

While Goldstein was sitting in Bodh-Gaya, Jack Kornfield was practicing vipassana in the remote jungles of Thailand. Kornfield had sought out Asia and meditation for reasons that he later realized related to his own stormy childhood. The oldest of four boys, Kornfield was born on a marine base in North Carolina, but his family moved around frequently. His father was a biophysicist who held a series of jobs at various East Coast universities, but it became clear to Kornfield early on that his father's route didn't deliver much satisfaction. "The people I knew in scientific, intellectual circles were unhappy," he told me during one of our first conversations. "It became very obvious to me even as a child that there was a difference between worldly success and happiness." Kornfield did well in school, but he felt painfully insecure and awkward in his relationships. Nor was his home life happy or easy. His parents fought a great deal, the atmosphere in the house was nearly always tense, and his own efforts to play the role of peacemaker weren't terribly successful.

At fourteen, Kornfield's mother gave him a copy of *The Third Eye*, a book of semifictional mystical tales about Tibet. Kornfield found the book both entertaining and intriguing, but it didn't occur to him that such an exotic life might be a reasonable alternative to his own. He arrived at Dartmouth College in 1963, intending to become a doctor but already looking for something more compelling to do with his life. In his first semester, he took a course called "Lao Tzu and the Buddha" from a handsome older professor named Wing Tsit Chan, who had been educated in China and could speak with authority about both Eastern and Western philosophy. Dr. Chan sat cross-legged on a desk at the front of the room and lectured on the Tao and other aspects of mysticism. Within a short time, Kornfield had decided to change his major to Asian studies.

He began to study Chinese, grew his hair long, dropped out for a year, and hitchhiked around Europe. In the summer of 1966, he spent four months living in Haight Ashbury. People were passing out LSD—which was still legal—on street corners, and Kornfield's psychedelic experiences gave him a powerful, often blissful glimpse of other states of consciousness. Although he eventually returned to Dartmouth to finish his degree, Kornfield was already determined to become ordained as a Buddhist monk in Asia after he graduated. "I was moderately unhappy in my life, my relationships with women were still really awkward, and I didn't know who I was," he told me. "What I did know was that the East somehow seemed an important part of the answer." Much later, he'd realize that a large part of his motivation was simply to escape the pain and confusion of dealing with life in the world. Kornfield arrived in Thailand in 1967, and almost immediately he began looking for a monastery where he could study when he wasn't doing his Peace Corps work.

"I didn't see [myself] being a monk for the rest of my life," Kornfield explained, "but I wanted to do the type of training that the Buddhist monks did to understand at a deeper level the texts that I'd been reading in college and the psychedelic experiences that I'd had. I wanted to step way outside my culture in the hope that I'd have a more compelling vision about my life." It was through an American whom he met in Asia that Kornfield was introduced to Achaan Chaa, a highly respected "forest monk." Achaan Chaa's practice had included several years as an ascetic, during which he begged for his food and slept under the trees. Strict and traditional, he required that his students abide by all 226 rules purportedly passed down from the Buddha. Kornfield was taken with the simplicity and austerity of life in a forest monastery hundreds of miles from any large city. His schedule began to revolve around meditating for long hours, walking five miles each day to collect food for his one midday meal—barefoot, regardless of the weather—and treating even the work of sweeping the paths around the monastery as part of his meditative practice.

After two years, Kornfield was ordained as a monk. With Achaan Chaa's blessing, he began to study with several leading Buddhist teachers. Among them was one of the senior teachers of the Theravada Buddhist master Mahasi Sayadaw, under whom Goldstein's teacher, Munindra, had studied. Kornfield also undertook an intensive silent retreat, living for a full year in a one-room hut, meditating up to twenty hours a day, and leaving only to see his teacher or to pick up his daily allotment of food. Like Goldstein, Kornfield found the initial experience of intensive meditation extraordinarily moving. "I had all kinds of difficulties in the beginning, including great physical pain, but I applied myself," he told me. "I was young, I had a bit of an ascetic temperament anyway, and I had a lot of interest in the practice. Eventually, I became incredibly open and clear. I felt intense openings of my senses and a really deep understanding of the Buddhist history and psychology that I'd been reading."

In 1972, after five years in Asia, Kornfield decided to return to the United States. He was determined to work out the stormy relationships with family and friends that he'd left behind. At the same time, he was intent on continuing to live in robes and shaved head as a renunciate Buddhist monk. The latter plan didn't last long. Two weeks after returning, Kornfield ventured outside in robes, carrying his begging cup, to meet his sister-in-law, who happened to be having a makeover at the Elizabeth Arden salon on Fifth Avenue. No sooner did he sit down in the waiting room than a group of eight to ten women gathered around him, staring in astonishment. The dissonance between the Eastern life he'd been living and the quintessentially Western world of Elizabeth Arden was instantly sobering. "At that moment," he wrote later and with considerable understatement, "it became clear that I would have to find a way to reconcile the ancient and wonderful teachings I had received at the Buddhist monastery with the ways of our modern world."

Within several weeks, Kornfield had discarded his robes, enrolled in a graduate program in psychology at Antioch, and taken two jobs to support himself: driving a taxi in Boston and working nights at a mental hospital. He also got involved in his first relationship with a woman since college and began living in a communal household. Very quickly, he came to a painful and disappointing realization. The deep understandings and the extraordinary states of clarity and well-being that he had experienced in meditation did not translate easily into worldly life in America. "My meditation had helped me very little with relationships," he wrote. "I was still emotionally immature, acting out the same painful patterns of blame and fear, acceptance and rejection, that I had before my Buddhist training, only the horror was that now I was beginning to see these patterns more clearly. . . . I had used the strength of my mind in meditation to suppress painful feelings, and all too often I didn't even recognize that I was angry, sad, grieving, or frustrated until a long time later. I had very few skills for dealing with my feelings, or engaging on an emotional level, or living wisely with my friends and loved ones." Or, as he summed it up for me: "There were big dimensions of the life I returned to that were quite uncooked and unfinished."

Ironically, Kornfield's practice under Achaan Chaa had focused specifically on how to bring a meditative awareness and qualities such as love and compassion into everyday life. Kornfield believes that he might have worked out more of his personal issues simply by studying longer with Achaan Chaa. But even then, he says, there were interpersonal issues that couldn't have been resolved in a retreat environment.

Joseph Goldstein's training, by contrast, followed a more classical path that accorded little priority to how one lived in the world and focused instead on nonattachment. "When you are engaged in practice," Goldstein was instructed by U Pandita, the fiercely classical successor to Mahasi Sayadaw, "you should be engaged without regard for body or life." Nonetheless, Goldstein is convinced that his austere meditative training in Asia had a positive impact on his ability to engage in relationships. He returned to America in 1974 assuming that he'd do some teaching but unsure in precisely what venue. "The actual stuff that happens in relationships still happened when I got back," he told me, "but it seemed much easier to deal with because of the practice." At the same time, it seems fair to say that intimate relationships simply weren't as important to Goldstein as they were to Kornfield. The Buddhist concept of nonattachment fit Goldstein's personal inclinations perfectly. Kornfield, by contrast, had always hoped and assumed that he would someday get married and have a family.

W hen Kornfield and Goldstein met in Boulder in the summer of 1974, their differences were far outweighed by their common ground. The occasion was the founding session of the Naropa Institute in Boulder, Colorado, a summer-long celebration that became the sort of defining event for the consciousness movement that Woodstock had been six years earlier for the rock 'n' roll counterculture. Both Goldstein and Kornfield—back from Asia for less than a year and still unsure what to do with the rest of their lives—were thrilled to discover such a receptive audience of young American seekers. Students flocked to their classes in part because they were among the first Western meditation teachers with authentic Asian training and also because each of them had a gift for making Eastern spiritual teachings seem relevant and accessible.

Naropa itself was the inspiration of the charismatic Tibetan-born Buddhist teacher, or *tulku,* Chogyam Trungpa Rinpoche. *Tulkus* are enlightened teachers—the Dalai Lama most notable among them—who are said to have taken rebirth from a previous incarnation solely for the purpose of awakening others. Identified as a *tulku* at the age of eighteen months, Trungpa spent his childhood in Tibet steeped in rigorous Buddhist training. In 1959, at the age of twenty, he is said to have helped three hundred fellow refugees escape Tibet, traveling at night to avoid detection by the invading Chinese army and eating boiled leather to stay alive. Trungpa settled first in India, but felt drawn to the West. With the aid of a benefactor, he moved to England to attend Oxford in 1963. He proved to be an extraordinary student, helped in no small measure by the powers of concentration and awareness that he'd developed through years of intensive meditation.

Trungpa arrived in the United States in May 1970, and very quickly, he set out on a lecture tour across the country. As he traveled, he was struck both by the intense spiritual hunger of the young Americans he met and by the level of their misunderstanding about the traditional Eastern approach to seeking wisdom. His lectures from that tour were eventually gathered in what remains his best-known and perhaps most influential book, *Cutting Through Spiritual Materialism.* "We can deceive ourselves into thinking we are developing spirituality," he wrote, "when instead we are strengthening our egocentricity through spiritual techniques. This fundamental distortion may be referred to as spiritual materialism."

The irony is that Trungpa's own behavior embodied these very contradictions. He smoked, drank heavily, ate whatever he pleased, and regularly showed up two hours late for lectures. Drinking in particular violated one of the five basic moral precepts of Buddhism. The cost, in his case, was ultimately catastrophic. When Trungpa died in 1987 at the age of forty-seven, the official cause was listed as cardiac arrest, but it was widely known that the real explanation was alcoholism. Far from apologizing, however, Trungpa insisted that even his shortcomings served as spiritual teachings for his students. Trungpa's virtues—his charisma, his penetrating intelligence, his broad knowledge, his accessible presentation, and his exotic lineage—prompted followers to overlook his excesses. Like Trungpa himself, his students ignored one of the essential messages that he had preached during his first lecture tour across America. "Whenever we begin to feel any discrepancy or conflict between our actions and the teachings, we immediately interpret the situation in such a way that the conflict is smoothed over," he argued, at the time. "We attempt to find a self-justifying answer for every question."

Trungpa settled with his English wife, Diana, in Boulder, and established a teaching center there. By 1974, with centers operating in several other cities, he decided to start a school in Boulder modeled on the ancient Indian Buddhist University. "The premise of Naropa Institute was that clear, hard thinking is central to a sane spiritual journey," explained Rick Fields, who eventually became one of Trungpa's devoted students. "What was needed was a crossroads where the intellectual-critical mind of the West and the way of experience and meditation of the East could meet head-on." College-age searchers—newly turned on to mysticism, through reading and their experiences with hallucinogenics—were immediately attracted to Naropa's course offerings in subjects ranging from meditation to anthropology, Sanskrit to tea ceremony. Several hundred students were expected to enroll when Naropa opened that summer. More than two thousand showed up.

The main attraction became the alternating twice-weekly

lectures by Ram Dass and Trungpa himself. Ram Dass still wore robes and a long beard, and he had attracted a large following based on the broad popularity of *Be Here Now,* published two years earlier. His Hindu devotional approach focused on joy, compassion, and opening the heart to higher truth, sometimes by way of ecstatic all-night chanting sessions. At the same time, Ram Dass preached a renunciate lifestyle. By contrast, Trungpa, looking more American than his Boston-born, Harvard-educated counterpart, gave talks about spiritual practice that were sober, austere, demanding, and full of references to suffering, the pain of illusion, and the need for rigorous discipline in meditative practice. Afterward, however, his followers often partied in the bars all night long.

"Ram Dass would give a lecture, and everyone would chant and think about God," Kornfield remembered for me nearly twenty years later. "And then the next night Trungpa would talk about how wisdom is not to be found in some vision of God but in cultivating mindfulness and facing impermanence. There was a tremendous creative tension between them, the sort you'd expect to see between two great dancers or musicians." Yet for all their surface contrasts, Trungpa and Ram Dass had much in common. Both spoke of shifting attention from outer pursuits to a more contemplative life; from relentless thinking to discovering truth in the stillness of meditation; and from seeking ever more ego-gratification to letting go of personal desire and moving beyond the ego.

Kornfield was invited to teach vipassana at Naropa by Trungpa himself, after they met at a cocktail party in Cambridge in 1973. Joseph Goldstein came to Naropa after running into Ram Dass—whom he'd gotten to know earlier in India—at a Berkeley restaurant just before Naropa began. Ram Dass suggested that Goldstein come and teach the meditation section of his lecture course. The first Naropa summer proved to be a heady experience for nearly everyone involved. "The seeds of the dharma," Goldstein said, using the Sanskrit term for "the truth" or "the way," "were widely scattered as a result of that summer." Kornfield felt equal enthusiasm at the time, but he looks back now with more reservations. "We all had this romantic, idealistic feeling that we were at the beginning of a consciousness movement that was really going to transform the world," he told me. "It was as if all you had to do was reach a high enough state of consciousness, and everything back down on earth would take care of itself. We were just very naive about what this transformation was going to take and what hard work lay ahead."

Still, many students were inspired by the mindfulness practices that Goldstein and Kornfield were teaching. By summer's end, the two teachers realized that their approaches were quite compatible. In September, Goldstein took off with Sharon Salzberg, whom he had met while practicing in India, to conduct a month-long meditation retreat in the Sequoia National Forest. Sixty students came along. The retreat was followed by a series of similar ones, which Kornfield helped lead, at various locations around the country over the next year. Kornfield and Goldstein alternated daily dharma talks on Buddhism and the practice of vipassana, and they met briefly each day with each student to discuss issues that came up in their practice. For the most part, however, students simply meditated fourteen to twenty hours a day, alternating periods of sitting with walking practice.

The growing popularity of the vipassana retreats prompted Goldstein, Kornfield, and several of their students to search for a permanent retreat center. In 1976, they purchased a former Catholic monastery with one hundred rooms, set on eighty acres in the rural Massachusetts town of Barre. The modest down payment on the $150,000 purchase price was cobbled together from supporters. They called the new center the Insight Meditation Society. "What IMS did was to give a lot of smart Jewish kids careers," said Eric Lerner, who helped find the Barre property. "We didn't want to be doctors or lawyers, and we weren't really prepared to live in the world, either. Here was an alternative. We could be missionaries: create a spiritual institution, bring Buddhism to

America without the robes and the gurus. The idea was to create a democratic place where people could sit, while different teachers would come and go."

Like all Buddhist teachings, those in the Theravada tradition can be traced back to the man who came to be called the Buddha. Siddhartha Gautama was born around 567 B.C. to a wealthy clan chief who lived in a palace below the Himalayan foothills. The story of his path to enlightenment remains one of the classic hero's journeys. Raised in the shielded privilege and luxury of a castle, he married young and soon had a son. Only then did he venture into the city for the first time. There he encountered experiences of suffering previously unknown to him, including a sick man and a corpse being carried to the burning grounds. That very day he resolved to leave his privileged life and go in search of an answer to the problem of suffering. Siddhartha spent six years wandering the countryside, living as an ascetic, meditating, and studying the sacred texts. Finally one day he found himself in the small Indian village of Bodh-Gaya. Frustrated by his failure to find answers, he determined to sit under a bodhi tree until enlightenment came to him. Just as the morning star appeared on that first night, he opened his eyes and realized he had found the answer within himself.

Siddhartha's central realizations have come to be known in Buddhism as the four noble truths. Both Goldstein and Kornfield have spent the last twenty years interpreting these truths for their Western students. The first noble truth is that all life is characterized by suffering, or *dhukka*. No matter how many distractions, escapes and pleasures we find for ourselves, we cannot avoid feelings such as anger, anxiety, ill will, and frustration. Beyond that, as we grow older, the body inevitably gets diseased and eventually dies. The second noble truth is that the cause of all our suffering is desire and attachment: to pleasure, to our own opinions, to preconceptions that prevent us from seeing things as they truly are, and most of all, to our belief that we have a solid and permanent self. The third noble truth is the recognition that this sense of self is finally an illusion—and that no amount of striving or accumulation or willpower can change that. "The mind stops grasping and clinging," Goldstein has written, "when the microscopic transience of everything is realized, and when we experience the process of mind and body without the burden of self." The fourth noble truth came to be known as the eightfold path—a systematic map pointing the way toward truth and freedom or what is simply called the dharma.

The eightfold path is built around cultivating a set of precepts and behaviors that clear the way to wisdom. "If we are engaged in actions that cause pain and conflict to ourselves and others, it is impossible to become settled, collected and focused in meditation," Kornfield has explained. "It is [also] impossible for the heart to open." Virtues in Buddhism are defined as qualities such as generosity and compassion that reduce suffering in one's self and in others and permit the mind to move more easily into a state of calmness and tranquillity. Hindrances are those qualities that promote suffering in one's self and others—anger and greed are examples—and so create disturbance and unrest in the mind. Ethical or moral behavior is not so much an arbitrary decree from above as the natural outgrowth of careful attention to the consequences of one's thoughts and emotions.

Thus, "right speech," as Goldstein explained it, simply means "not speaking what is untrue . . . rather speaking words which are honest and helpful." "Right action" includes not killing or stealing or "causing suffering to others out of greed or desire for pleasant sensations." "Right livelihood" refers to ethical behavior in one's work life—specifically, "doing that kind of work for support and maintenance which is not harmful to others." Finally, "right effort" refers to a subtle form of discipline in the service of a goal—"to be persistent and persevering but with a relaxed and balanced mind, making the effort without forcing." Each of these behaviors enhances the mind states that constitute the final two steps of the eightfold path. *Concentration* refers to the capacity to stay focused on one thing at a time. *Mindfulness* implies an awareness of what is happening in each moment, without attachment to any of it.

Underlying the noble eightfold path is the Abhidhamma or classical Buddhist psychology, a system for understanding everyday mind states. This model posits that there are some fourteen "unhealthy" factors that stand in the way of wisdom, along with fourteen corresponding "healthy factors" that literally prevent the unhealthy factors from arising. Doubt, for example, is counteracted by faith: restlessness by composure; and envy by impartiality. In the Abhidhamma, three central factors lie at the root of all unwholesome activity and suffering: greed (desire), hatred (aversion), and delusion (ignorance).

Greed, as Goldstein has described it, includes clinging, wanting, and attachment. These qualities are offset by the wholesome factors of generosity, nonattachment, and nonpossessiveness. Hatred includes aversion, ill will, and anger, which can be counteracted by the healthy factors of love, goodwill, and friendship. Finally, delusion is the lack of awareness that stands in the way of perceiving what really is. It is counteracted by wisdom—which leads one to see more clearly the truth. Each unhealthy factor leads to a specific mind state that stands in the way of well-being. Hatred or aversion, for example, fills the mind with turbulence, anger, and even violence. Lusting after pleasure, whether for a material object or a specific sensation, keeps the mind agitated and focused outward. "Every act of condemning the hindrances strengthens the enemy," Goldstein has written. "Mindfulness makes them all inoperative. They may continue to arise, but they do not disturb the mind because we are not reacting to them."

Perhaps no Westerner has written more accessibly about the difficulties and rewards of vipassana practice than Roger Walsh. Now in his mid-forties, Walsh grew up in Australia, where he earned his M.D. and his Ph.D., then came to the United States to do his psychiatric training at Stanford University. In addition, he entered psychotherapy and began sampling the myriad offerings of the human potential movement in the early 1970s. He took his first extended silent retreat at IMS in 1976, shortly after his thirtieth birthday. The experience was transformative. "I learned more about the mind in those ten days than I'd learned about it in three years of psychiatric training," he told me when we sat down to lunch at a restaurant near his home in Mill Valley, California. Walsh began sitting in longer meditation retreats, and the following year he started an annual tradition of sitting each fall for the full ninety-day silent retreat at IMS.

In 1977, he published perhaps the most comprehensive Western description yet of the experience of long-term meditation, in two long articles for the *Journal of Transpersonal Psychology*. Walsh's initial observation was that beyond a superficial level of integration, the mind operates chaotically. Gaining control of attention, he discovered, is a huge challenge, even for a highly disciplined and experienced meditator. "I was lost in fantasy most of the time," Walsh wrote. "When I got myself out I'd fall back in. I was driven by desires, and doubts and most of all by fears. There were depths of mind I could get glimpses of—moments of quiet and clarity and peace—but I didn't have the attention or control to sustain them. The most astounding insight for me—as I became more sensitive—was that the mind was totally out of control and I'd been totally unaware of this my whole life."

Although Walsh went on to become a professor of psychology at the University of California–Irvine, the meditative practice of mindfulness—rather than psychotherapy—became his own primary tool of awakening. "Day ten in retreat is easier than day one," he told me. "When you go inside, it's like turning on a faucet that hasn't been used for a long time. What comes up first is gunk. Most people's immediate response is to turn the faucet off and say, 'Yeech, I don't want that stuff.' But as you allow yourself to confront fears and anxieties, and your worst fantasies don't come true, the trust in the process begins to grow." With disciplined practice, Walsh discovered, the rewards of mindfulness are very rich. "You get," he told me, "a greater appreciation of the vastness of mind, a deeper level of insight, incredible subtlety of perceptions, a significant improvement in the capacity for focused attention, and short-lived periods of intense peace and tranquillity that are immensely satisfying. But the real insight from the practice is that there is such a thing as liberation—that we can get a glimpse of our true selfless nature."

My own introduction to vipassana came in a weekend workshop taught by Goldstein and Sharon Salzberg, held in a cramped and crowded room overlooking New York's Times Square. By then, I'd been meditating for about a year, using the simple concentration practice of repeating the word *one*. The practice of vipassana, I soon discovered, was far more challenging. Yet even with the distraction of fellow students close by my side and the dull roar of traffic below, I recognized very quickly that cultivating mindfulness—what Buddhists call the witness or inner observer—provides a remarkable window into the way that my mind works. It was a novel experience to simply watch, without interference or judgment, the arising and passing of my thoughts, emotions, and sensations. Often, for example, I found myself observing not just a thought but my own inclination to judge the thought. Never before had I so systematically observed the pattern of preoccupations, obsessions, habits, worries, fears, hopes, regrets, muscle aches, fantasies, and daydreams that so often dominate waking life. Suddenly, I saw how little control I had over the patterns of my mind.

Both Goldstein and Kornfield believe that it takes anywhere from two days to several weeks of sustained meditation for the mind and body to begin to experience extended periods of quiet. IMS offers retreats of varying length, including a ninety-day silent retreat that regularly attracts nearly one hundred people. Given my family obligations, I simply didn't feel able to commit to such a long time away. Instead, I decided to shift my daily meditation practice from a breath-counting concentration technique to vipassana. For more than two years, I practiced mindfulness twenty to forty-five minutes every day, sometimes twice a day. I also attended several shorter one- and two-day retreats, led by Goldstein and Kornfield. While I never experienced any of the deepest and subtlest understandings I'd read about—most notably, the direct, boundless experience of true emptiness—I did begin to appreciate the unique power and perspective that emerges through the practice of mindfulness.

Early on, for example, I was acutely aware of the pains and tensions in my body when I sat for any extended period. These tended to focus in my lower back, neck, and shoulders. When I followed the instruction to simply label whatever arose in my consciousness, I sometimes found myself noting the same sensation arising over and over—"back pain, back pain, back pain"—until the pain seemed to completely dominate my mind. Then one day, during a day of meditation led by Goldstein, he gave a talk about the nature of physical pain. Instead of labeling a sensation "back pain" or "neck pain" as it arose, he suggested that we observe the sensations more closely. What form precisely did the pain take? Was it stabbing, shooting, pulling, itching, burning, tightness, or spasm? And where exactly was the pain? What physical shape did it have? By this sort of close moment-to-moment observation, he told us, we might discover that the pain wasn't as relentless, pervasive, or immutable as we'd previously assumed it was.

Sure enough, I noticed that when I observed more closely, the nature of the pain I might be experiencing shifted from moment to moment, and so did its exact location. When I observed it very carefully and without judgment, I realized that there were breaks in my experience of the pain. Something else—another thought or a feeling—arose intermittently and commanded more of my attention. I began to see that even the most painful sensations had a transitory quality. I suffered far more if I lumped them together under the broad concept of "pain"—the sort of suffering that feels indefinite and oppressive—than if I observed my changing sensations moment to moment. Not only did the pain begin to come and go, but there were times when it disappeared altogether. This was, I eventually realized, my first direct experience of both impermanence and nonattachment. Until then, both concepts had seemed abstract. But here I found myself experiencing impermanence in the form of constantly changing sensations that I'd previously thought of as fixed. The feeling of nonattachment became palpable when I managed to let go of my fixed ideas about the nature of pain, in favor of simply observing whatever arose and passed. I literally began to feel less identified with the pain—and less plagued by it.

But what then of the strong emotions that came up during meditation—anger, sadness, and anxiety? Was it possible to treat these with similar nonattachment, merely as feelings to be observed rather than expressions of the essential me? My first insight, as I began mindfulness practice, was that most of the time, there was no distance at all between me and my thoughts or my emotions. When I was angry, I didn't observe my anger—I just felt angry. When I was anxious, I didn't note an anxious thought, I became preoccupied by it. Although the challenge in vipassana was to observe what arose and passed, more often I found myself getting absorbed in whatever came into my mind and losing the witness stance altogether.

I might find myself drifting off into thoughts about this book, for example, and even composing sentences in my head. Or I'd find myself thinking about how a certain section I'd just written didn't quite work. After that, I'd begin to feel a more generalized worry—the possibility that I'd never finish the book, or that critics would hate it, or that no one would read it. That, in turn, might prompt worries about paying my bills. Then suddenly, I'd snap to, almost as if someone had thrown cold water on my face. Abashed, I'd realize that I hadn't been observing any of these thoughts or emotions and couldn't even remember their sequence. Fortified by this insight, I'd go back to watching. But soon enough, I'd drift off again—to a problem that one of my daughters was having in school, or to a conflict I was feeling in a relationship, or to the pain of a tense muscle. Before I knew it, I was lost again in my thoughts and feelings. In the course of thirty minutes of meditation, I'd often have this same experience a dozen times or more.

But then there were days when my mind was a little clearer and quieter and my anxieties and preoccupations not quite so intense. In those instances, I found, I could observe whatever came up a little more closely, without getting lost in its content so quickly. This had a remarkable effect. It was like moving from an overcrowded, noisy corridor into a quieter, more spacious room. As soon as I felt less anxious and less bombarded, my awareness became sharper and more focused. Say, for example, that a typical fearful thought about the outcome of this book came up. Rather than being swept away on a wave of emotion and fantasy, I might simply note the thought ("worry, worry"), then let it go. When it came back up again, I'd note it once again and let it go. Whenever I reacted strongly to a worrisome thought or emotion, I invariably gave it more energy and ended up preoccupied with it. In the detached role of observer or witness, I was able to see that this fear was just one among many thoughts and emotions—often as not an automatic negativity with no rational or reasonable basis. Merely observing the thought arising and then passing, even if it resurfaced a half-dozen times, seemed to defuse its electrical charge. When I truly adopted the witness stance, I felt a larger perspective and a broader sense of identity. Distracting or upsetting thoughts still arose, but they no longer felt like the whole story—or even the most important element.

Sometimes mindfulness meditation opened an even more spacious perspective. When I found myself able to coolly observe even a highly threatening emotion—the experience of a rejection, for example—other ways of dealing with the issue invariably occurred to me. So long as I didn't react with alarm or try desperately to solve the "problem," I found that events had a way of unfolding in their natural course. The imagined negative outcome might still occur, but by the time it did, I had often already seen that the issue wasn't really important or that the outcome wouldn't have served my best interests after all. What seemed highly threatening in the short term often proved to have a value or a dimension that I hadn't anticipated at first. The main cost of reacting instantly and automatically was that by doing so, I lost connection with a more equanimous self-observer—a calmer, more secure inner core that didn't get fazed much by the shifting tide of everyday events.

There was one additional Buddhist meditative practice that both Goldstein and Kornfield spent time teaching. *Metta* is the Sanskrit word for love, and metta meditation focuses on consciously evoking feelings of love and compassion—both for one's self and for others. I'd learned a variation on this technique in my first retreat in Utah. Metta practice is built around repetitively reciting a series of phrases to one's self: "May I be filled with love and kindness," "May I be free of suffering," "May I be peaceful and at ease," and "May I be happy." After a certain period, one is instructed to replace the "I" in each phrase with specific family members, then friends and acquaintances, and eventually even one's enemies.

My initial instinct had been to dismiss this technique as mechanical and simplistic, even irritating. However, it prompted a very palpable, welcome emotional shift when I tried it that first day in Utah. Eventually, I began to alternate metta regularly with my vipassana practice and the results were sometimes very powerful. If the phrases that I repeated remained abstract ideas, they had a limited impact on me. But when I managed to connect feelings and images to the words I recited, I could literally feel my heart softening and my anger, anxiety, or even fear diminishing. At other times, I felt so agitated when I sat down that my mind wandered off the phrases even as I recited them, and it was nearly impossible to sustain any images in my mind. But that, too, was revealing. It became an unmistakable sign for me that I was carrying a lot of anger. Inevitably, this feeling of alienation created a distance between me and other people. My capacity to freely extend love depended first on becoming more aware of these underlying negative emotions. Through metta, I could then sometimes evoke more positive feelings.

Useful as I often found this technique—along with my ongoing practice of mindfulness—there remained a level at which neither practice fundamentally transformed the underlying feelings that troubled me. It wasn't finally enough to work just on shifting my placement of attention. Through sitting in mindfulness practice, I did often gain some distance from my envy, or my doubt, or my fear, or my grief. When I felt less overwhelmed by these thoughts and emotions, I was less compelled to react to them. Through metta practice, I was specifically able to let go of anger and even to feel a flood of love and compassion for people I'd been holding at bay or toward whom I'd been harboring resentment. But where my negative emotions ran deepest, they invariably resurfaced, particularly in times of stress and in my closest relationships. No amount of meditation seemed to resolve these familiar and repetitive conflicts.

It was precisely this issue that eventually began to come between Kornfield and Goldstein. For nearly a decade, they both taught vipassana at IMS based on the traditional Buddhist teachings. They devoted limited attention to translating insights derived during silent meditation practice into the everyday world of relationships and work. For Goldstein, who himself continued to sit in long retreats, this approach remained the purest path to freedom. "Something can be true—say, the idea of impermanence—and not necessarily [be] palatable in our culture," he told me. "For me, what's been most important is to aim for the highest liberation of the mind. I see a tendency to let go of that goal and instead become satisfied with something less: doing good in the world, having more harmonious relationships, seeking a happier life. That's all beautiful, but in my view, it misses the essential point. My teacher U Pandita, who is not at all concerned with pleasing people, likens vipassana practice to bitter medicine. Often it doesn't taste good, but it's effective. Our minds have been conditioned for countless aeons, and we're working to awaken from that. Transformation takes practice, effort, and commitment." Truly understanding the concept of impermanence, Goldstein told me, not only prompts the experience of liberation but changes one's behavior in the world. "As there is less identification with the concept of 'I' or 'me,' there is inherently less feeling of separateness," he explained. "Compassion in the world becomes a spontaneous response to the experience of connectedness."

Kornfield, by contrast, grew more skeptical that vipassana practice by itself could transform people's lives—including his own. Before founding IMS, he had entered psychotherapy in addition to studying psychology in graduate school. "I knew that meditation didn't touch some of my deep personal and interpersonal issues," he told me. "I also knew that it would be healthy to deal with those issues in our community at IMS. But somehow I wasn't ready to do so, nor were the other teachers. In my case, I wasn't mature enough, and it scared me too much. So instead, I taught what I knew how to teach well, which was meditation." Even devoted students observed that there was a disparity between Goldstein and Kornfield's considerable skills as meditation teachers and their capacity to translate their understanding into their daily lives. Mark Epstein, a psychiatrist who sat in retreats at IMS beginning in the 1970s and grew friendly with both Goldstein and Kornfield, recognized this issue early on. "They could both move into more peaceful, balanced states in meditation than most people I knew," Epstein told me. "But that didn't necessarily make them more peaceful and balanced in their lives."

While Goldstein remained inspired by U Pandita's uncompromising approach to liberation—which he taught in retreats held at IMS and in India—Kornfield grew more vocal about his dissatisfactions. "U Pandita was very skillful in his particular style, and those of us with the ability to be very concentrated had deep experiences with him," Kornfield recalled. "But he was also very traditional and very conservative. His view of the dharma was 'Either you do it this way, or you don't get enlightened.' He taught that life was suffering, the body was bad, emotions weren't important, and all that mattered was letting go of attachment and reaching the cessation state of nirvana. He saw himself as a warrior teaching us to use our minds to fight and uproot the defilements of greed, hatred, and delusion. But at the same time, he was not always kind to students. As one of his senior students once put it, he had a kind of Stone Age psychology. By the time I finished a retreat with U Pandita, I felt appreciative of his teaching skills but not very appreciative of his perspective."

The more Goldstein and Sharon Salzberg embraced U Pandita's hard line, the more Kornfield began exploring other approaches to wisdom. "Joseph and Sharon's dharma talks began to focus more and more on the defilements," Kornfield explained. "I was more interested in teaching the dharma from the heart, by engaging feelings and applying experiences to everyday life. These are very different visions. Joseph is very good at getting you to step out of your whole personal drama, but I don't believe that's completely liberating." Not surprisingly, Goldstein saw it differently. "Sometimes people are so stuck psychologically that it's a real obstacle to their ability to pay attention and be mindful, and then therapy can help. But unless it's done very skillfully, psychological work can reinforce a sense of self—me, my story, my problems—which I believe is a basic misconception. It might make life more comfortable, but it wouldn't be leading to real freedom. One difference between me and Jack may be in his emphasis on humanistic values versus mine on the values of liberation. Where they conflict, I hold the values of liberation to be the highest. All others are secondary."

Friends came to see their diverging paths as reflective of two very different temperaments. "Intellectual curiosity is Joseph's strong suit," one close friend of both men told me. "He's investigated the universe from an outsider's perspective, almost as a way to distance himself from it. He has a very gentle quality. There's the feeling about Joseph of a monastic, someone who wants to get off the wheel and isn't that concerned about going back to live in the world. He's been more deeply committed to meditation than Jack, and he's been very brave about pursuing that passion. Jack began to see meditation and retreat as just one part of it. Sitting in long retreats didn't solve his problems, and he came to believe that work on the heart is what Westerners need most. So he has emphasized the emotions and embodiment—how to go back into the world and live. Jack is less interested in pointing you to an out-of-body trip than he is to an 'in-the-body experience.'"

Indeed, Kornfield began to supplement classical Eastern notions of liberation with a more psychodynamic approach—emphasizing consciousness at all levels rather than focusing solely on achieving higher states or the traditional Eastern notion of enlightenment. "Awareness doesn't translate automatically from one realm to another," Kornfield told me. "You can be extremely conscious of your body and still be emotionally ignorant. You can have a great deal of emotional understanding and still be spiritually bereft. I've known dozens of meditators who can go completely empty in meditation, dissolve their bodies and mind into pure void and bliss—but then come back into the world and still act like emotional infants and sexual idiots in their relationships. In my view, they've done only half the dharma. There has to be a wedding of the personal and the universal. We need to bring our personal lives—the way we treat others and live our lives—into harmony with universal truths." In part, Kornfield was describing his own challenge. For all his insight and intelligence, he continues to struggle, as one friend puts it, "with the dissonance between what he teaches so effectively and how he sometimes behaves."

"Many people first come to spiritual practice hoping to skip over their sorrows and wounds, the difficult areas of their lives," Kornfield wrote in his most recent book, *A Path with Heart*. "They hope to rise above them and enter a spiritual realm full of divine grace, free from all conflict. . . . [But] as soon as practitioners relax in their discipline, they again encounter all the unfinished business of the body and heart that they had hoped to leave behind." Certainly, I saw this in my own life. Mindfulness proved more valuable as a technique for allowing me to engage and explore my automatic behaviors and reactive emotions than as a means to rising above them or gaining a permanent detachment from them. It was necessary, I found over and over again, to truly experience my fear, grief, or anger in order to begin to tap the hope, love, and strength that lay beneath. "In the end spiritual life is not a process of seeking or gaining some extraordinary condition or special powers," Kornfield concluded. "In fact such seeking can take us away from ourselves. If we are not careful, we can find the great failures of our modern society—its ambition, materialism and individual isolation—repeated in our spiritual life."

In the end, Kornfield found that failing to address one's personal issues undermines even meditative practice. "When we have not completed the basic developmental tasks of our emotional lives or are still quite unconscious in relation to our parents and families," he explained, "we will find that we are unable to deepen our spiritual practice. . . . We will not be able to concentrate during meditation, or we will find ourselves unable to bring what we have learned in meditation into our interaction with others." As many as half of the students who attend each year's ninety-day silent retreat at IMS, Kornfield told me, prove unable to do the traditional insight or mindfulness practice. In the course of sitting, too many unresolved emotional issues arise that demand more direct attention—and often the supportive help of another person.

B y the early 1980s, the philosophical differences between Goldstein and Kornfield were spilling into the IMS community. One of the most painful events centered on Goldstein's first teacher, Munindra, who occasionally came to IMS from India to give retreats. All the retreats included a vow of celibacy. At the end of one, in 1983, a female student who attended told several people, including Goldstein and Kornfield, that she'd had sex with Munindra during the retreat. The woman had already been experiencing significant psychological distress, and the Munindra affair proved to be a further trauma. A schism soon developed among the American teachers at IMS over how to deal with the situation. "My unofficial role in the community was to bring up things that were difficult," Kornfield told me. "Partly it was just my temperament. I wanted the affair to be looked at, and I found that Joseph and Sharon and some others were less willing to deal openly with this shadow side of our practice and our community. They wanted to keep secrets, and I got very frustrated and angry."

Goldstein is reluctant to resurrect the issue a decade later, believing that it has long since been resolved. But when pressed, he reluctantly tells his own version of the events. "I think Jack's and my main difference was over how much of the larger community to bring it to," Goldstein told me. "It wasn't a black and white issue, and I thought that in dealing with it, we needed to have respect for each of the people involved. I was concerned that there was a strident energy among some at IMS who seemed to convict and sentence Munindra without even speaking to him." "I would have waited until his planned return nine months later to talk with him."

Kornfield would not buy that approach. "I felt that the reluctance to confront the issue came from fear. If parts of one's life are quite unexamined—which was true for all of us—and something like this comes up about a revered teacher, it throws everything you've been doing for years into doubt. It's threatening to the whole scene." Eventually, Kornfield was chosen by the IMS board—including Goldstein—to fly to India and confront Munindra directly. The teacher acknowledged what had happened and agreed to apologize to the community as a whole. For Kornfield, the lesson was clear. "We must tell the truth to ourselves," he concluded, "and we must speak the truth in our communities."

In the aftermath of the Munindra incident, the teachers at IMS and in the vipassana community more broadly adopted a set of ethical guidelines for themselves. Built around basic Buddhist teachings, these guidelines included refraining from sexual misconduct; not abusing alcohol or drugs or misusing money; and maintaining a commitment to open and honest exchange. In addition, the community appointed its own ethics committee and charged it with evaluating and ruling on any serious accusations of misconduct against any teachers. Since that time, no incidents have been reported. Perhaps because the vipassana communities do not invest any single teacher with absolute authority, they have remained unusually free of the cultlike atmosphere that characterizes so many guru-based spiritual communities in

America. Even so, there are some critics who argue that institutionalizing the search for meaning almost guarantees that a certain amount of dogma, doctrine, and hierarchy will ultimately replace the free, unfettered search for truth.

In 1984, Kornfield left IMS and Barre after nearly a decade. He had just gotten married, his wife was pregnant, and he was determined to start a new life in northern California, where he'd already spent a good deal of time teaching. IMS continued to thrive. Its retreats nearly always filled to capacity under the leadership of Goldstein and Salzberg. For several years, Kornfield taught retreats up and down the West Coast, incorporating psychotherapeutic techniques, and he also saw clients privately. In 1989, after searching for several years, he and several fellow teachers finally found a site on which to build their own center, which they named Spirit Rock, just minutes from Kornfield's home. Ground was broken the following year, and Spirit Rock began operating with temporary buildings almost immediately.

Kornfield was determined to offer not just traditional silent retreats but classes focused on how to live the tenets of Buddhism—the dharma—in the world. Some three hundred people show up each Monday night for the talks that Kornfield has been giving for the past several years. Spirit Rock has also begun offering programs that deal with subjects such as the intersection between meditation and psychotherapy; parenting; the role of service; right livelihood; and the pursuit of work that is consistent with one's deepest beliefs.

Even in meditation itself, Kornfield is committed to a highly flexible approach to practice. "If very painful memories are coming up for someone who is sitting, I might help that person work just with grief for an extended period," he told me. "That might mean weeping or drawing or taking walks in the woods. The idea would be to find ways to help the person stay in touch with the feeling until it moves. At that point, you might go back to another level of the process—watching without attachment. For me, the practice always has to do with engaging the truth of what's going on in the present. The real challenge is to bring attention to every dimension of life. Wherever there is difficulty, wherever you are unconscious, you bring your attention there." Kornfield now views even the most profound meditative insights merely as one step on the path to wisdom. "No matter how tremendous the openings and how strong the enlightening journey," he wrote in *A Path with Heart,* ". . . one inevitably comes down, [and] must re-enter the world with a caring heart."

Goldstein himself is also focusing attention on the challenges of living in the world. "If liberation is the central aspiration of your life, periods of intensive meditation practice can be of inestimable value," he writes in his most recent book, *Insight Meditation: The Practice of Freedom.* "But there are also cycles of living actively in the world, developing generosity, morality, truthfulness, and compassion, qualities more easily expressed in daily life than in retreat." Indeed, the final section of his new book is titled "Practice in the World," and in it he devotes attention to everyday issues such as relationship with one's parents, the role of humor, and the art of communication. Goldstein and Kornfield remain friends, and continue to teach together at least once a year.

On a more personal level, Goldstein has begun studying with teachers outside the vipassana tradition, and he has even spent some time in psychotherapy. "My experience in meditation," Goldstein told me, "is that it deals with the issues that arise organically, but it doesn't necessarily focus one's attention on them, or pursue them, or dig into them. For me, therapy has been a way of focusing on particular issues—in my case, particularly around what it means to be a man. Nonetheless, Goldstein remains more passionately committed than ever to what he calls awakening or liberation, through the traditional mindfulness practice of letting go of attachment and not identifying with what's arising. To that end, he is spending longer periods than he has in many years pursuing intensive meditation practice.

As a teacher, Goldstein takes an increasingly broad view of how students can best deal with the issues that arise in their lives and in their practice. "The path is really about awakening from ignorance and I just see the appropriateness of a range of skillful means in dealing with what comes up," he told me. "In some ways, it could be said that the dharma—the way things are—is a double helix consisting of relative truth and absolute truth and that they keep winding around one another. To the degree that one has the wisdom or perspective of absolute truth, it facilitates work on the relative or personal level. Then the more we actually deal with our issues on the personal level, the greater access that gives us to absolute truth. It's easy to go too far in either direction. On the one hand, there's a danger of getting so enmeshed in the personal level that one loses sight of the bigger perspective—the essential emptiness and impermanence of it all. But there's also a danger of getting attached to the concept of emptiness, and then wrongly assuming that because everything is ultimately empty, nothing really matters."

9

PUTTING CONSCIOUSNESS
ON THE MAP

How Ken Wilber Married Freud and the Buddha

*To know that what is impenetrable to us really exists,
manifesting itself as the highest wisdom and the most
radiant beauty which our dull faculties can comprehend
only in their most primitive forms—this knowledge, this
feeling, is at the center of true religiousness. In this
sense, and in this sense only, I belong to the ranks of
devoutly religious men.*
—ALBERT EINSTEIN

*The ultimate metaphysical secret, if we dare to state it so
simply, is that there are no boundaries in the universe.
Boundaries are illusions, products not of reality but of
the way we map and edit reality. And while it is fine to
map out the territory, it is fatal to confuse the two.*
—KEN WILBER

NO one has described the path to wisdom more
systematically and comprehensively than Ken
Wilber. Almost completely self-educated, he
wrote his first book, *The Spectrum of Consciousness,* at the age
of twenty-three. During the two decades since then, Wilber has
meticulously mapped the stages of human development in a dozen
books aimed at synthesizing Western psychology and the Eastern
spiritual traditions. His work is testament to the value of rigorous,
discriminating thinking in the pursuit of a more complete life.

Wilber's "full spectrum" model is based on the premise that human development unfolds in predictable stages that extend beyond those recognized by most Western psychologists. Only by moving successfully through each stage, he argues, is it possible first to develop a healthy sense of individuality and ultimately to experience a broader identity that both transcends *and* includes the separate self.

Acknowledged by most colleagues as the leading theoretician of consciousness, Wilber is known to them mostly through his writing. Now in his mid-forties, he lives alone in Boulder, Colorado, spends most of his waking hours writing and meditating, declines all offers to speak and teach, rarely gives interviews, and limits himself to a small circle of friends who themselves often have trouble reaching him by phone. No one I sought out for this book was harder to get to than Wilber. Once he had agreed to talk, however, no one gave more generously of his time. Eventually, we spent dozens of hours discussing his ideas and those of others. What Wilber brings to the seach for wisdom is an extraordinarily penetrating, synthetic, and discriminating intellect; a nearly encyclopedic knowledge of psychology, philosophy, mysticism, anthropology, sociology, religion, and even physics; and vast personal experience with the states of consciousness that can be accessed through meditation.

Because he is not tied to any particular dogma, Wilber functions as both a theoretician about consciousness and a critic of the individual strengths, myths, pretensions, shortcomings, and outright falsehoods contained in any given approach to wisdom. At the same time, he makes his personal preferences clear. He is more passionately interested in the higher stages of consciousness than in the personal levels of ego development, and he is more drawn to the intellectual and spiritual realms than to those of the heart and body. He spent several years in psychotherapy in his twenties and has read the literature exhaustively, but for the past two decades, by far his main practice has been meditation: at least two hours every day, along with dozens of longer retreats. Wilber counts many gains from meditation—a greater sense of freedom, equanimity, clarity, and inner quiet; a more focused yet spacious awareness; and an increased capacity for even-handed self-observation. But finally it is the spiritual dimension that has moved him most. "Meditation was invented as a way for the soul to venture inward, there ultimately to find a supreme identity with Godhead," he has written. "Whatever else it does, and it does many beneficial things, meditation is first and foremost a search for the God within."

I deeply wanted to believe that the sort of truth and meaning I was after could finally be explained logically in words—and it was with that in mind that I sought out Wilber. He came far closer to doing so than anyone I encountered. His maps of the route to wisdom cover more of the *observable* territory than any other theoretician. But detailed and encompassing as they are, they still cannot capture the full range of human experience and possibility. Wilber does not spend much time, for example, addressing the more subjective realms of everyday experience—among them, the intuitions of the body and the passions of the heart, both of which resist systematic observation and developmental logic. Even so, the observations he has made in these areas are characteristically trenchant.

For a long time, Wilber and I had a somewhat formal relationship in which he served as teacher and I willingly played the role of student. He had an enormous store of knowledge, I had a huge appetite to learn, and in response to my questions, he was invariably logical, cogent, and intellectually persuasive. Over time, I discovered that Wilber can also be warm, charming, patient, generous, funny, insightful, and entertaining. Eventually, we began to talk nearly as much about relationships, movies, and mutual friends as we did about wisdom. Although our relationship was conducted mostly through phone and by fax, we developed a closeness on many levels. In turn, I came to understand that Wilber can't simply be pigeonholed as an intellectual. While he lives a mostly solitary life built around the mind, he has many other dimensions. When his personal circumstances changed suddenly and dramatically in the fall of 1983, for example, he gracefully embraced an entirely different role. Less than a month after he was married to Treya Killam, she was diagnosed with breast cancer. During the next six years, he gave up his routine of writing and meditating almost entirely in order to care for her. Treya died in 1989, and he tells the story of their relationship in his moving and uncharacteristically personal memoir, *Grace and Grit: Spirituality and Healing in the Life and Death of Treya Killam Wilber.*

At the same time, Wilber makes no apologies for the highly theoretical emphasis that continues to characterize most of his work. He leads, he says, with his strongest suit—the capacity to absorb, synthesize, categorize, and make sense of vast amounts of information from disparate fields. For twenty years, his central goal has been to objectively document the *stages* of consciousness development—the deep unvarying structures—including those beyond the ego levels described by Freud and Western psychology. The result is the most comprehensive cartography of consciousness yet produced—a map that spans the spectrum of human possibilities as they have been defined in both the East and the West.

Wilber readily acknowledges a broad group of great thinkers and sages whose work he has drawn on and sought to connect. His Western influences include Sigmund Freud, Carl Jung, R. D. Laing, Jean Piaget, and Alan Watts. The Eastern influences include Krishnamurti, Ramana Maharshi, D. T. Suzuki, Sri Aurobindo, and perhaps most important, the Buddha. Wilber has also drawn on other developmental mappers, most notably Lawrence Kohlberg and his onetime student Carol Gilligan, who have systematically charted the moral stages of development. It is by integrating and elucidating these disparate thinkers that Wilber has come to be seen as the leading theoretician in a field known today as transpersonal psychology.

The notion of a psychology dealing with the issues that transcend one's ordinary sense of self originated with a remarkable man named Anthony Sutich. His personal search grew out of desperate circumstances. Born in 1907, Sutich had an accident at the age of twelve, while playing baseball, that led to a progressive rhematoid arthritis. Sutich's formal education ended in the ninth grade, and by the time he reached eighteen, he was totally physically disabled. Hospitalized and told he had only a few months to live, he found that the hospital nurses would stop by to talk with him, pouring out their woes and seeking his advice. Sutich not only survived but went on to live an incredibly productive life for the next fifty years—even though he remained permanently confined to a gurney, largely unable to move.

Despite these awkward physical circumstances, people continued to be drawn to Sutich's instinctive empathy and insight, much as the hospital nurses had been. At the age of thirty-one, he became a group counselor for the blind, and three years later, he opened a full-time private practice as a counselor. In addition to his clinical work, he pursued a rich intellectual life. Sutich was a voracious reader, particularly in psychology and philosophy, and he kept up a prolific correspondence with psychologists, writers, politicians, and various intellectuals. It was in 1949 that he made his first contact with Abraham Maslow. They became immediate friends. Together—at Sutich's instigation—they founded both the Association for Humanistic Psychology and the *Journal of Humanistic Psychology* in 1961. Built around the theories of psychologists such as Maslow, Carl Rogers, Rollo May, and Fritz Perls, humanistic psychology focused far more on nurturing the human potential than on exploring psychopathology.

In 1966, Sutich—still on his gurney—attended the infamous Esalen seminar at which Maslow hoped to begin developing a new language for the higher human possibilities that he'd long been studying. Michael Murphy had reluctantly invited Fritz Perls as a participant, and Perls ended up taunting Maslow for being overly intellectual. For Sutich, the experience—along with a seminar earlier that week devoted to the relationship between humanistic psychology and theology—was both upsetting and inspiring. In the months that followed, Sutich began to reconsider his commitment to humanistic psychology. Perhaps it wasn't as embracing as he had thought. He had already begun to read widely in the Eastern and Western mystical literature, including books on yoga, Buddhism and Theosophy, as well as classical texts such as the *Bhagavad Gita* and the *Upanishads*. He had spent time with leading thinkers about the East, including Alan Watts and Krishnamurti. "The concept of self-actualization was no longer comprehensive enough," he wrote later. "I felt that something was lacking in the orientation, and that it did not adequately accommodate the depths of the cultural turn toward the 'inner-personal' world or give sufficient attention to the place of man in the universe or cosmos."

Soon after the Esalen experience, Sutich wrote to Maslow suggesting that they launch another new field together. He proposed the name "humanisticism"—an awkward attempt to blend humanism and mysticism. Enthusiastic about the concept, Maslow replied by suggesting that the field instead be called "transhumanism." Maslow had been reading widely in the mystical literature himself, and he and Sutich continued to correspond about the new field's possibilities. In the fall of 1967, Maslow gave a speech titled "The Farther Reaches of Human Nature," to a thousand people at the San Francisco Unitarian Church. In it he shared for the first time his thoughts on what he termed a "fourth force" in psychology—beyond behaviorism, Freudianism, and his own third force of humanism. Specifically, Maslow argued for the need to evolve a psychology of transcendent experiences and transcendent values. "The fully developed (and very fortunate) human being, working under the best conditions," Maslow said, "tends to be motivated by values which transcend his self."

Inspired anew by Maslow's talk, Sutich set out to formally define the field. This emerging fourth force, he concluded, should be concerned with everything from ultimate values, self-transcendence, unitive consciousness, and mystical experiences, to peak experiences, ecstasy, awe, wonder, spirit, and ultimate meaning. Stanislav Grof, drawn to the psychology of higher states through his own experiments with clinical LSD research, came up with the word *transpersonal* during a meeting with Maslow. "The more I think of it," Maslow wrote Sutich afterward, "the more this word says what we are all trying to say, that is, beyond individuality, beyond the development of the individual person into something which is more inclusive." The first issue of the *Journal for Transpersonal Psychology* was published in 1969. Sutich served as editor, and Michael Murphy as associate editor. The rest of the editorial board constituted a who's who of the consciousness movement—among them Grof, Maslow, Alan Watts, Huston Smith, and psychosynthesis founder Roberto Assagioli. The lead article in the first issue was a reprint of Maslow's lecture at the Unitarian Church. Meanwhile, the Association for Transpersonal Psychology was founded that same year, and Elmer Green's wife, Alyce, was elected its first president.

In the years that followed, several key researchers helped put transpersonal psychology on a firmer scientific footing. Elmer Green was certainly one, particularly through his work with theta biofeedback, which helped give a measurable framework to the transpersonal realms. Another was Stan Grof, through his continuing experiments using LSD as a psychotherapeutic tool. Grof discovered, for example, that under the influence of LSD, patients typically first experience vivid regressions to childhood and infancy. After reliving and working through the conflicts from these periods, subjects frequently moved next to perinatal experiences, including birth itself. This process, Grof discovered, directly parallels the classical spiritual descriptions of death and rebirth. Reliving the stages of birth, he went on to argue, often leads subjects directly into the transpersonal realm.

"In my experience," he wrote, "everyone who has reached these levels develops convincing insights into the utmost relevance of the spiritual and religious dimensions in the universal scheme of things." For those subjects who did experience the death-rebirth sequence, Grof found that subsequent sessions typically focused exclusively on the transpersonal realm. "The common denominator of this otherwise rich and ramified group of phenomena," he has written, "is the feeling of the individual that consciousness expanded beyond the usual ego boundaries and limitations of time and space."

A third researcher, Charles Tart, has done more than anyone to establish *states* of consciousness—including those in the transpersonal realm—as a legitimate field of scientific inquiry. Over the past thirty years, Tart has made it his mission to measure and document an array of nonordinary states of consciousness in which unique capacities emerge—among them psychic states, hypnotic trance states, out-of-body and near-death experiences, various forms of dreaming, psychedelic drug states, and a variety of meditative experiences. Cultivating voluntary access to more states of consciousness, Tart has argued, expands the range of human possibility and thus represents a key step on the road to a more complete life. His best-known book, *Altered States of Consciousness,* brought together thirty-five articles on a variety of nonordinary states, including the hypnagogic or theta state, dreaming, meditation, hypnotic trance, and the psychedelic experience. Tart also included an article about the effects of autogenic training, as well as three of the earliest studies of the effects of meditation and biofeedback on brainwave activity. "This data cannot be ignored," he concluded, "if we are to develop a comprehensive psychology."

While Ken Wilber is widely seen as transpersonal psychology's leading theorist, he views himself in a broader perspective. His influences come as much from traditional Western psychology and philosophy as from the Eastern contemplative traditions, equally from Freud and the Buddha. While his transpersonal colleagues have focused on establishing the legitimacy and value of nonordinary states of consciousness, Wilber has been more interested in establishing a model of consciousness development that begins with the prepersonal stages of infancy, extends through the ego levels, and continues up to the highest stages of transpersonal realization. While the overwhelming majority of his transpersonal colleagues focus on the highest stages of development, Wilber is more interested in what he calls the "full spectrum."

Like Michael Murphy, Wilber began on a conventional road to success and established all-American credentials early in life. His father was a career officer in the Air Force, and the family moved to a new town nearly every year, but Wilber managed to adapt quickly and easily. He was elected student body president at two different schools, captained the football team in junior high school, graduated at the top of his class, and gave the valedictory speech. Just to keep his bases covered, he also ran with the wilder jocks, drinking beer, smoking cigarettes, and making trouble. "I was very attuned to the outer world, very outgoing, and very eager to be liked," he told me. Moving so frequently was painful—Wilber still remembers sobbing almost continuously for several days when he had to leave one town—but it had its compensations. "I learned to get involved with people very quickly and intimately," he explained, "but also to hold everything lightly. It was a real Buddhist education: to be open, and yet to know that everything comes and goes."

The pain of moving was softened, Wilber believes, by a certain level of security that his parents provided. "My father was abandoned by his own father when he was four, his mother died of tuberculosis soon after, and he was raised by an uncle until high school when his father came back. Yet he never blamed any of life's difficulties on his father's leaving him or his mother's death. He always struck me as a very together guy: handsome, likable, and respected, someone who did very well despite his setbacks. My mother was one of four sisters, all drop-dead gorgeous and all very close to each other. She was a housewife, and she was very devoted to me. When it came time to really let me go, that became a real problem. But what I really appreciated about both of my parents as I grew up was that they supported me, and they gave me intellectual freedom. They were proud of what I accomplished, but neither of them ever pushed me or even said, 'Do your homework.' The result was that I ended up following my own interests—and pushing myself very hard."

After graduating from high school in Lincoln, Nebraska, Wilber went off to Duke University in the fall of 1967, intending to become a doctor. Throughout high school, he'd been passionate about science, building chemistry laboratories in his basement and winning prizes at science fairs. "I fashioned a self that was built on logic, structured by physics, and moved by chemistry," he wrote later. "My mental youth was an idyll of precision and accuracy, a fortress of the clear and evident." But no sooner did Wilber arrive at Duke than he realized he had no desire to be there. "I knew what science had to offer—objective knowledge—and it didn't interest me anymore. I wanted knowledge about interior, psychological, spiritual questions, although I didn't yet formulate it that way. I just knew from the very first day that there was nothing the university was teaching that I wanted to know. It was a classic global existential crisis. I was looking for meaning—for God—and I'd run through all of the outer places you can find it."

In search of other answers, Wilber happened one day to pick up a small classic work by the Chinese philosopher Lao Tzu. The opening lines of the *Tao Te Ching* include these:

> Truly, only he that rids himself forever of desire
> can see the Secret Essences;
> He that has never rid himself of desire can only
> see the Outcomes.
> These two things issue from the same source,
> but nevertheless are different in form.
> This source we can but call the Mystery.
> The doorway whence issue all secret essences.

Here suddenly was an entirely different way of looking at the world: a focus not on external goals but on an exploration of deeper meaning beyond logic, beyond science, even beyond the ordinary definitions of self. Wilber began reading voraciously in the mystical literature. "It was as if my previous lifelong 'repression of the sublime' . . . was now compelling me to redress the balance with an almost pathological seriousness," he wrote later.

He devoured mystical texts such as the *Bhagavad Gita* and the *Kabbalah,* the writings of East-West synthesizers such as Aldous Huxley and Huston Smith, and those of the Zen-inflected beat poets such as Gary Snyder. He studied Sufism, Hinduism, and Buddhism. Reading Alan Watts led him to the Indian mystic Krishnamurti and the Western philosopher Norman O. Brown, who pointed him in turn to Freud. Mesmerized by Freud's insights about the early stages of development and the role of the unconscious, Wilber devoured his entire collected works. "I hadn't known anything about Freud or about systems of meditation," Wilber told me, "but now I had this intellectual puzzle: How do all these people and ideas fit together? It was absolutely fascinating to me. Suddenly, I wasn't just tinkering with chemistry. I was on to something that had to do with my own happiness, my own salvation, what life was really about."

Wilber quit Duke after his sophomore year and returned to Nebraska, where his family was still living. He was committed to pursuing his self-education and had no real interest in returning to classes. However, in order to get a deferment from the draft—and still conventional enough to want a college degree—Wilber enrolled at the University of Nebraska. He decided to major in chemistry and physics simply because they came so easily to him. Dispensing with his required assignments in short order, he spent the rest of each day—five, seven, even ten hours—reading his own syllabus of Eastern philosophy and Western psychology. He ordered books by mail, a dozen at a time, from the Shambhala Bookstore in Berkeley, which specialized in esoteric texts. "I was not doing this for a college degree, a career, tenure, or even a pat on the head," Wilber explained. "I was doing it because I felt I must; for me it was a Grail search."

During this same period, Wilber began therapy with Bob Young, an eclectically trained, intellectually wide-ranging psychologist. The main issue that Wilber found himself struggling with was anger—more specifically, his difficulty in expressing it directly. "I was very angry, at everything and everyone," he told me, "but it tended to come out in snideness and sarcasm—or simply as anxiety. I went into therapy to deal with all of that." Before long, the therapy focused on his relationship with his mother. "My biggest complaint was that I felt smothered by her, and oversheltered," he explained. "My father wasn't around a lot when I was growing up, and I became not only my mother's darling kid but almost a substitute husband. She did the best job she could have, but I still felt overwhelmed. I needed to establish my own space—without feeling that I'd be abandoned."

Young was unconventional in his techniques, and in time he and Wilber became close friends, even as their therapeutic relationship continued. "Bob was in his sixties when we met, and he became my mentor in the best sense," Wilber explained. "He was someone who asked the big questions. I talked over everything I was reading with him, and he encouraged me to explore other techniques—Perls's Gestalt, Ira Progoff's intensive journal work, which was my experiential introduction to Jung; and eventually Zen and meditation." At the same time, Wilber continued on a traditional academic track. After graduating from college, he got a master's degree in chemistry and began working toward his Ph.D. To support himself, he tutored undergraduates on the side. One day a brash, very attractive young woman named Amy Wagner arrived at his house for her first lesson—and never left. A year later, in 1972, she and Wilber were married. Bob Young was their best man.

In time, Wilber realized that while he felt better about his life, he was now suffering from what he termed "a severe case of cognitive dissonance." On the one hand, his academic work was yielding fewer and fewer rewards. "I had spent my entire life studying science," he later wrote, "only to be met with the wretched realization that science was, not wrong, but brutally limited and narrow in scope. If human beings are composed of matter, body, mind, soul and spirit, then science deals handsomely with matter and body, but poorly with mind and not at all with soul and spirit. . . . I wanted some meaning in the mess of facts I was ingesting." At the same time, Wilber found himself struggling with how to reconcile the brilliant but seemingly contradictory ideas espoused by people as diverse as Freud, Fritz Perls, and the Buddha.

"Most of these thinkers were trying to disprove what everyone else had to say," Wilber told me. "The Freud people hated the Zen Buddhists, the Zens hated Freud, Perls hated them all, and each of them claimed to have the ultimate truth. My problem was that I felt that they were all saying something true, but that *none* of them had it entirely figured out." As Wilber read more deeply and eclectically, the pieces started to fall together. "It slowly dawned on me that these people weren't all addressing the same *level* of consciousness," he explained. The question was no longer "Who is right and who is wrong?" but "How do all these truths fit together?" In a wonderfully appropriate moment, the answer came to Wilber one day in a biology laboratory where he was cutting the eyes out of cows—in order to study the mechanism of vision. "I finished in the lab that day, cleaned up, went home, walked into my kitchen, and told Amy, 'I'm quitting graduate school and I'm going to write a book.' " He was twenty-three years old.

Wilber wrote *The Spectrum of Consciousness* in longhand in three months, working twelve hours a day and rarely revising. The process, he felt, was a sufficient reward. "When I was writing, I was expressing my own higher Self; I had no doubt about that at all," he explained. "Two paragraphs into the writing . . . I knew I had come home, found myself, found my purpose, found my God. I have since never doubted it once." Wilber's faith was truly tested. It took him more than three years to get the book published, and it was rejected by twenty publishers before it finally found a home. Although he was just twenty-seven when *The Spectrum of Consciousness* came out in 1978—and while he boasted no formal credentials in psychology or philosophy—the book attracted immediate attention and extraordinary notices. James Fadiman, a founder of the Association for Transpersonal Psychology, concluded that "Wilber has written the most sensible, comprehensive book about consciousness since William James." In a systematic way, Wilber synthesized the thinking of dozens of

Western psychologists and Eastern mystics to lay out a model of human development from infancy to enlightenment. Less than two years later, he followed up with *No Boundary,* a leaner, more accessible description of his full-spectrum model of consciousness. Over the next ten years, he produced an average of about one book a year—each one relating his developmental theories about consciousness to a different field, ranging from evolution to sociology, from anthropology to physics.

I first came to deeply appreciate Wilber's work during three marathon days that we spent together at his home in Boulder in the summer of 1991. By that point, I'd spent more than a year pursuing him, and we'd spoken twice by phone. In response both to my persistence and passion, Wilber had finally agreed to sit down with me. In person, he made an instantly memorable impression. I'd seen pictures of him, but when he came to the door of his large, airy, modern house on a hill overlooking Boulder, I was still surprised. At six foot four, he is tall, lean, and muscular from working out with free weights every day. The most striking thing about him, however, is his head. It is totally shaved, making it look especially large in relation to his body. He began shaving it in his early twenties, during a period when he followed a strict ascetic Zen practice that included living on brown rice, working at a manual job, and sitting in meditation for long hours. Over the years, this practice gave way to a more worldly lifestyle, but by then his hairline had begun to recede and he'd grown used to a shaved head.

We didn't spend much time in idle chatter. Instead, we sat down in his living room and began to talk about his work almost immediately. I never sensed a time limit, and Wilber never seemed to tire. The only times we broke were to eat, and he turned out to be a solicitous host, having prepared quiches and pasta salads for us in advance. It soon became clear that whatever Wilber does, he brings to it an exceptionally engaged attention. During the fifteen to twenty hours that we spent together over the next several days,

I realized that I'd become the beneficiary of the singular focus that he ordinarily brings to his writing, reading, and meditation.

More than any theoretician who has analyzed the path to wisdom, Wilber makes a powerful case that the stages of human development unfold in a predictable, consistent sequence. Even after one reaches the highest stage of personality development— the fully integrated ego described by Freud and others—Wilber argues that it is possible to cultivate equally well-delineated stages of transpersonal development. At the same time, he says, no stage replaces or negates an earlier one. "The higher stage always has access to those below it," Wilber told me. "Each succeeding level has all the capacities of the previous level, and then it adds something extra. That something extra is what makes it transcending in relation to the previous one. What's negated is not the previous stage but its limitations. Each stage transcends *and* includes."

This explains how it is possible to simultaneously experience both a separate self and a sense of unity or oneness with a larger whole. "At the first transpersonal stage, the mind quiets down and you palpably feel yourself as one with all manifestation," Wilber told me. "But that doesn't mean you don't know where your body or mind are. Even in this higher state, you can respond accurately when someone says, 'Where are you?' and you can be perfectly aware of your own body. The shift is that you're no longer so *identified* with your separate self—or with your thoughts." Another way to conceive of it, Wilber said, is to think of each stage as a broadening of identity. "To be part of a larger whole doesn't mean that the part evaporates," he has written. "You are an individual, yet you also feel that you are part of the larger unit of a family, which is a larger part of a society. Mysticism is just the even larger identity of also feeling part of the cosmos at large, and thus finding even greater meaning and value."

For Wilber, this insight lay at the heart of his developmental approach. "If one philosophical system can embrace another but not vice versa, then the more encompassing is the more valid," he told me. "I tried to look at all the Western developmental studies, as well as what's been written about the Eastern stages of growth, and then create a master template—a comprehensive psychology of matter, body, mind, soul, and spirit. I also did this cross-culturally. While the surface structures are very different, I found strong similarities in the deep underlying structures in every culture and throughout history. The fact that each stage of development transcends and includes its predecessor gives coherence to the whole model, a unity to the unfolding of consciousness. What it really means is that the universe hangs together. In essence, I picked up where Maslow left off with his developmental hierarchy. I set out to plug modern Western psychology back into the Great Chain of Being—what Huxley called the perennial philosophy."

The set of truths that form the perennial philosophy have been embraced by virtually all of the great contemplative traditions, West and East. Among dozens of areas of common philosophical ground, Wilber ferreted out seven that he considers central. First, Spirit, or God, or a Supreme Reality exists. Second, it is found within one's self. Third, most of us don't recognize this Spirit because we live with an illusory sense of separateness from others and from the universal ground of all being. Fourth, the path to liberation requires building a broader identity in which the wholly separate sense of self is surrendered. Fifth, if this path is followed to its conclusion, it leads finally to rebirth, or enlightenment—in the form of either a direct experience of the Spirit within or oneness with God. Sixth, this experience marks the end of suffering. And seventh, the natural outgrowth of such enlightenment is a life grounded in compassion and directed toward selfless service.

Wilber went on to characterize ten broad stages of the development of consciousness. Drawing on developmental psychologists including Piaget, Jane Loevinger, and Margaret Mahler, Wilber first delineated the early stages of consciousness development. Stage one, he said, is marked by the newborn's first capacities for sensation and perception. The development of impulses

354

and emotions and the capacity for thinking in images emerge in stage two, between the ages of one and three. In stage three—usually from ages three to six, the child begins to use the symbols and concepts that form the heart of language. Taking on the role of others and performing rule-based tasks begins at stage four, around age six or seven. Stage five—the highest level of development that most Westerners reach—is marked by the capacity for rational understanding, introspective thinking, deductive reasoning, and socially acceptable behavior. This usually starts around adolescence, ages twelve to fourteen. Stage six, Wilber concluded, represents the highest potential stage of personal development. It is characterized by a more integrated form of thinking, including the ability to synthesize concepts, connect ideas, and relate truths to one another. It is also the first stage at which a genuine mind-body integration occurs.

Wilber's main theoretical breakthrough was to suggest that this development can continue beyond these first six levels to the transpersonal stages, which also unfold sequentially. None of these higher realms are generally recognized by Western psychologists or cultures. Instead, the norm or center of gravity in modern Western culture is what Wilber calls stage five. "Society creates a subtle pressure to evolve up to that level," Wilber told me. "If you don't, you are regarded as retarded. But society exerts an equally strong pressure not to evolve beyond that level. The magnet at stage five pulls both ways—up for those below it, down for those who move above. To develop the higher stages, you're on your own. You have to go against society's norms."

While the higher transpersonal stages of consciousness have long been described in the Eastern literature, Wilber was the first theoretician to map them as a continuation of ordinary ego development and to describe their qualities in accessible psychological terms. By Wilber's model, the seventh or *psychic* stage—one in which psychic capacities may indeed emerge—refers to the beginning stages of transpersonal awareness. This is the level at which one has the first direct apprehension of God or a higher Spirit in the universe. "You sense—for a few seconds or even a few hours at a time—that there is something utterly divine about the entire cosmos, and you might even experience that oneness directly," Wilber told me.

Stage eight is called the *subtle* level. Subtle refers to the notion that there are processes of consciousness more subtle than everyday, outer-directed experience. States of intense and luminous inner light may arise, for example. "This stage is one in which you touch divinity, even unite with divinity, in an all-encompassing love," Wilber explained. In his system, seven and eight represent the two stages of "soul" development—"a halfway house between the personal ego-mind and the impersonal or transpersonal Spirit," he told me. "The soul is one's deepest, archetypal essence. It is also the home of the Witness, or more specifically the capacity to observe one's thoughts and emotions without attachment or identification."

The *causal* level—stage nine—is not just a union of soul and God but a "supreme identity" or pure Spirit. This occurs, Wilber concluded, when union is so complete that there is no sense of self at all, a state of consciousness akin to deep dreamless sleep or pure emptiness. It is also the last stance of the pure witness—but without any separate objects of attention. Paradoxically, it is characterized by an expansive awareness. "Nothing is happening," Wilber told me, "and yet it is the fullness out of which everything emerges." The tenth and highest stage—nonduality, or the absence of any split between subject and object—is both the easiest and the hardest to explain. "The tenth really isn't a separate stage," he explained, "but the ground and reality of all stages, high or low, sacred and profane. It is simply the reality or the 'isness' of everything. It's extraordinarily *ordinary*. The sages at this point are always depicted as so utterly ordinary that you can't even spot them in a crowd. There appears to be nothing special about them because they are simply one with whatever arises."

Both stages nine and ten reflect the level of Spirit. "Once you push through the soul level, then the Witness itself collapses into everything witnessed," Wilber told me. "You don't witness the clouds, you *are* the clouds. The wind doesn't blow on you, it blows through you, or within you. There is no gap between you and what you are aware of. You're the sum total of everything that arises from moment to moment. This radically simple and nondual awareness is, as Zen would put it, the 'Original Face'— the one you had even before your parents were born. It's your timeless and primordial state. You are not entering this state, because you never left it. You are simply recognizing it. The entire universe is a reflection in your mind's own mirror." Distinguishing between these stages is critical, Wilber argues: "What you get at each of these four transpersonal levels are four different types of mystical experiences that have usually been lumped together. In reality, each one is reached by different techniques and leads to a radically different understanding and experience."

As Wilber sees it, nearly all theorists and wisdom traditions, both Western and Eastern, have promoted the value of certain stages while repudiating or neglecting others. Western psychology, most profoundly through Freud, has evolved a highly sophisticated understanding of the development of a healthy ego, as well as the disruptions and pathologies that may occur at each stage along the way. At the same time, Freud considered any so-called mystical experiences to be primitive, infantile, and even pathological rather than encompassing and transcendental. The Eastern meditative traditions, by contrast, have focused with great subtlety on techniques for developing the transpersonal stages of consciousness. However, they've almost uniformly overlooked the issues of personal development, contending that any such attention only reinforces the illusion of a truly separate self. "Freud is unmatched in his understanding about the early stages, but he doesn't come close to some of the insights the Buddha had about the higher states," Wilber told me. "The Buddha, for all his brilliance, never had any of Freud's seminal insights about early development and the role of the repressed unconscious."

Wilber makes a distinction between moving to higher stages

of consciousness and nurturing specific human potentials. "The right and left hemispheres, as just one example, are not levels of consciousness," he argues, "although they are constantly mistaken for that. Rather, left and right are two aspects of consciousness that are present on all levels—except the very lowest and highest ones. It's important to develop the potentials of both the left and right hemispheres—and you miss something if you do not—but they'll tend to be expressed at whatever level you happen to be at. Gaining more access to the right hemisphere or the left does not specifically lead to higher development."

Similarly, in Wilber's model, dreams occur at all levels of consciousness except the lowest and the highest. "A dream symbol," he told me, "can represent an important message from any of the major levels of consciousness, and all of these various interpretations need to be checked out in order to unlock the dream message. The higher one's level of development, the more likely it is that one can make use of the dream in more varied, richer, and broader ways. At the same time, dreams can always remind you of problems on the lower levels that you have neglected." In a similar way, Wilber contends that the experience of flow, or the ideal performance state, represents a powerful human potential but doesn't necessarily reflect higher development. Flow can occur at many different levels of consciousness, including relatively primitive ones.

Wilber's model has a wonderful theoretical orderliness. Only after one successfully negotiates a given stage, he maintains, is it possible to fully inhabit the next one. "Just as sitting precedes standing in physical development and letters are always learned before words in intellectual development," he says, "so the stages of consciousness unfold in sequential fashion. You can't bypass any of them. Until you work out unresolved issues lodged in the unconscious, they stand in the way of higher development. If you have large repressed material from the lower stages, it will just eat up your attention and energy. The more consciousness that is trapped in these lower stages—say, in some unresolved issue with your mother at the age of four—the less consciousness you have available to find a home in the stages beyond ego."

When development proceeds smoothly, Wilber told me, identity grows progressively broader and more encompassing. At the first transpersonal stage, for example, the witness begins to emerge. "In a sense, the individual [is] able to let go of his individual concerns and view them with a creative detachment and indifference, realizing that whatever problems his personal self faces, his deep self can transcend," he has written. "He would find, haltingly at first but then with an ever increasing certainty, a profound center of awareness that persists unperturbed, like the depths of the ocean, even though the surface waves of consciousness be swept with ripples of pain, anxiety or despair." This model takes into account certain aspects of emotional development, including the role of love. "At the personal level, you might feel love for your wife," Wilber explains. "As you move to a higher stage, you don't give up that love but you are able to expand it to include the community and ultimately the universe. At the highest level, the statement 'Love thy neighbor as thyself' is not a moral injunction but a description of a state of consciousness in which you and your neighbor are experienced as one and the same."

In everyday life—as Wilber himself readily acknowledges— development takes place far less smoothly, predictably, and sequentially. Needs fail to be met in the lower stages, repression occurs, blockages build up. But unless these disruptions are severe, Wilber believes, people still tend to move up the ladder of development. "All you need is a passing grade to get to the next stage," he told me. New capacities that emerge at any given stage may be used not only to broaden consciousness but also to avoid issues left unresolved at a lower stage. The emergence of logical and rational powers are a potential tool of greater wisdom and depth, for example, but also a means by which to rationalize, intellectualize, and distance oneself from painful feelings and impulses that persist in earlier stages.

Similarly, a taste of a transpersonal stage—the glorious experience of oneness and unity, for example—may provide a broader identity and a larger perspective, but it can also be an excuse for avoiding unresolved issues of self-esteem or anger. Rather than transcend and *include* the capacities of the previous stage—as Wilber characterized ideal development—people often transcend and *exclude* the conflicts they leave behind. "A lot of people seek out meditation as a way of spiritually bypassing the lower stages, but it simply doesn't work," Wilber told me. "The issues persist, and they eventually find ways of expressing themselves."

Wilber rejects the classical Eastern teaching that the stages of ego development are inferior and that the separate self is somehow suboptimal. "That's like saying an acorn is a suboptimal oak," he says. "In fact, the acorn is perfect just as it is. The ego is basically an acorn for one's spiritual self. It's a perfect stage in a larger process, fine as far as it goes, as optimal as you can get an ego to be. If you destroy the acorn—or the ego—you destroy the possibility for an oak—or a higher self." In practice, even the higher stages have limitations. It is possible, Wilber argues, in much the way that Kornfield does, to cultivate a very high degree of consciousness and understanding at a transpersonal level, yet to be very unconscious and primitive at another. Likewise, it is not uncommon to act with selflessness, sophistication, and compassion under conditions of security, and to regress to a lower stage under more stressful circumstances. The path to wisdom, in Wilber's model, is built around progressively broadening one's boundaries and thus enlarging one's sense of self. "The aim is to remember something of ourselves that we had formerly forgotten. To remember is simply to re-member and re-collect . . . to make whole that which was split and fragmented."

From the moment that *The Spectrum of Consciousness* was published, Wilber found himself besieged with offers to teach, lecture, give interviews, and appear at conferences. After accepting several speaking dates, he quickly pulled back. "It was completely unbalancing," he told me. "What you get are a lot of people telling you how great you are. Within a short time, you start believing them, and then you're headed for disaster. I simply didn't feel competent to appear in public as a teacher. I might have theoretically understood the big picture, but that doesn't in any way guarantee that it will permeate your personal life. There was a lot of growth and personal work I still had to do. I wasn't about to appear in public as an exemplar of the full spectrum person."

Instead, Wilber stayed home in Lincoln and focused on his writing and his continuing inner work. He kept up therapy with Bob Young and tried a variety of other self-exploration techniques, including dreamwork and work in groups. He also continued to meditate in a classical Zen practice that was very demanding—and not immediately rewarding. "I finally got so I could sit in full lotus for twenty or thirty minutes at a time, but I didn't have a single positive piece of feedback for many months after I first started," Wilber told me. "I'd try to watch my mind, and I'd get lost. I learned to keep count of my breaths from one to ten, but nothing came of it. Three or four years went by before I got my first real rush. I don't even know why I continued, except I was absolutely convinced that this was the thing to be doing—that it was the route to my salvation." To help pay his share of the rent, Wilber worked part time at a series of menial jobs—washing dishes, pumping gas, stocking grocery shelves. "It was very grounding for me to get out of the house," he explained. "The work I did was often difficult and gruesome, but I never minded it. And the advantage was that when I left work each day, it was done. Any other job would have invaded the rest of my life."

His primary passion remained his writing. During the next decade, Wilber not only published ten books but wrote dozens of articles for academic journals. He was well aware that he had chosen a highly intellectual approach to the search for wisdom, but he made no apologies for it. "When people say to me, 'Aren't you leaving out feelings and the personal dimension in your work?' or 'Don't you use writing to avoid your personal problems?' my response is, 'Maybe I do, and maybe I don't.' The fact is that I have these ideas, and for me, tying them together is what seems most important. The main work I do in the world is writing. I average six to ten hours a day, seven days a week, 365 days a year. On intense writing days, I go up to fifteen to eighteen hours. When I first started meditating, I sat for three to four hours a day. Once a week, I'd take a whole day and sit ten or twelve hours. I still sit every day for at least two hours. These are my two main practices: meditating and writing. They are very solitary, and what I do is very cognitive. My strong point is my mind, no question. That's the talent I was given. If I could sing or sculpt my ideas, maybe I'd do that. I just happen to believe that the main component of human growth and development is through consciousness, and that the main way to get these ideas across is through my writing."

On a practical level, Wilber's greatest contribution may be as a critic of teachers, gurus, techniques, ideas, and systems that promise routes to encompassing truth but are in fact incomplete, misleading, or misguided. "I'm the guy," Wilber told me only half-jokingly, "who comes in after the party and tries to straighten up the mess. If you don't have any map when it comes to consciousness, you can wander around and get hopelessly lost. Some people have charted the road better than others, but I found all of the maps to be incomplete and insufficient. I tried to take *everyone's* map, put them all together, and fill in the voids. That's what a full spectrum map is."

With a vast base of knowledge and a highly discriminating mind, Wilber has an unusual capacity to assess both the strengths and the shortcomings of any given approach to wisdom. One of his most penetrating and broadly useful insights is into what he terms the "pre-trans fallacy." *Pre* refers to the early stages of development that precede both language and the capacity for logical thinking. *Trans* refers to the transrational or transpersonal stages in which one acquires a broader perspective beyond personal concerns—without sacrificing rational capacities or a strong sense of self. In the pre-trans fallacy, Wilber argues, these two totally different stages of development are seen as one and the same.

"Since prerational and transrational are both, in their own ways, *non*rational, they appear quite similar or even identical to the untutored eye," Wilber has explained. Put simply, genuine transcendental awareness sometimes gets dismissed as primitive and neurotic, while more childlike, prerational experiences are often mislabeled and exalted as transcendental. The fallacy, Wilber argues, "exists to this day in both the attempts to champion mysticism and the attempts to deny it."

Wilber cites both the human potential movement and the psychedelic drug culture that sprang up in the 1960s and 1970s as hotbeds of the pre-trans fallacy. He argues, for example, that when Fritz Perls urged his students to "lose your mind and come to your senses," Perls was promoting a prerational approach in the name of higher personal growth. A transrational approach, argues Wilber, would have meant integrating the mind *and* the senses, thinking *and* feeling. In a similar way, Wilber believes that Ram Dass's call to higher consciousness—"Be here now"—was translated typically as a prepersonal, rather than a transpersonal challenge. "Most people," Wilber told me, "took 'Be here now' to mean 'All that matters is what I'm feeling and experiencing now. I don't need to be worried about tomorrow or to feel guilty about anything I did in the past.' That misses the whole meaning of the higher stages of consciousness, which transcend rationality but also embrace it. Simply to 'Be here now' isn't beyond logic, it's *beneath* it. In the transpersonal realm, you are fully aware of the present but also of the past and the future. And you aren't attached to any of it."

Wilber doesn't discount the possibility that people can break through temporarily to higher levels of development. "A peak experience—whether it's in meditation, or on a drug, or watching a sunset—is like a transfusion," he told me. "It reaches down and cracks the hell out of your present way of understanding the world. What you get is a miniature 'satori,' a little hit of a higher stage. It's not the same as transformation itself—which is permanent—but it can be a very important starting point. Your life gets jazzed around. You become more aware of new possibilities and of the limitations of the stage you're at. That's why suffering can be the first grace. If you get a glimpse of a higher stage, it tends to make you feel a little more unhappy with your present translation—the way you experience the world at whatever stage you're at. Put simply, when translation fails, transformation ensues—either up or down."

Only a tiny percentage of people, Wilber believes, finally transform to the higher stages. "Most peak experiences simply make the ego feel better—a little more secure and meaningful—by giving it a small glimpse of a bigger view," he told me. "If you're lucky, this can lead to a relatively more benign, humane way to live at the level you're already at. It can also make people self-righteous and insufferable. Unless you take on the arduous work of an ongoing practice designed to sustain the glimpse you get from a peak experience, the effect will eventually wear off. It's a fundamental error to assume that moving into the higher stages of spiritual development is easy—something you can do in a weekend workshop, or by reading a book, or by taking LSD. Only through long-term disciplines can you make these experiences stable, permanent structures of consciousness. It's very hard work. The truth is that transforming oneself is a long, laborious, painful process."

Peak experiences can also be profoundly misleading and diverting. "It's easy to see what an unbalancing effect they can have," Wilber told me. "Say you get a real glimpse—perhaps through meditation or even LSD—of the fact that you are not merely this individual bodymind, that some part of you is one with the universal being. You're ushered into new realms, and it's thrilling. But then inevitably, the experience fades. This is truly what is meant by the dark night of the soul. The fading is often an agony greater than the ego can accommodate. What happens is that many people end up wanting to shun all the lower levels—when in fact they've still got a lot of work to do there. They choose the spiritual bypass, and it's just as inadequate a solution as ignoring the higher stages altogether."

Wilber argues that two antagonistic movements have dominated the historical search for enlightenment, East and West. One is "ascending," the other "descending." The ascending movement—puritanical, monastic, ascetic—has shunned embodiment in favor of transcendence and has discounted the possibility of finding happiness in the material world. The descending movement has done just the opposite, celebrating the senses, the body, sexuality, and self-expression and rejecting the possibility of any higher or transcendental truth. "The point is to bring these two currents into some sort of balance and harmony," Wilber told me, "so that both wisdom and compassion can join hands in finding a Spirit that both transcends and includes this world. It is in the union of the ascending and the descending that harmony is found not in any brutal war between the two."

As an example of the descending current, Wilber points to the movement of modernism—and postmodernism—in the West. On the one hand, these currents have led to greater democracy and to liberation movements, to more rational legal institutions, and to scientific advances on countless fronts. But the cost, Wilber says, has been to cut people off from their own transcendental source of meaning. "Salvation—whether offered by science, earth religion, tribalism, Marxism, consumerism or sexuality—can be found only on this earth," Wilber explained, summing up the limits of modernism's descending perspective. "There is no higher truth, no ascending component, nothing transcendental whatsoever. Men and women's transcendental, spiritual impulses were toppled to an infinite grasping forward in the merely finite realms—an impossible situation, Faustian to the core."

The ascending currents, by contrast, offer routes to a higher level of truth and meaning but at considerable potential cost in the everyday realm. As perhaps the most influential of the ascending paths, Wilber cites vipassana meditation. "By simply witnessing one's thoughts, emotions, and sensations, one begins to transcend them and gain a calm detachment," he explains to me. "However, the final goal of this meditation is to entirely suspend ordinary thoughts and emotions. The personal dimensions are ignored altogether, and in traditional practice there is scant attention paid to how to integrate these higher states into ordinary life and practice."

A similar issue arises with the simplest and best-known form of Eastern spiritual practice—Transcendental Meditation. The teachers of TM, starting with the guru Maharishi Mahesh Yogi, assert that the highest levels of wisdom can be reached through mantra-based practices aimed at quieting the mind. "It's a good step in the right direction," Wilber told me. "TM introduces people to deep states of relaxation, which can reduce their anxiety and loosen their defenses. It also induces healthy physiological changes that have been measured and verified scientifically. That's all most people are seeking, and they derive these gains by sitting twice a day for twenty minutes at a time." It is even possible, through TM, to cultivate the highest stages of consciousness beyond ego, says Wilber. But even then, he argues, there are limits to the practice.

"Because the TM path aims basically at this ascending movement," he explained, "it accords very little value to the personal domains and simply assumes that they will straighten themselves out, the more relaxed one becomes. Instead, what you often get are very relaxed neurotics." Like most ascending practices, both East and West, TM simply ignores the issues of personal development. "In effect, they're blindfolding people, putting them in a chair lift, and sending them up to the top of the mountain," Wilber told me. "People may ascend to the top, but they don't get to see anything along the way, and once they arrive, they have no idea how they got there—or how to cope with the issues that continue to arise once they've experienced the highest possibilities."

Even those committed to a more conscious and complex pursuit of wisdom face considerable obstacles, says Wilber. In part, the problem is that each level of transformation requires experiencing a form of death. "In order to advance to a higher stage of development," he told me, "you need to 'die' to the worldview of the previous one. At the early stages, this happens more or less automatically. But the more conscious you become, the more frightening it is to let go of what you've already got—your sense of self—however inadequate or limited it may be." At the same time, Wilber says, Western culture provides few role models. "We don't have many 'pacers'—people who have developed beyond stage five or so—and there is no collective magnet to help pull us above that level."

The practical challenge for most people, Wilber has concluded, is not so much to transcend their boundaries as to make them more permeable. It is less to attain the highest levels of consciousness than to learn to move more freely between a range of states and stages of consciousness. This requires acknowledging and accommodating the play of opposites that characterizes everyday life. Most notable is the tension between individual concerns and more universal or transpersonal ones. A person's healthy sense of self, for example, ideally coexists with a capacity to move beyond his or her narrow agenda and to act selflessly in the service of others. The pursuit of one's highest possibilities must be balanced by the willingness to acknowledge and engage one's darker or shadow side. "The question is not just what floor of the building you're living on," Wilber told me, "but how many floors you have ready access to as you negotiate your way through life."

W ilber's own resiliency was never deeply tested during the first three decades of his life. He was successful at nearly everything he undertook. His marriage to Amy ended in 1981 after nine years, when they realized that they'd grown in very different directions. But even then, the split was amicable and they remained friends. After a year on his own—during which he lived in Cambridge, Massachusetts, and edited *ReVision,* a journal devoted to consciousness—Wilber returned to California, and moved in temporarily with Roger Walsh and his wife, Frances Vaughn. It was at their house in Mill Valley, California, that he met Treya Killam in August 1983. Wilber was thirty-three years old, and from the first night he and Treya spent talking, he felt certain that he'd met the love of his life. "When I put my arm around her, I felt all separation and distance dissolve," he wrote much later. "It was as if Treya and I had been together for lifetimes." Ten days after their first meeting, Wilber proposed marriage. "If you didn't ask me," Treya responded, "I was going to ask you." They were married in November and made plans for a honeymoon in Hawaii. Almost immediately, however, their lives were turned upside down.

Treya was diagnosed with breast cancer one week after the wedding. Despite intensive radiation, the disease proved vicious and relentless. When the cancer recurred a year later, Treya had one breast removed, but the prognosis remained grim. The likelihood of a third and fatal recurrence within nine months, the couple learned, was 50 percent. Both Treya and Ken were inclined to address the illness at every level—physical, mental, psychological, and spiritual. They began simply by gathering as much information as possible about the cancer—and soon discovered that there was little of much practical use, save that survival for more than five years after the initial diagnosis was very rare. Given the perniciousness of her cancer, they decided first to make the most radical intervention possible. "These tumors are the Nazis of the cancer crowd, and they are not terribly impressed with wheat grass juice and sweet thoughts," Wilber told me. "You have to nuke these bastards if you're going to have any chance at all—and that's where white man's medicine comes in."

At the same time, they began investigating virtually every form of alternative treatment available: from macrobiotic diets to meditation, from faith healing to laetrile, from massive doses of vitamins to visualization. Fiercely determined to beat the cancer and open to the possibility that it might have multiple causes, Treya experimented with a variety of treatments, in addition to conventional radiation and chemotherapy. These included a low-fat diet, megavitamin therapy, daily meditation and visualization practice, recording her dreams, writing her thoughts and feelings in a journal, and following a regular exercise regimen. She was particularly concerned with how her own psychological conflicts might have contributed to her illness. "Was there some secret death wish here?" she wrote in her journal soon after her diagnosis. "Had I been too hard on myself, too judgmental, too nice, repressing my anger and my judgments, so they eventually manifested as a physical symptom? Was I being punished somehow for having been given so much in this life? . . . Had I somehow earned this through the karma of some previous lifetime? Did this experience contain in it a lesson I needed to learn or the necessary push to move on in my spiritual evolution?"

Wilber took a more spacious view, focusing simply on how best to nurture Treya's own healing capacity. He was inclined to believe that emotional and spiritual factors do play some role in illness, but that guilt and self-recrimination serve no useful function. "Since nobody knows what caused your cancer," he told Treya, "why don't you use cancer as a metaphor and a spur to change all those things in your life that you wanted to change anyway? In other words, repressing certain emotions may or may not have helped cause the cancer, but since you want to stop repressing those emotions anyway, then use the cancer as a reason." In particular, he dismissed the radical but increasingly popular New Age view that we literally create our own reality and thus our illnesses. This, he said, is another pre-trans fallacy: infantile grandiosity and narcissism masquerading as higher understanding.

Over time, Treya herself began to find oppressive the well-meaning friends and acquaintances who were eager to help her find meaning in her illness, or urged her to think positive thoughts rather than feel her fear and pain, or tried to convince her that she could overcome the disease with her mind and will alone. "I needed to be around people who loved me as I was, not people who were trying to motivate me or change me or convince me of their favorite idea or theory," she wrote in an article titled "Attitudes and Cancer: What Kind of Help Really Helps?" "Certainly I worked hard to achieve physical health," she went on, "but true healing has to do with how each of us lives our lives on all levels, in all dimensions, and physical health is clearly not more important than emotional or spiritual health." Still, the advice kept right on coming. "Everybody had some theory about it; it hung in the air always," Wilber lamented. "It became an unwanted but inescapably dominant theme of our lives."

Even so, neither Ken nor Treya foresaw how overwhelming their life together would become. In 1985, they moved from California to North Lake Tahoe, Nevada, and entered a period that proved physically and psychologically devastating for both of them. Treya continued to undergo intense and punishing chemotherapy. In an unfortunate coincidence, a bizarre and still-unexplained disease blew into North Lake Tahoe in 1985 and prompted debilitating illness in more than two hundred people. Wilber was one of them. For the next two years, his symptoms, comparable to those that characterize chronic fatigue syndrome, included low-grade chronic fever, muscle dysfunction, night sweats, sore and swollen lymph nodes, and sheer exhaustion. The combination of Treya's advancing cancer and the failure to have his own illness effectively diagnosed caused Wilber to fall into a deep depression.

He found that he could not write—even though he'd never before experienced any blocks. "As men often do," he wrote later, "I defined myself by my doing, by my writing, and when that suddenly stopped I was suspended in midair without a net." Wilber also lost the motivation to meditate. "The strong taste I had of the Witness slowly evaporated," he explained. "I no longer had easy access to the 'center of the cyclone.' I only had the cyclone. When I lost access to pure open awareness—to the Witness, to my soul—I was left only with my self-contraction, with Narcissus, hopelessly absorbed in his own image." Wilber began to drink from the time he woke up until he went to sleep—vodka, beer, wine, and brandy—while sitting for hours in front of a television. "I felt I had lost all control of my life," he said. "Off and on for months I felt suicidal."

Perhaps inevitably, Ken found himself blaming Treya for his woes—at precisely a point when she had limited strength even to deal with her own more life-threatening problems. It was a terrible bind for both of them. The very source of Treya's helplessness—a pernicious cancer—gave Wilber the feeling that he had no right to assert his own growing needs or to deal with the feeling that he'd lost his own center. This, in turn, only undermined his capacity to be supportive to Treya. The relationship reached a nadir one day when Wilber got so angry that he hit Treya in frustration—the first and only time he's ever struck a woman. It proved to be a turning point for both of them. Humiliated and at wit's end, Wilber left for San Francisco, unsure what to do next but desperate for a change. Treya followed almost immediately. They went into therapy together in California, and their burden began to lift. Treya enjoyed a brief period of remission, Ken's illness finally resolved itself, and their closeness as a couple returned.

But while their relationship remained strong, Treya's physical health did not. In late 1985, several months after they settled in San Francisco, she was diagnosed with diabetes, likely triggered by the chemotherapy. It was another blow, but one that they both absorbed more easily. "One more wave to the surf," Wilber concluded at the time. Then in November 1986, there was a recurrence of the cancer, just as Treya turned forty. "Life knocked her down, she got right back up," Wilber wrote in his own journal. "If anything the events of the last year had increased her enormous resilience."

Wilber, in turn, found himself slowly accommodating to the role of full-time support person. "Everything I'd figured out theoretically paled at this point," he told me. "This was extremely concrete, very real, and very difficult. Dealing with Treya and her illness, being there for her, demanded that I truly drop everything I'd always defined myself by. I'd been completely driven to write and to be productive in my work, and in the end, I had to die completely to those desires. It was a really profound introduction to the Buddhist concept of emptiness, and I think that it served me well. Now I can do my work or not do it. I don't feel like my life depends on it."

Despite several experimental treatments, Treya's cancer continued to spread. In the summer of 1988, they returned to a new home that they'd purchased in Boulder, after an extended period during which Treya tried an experimental chemotherapy protocol in Germany. By this time, they'd both come to some sort of acceptance. Treya was simply happy to be alive, day by day, and her efforts focused not just on taking care of herself but on reaching out to others through a group called the Cancer Support Community, which she co-founded in San Francisco. "This growing acceptance of life as it is, with all the sorrow, the pain, the suffering, and the tragedy, has brought me a kind of peace," she said in a talk that she gave to others with cancer during this period. "Because I can no longer ignore death, I pay more attention to life."

Wilber himself resumed intensive meditation, and he soon felt a wider perspective return—the capacity to watch his own drama with some detachment and equanimity. "Treya's facing a potentially lethal disease is an extraordinary spur to meditative awareness," he wrote, in an article describing his experience as a support person. "Treya's cancer is a constant reminder that death is a great letting go, but you needn't wait for actual physical death to profoundly let go of your own grasping and clinging in this moment, and this moment, and this." For the last months of Treya's life, Wilber's earlier complaining, his resentment, and even his deep sadness gave way to a simple selfless desire to serve his wife. It was a phenomenon that he'd often read and even written about but never before experienced at such a personal level. Effectively, his life became a meditation-in-action. Wilber felt prepared to continue in this role indefinitely—and indeed never believed that Treya was going to die until the last forty-eight hours of her life.

By then, he'd come to see Treya—almost literally—as his other half. "In [her last] years," he wrote, "she had returned to her roots in the earth, to her love of nature, to the body, to making, to her femininity, to her grounded openness and trust and caring. I had remained where I wanted to be, where I myself am at home—in the Apollonian worlds of ideas, of logic, of concepts and symbols. Heaven is of the mind. Earth is of the body. I took feelings and related them to ideas; Treya took ideas and related them to feelings. I moved from the particular to the universal, constantly; Treya moved from the universal to the concrete, always. I loved thinking, she loved making. I loved culture, she loved nature. I shut the window so I could hear Bach; she turned off Bach so she could hear the birds."

Wilber grew convinced that the highest stage of consciousness—what he calls Spirit—is found neither solely in heaven nor on earth. "Only the balance of the two, found in the Heart, could lead to the secret door beyond death and mortality and pain," he concluded. "And that is what Treya had done for me; this is what we had done for each other: pointed the way to the Heart. . . . Far from being whole and self-contained people, we were each half-people, one of Heaven, one of Earth, and that was exactly as we should be. . . . I will always be at home in ideas. Treya will always be at home in nature, but together, joined in the Heart, we were whole; we could find that primal unity which neither alone could manage." It was this last realization—shortly before her death—that Wilber found most bittersweet: "With Treya, I thought to myself, I am beginning, just beginning, to find my Heart."

In the five years since his wife's death, Wilber has put his heart into developing and refining his full spectrum model of human potentials. He has not only addressed the levels of the spectrum—matter, body, mind, soul, and spirit—but has attempted to integrate ascending and descending currents; interior and exterior; masculine and feminine; the individual and the social. In early 1994, he published the first volume in what he calls his "Kosmos" trilogy, titled *Sex, Ecology, Spirituality*. To take on this enormous challenge, Wilber has returned to a writing schedule that runs to ten hours a day, seven days a week, and to a relatively monastic life.

But if his work is largely theoretical, his ultimate intent is also worldly and practical. "I am attempting to draw as comprehensive a map of human potentials as possible, and a good one helps chart the way," Wilber told me. "We have so few comprehensive maps available that we don't even realize the full range of what's available to us. If you don't know the Bahamas are even there, you'll never try to reach them. Still, I don't suggest the mere study of maps. What I actually recommend is finding and engaging a practice that speaks to your potentials and shows you the actual territory. The more full spectrum the practice is, in my opinion, the better. Usually, that means some combination of psychotherapy and meditation, so that it integrates ascending and descending currents. But the practice could be anything—art, community service, raising sane kids, writing novels, sports—so long as it also pulls you out of yourself and into a larger being. The point is that each of us has to take the actual journey, in our own way, in our own time, at our own pace."

10

PERSONALITY AND ESSENCE

Helen Palmer, the Enneagram, and Hameed Ali

> *Man's higher nature rests upon man's lower nature,*
> *needing it as a foundation and collapsing without this*
> *foundation.*
> —*ABRAHAM MASLOW*

> *The goal of man is Truth. Truth is more than happiness.*
> *The man who has Truth can have whatever mood he*
> *wishes, or none. . . . We have pretended that Truth is*
> *happiness and happiness Truth, and people have be-*
> *lieved us. Therefore you, too, have until now imagined*
> *that happiness must be the same as Truth. But happiness*
> *makes you its prisoner as does woe.*
> —*SUFI TEACHING*

AS powerfully as anyone I met in my search, Helen Palmer and Hameed Ali make a compelling case for the inextricable connection between Western psychological insight and Eastern spiritual understanding in the search for wisdom. Each uses Western psychological techniques to penetrate more deeply what stands in the way of something they call "essence"—a more authentic experience of the true self. While they work in very different ways, each views the personality, or ego, not just as an obstacle to essence—a false self—but also as the central vehicle through which to uncover one's true nature. In many ways, Palmer's and Ali's work represent pioneering examples of Wilber's call for a full spectrum approach to wisdom.

By the time I met Palmer, three years into my search—a year before I met Hameed Ali—I was still struggling to reconcile very contradictory experiences. Through meditation, I'd found that it was possible to tap a deep state of well-being. I'd experienced moments of great peacefulness, exhilaration, and even boundless love. But it was equally evident to me that these states were fleeting. The everyday emotions that most stood in my way—a quickness to anger, an edgy mistrust, a reluctance to open my heart—often resurfaced when I returned to the world. At the same time, I'd seen that no amount of psychological insight—nor even an improved ability to function in the world—seemed to fully address the hunger for meaning that prompted my search in the first place. I was drawn to Palmer and Ali both because they valued Western psychology as a tool for understanding personality conflicts—and because they recognized a more essential level of truth that a focus on personal concerns never addresses.

In Palmer's case, it was her work with the Enneagram, an ancient system for understanding personality types, that most interested me. The word *ennea* is Greek for "nine," and the Enneagram is a diagram of nine personality types and their interrelationships. Widely believed to have roots in the Eastern Sufi mystical tradition, the Enneagram was introduced to the West by the Russian mystic George Gurdjieff in the early 1900s and in a more accessible form by two psychiatrists, Oscar Ichazo and Claudio Naranjo, in the 1970s. Each personality type on the Enneagram is marked by a central fixation or passion—a defensive survival strategy—that prompts a very narrow, habitual, and limited way of perceiving and responding to the world. Discovering my own type, and the constellation of patterns associated with it, helped me to understand—in a way that no therapy ever had—a lifetime of puzzling, repetitive, and often self-destructive behaviors. No single tool I came across in my search for wisdom has so richly revealed the specific obstacles we each face.

Palmer's most important contribution has been to bring together panels of each personality type and to interview them in depth before students. Her book, *The Enneagram,* based on thousands of interviews, contains the most detailed and insightful descriptions of each of the nine types that I have yet come across. Even so, it is in what she calls the "oral tradition"—Palmer's way of teaching through live interviews with people—that she makes most vivid the psychological characteristics of each type and their predictable patterns of perception and behavior. The impact of watching panels is very powerful—at first, simply by giving one the experience of solidarity with other people who share a specific view of the world. Beyond that, it is startling to discover how automatically and often unconsciously each type responds to a given situation. Perhaps most important, it is both humbling and enriching to discover that there are at least nine very different ways of perceiving the same experience. Palmer's work with panels makes clear how much our fears, hopes, prejudices, and preoccupations shape our view of the world and narrow our experience.

Unlike other psychological systems, the Enneagram treats *all* personality types as inherently defensive structures. Our acquired personalities, Palmer explains, serve to mask, mimic, and protect from further harm the more essential potentials that we inherit at birth but from which we're increasingly cut off in the course of growing up. By characterizing the defensive characteristics of each personality type so precisely, the Enneagram is a unique tool for self-awareness. Most traditional psychotherapeutic techniques seek to make patients aware of unconscious defensive patterns. Moreover, the system can be used not just to identify and loosen destructive personality fixations such as fear, anger, and deceit but to convert them into their higher opposites—qualities of essence such as courage, serenity, and truthfulness. It provides a route not just to more adaptive behavior in short but to an experience of a truer self.

Palmer was in her mid-fifties when we first met in 1991, and she brought to her teaching a rare blend of skills. Trained initially as a psychologist, she became interested in consciousness and the Eastern wisdom traditions after leaving New York City and settling in Berkeley in the late 1960s. She got a job teaching psychology at a local community college, and also began to experiment with cultivating other states of consciousness. Palmer undertook a rigorous meditative practice with a Zen master and began studying the martial arts discipline aikido. It was in the course of her meditative training that she discovered an extraordinary psychic or intuitive capacity. For more than a decade beginning in 1972, she earned a living largely by giving intuitive readings to clients. Palmer became well known for both the accuracy and the specificity of her information and for the depth of her psychological insights. During this same period, she began studying the Enneagram. By 1975, she was gathering panels of people representing each type in her living room. Today, she spends nearly all of her time teaching the Enneagram both in the United States and in Europe—most especially to prospective teachers of the system.

From the day that we met, I was struck by Palmer's febrile intensity and her extraordinary powers of focus, clarity, and precision. A short, compact woman with shoulder-length dark blond hair and large blue eyes, Palmer had arranged to see me during a lunch break from an Enneagram workshop she was giving near Palo Alto, California. She wasted no time. I asked a series of questions, and she answered them rapidly and directly, never hesitating or stumbling or backtracking. Cool and businesslike in her manner, she rarely met my gaze directly, and it was some months before I began to feel the beginnings of a more personal connection with her. Still, from that first meeting, I sensed Palmer's passionate commitment to her work, as well as her fierce intelligence and her wide-ranging knowledge.

The roots of the Enneagram remain both mysterious and eclectic. The fixations or passions of seven of the Enneagram types, for example, correspond to Christianity's seven deadly sins—anger, pride, envy, greed, gluttony, lust, and sloth or laziness. As far back as the thirteenth century, in the "Purgatorio" section of *The Divine Comedy,* Dante wrote about the seven deadly sins and their higher opposites. He also described the sins of fear and deceit, which are the fixations of the remaining two Enneagram types. A century later, Geoffrey Chaucer listed in *The Canterbury Tales* the antidote for each of the seven deadly sins—pairings that mirror almost exactly the central defense and the higher opposite of each Enneagram type.

The Enneagram was introduced to the west by George Ivanovich Gurdjieff, a secretive, Russian-born mystic and teacher. Born in 1870, Gurdjieff spent much of his life traveling the world, intensively studying a variety of Eastern and Western wisdom traditions. He supported himself for many years through odd jobs, ranging from trading carpets to selling pickles to doing household repairs. As his powers of attention became more developed through his studies, he went on to work as a magician and a hypnotist. In 1918, Gurdjieff settled in Paris and founded a school devoted to his work, the Institute for the Harmonious Development of Man. Although he drew on many practices and traditions, Gurdjieff's main influence appears to have been the Islamic mystical school of Sufism. This was the source, he told followers, for his introduction to the Enneagram—specifically, through an ancient and secretive Sufi sect of wise men in Afghanistan known as the Sarmouni Brotherhood.

Gurdjieff "Work," as it came to be known, was built around his belief that most of us are asleep to our true selves—our essential nature. Gurdjieff distinguished the attributes of essence from the set of qualities that make up what he called the false personality—or ego, in western psychological terms. "It must be understood that man consists of two parts: essence and personality," wrote P. D. Ouspensky, perhaps Gurdjieff's most famous student. "Essence in man is what is his own. Personality in man is what is 'not his own.' A small child has no personality as yet. He is what he really is. He is essence. His desires, tastes, likes, dislikes, express his being such as it is." Most people, Gurdjieff theorized, become so identified with their personalities that they lose all connection to their true selves. The result is that they begin to behave in rote, reflexive ways and become stuck in automatic patterns that grow out of their defensive needs. The chief challenge in life, Gurdjieff argued, is to wake up from this unconscious state by becoming more aware of the habits, roles, preferences, prejudices, desires, and perceived needs that make up the false personality. To that end, Gurdjieff evolved a series of practices—including meditations, patterns of movement, and even tasks of physical labor—all aimed at what he called "self-observation" and "self-remembering."

Gurdjieff's emphasis was on prompting students to become more aware of their particular fixation, which he called the "Chief Feature." Ingenious at spotting this quality in students, he would take steps to force the defensive behavior out into the open, largely to reveal its distorting impact in all facets of a person's life. Much later, Palmer envisioned the Chief Feature as a potential teacher. "The hope," she has written, "is that by naming our own Chief Feature we can learn to observe the many ways in which this habit has gained control of our lives. Then our neurotic skew of attention can be enlisted as an ally whose presence makes us suffer and causes us to remember what we have lost."

Gurdjieff didn't believe that his students were capable of working on their own with the Enneagram. He identified students' Chief Features, but passed on no formal means for using the system. The result was that after his death in 1947, it lay dormant for many years. Finally, two decades later, the Enneagram was reintroduced to the West by a Bolivian psychiatrist named Oscar Ichazo—this time in a far more psychologically sophisticated form. Like Gurdjieff, Ichazo has long been somewhat secretive and elliptical about his past. Born in La Paz in 1931, he began suffering at the age of six from cataleptic attacks—painful bouts that left him conscious but unable to move. Finding a way to overcome this intractable pain became his life's mission. Ichazo first studied medicine and psychiatry, neither of which proved useful. He went on to explore consciousness, experimenting with psychedelic drugs and studying Zen meditation, Sufism, shamanism, yoga, and other mystical disciplines. By the age of eighteen, he had learned sufficient skills of self-control to bring his attacks to an end.

For years, it was assumed that Ichazo had learned about the Enneagram from the same Sufi source that Gurdjieff did. In a recent interview, however, Ichazo announced that most of his insights about the system came to him in the form of visualizations that he conjured up in deep states of concentration. This occurred, he said, while studying esoteric practices with a group of intellectuals in Buenos Aires, Argentina, beginning in 1950. Whatever the source of his knowledge, Ichazo was able to map each of the personality fixations on the Enneagram's nine-pointed star—he termed the types "Enneagons"—and to demonstrate how they relate to one another. He concluded, for example, that one's type is often influenced by its wings—those types directly adjacent to it. In addition, certain types are linked to others in a predictable pattern. The central triangle of the Enneagram, for example, is formed by types Three, Six, and Nine. Under conditions of stress, Ichazo determined that the Six tends to take on characteristics of the Three, the Three goes to Nine, and the Nine goes to Six. The same pattern occurs in reverse under conditions of security. In that case, the Six tends to act more like the Nine, and so on.

Ichazo's work remained largely unknown until 1969, when he delivered a series of lectures to the Chilean Psychological Association. Among those in attendance was a Chilean psychiatrist named Claudio Naranjo, who had been experimenting with blending Western psychological techniques and Eastern meditative practices. Naranjo first visited the United States in the mid-1960s, and he eventually found his way to Esalen, where he studied Gestalt therapy under Fritz Perls and explored body-based practices and meditation. In time, he became a popular teacher at Esalen. After hearing Ichazo speak in Chile in 1969, Naranjo returned to Big Sur full of enthusiasm about his teachings, particularly the Enneagram. In the summer of 1970, fifty-four Americans—most of whom Naranjo recruited at Esalen—traveled to the small desert town of Arica, Chile, to undertake ten months of intensive training under Ichazo.

Much like Gurdjieff, Ichazo maintained sole authority to tell people their types, which he claimed he could do simply by looking at a photograph. Once he'd typed the members of his training group, Ichazo had them divide into groups in order to work on issues specific to their fixation. "He could say very original things in connection with particular people. And that hit some people very seriously," Naranjo explained recently. After seven months, however, Naranjo had a major falling out with Ichazo and was forced out of the training. They have not spoken since. Ichazo went on to form a school of his own, the Arica Institute, which flourished in the 1970s and still has students and offices in a number of cities across America. Ichazo himself lives reclusively in Hawaii and communicates with his students mostly in the form of long esoteric treatises that he writes on various subjects. While he has never published anything about the Enneagram, Ichazo has been extremely aggressive in bringing suit against other Enneagram teachers, charging them with plagiarism. A protracted suit that Ichazo and Arica brought against Palmer, for example, was finally thrown out by a New York circuit court judge in 1992.

Naranjo, meanwhile, returned to Berkeley after his split with Ichazo and immediately began incorporating the Enneagram into his own teaching. One of the techniques he developed was to interview highly self-aware students about the nature of their preoccupations. In contrast to Gurdjieff and Ichazo, Naranjo encouraged his students to figure out their own type-related fixations. Naranjo's interview method provided a means for fleshing out the varied psychological attributes of each type. In the process, he was able to map the major defense mechanism associated with each type, using classic Western psychodynamic categories such as obsessive-compulsive, sociopathic, and paranoid.

Naranjo's classes also explored the notion that a better understanding of the defensive patterns of the personality is a route to accessing one's underlying essence. Among the students in Naranjo's earliest classes was the psychologist Charles Tart, who later taught his own Gurdjieffian classes in self-remembering.

"The fact that the Enneagram of personality went beyond ordinary life, that it discussed the existential and spiritual virtues that could be developed if we recaptured the essential energy that was going into pathological defenses against our real nature, was one of its primary attractions," Tart wrote. "It was clearly the most complex and sophisticated personality system I had ever run across." Tart was especially moved by his own experience in Naranjo's workshop. "When the nature of my type was explained to me, it was one of the most insightful moments of my life," he went on to explain. "All sorts of puzzling events and reactions in my life now made excellent retrospective sense to me. Even more important, I could see the central way in which my approach to life was defective and I had a general outline of the ways to work on changing it." Another student in Naranjo's class was Robert Ochs, a priest who later helped introduce the Enneagram to the Jesuit community. Finally, Naranjo's classes included two people whose work connecting essence and personality eventually proved most compelling to me. One was Hameed Ali, then a young physics graduate student from Kuwait. The other was Helen Palmer.

The roots of Palmer's passion for personal transformation can be found in her frightening and difficult childhood and the defenses she built to survive it. As an infant, she was abandoned by her natural parents at the pew of a church. She spent her first three years being shuttled between foster homes, until she was adopted by a young childless couple in New York City. They lived in a tenement in an Irish neighborhood under the Third Avenue El and barely had enough money to get by. Palmer's adoptive mother was a talented musician who was debilitated by severe alcoholism. As a child, Palmer was humiliated by her mother's public drunken outbursts and frightened by the effects of her private drinking. Palmer still remembers vividly coming home from school one day to discover her mother in a stupor, having fallen and broken through a window. Her adoptive father, meanwhile, was a passive and reclusive man who had little external success and experienced great difficulty in any social situation. "Both of my parents were afraid of the world and not very equipped to cope," Palmer told me. "I never felt that they could protect me."

Grim as this scenario sounds, Palmer resolutely refuses to feel sorry for herself and insists that she feels none of the bitterness or sense of deprivation that one might expect. "People endure so much pain and difficulty that what happened to me doesn't seem so out of the ordinary," she told me. The saving grace in her childhood, she believes, was her father's devotion to her. The two of them would escape her mother's binges and erratic behavior by spending long hours together, virtually hiding out. "My father was very loving and maternal, and I adored him," Palmer says. At bedtime, in particular, her father entertained her with endless epic stories and fairy tales. Instinctively, she would create images from these stories and project them like movies onto the ceiling of her bedroom, much the way she did when she listened to serial dramas on the radio. Palmer's imagination was a source of pleasant escape. Much later, her ease at visualizing became a valuable tool in accessing other states of consciousness, including the intuitive capacity.

Her intelligence was evident from an early age. "It was my leading feature as a kid," Palmer told me bluntly. At the age of six, she was accepted at Hunter, a New York City public school for gifted children, where she remained through high school. "I had a good school experience," she says. "It was an escape into a different territory, and I was there until six P.M. every day." She moved out of the house at eighteen and began college at what is now the City University of New York. She also got married to a fellow student, who later became a minister. Nearly broke, they found a cold-water flat on New York's Bowery, and Palmer worked part-time at clerical jobs, fitting her hours around her classes. Motivated in part by the desire to better understand her mother's mysterious and erratic behavior, she became increasingly interested in psychology. Shortly after graduating in 1960, she gave birth to a son. Six months later, she enrolled at the New School for Social Research, where she got a master's degree in psychology.

By the mid-1960s, as opposition to the war in Vietnam was heating up, Palmer's antiestablishment instincts drew her to the antiwar movement. In 1966, she began working with an underground radical group that helped smuggle draft resisters across the border into Canada. It was terrifying work, but the fear had an unexpected result. Early in life, to protect herself against her mother's alcoholic outbursts, Palmer developed an acute sensitivity to subtle signals that things were about to take a turn for the worse. In the course of her resistance work, she began to experience similar danger signals. On certain nights, when she was scheduled to help move someone across the border, she'd suddenly sense that they were about to be busted or that a resister was actually a government informer. Quite literally, she'd see the scene unfold in her imagination. Rather than ignore her fears, she'd find herself paralyzed and unable to leave her apartment.

"On the nights that I had these visions and didn't go along," Palmer told me, "I'd invariably hear that the arrests had come down just as I'd envisioned them. Others saw me as simply lucky, but I sensed something different. Through the intense focus of attention prompted by my fear, I was accessing some other, deeper level of knowing that was beyond thinking and logic." Meanwhile, pressure on the resistance movement continued to grow, her marriage was foundering, and in 1969, she decided to take her son and move to the West Coast.

Palmer quickly got a job teaching psychology at a junior college near San Francisco. The prospect of lecturing before a large class was so terrifying that merely thinking about it made her physically ill. Determined to teach herself to relax, Palmer enrolled in a local free university course in self-hypnosis and began diligently practicing the techniques at home. The class was taught by an ex-motorcycle traffic cop, and Palmer was particularly moved by the fact that he himself had used hypnosis to overcome his alcoholism. The technique was built around learning to detach from thoughts and sensations, and even from awareness of the immediate physical environment, in order to move into a deeply absorbed trance state. When this shift occurred, Palmer was instructed to imagine herself in a classroom, actually giving a lecture while remaining calm and relaxed. Very soon, she was able to enter this state while teaching in the classroom. The technique of deeply quieting her mind, she realized, represented a way to finally escape the fear that pervaded her life. "If my pain, worry, and anxiety came from my thoughts," she told me, "it seemed to me that the challenge was to learn to get empty of thoughts, to be able to shift into this state of mind where there wasn't any anxiety."

The self-hypnosis work had a second, unexpected result. In the course of practicing the techniques, she began to see certain events in her mind's eye—only to have them come true days later. Palmer soon began to work at developing this intuitive capacity under another teacher. Her approach to intuitive work was characteristically disciplined, rigorous, and systematic. "You begin by emptying yourself of thoughts and feelings," she told me. "Then you focus on a name or a place or a point in time that a person has asked about and get that fixated in your consciousness. Next, you become one with it, so that your own inner observer and the object of your attention merge. The task is to identify your consciousness with this event or person or place so totally that information about it is relayed to you through an inner vision or a sensation or a feeling. In my case, it's a form of dreaming— except that I can access the dream mechanism voluntarily. Then I recover this information the way one does after a dream: by 'waking up' and recording it. The final thing I do is put into words what I've seen."

At a certain point, Palmer's teacher began inviting people she did not know to stop by and bring along questions about their lives. Palmer attempted to answer, based on the dream images that came to her. The results were so good that she decided to start seeing clients privately.

Six months after she began conducting sessions at her home

in 1972, Palmer had a waiting list more than a year and a half long. By this point, she'd also begun a rigorous meditation practice under a Zen Buddhist teacher, in addition to learning techniques from a Tibetan teacher aimed at enhancing her capacity for visualization. It was a very intense period in her life. "I saw immediately that I had an aptitude for this inner work," she told me. "I spent many hours a day in meditation practices. It was as if something in me craved it. I felt I was onto something bigger than myself. It was very powerful that something could so take hold of me, set up such a calling inside. Emotionally, it was like a love affair, a sweeping of the heart, and it went on for years. Most people don't live like that, but I found the call so strong that I had to respond." Palmer's spiritual teachers were less interested in her intuitive work. Such *siddhis,* they told her, are a common by-product of learning to quiet the mind, but ultimately they divert attention from the real work of transcending the ego. Palmer rejected this advice, believing instead that developing her intuitive capacities actually served her spiritual search.

"I always saw my intuitive work as a staging ground for the next leap, a stepping stone to higher capacities that began to emerge while I was in this highly focused, intuitive state," Palmer told me. "I logged six to eight hours a day letting go of thoughts, building up my ability to become absorbed, and learning to control the placement of my attention. One reason I liked the intuitive world was that the feedback I got from my readings became proof that these higher capacities are real. This kind of evidence was very important to me. Intuition is the intermediate state between ordinary consciousness and higher consciousness—a way to distinguish between projections and a genuine contact with essence. It is a form of direct knowing. My search has always been to see the truth, to overcome my doubt, to get past my neurotic projections. From the time I began doing intuitive work, my faith that I could move beyond the biases of personality to a deeper level of truth has never flagged."

As it happens, Palmer's intuitive capacities have never been tested in any scientific way. Curious to see for myself, I asked her if I might fashion a test of her abilities, and she agreed. Over the telphone one afternoon, I provided her with the first names of a half-dozen significant people in my life, one at a time. Then I asked her to describe each of them to me in as much detail as possible, including the circumstances of their lives. I offered no further information. Since we were speaking by phone, Palmer couldn't take any cues from my facial expressions or body language. Because I offered only first names, there was no way that she could have known the individuals I asked her to describe for me. Nor did I give her any feedback.

In all six cases, the information that Palmer provided was startlingly on target. It was often very specific. For example, she described an unusually handsome, charming, and successful friend of mine as "a very good-looking dude, sociable and gracious, a real fast study who can do a lot of different things." This was right on target, but then Palmer went on to pinpoint a more profound and subtle truth about him. "He has an odd superficiality," she told me. "It's as if he's almost circulating on the edges of seriousness, not really wanting to go into depth because that's too frightening. Yet he doesn't know that. He's not aware that he can't hack staying with anything that stirs him deeply." I couldn't have captured this longtime friend's psychological profile more accurately myself.

Palmer also honed in on a female friend's as-yet unarticulated belief that her husband's failure to provide financial and emotional support was beginning to seriously threaten their two-year-old marriage. Sure enough, a year later, they were divorced over precisely this issue. Speaking of another female friend, Palmer described dead-on this woman's need for intellectual invincibility and the profound lack of self-confidence that it covered. Palmer also noted the way in which this woman chose friends more daring than she, only to compare herself with them invidiously. In the case of yet another person on my list, Palmer focused immediately on the career crisis that he was facing after years of steady success. Less than a year later, he quit his longtime job.

It was in 1973 that Palmer began to study the Enneagram, after several clients familiar with the system suggested that she spoke its language in her readings. They were referring to the fact that Palmer instinctively focused her comments on the chief feature or central fixation in any given client's personality. "Through my intuitive work I saw how the same pattern operated in every dimension of a client's life," Palmer told me. "I'd be able to hook all these seemingly disconnected experiences together— why they felt envy in this situation and unresolved anger in another and a sense of something missing in another. People who came to me got extremely good, useful information about their lives." At the same time, she recognized certain dangers in continuing her intuitive work. "I worked very hard to develop this aspect of myself, and you *do* get attached to it. You say 'Hey, wait a second, I can do something others can't do.' And then people are lining up for two and a half years to see you. It's very hard to stay even with it all."

As Palmer began to study the Enneagram in Naranjo's class, she found a psychological explanation for what she had been picking up intuitively about her clients. A person's particular personality type emerges, she began to understand, as a means of survival. Challenged with filling physical needs for food, shelter, and safety, and then emotional needs including caretaking, security, love, and acceptance, even a small child's attention starts to turn to the external world. Ultimately, these coping mechanisms evolve into an ego style—and a set of fixations. "Once personality is formed, attention becomes immersed in the preoccupations that characterize our type," Palmer wrote later. "We lose the essential childlike ability to respond to the world as it really is, and begin to become selectively sensitive to the information that supports our type's world view. We see what we need to see in order to survive and become oblivious to the rest." By this view, each personality type reflects an alternative strategy for getting one's needs met and of compensating for the pain of lost essence.

While any brief summary of Enneagram personality types necessarily oversimplifies a complex and sophisticated system, doing so at least provides a starting place. The perfectionist Ones, often reacting to a history of being severely criticized, try to recover a sense of essential value by attempting to behave perfectly—only to become their own severest critics when they inevitably fall short of their ideals. The giver Twos, rewarded early in life for being pleasing and self-sacrificing, seek affection and approval by putting other people's needs first—but always with the unspoken expectation that they will get something in return. The performer Threes, prized as children for their success and accomplishment, come to value achievement and image above all else, and lose touch with their own underlying feelings and emotional needs. The tragic-romantic Fours, beset by a sense of early abandonment and loss, believe that intense, passionate relationships are the key to escaping depression and finding happiness—but forever feel unfulfilled and let down. The observer Fives, intruded upon or simply ignored as children, conclude that cultivating detachment and minimizing needs is the best way to avoid being overwhelmed either by their own feelings, or by the demands of others.

The fearful Sixes, raised by authorities who proved untrustworthy and even humiliating, conclude that constant vigilance and careful attention to the motives of others is the key to warding off harm and insuring safety and security. The dilettante Sevens convert frightening early circumstances into selectively happy memories and live in an idealized and self-absorbed world, resisting deep commitments and focusing attention instead on all of the possibilities ahead. The combative Eights, dominated by powerful and demanding people early in life, conclude that the key to feeling safe is controlling others, exerting power, and avoiding any feelings of dependence and vulnerability. The mediator Nines, overshadowed and often neglected early in life, react by discounting their own needs and merging instead with the agendas of those around them—resisting only in a passive form.

To enrich and deepen these profiles, relying partly on her

intuition, Palmer developed a line of questioning designed to draw out the preoccupations that reveal a person's type. For example, she recognized herself almost immediately as a Six—preoccupied for much of her life with fear and mistrust, centered in her mind, and predisposed to look vigilantly and suspiciously for people's hidden agendas. "The value of this oral tradition," Palmer told me, "is that it makes a great deal of psychological understanding immediately available to people, and it puts the emphasis not on a guru who is all-knowing but on people's own powers of self-observation." Hearing hundreds of people talk about themselves demonstrated to Palmer, for example, that all types are influenced by at least one of their wings—the types on either side. Any given Two, for example, will tend to have some of the flavor of either the One or the Three.

Drawing on Gurdjieff's theory that we are all born with three forms of intelligence—intellectual, emotional, and belly-based—Palmer also found that the Enneagram types could be clustered according to whether they tend to experience the world primarily through their minds, their hearts, or their bellies, which correlate with a penchant for action in the world. Types Eight, Nine, and One tend to be belly-based; Two, Three, and Four are heart types; and Five, Six, and Seven are head types. Completeness, Palmer concluded, implies ultimately cultivating all three forms of essence—the intellectual and visionary capacities of the mind, the love and compassion of the heart, and the energy and will of the belly.

Palmer actively cultivated all three of her own centers—head, heart, and belly. Still, she was aware, sometimes painfully, that the challenge was greater in some areas than others. "I have more access to the power in my belly and to the focus and concentration in my mind than to the current of feeling in my heart," she told me. "That empathic current is open, but it's weaker than the other two. Many students expect that I should be strong and precise and courageous and also peaceful and compassionate and loving. The fact is, I only am what I am. I'm not all of these things equally, but we all project these idealized expectations onto people who help us. You might find a guru or a lama who has great access to compassion, for example, but who lacks intellectual precision. The tendency is to throw the baby out with the bathwater—to say, 'Well then, he's nothing.' But that's not so. So maybe he doesn't have intellectual precision. But he has compassion. He does have something to offer."

As a teacher, Palmer was moved most by the possibility of using the information revealed by the Enneagram to help her students nurture a connection to states of essence. But the first step, she quickly concluded, was to develop an awareness of the particular fixations or defenses that characterize each type yet often remain unconscious. This sort of awareness was the emphasis of the first workshop of Palmer's that I attended—an intensive five-day event that took place at Esalen in the summer of 1992. For most of my search, my wife Deborah had kept a certain distance from my enthusiasms, curious but skeptical. Something about my description of the Enneagram, however, caught her attention, and she decided to accompany me to Esalen. We were joined by nearly forty other people.

The workshop was built largely around listening to Palmer interview panels of each type, most of them participants in the workshop. She also spent at least an hour of each day lecturing about the Enneagram and introducing us to attention practices aimed at developing what she calls the "inner observer." Familiar to me from my vipassana meditation, the inner observer is the vehicle by which one learns to witness one's thoughts, emotions, and sensations without becoming lost in them, reacting to them compulsively, or mistaking them for one's true self.

"The hardest thing," Palmer told our group, "is to see exactly *when* we begin to move into these automatic behaviors characteristic of our type. It's very easy to know retrospectively what we have done. It's much harder to be aware when it's happening—to watch the habit or pattern of the emotion arise without reacting to it—or acting on it." All of us, Palmer said, look at the world through the narrow frame of our particular personality type, constantly reinforcing our fixed beliefs rather than fully experiencing the world in all its richness. "It can be astounding to realize," she writes in *The Enneagram,* "that we perceive 360 degrees of reality in a very limited way and that most of our decisions and interests are based on highly sophisticated habits rather than on real freedom of choice."

Unlike many people attending the workshop, who had worked with the Enneagram before, my first challenge was simply to identify my type. It is never easy to recognize one's own defensive patterns, and neither Deborah nor I had been able to clearly locate ourselves on the Enneagram, even after reading the long descriptions of each type in Palmer's book. On the first night of the workshop, Palmer suggested that those uncertain of their types simply listen to the panels, during which we'd almost certainly begin to recognize ourselves.

Late that night, I reread her descriptions of the types that rang bells for me, went to sleep thinking about them, and awoke the next morning having remembered two upsetting but revealing dreams. In the first, I was in the basement of my mother's house when I learned that she intended to kill me, that my father would be unable to protect me, and that I'd have to escape on my own. Somehow, I finally did. In my second dream, I once again found myself in the basement of a house, this time with a psychic. I began asking her about the meaning of my first dream and my childhood. She parried my questions, dawdled for a while, and finally told me that she was tired and wouldn't be able to continue her reading.

No sooner had I written down these dreams than it occurred to me that I was—like Palmer herself—a Six on the Enneagram. If I could dream so believably that my mother wanted to kill me and that my father couldn't protect me, it seemed clear that my primary emotion from childhood had to be fear. Although fear is one of the two emotions considered generic to all types on the Enneagram—deceit is the other—it is the primary passion only for the Six. As Palmer put it: "Sixes . . . remember being afraid of those who had power over them. The common theme is that of a child who felt unprotected, without a safe place to go . . . without a strong figure who would offer protection."

This felt very familiar to me, and so, suddenly, did everything about her description of Sixes. More than other types, Sixes have two distinctive shadings. The more phobic Six deals with fear by withdrawing from confrontation and seeking a strong protector, while the counterphobic Six responds to fear by aggressively challenging authority and asserting strength. The latter described me. Nor was it terribly surprising that I'd been unconscious of this deep underlying fear. My way of dealing with it, after all, had long been to aggressively push fear away in order to avoid the threatening feeling of vulnerability.

When I told Palmer about my dream and my interpretation the next morning at breakfast, she couldn't resist smiling. Although she purposely avoids telling students their type, it was plain that she, too, believed I was a Six. Indeed, when I went back later and reread the transcript of an intuitive reading that Palmer had given when we first met some months earlier, it was filled with her descriptions of my Six-like beliefs and behavior. The word *fear*, for example, came up in her reading more than a dozen times. So did other Six-like issues, including my tendency to focus on the worst-case scenario; my fears about success based on the belief that it tends to prompt envy and isolation; and my intense hunger for faith in the goodness of others, and doubt that it is merited.

It was also clear that my childhood experiences were characteristic for a Six. As my dream suggested, my mother was an immensely powerful but unpredictable presence as I grew up. She could be fiercely protective and supportive, and I identified with her strength and drive. But she was also controlling, critical, and capable of exploding in anger for mysterious reasons and then disappearing behind a locked bedroom door for hours, only to reappear without explanation. I felt as terrified by her growing up as I was hungry for her love. My father was a softer and sweeter presence, but he dealt with my mother's behavior passively, mostly by withdrawing. I never felt protected by him, nor did he help me to better understand my mother's outbursts.

Recognizing for the first time this pattern of fear in my life hardly seemed a cause for celebration. Still, I found myself feeling oddly exhilarated. My anxieties, compulsions, and most of all the hostility that often surfaced without warning had often baffled me. Suddenly I had a whole new window into why I reacted in the defensive ways I did. I began to see how my personality—and most notably, my fixation—had been shaped by my lack of trust, by the constant fear of being hurt, and by my desire to avoid the pain of judgment and rejection. For the first time—odd as it may seem—it dawned on me that my way of seeing the world wasn't necessarily accurate or complete. Far from prompting a sense of despair, this discovery filled me with hope. Suddenly I saw the possibility of moving beyond the limited defensive perspective that I had always taken for the truth, the narrow worldview that had so severely circumscribed my experience. Some of the challenges ahead became clearer: to convert fear into faith, doubt into trust, imagined negative scenarios into more realistic assessments—and perhaps above all, to find a better balance between my mind—which I'd long relied on—and my heart.

At almost the same time, Deborah had an epiphany about her own type. She was, she realized, a perfectionist One. She went to great lengths to do the right thing, to be well liked, and to avoid criticism. At the same time, the image that she projected to the world was directly at odds with her central underlying passion. What she'd rarely allowed herself to experience or express was her resentment and anger at having to maintain an image of perfection in order to feel lovable. No matter how hard she tried and how much positive feedback she might get, she still felt in some measure undeserving. Nor did the image that she projected ever feel fully authentic. The challenge for Deborah was not so much to ventilate her anger and resentment as to become more aware of it, and more willing to own it. Beyond that, the One's challenge is to give up the internalized demand to meet the impossible standards that prompt resentment in the first place. In short, the One is challenged to feel acceptable even though he or she isn't perfect, much as the Six seeks an internal experience of safety, even though not everyone merits trust.

As it happened, the Sixes were the first panel that Palmer interviewed. Suddenly I found myself alongside others who viewed the world just as I did. We each described how we automatically envision the worst possible outcome—partly to protect ourselves against the disappointment that we consider inevitable. We talked about living with the expectation that at any moment a person or situation can turn against us. We shared an acute sensitivity to potential danger and personal slights, and an instinctive suspiciousness of people's affection and good intentions. I'd never assumed that everyone sees the world as darkly as I do—Deborah, for example, is sunny and optimistic—but I was convinced that my pessimism was simply a form of realism and that all optimism is really just a form of denial.

Sitting on the panel made clear to me how much these views support a fixed set of beliefs and how little they often have to do with external events. My doubt and fear were less a reflection of objective reality than a response to my own limited and defensive perceptions. "Above all a fearful person wants an intellectually correct stance from which to fend off possible opposition," Palmer explained. "In the intellectual arena, healthy skepticism produces good sciences, testable procedures, and clearly defined rationales. Those who are overly attached to skepticism, however, can obliterate their own genuine inner life experiences by doubting them out of existence."

For the first time, I began to see that my passionate desire to write a book about wisdom grew out of a very personal hunger to overcome my chronic doubt and to find something that I could truly believe in. At the deepest level, I longed to recover the wordless faith and trust in the world that had been so injured in my childhood. I began to see why quieting my mind in meditation was especially challenging for me. As soon as I started to relax and let go of my self-protective vigilance, I felt vulnerable to attack. My fear came rushing back, and my defensive strategies sprung into action: thinking, worrying, doubting, and judging. Conversely, I understood better why it was so exhilarating to set thinking aside even briefly during meditation. When my mind did quiet down, I sometimes moved beyond doubt. What I experienced in those moments was faith, pure and simple. I regained my sense of essential trust. I felt at home in the world.

Yet another window opened up in those first few days of the workshop. It came from listening to other types describe their own fixations. I was especially taken, for example, with the Sevens—in part because I now realized that several of my friends were Sevens, and in part because Sevens seemed to have such an easier time than I did in life. The Seven is the type of the eternal child—Puer Aeternus, Peter Pan. Sevens appear free of fear and anxiety and tend to radiate good spirits, fun, charm, and endless possibility. "They have sensitive tastes and want to sample the best that life can offer," Palmer writes. "Sevens like to keep up their spirits. They want adventure and to keep their expectations high."

As I listened to the Sevens, I started to see why I'd so often been attracted to people with these qualities. Where I envision the worst, they see the best. Where I feel instinctively wary of new experiences, they thrive on adventure. Where I procrastinate and worry, they simply jump in. Because they seem so fearless and optimistic, being around them can raise my spirits. There are even times when I identify with them. Seven is one of my wings, and like the Sevens I am given to sudden new enthusiasms and to fantasies about the boundless future. The difference is that my attention soon turns to the things that can go wrong. For years, I found myself envying my Seven friends their eternal good spirits and the fact that they seemed to be so free of doubt, so able to enjoy life in an uncomplicated way.

What I failed to appreciate, the Enneagram made clear, was the degree to which the Sevens' relentlessly upbeat stance is itself a defensive posture. As I understood the Sevens better, I recognized that in their own way, they are as driven to keep their spirits high as I am to conjuring the worst-case scenario. As I heard their stories, I was surprised to discover how frequently they, much like the Sixes, described frightening childhood circumstances. Focusing exclusively on the high side of life becomes their way of defending against the experience of fear and pain. Any let-up in activity and excitement makes them vulnerable to the troubling feelings that lie underneath. Sevens, in turn, devote enormous energy to keeping the shadow side of life at bay. Characteristically, they are reluctant ever to slow down the pace or delve too deeply into anything, whether in relationships or in work. They are terrific at romance and courtship, inspired ideas, and lofty plans, but they find it far more difficult to make sustained commitments in their careers, or to cultivate truly intimate relationships. It dawned on me that I rarely experienced a close, heartfelt connection with my Seven friends and that we almost never talked about intimate subjects. Happy as they appear, they're often afraid to stop running long enough to really connect.

I recognized another variation on this theme when I listened to the members of the Three panel. More than any of the nine types, the Three embodies the American dream: driven, hard-working, optimistic, status-conscious, externally focused, and often high-achieving. Threes tend to be leaders in any given situation, and like Sevens, they keep themselves intensely busy and active, even on weekends and vacations. Unlike the Sevens, however, who are oriented to enjoying themselves, the Threes are most concerned with power, credentials, and respect. Prized as children for their accomplishments, they become intensely image-conscious, hungry to do whatever is necessary to win the acclaim and respect of others. This was a familiar feeling to me. Under conditions of stress, the Six takes on the flavor of the Three, and this helped me to understand why, when I find myself feeling threatened or insecure, I so often become preoccupied with power, recognition, and external achievement—or envious of those who have it.

In a sense, the Three is the quintessential "false personality."

The Three's central defense is deceit. As Palmer explained it, we all seek in some measure to fill externally what we feel is missing internally. For the Three, however, this becomes a full-time job. The problem is that by focusing so much of their attention on winning external approval, Threes often sacrifice a sense of connection with their real feelings, desires, and deeper needs. They become so identified with what they *do* that they lose touch with who they *are*. The discrepancy between image—what they want to project—and reality—who they really are—typically pervades even their closest relationships. "Threes can project the image of being an intimate partner, while at the same time being aware of performing a role," Palmer explained. "They can make honest and enduring commitments to their intimates . . . without being truly connected to the emotions they describe."

I was struck, more broadly, by how the most socially positive and adaptive personality types—the Three and the Seven among them—still carry underlying, often unconscious experiences of deprivation. It also became clear how the personality types that receive the most cultural reinforcement—types more inclined to achievement, more buoyant by temperament, or more oriented to the welfare of others—are often the least motivated to look within for a deeper level of truth. By conventional terms, these types are typically among the more productive and upbeat members of society, and that is certainly a value in and of itself. But from the Enneagram perspective, the outer-directedness of such personality types may also serve as a way of defending against any inner experience of emptiness or inadequacy—and from the motivation to face their pain and loss of essence.

U sing the Enneagram to become aware of personality fixations is, for Palmer, just the first step. Her primary mission, she told our Esalen group, is to help her students convert fixations to their higher opposites—the essential qualities that the defenses tend to mask. For the One, the challenge is to transform anger into acceptance and serenity; for the Two, pride into humility; for the Three, deceit into truth; for the Four envy into equanimity; for the Five, avarice and detachment into the capacity for deep connection; for the Six, fear into faith; for the Seven, gluttony into moderation; for the Eight, the need for control into tenderness; and for the Nine, sloth into action.

Initially through her experiences as an intuitive, Palmer found that if one learns to shift attention away from the central defensive emotion when it arises—to a neutral place in the belly—the underlying essence quality that is called for tends to arise. These essence qualities are not to be confused, she argues, with simply learning to function more honestly or ethically or thoughtfully, virtuous as all that may be. "We are in our essence at those times when our body moves correctly before we know what we should do, and we speak the truth before we know what we are going to say," Palmer explained. While this approach sounded faintly mystical, Palmer envisioned it in very practical, straightforward terms. "When you find yourself moving into anger or fear or pride or lust," she told our group, "the first step is just to be mindful, to observe what is happening in the moment and shift attention to the neutral place in the belly. You follow your breath down and in. Then you simply wait, so that your energy does not go out reactively and create its inevitable backlash consequences. At the very least, you convert the negative energy into a neutral place, which allows you to more easily see someone else's point of view. Eventually, when you can maintain that neutrality under pressure, an experience of essence can arise."

I was familiar with this experience in at least one area of my life. Without a specific imminent writing deadline, I often procrastinated, struggled to focus my ideas, and became easily distracted by various anxieties from other parts of my life. Under the pressure of a close deadline, however, my burden seemed to lift. The more difficult the challenge, the more easily I responded. In twenty years as a journalist, including many years working under daily deadlines, I almost never missed one. Much like Palmer, a certain kind of intense pressure sharply focused my attention—and took me out of my conscious mind. When the task simply had to be done, I was liberated from doubt and distraction, and I often produced at a level beyond what I rationally assumed was possible. Sentences that had eluded me for days seemed to flow out in perfect rhythms. Ideas suddenly tied together. Plainly, I was transforming energy that all too often got dissipated in a half-dozen directions. In the process, I managed to access potentials beyond everyday thoughts and emotions—the realm that Palmer termed essence.

Palmer's approach to transformation relies on developing a very powerful and stable access to one's inner observer. She herself developed these capacities through many years of rigorous meditation, and remains deeply committed to the value of disciplined, solitary inner work. "No pain, no gain. No focus, no reward," she told me bluntly. "I like my family and my friends, but I also like being alone. I can stay in the house for long periods quite happily."

Palmer is less drawn—in her own life and in her teaching—to the more classical Western psychological approaches: deeply exploring the origins of one's personality fixations, understanding better what makes them arise, allowing oneself to fully experience painful feelings, and working through them in the context of a relationship with a therapist. On the one hand, she acknowledges that dealing with such material is necessary. "As you develop your observer and become more aware of your fixation," she said, "you do have to deal with the fallout—the unconscious material that comes up—through good psychological work." Still, she gets impatient with dwelling too much on the past.

"Each type does follow a trajectory from deep pathology to enlightenment, but I am more interested in demonstrating the types themselves than in investigating the nature of the trauma that caused them," Palmer told me. "No matter what one's level of psychological development, I still believe the challenge is to bring the defenses and passions that underlie type to consciousness. You don't have to be a 'good person' to be good spiritual material. In the mystical traditions, there are many examples of thieves and murderers who had the ability to shift their awareness and so could transform their fixations to their higher opposites. What I think of as spiritual capacity may be different than psychological health."

Other Enneagram theoreticians have focused more attention on the latter. The most notable is Don Richard Riso, a former Jesuit who first learned about the Enneagram while studying at a seminary in Toronto in 1973. It became his primary passion and prompted him to give up his plans to become a priest and to spend more than a decade writing his first book, *Personality Types*. Riso's key contribution has been to evolve a highly sophisticated map of the levels of psychological development for each personality type, from the most pathological to the most healthy. In recent years, he has refined this work in conjunction with a partner, Russ Hudson, focusing on what they call the "core dynamics" that characterize functioning for each type, at each level of development.

Riso's ideas took shape in the mid-1970s, when he began to think about the nine types and to observe patterns of behavior among those he encountered. In time, he started noting specific qualities for each type on index cards. "Instinctively," Riso told me, "clusters of qualities began sorting into nine different piles." The lowest three, he concluded, reflected unhealthy levels of functioning, the middle three average levels, and the top three the most healthy levels. These distinctions helped Riso to understand, for example, why two people of the same type, characterized by the same basic defense, often behave very differently than one another. A healthy Two, for example, might evidence a capacity for selfless love and humility, while a less healthy Two can be smothering and self-important.

Riso also theorized that people do not simply fixate at one level of development, but rather reach a center of gravity from which they tend to move up or down, even within a given day. A significant stress, for example, might prompt a person to exhibit more low-level defensive traits than usual, while a feeling of unusual security might lead to more selfless, less defended, higher-level behaviors. Riso also speculated that severe stress can cause a sudden and sustained drop in one's center of gravity. Conversely, he says, a permanent move to a higher developmental level requires sustained psychological and spiritual work.

In my own emerging vision of a complete life, I was more drawn to this step-by-step developmental mode than to Palmer's focus on developing higher spiritual capacity regardless of one's initial level of psychological health. The most profound inner transformation strikes me as inconsequential if it does not eventually prompt a corresponding shift in external behavior. It is one thing to develop the capacity for inner shifts of attention through disciplined meditative practices. It is quite another to be able to make such shifts in the crucible of love and work relationships—and particularly under stress. For example, Palmer's central fixations as a Six—fear, doubt, and mistrust—remain powerful, for all her meditative work. More broadly, I saw little evidence that the capacity to shift the placement of one's attention necessarily results in being able to open the heart more deeply to others, for example, much less that it transforms the personality.

To the extent that unconscious childhood conflicts still feed people's defenses, I found over and over, such issues tend to arise under pressure, regardless of one's meditative training. At the same time, I increasingly appreciated the power and value of cultivating the inner observer, and of being aware of powerful emotions without reacting to them. In the very last hour of the workshop at Esalen, I got an unexpected opportunity to experience directly the way Palmer uses meditative techniques to work with particular fixations.

An intense, diminutive man about my age—let's call him Richard—was sitting in the center of the room describing the way that he, as a highly analytic Five, handled a certain situation. As he spoke, I got the sense that he somehow felt superior to the rest of us. Without thinking, I blurted out this observation. In my own mind, I was groping for a way to understand him better, to bridge the gap between us. In the course of the week, I sensed he had a harsh, impatient side, but he also struck me as bright and feisty, and I was drawn to him. No sooner had I spoken up, however, than Richard flashed back in red-hot anger, accusing me of imposing my views on him and misunderstanding what he'd been saying. This was the second time during the week I'd done so, he said. I believed that it was he who had misunderstood me, but from the murmurs around the room, it seemed clear that others in the group agreed with Richard.

Our brief exchange made me feel terrible, not least because the week had been such a positive experience for me and I hated to have it end on a hostile note. As we got closer to the end of the session, I raised my hand and asked Palmer if I might come out and discuss with Richard what was on my mind. In recent years, Palmer has begun to experiment with interactions between types, both as a way of exploring how their fixations play out in real life, and in an attempt to work through the conflicts that arise. While Palmer didn't seem eager to cap the week with a confrontation, she finally relented. I walked out to the middle of the room and sat down across from Richard. Palmer was between us. In my urgency to set things straight, I started to lean toward Richard, who was significantly smaller than I. I felt my adrenaline rising, but just as I was about to say something, Palmer literally pulled me back.

"Instead of putting your energy out here in the room," she said gently but firmly, "I want you to try first to follow your breath down and in—to come inside. When you've done that, just say what you're feeling, simply and from your heart." It was like stopping in my tracks, but I tried to follow Palmer's instructions by consciously pulling my energy back in, and following my breath down into my belly. As I did so, the room began to disappear and I lost track of whatever had been on my mind. Instead, I felt a wave rising inside me—a powerful, cresting wave of sadness that began to fill my body. I tried to say something, but I discovered that I was too choked up. Suddenly, tears started to stream from my eyes. They took me utterly by surprise. I attempted to compose myself, but it was no use. For what seemed a very long time, I just sat filled with these overwhelming emotions and waited. Finally, Palmer turned to me and said quietly, "Just say what you're feeling."

"I feel bad," I heard myself say. "I feel like I could have made a connection with Richard, but I lost the opportunity. Somehow I got him angry, and now I've ended up with just the opposite of what I wanted. The opportunity has passed. I also realize this has happened to me a hundred times. And it just makes me very sad." Under ordinary circumstances, I'd have found acknowledging this much vulnerability intolerable—especially with a large group of people looking on. Had Palmer permitted me to say what was on my mind when I first came out to confront Richard, we would almost certainly have ended up in an angry exchange. With a very simple gesture, Palmer had helped me to take the energy of my passion—born of the fearful conviction that someone had turned against me—and to direct my attention instead to the painful feelings that this passion served to cover. Richard, who had clearly braced for a confrontation himself, looked bewildered by my tears. "I didn't have any idea you felt this way," he told me. "I'm just amazed."

I had no sense of how much time had passed when the interaction ended and the room came back into focus. The first person I saw was Deborah, and I could tell that she, too, had been crying. Slowly, I realized that many people in the room had tears in their eyes, and that nearly everyone was emotionally shaken by the experience. All week, I had been playing my usual role as an aggressive, sardonic tough guy. Now suddenly I'd come face to face with the fear and sadness that lay beneath this defensive mask. I'd allowed myself to experience my pain—my sense of loss—instead of running from it. Far from being disparaged or rejected for doing so, I felt the very connection I'd been seeking—not only with Richard but with many others in the room. For a few moments, I realized, my barriers had come down, and I'd been able to tap into an aspect of my own essence. The experience was bittersweet: achingly sad in what it revealed about the barriers I so often erected but utterly authentic, rich and deep in the possibilities that it suggested. More than a year later, the encounter remains vivid in my memory.

By the time Hameed Ali and Helen Palmer took Claudio Naranjo's Enneagram class in 1972, they already shared some common interests. Both, of course, felt drawn to the Enneagram as a tool for transformation. Both sensed that the search for wisdom could be accelerated by a better marriage between Western psychology and the Eastern spiritual traditions. Both were moved by the Gurdjieffian distinction between personality and essence. Both were served by highly analytical minds, and both were looking for a path to a more complete life. Over the years that followed, they lived just a couple of miles from one another in Berkeley, and, more recently, they have become friends.

Where their work diverged was over how to use the insights of Western psychology in the service of accessing essence. Ali grew convinced that because the ego or personality is so incredibly entrenched—because people's unconscious fears and conflicts so stand in their way—meditative practices are rarely sufficient as a route to recovering one's true nature in everyday life. Many people do a great deal of meditation, he found—only to remain stuck in their personalities, and unable to let go of their fixations. "I look at the interplay between the psychological and the spiritual, the personal and the transcendental," Ali told me. "The way we get to our essential nature is not primarily through spiritual exercises but through psychological work to penetrate parts of the personality that are connected to underlying essential aspects of ourselves. Psychological inquiry leads to spiritual realization. Meditation supports this inquiry and sharpens it, but the psychological work is inseparable from the spiritual practice. This makes my work particularly Western."

To do his work, Ali employs a wide variety of techniques in addition to the Enneagram, ranging from breathing practices aimed at loosening the defenses, to more intellectual inquiry into the nature of one's conflicts, conducted in small groups.

Cultivating the inner observer and developing the capacity for focused attention, Ali found, were valuable less as a way to transcend the personality than as a means of exploring more deeply the nature of one's fixed beliefs, habitual behaviors, and areas of resistance. "The effectiveness of the [meditative] schools has been limited by a lack of knowledge of the specific unconscious barriers which prevent us from experiencing the corresponding essential states which make up our true nature," he has written. "The effectiveness of psychotherapy has been limited by its ignorance of essential states, so that resolutions occur on the levels of ego and emotions, which are not the level on which we are ultimately satisfied."

Ali was nearing fifty when we met for the first time toward the end of my travels. I had been drawn to his theories and practices by reading his books, which he writes under the pen name A. H. Almaas. They describe an approach to the complete life that I found as broad, clear-headed, and practical as any I've come across. We spoke at length by phone several times before I finally went to visit him at his sprawling pink Mediterranean home high up in the hills of Berkeley. Soft-spoken, direct, and unaffected in his manner, he put me immediately at ease. I'd found him youthful looking in the videotapes I'd seen of his talks, but he'd just grown a gray-flecked beard that made him look somewhat older. Sure enough, the beard's purpose, he told me with a smile, was to make him feel more like the grandfather he was about to become. I was drawn most to his eyes. From the moment I walked in, I saw in them a lively alertness and a focused intelligence but also a certain twinkle—a sense of lightness and fun. He struck me as a reserved and serious man but not self-serious. We met in a large room that he uses for his work. It contains bench-style seating along the walls for group meetings, and a large open area in the middle with mats where he can do body-oriented work with individual students. Hanging on the walls were photographs of the eclectic thinkers who have influenced his work—among them Sigmund Freud, the Dalai Lama,

Gurdjieff, the mystic Ramana Maharishi, and the Zen master Suzuki Roshi.

Born in Kuwait, Ali grew up in a middle class Muslim household, the oldest of eight children. His father was a successful businessman, his mother was a homemaker, and he remembers his childhood more for its nurturing qualities than for its deprivations. "I grew up in a traditional culture where family was important, respect for one's fellow human beings was valued, and materialism hadn't yet arrived," Ali told me. "I was also fortunate that I had parents who truly wanted me as a child and gave me a great deal. Even so, I developed my own personality fixations. The way I understand it, developing an ego structure, a personality, is a necessary part of the development of the human soul. It's not abnormal. The problem is that most of us get stuck in this ego stage. It's a form of arrested development."

One of the most powerful shaping events in Ali's life occurred when he was eighteen months old and contracted polio. No vaccination had yet been invented, and he was left with one leg paralyzed and virtually useless. Today, he uses a single crutch to get around. "At the beginning, I had a lot of difficulty with the disability, the limitations it caused, and its effect on my self-esteem," Ali told me. "I had to struggle with that a lot in the psychological work I did, but at some point, it became an asset. Because I couldn't be that active in the world, I became active inside. Also, because I walk with a crutch, my body is not symmetrical, and that affected my physical tension patterns— what Reich called character armor. Most people get adjusted to the tension and holding patterns in their bodies and don't notice them after a while. But I always had a little discomfort and tension in my body, and I learned to work with it—to inquire into what it was about."

Ali arrived in California in 1963 to study physics at Berkeley, the same path that Elmer Green had once taken, and for many of the same reasons. "I was interested in knowing 'What is reality?' and 'What is truth?' " Ali told me. "At the time, I thought physics was the best way to study these questions. It wasn't until graduate school that I realized the reality I was learning about in physics wasn't exactly the one I was after. It was called 'objective reality,' but I could see that it wasn't really objective." With the human potential movement beginning to take shape around him, Ali started attending workshops at Esalen in various disciplines. Shy, somewhat withdrawn, and very much centered in his mind, he soon realized that he was disconnected from his body and his emotions. "I began to study bioenergetics, which had grown out of Alexander Lowen's work with Wilhelm Reich," he explained. "It was very powerful for me to work at letting my physical armor down, opening to my body. In the process, I began to feel my own emotions more deeply and to express them in a freer way." Awakened to this deeper experience of himself, Ali was inspired to keep digging.

The classes that Claudio Naranjo offered when he returned from his Arica training in 1972 were a blend of bodywork, Gestalt therapy, meditative practices, and above all, the Enneagram. For Ali, the Enneagram became a vehicle through which to explore intensively his childhood experience and how it had shaped his personality. He quickly discovered that he was a Five—the most self-contained, cerebral, and emotionally withdrawn of the Enneagram types, the type most drawn to intellectual models and systems that explain human behavior. Typically, the Five fixation emerges in response to a sense of being abandoned by one's caretakers in childhood—plainly not Ali's experience—or from being overly intruded upon. This was certainly plausible, given the size of his family. Fives, in turn, become fearful of emotional demands and respond by cultivating detachment and privacy in their lives. Perhaps fittingly, Ali wasn't inclined to talk with me in any detail about how precisely these defensive patterns developed. Nonetheless, between bodywork, Gestalt, and the Enneagram, he moved very directly against his central fixation. "I spent two or three years doing this work in Naranjo's group," he told me, "and it was very extensive and deep."

Ali went on to work with a variety of other Eastern and Western teachers. He studied meditation with Tarthun Tulku

Rinpoche, a renowned Buddhist teacher, and did a subtle form of breathwork with a Reichian therapist named Phillip Curcuruto. He also worked with Henry Korman, who blended Freudian psychoanalytic exploration with Gurdjieffian techniques. During this period, Ali began to have experiences that none of his teachers seemed to fully appreciate but that he himself eventually recognized as the spontaneous arising of essence. "They would happen when I was meditating or walking or sometimes even when I was relaxing by watching TV," Ali told me. "What came to me, full force, was the recognition that this was me, my true nature—a felt experience beyond words. It became clear to me that my teachers weren't familiar with what I was experiencing. Over time, this apprehension of essence—of being fully myself, a state that was finally beyond words—became more and more established, more and more permanent."

Ali didn't experience essence as a broad transcendence or a sudden enlightenment. Rather, he found that there are many individual qualities of essence—among them love, strength, will, joy, understanding, compassion, awareness, clarity, truth, value, pleasure, and consciousness. Sufism, he concluded, had the clearest and most precise understanding about the nature of these qualities—and their application to everyday life. The Sufis describe the aspects of essence through a system called the *lataif,* which refers to five centers of perception, each associated with a specific physical location in the body and a different color. Yellow, in the heart, is associated with essential joy and delight; red, on the right side of the body, with strength and vitality; silver, in the solar plexus, with will; black, in the forehead, with clarity and objective understanding; green, in the chest, with compassion and loving kindness.

Deborah first experienced one of these aspects of essence during a guided meditation conducted by a student of Ali's work. The focus of the meditation was compassion—what the Sufis call the "green essence." The student, John Harper, set out to prompt the experience of compassion—not just for others, but for oneself. As the meditators sat around a circle with their eyes closed, and music played in the background, Harper began to describe a series of life circumstances in which we tend to doubt and disparage ourselves. In each instance, he evoked an image of being washed by a steady rain of compassion. "And the green rain says 'I know,' " Harper repeated in a gentle, rhythmic chant.

For Deborah, the impact was stunning. She began to cry and couldn't stop. Later, she told me that she'd always thought of compassion as something reserved for others, but never entitled to herself. To experience the sense of deep self-acceptance that the meditation elicited—to feel her heart opening to herself—was something wholly new for Deborah and very moving. Several days after returning home, she still felt suffused by the experience, and it showed. I was intrigued. Finally, one night I asked if she might try to take me through the same meditation. We set aside time one evening after putting our children to bed, and Deborah served as the guide. Within a few minutes, the tears were streaming down my face just as they had hers. In effect, I'd been introduced to a source of comfort and understanding that I hadn't realized I carried inside myself.

Ali theorized that these interconnected qualities of essence represent the components of a complete life. "It is as if they are different organs of the same organism," Ali has written. "They are all necessary, and the being is incomplete without any of them." At the same time, Ali concluded that the personality—and the mind—are necessary components of the mature development of essence. "One of the purposes of developing an ego," he told me, "is that it makes possible the capacity for self-reflection. Infants don't have that, and without self-reflection there can be no passing on of knowledge nor any evolution of consciousness. A person needs to be able to reflect to understand and value his experience. Still, it is a double-edged sword. Self-reflection can also separate a person from his true nature. We need this capacity in order to grow, but it often gets misused."

A central breakthrough for Ali was his realization that it isn't necessary to seek essence all at once. "Most spiritual disciplines talk about our lack of true nature or essence in a general way," he told me. "In our approach, we talk not about an overall lack but about very specific ones. We work with the idea that each essential aspect—love or peace or will or strength—is blocked by a certain part of our personality. Right away people have something that they can relate to. Doing some psychological piece of work—understanding and penetrating a particular aspect of the personality—leads directly to experiencing essence in some form. This, in turn, transforms some part of the personality. The person who is shy stops being scared. The one who is angry becomes compassionate. It's a very interconnected process."

In the course of his own work, Ali also saw that before it is possible to experience the true self, it is first necessary to get in touch with one's feelings. "Many people do not even experience their emotions, and the ones who can usually don't experience them deeply or fully. The emotions are usually so distorted and dominated by negativity that it takes a lot of hard work to start feeling them both deeply and in a balanced way," he has written. "Balanced emotional growth is necessary for finding and developing one's essence. However, the emotional life is not the essential life. The emotionally developed normal person is superficial, incomplete and still a child in terms of the potential of the human being."

At any level of work, Ali came to believe, one must respect the enormous intelligence of the ego and its determination to remain dominant. "The personality will do anything in its power to preserve its identity and uphold its domain," he explained. "This need is literally in our flesh, blood, bones, even our atoms. The power of the personality is so great, so immense, so deep, so subtle that the person who contends with it for a long time will have to give it its due respect." In effect, Ali believes that the personality never simply throws up its hands and cedes territory to essence. "Ego death is a repeated and in time a continual experience," he concluded. "There is no end to the development and unfolding of essence. This development proceeds by exposing more and more, perhaps in time very subtle aspects of the personality. . . . It is not that the personality is gone and now essence develops. It is rather that the more essence develops, the more personality is exposed and its boundaries dissolved."

Ali named his work the Diamond Approach, partly to reflect the notion that like a diamond, essence has many facets, and partly because he wanted the approach to have the precision and clarity of a diamond. One of my first direct experiences with Ali's work came when I attended an introduction to the Diamond Approach in San Rafael. Held on the campus of a small college, it was taught by a woman named Sandra Maitri, who is one of Ali's senior teachers. Like Ali, her style is understated, unpretentious, and exceptionally lucid. I felt comfortable with her immediately. The weekend was built around what Ali calls the "theory of holes."

As Maitri explained it, we experience essence from birth, but in our earliest years, we lack self-awareness or the capacity to see who we are. Infants, in short, are not *aware* of their own essence. In theory, adults can develop a deeper, richer, more mature and powerful experience of essence that is only a potential in babies. In practice, Maitri told us, our essential development almost invariably gets aborted. In the course of growing up, physical and emotional survival become important, and so does building an individual identity and winning social acceptance. "As consciousness begins to form, we take on a personality, and in the process we lose touch with our essential qualities," Maitri told us. "Because our parents are usually hopelessly out of touch with their own essential depths and have never experienced these qualities in themselves, they can't mirror them back to us. When a certain essential quality is not seen in us, or it's devalued, we tend to lose contact with it."

In turn, this lost connection is experienced as a hole. "It is an absence, a lack, a sense of something missing, and it literally *feels* like a hole," Maitri told us. "What happens is that we end up filled with holes." As Ali came to see it, we build our lives—mostly unconsciously—around finding ways to compensate for our sense of deficiency. "What you fill the holes with," he has written, "are the false feelings, ideas, beliefs about yourself, strategies for dealing with the environment. These fillers are collectively called the personality—the false personality or what we call the false pearl. . . . But after a time, we think that is who we are. Everybody thinks that's who they are, the fillers. The false personality is trying to take the place of the real thing." Or, as Maitri elegantly summed it up: "After many losses of contact with who we are, we begin to take ourselves to be what we are not."

Most people, Ali found, go to enormous lengths to avoid feeling their holes at all. "They think the hole, the deficiency, is how they really are at the deepest level and that there is nothing beyond it," he explained. "They believe that if they get close to the hole, it will swallow them up." The culture, in turn, conspires to help people avoid their holes by offering endless external ways to fill them: through taking drugs, or drinking excessively, or overeating, or watching endless television. But it is also possible to fill holes, Ali concluded, in subtler ways that aren't so obviously pathological and may even be relaxing or socially productive: meditating for long hours, working obsessively, or even devoting ourselves to others to the exclusion of focusing on our own deepest needs. "People don't know," he wrote, "that the hole, the sense of deficiency, is a symptom of a loss of something deeper, the loss of essence, which can be regained."

Much of our weekend workshop focused on this issue. "We need to dive into these holes—not fill them, but feel them," Maitri told us. "When you let yourself experience a hole—stop rejecting it and just let it be—a sense of openness begins to emerge, a relaxation, a spaciousness. Whatever quality of essence this hole developed in response to begins to arise spontaneously." Or as Ali put it: "If you go all the way into that sense of emptiness, through the fear of feeling it—all the way—you will get to the quality which has been lost to you."

As an example, Ali pointed to the common feeling of anger—an aspect of personality. Begin looking into why this emotion recurs, Ali told me, and one might discover that at the surface level it is simply a way of asserting strength—of feeling separate and independent from other people. Explore a little more deeply, he elaborated, and it will turn out that the anger covers up an underlying experience of fear and weakness. "If you stay with that sense of weakness," he explained, "you'll begin to experience a hole in the belly, an emptiness, the feeling that you can't stand your ground, that something is missing. And if you feel that emptiness, [and] you don't fight it or react to it but just stay with it, the hole will begin to fill with a certain quality of essence. It feels literally like liquid fire. And then what you will feel is a real strength. Just by truly being yourself, you are strong. And that essential strength gives you the capacity to be truly independent without feeling angry."

Qualities of essence can be realized, Ali concluded, by steps and degrees, through work on specific sectors of the personality, just as essence is lost in childhood, aspect by aspect. As essence is recovered, he argues, the need for the personality diminishes. "A person who is this essence," Ali has written, "does not need to use the linear mind and rack his brain over certain important situations. The direct knowing is just there, available [with] clarity and precision."

As he studied other schools of Western psychology, Ali found that few of them acknowledge the existence of anything akin to essence. "Psychotherapy is oriented toward making the personality healthier and stronger, making it function better," he told me. "The empty hole is almost never approached. Rather, the person learns to find better and more effective ways to fill the hole." Nonetheless, certain Western therapeutic approaches provide a very sophisticated understanding of specific personality deficiencies that Ali came to correlate with lost qualities of essence. Freud, for example, paid particular attention to issues such as castration anxiety and fears about aggression. By drawing on Freud's insights in these areas, Ali found that students not only got relief from their pain—the traditional psychotherapeutic goal—but could be led to the recovery of the related essential qualities: will and strength, respectively.

Ali was also influenced by Wilhelm Reich, whose body-oriented therapy was concerned with the loss of the capacity for depth of emotion—and particularly pleasure. Reich recognized the need to break through the physical armor that we build up to protect ourselves from pain. Ali, in turn, discovered that the qualities of essence can be experienced only in the body and not in the mind, abstractly. To illustrate this point, he described for me the process that follows a child's early loss of intimate connection to the mother. This is inevitable in development and always painful, but it is especially traumatic for the child who is not sufficiently valued by the mother or who is explicitly rejected. "To avoid experiencing this intolerable hurt," Ali told me, "we deaden a certain part of our body, and in that way we are cut off from that sweet quality of love in ourselves. Where that love should be, we have an emptiness, a hole. What we do then, to get the love we feel lacking, is to try to get it from outside ourselves. Inevitably, we are frustrated, since the true source is within."

The Diamond Approach is built around a very straightforward form of inquiry into experience. "We start with whatever is arising in the moment, our lives as they are without trying to change them," Maitri told us. "The method is to see and experience where we are, opening to the whole realm of our experience instead of narrowing it. We bring a spirit of curiosity and inquiry and openness to the process, and the mind is used only as a tool to help do that more deeply. Patterns don't change by pushing or prodding but by seeing why we think we need to do what we do; by really feeling the part that holds on and what we're getting from it; and by understanding why we believe it's not okay to behave any differently." What we suffer from, Maitri told us, is finally a case of mistaken identity—and a limited worldview. "The personality is based on a fixed set of beliefs about what reality is," she said. "It's a trap, a jail, a confinement in a particular band of reality. When we stay with what is happening moment to moment—without beliefs, images, and conceptualizations about who we are—then we begin to experience a miraculous unfoldment. The heart knows when we're getting closer to the truth."

Throughout the weekend, our inquiry took the form of exercises in which we broke up into groups of two or three and attempted to answer a specific question—sometimes in monologue form, sometimes in response to having the question posed to us repeatedly by a partner. Maitri asked that as listeners, we refrain from commenting or reacting in any way to what the speakers were saying. "The idea is to explore the truth about a particular issue," she said, "and the biggest assistance we can give each other is to be present, open, and allowing. When you're speaking, don't worry about how you are perceived or what happens to you. Just be with your own experience."

The first exercise was framed as a repeating question: "Tell me something that stops you from being here now." To my surprise, I soon discovered that most of my answers focused on my concern with how what I say is received. I had never thought of myself as highly concerned with the approval of others. Forced by the nature of the exercise to keep digging deeper, however, I began to uncover all of the subtle ways that I adjust what I say to make it more acceptable. I also saw that my underlying motive was less approval than it was assuring that I wouldn't be rejected or seen as wrong and thus endangered. It became clear that I rarely simply connect to what I feel most deeply and say it straight out.

The second repeating-question exercise was even simpler: "Tell me something you are experiencing now." This time I saw quickly how many conflicting concerns, preoccupations, and habits stood in the way of my simply getting immersed in the moment. I also saw that the more I exhausted the answers that came immediately and glibly to mind, the more I felt pulled into the frightening territory of the unknown. This was also the domain of a deeper level of truth. Over the course of the two days, we did a series of similar exercises that prompted us to probe more and more searchingly into our fixed beliefs and habitual ways of responding. The questions ranged from "What pattern is repeated over and over again in your life?" to "Who do you take yourself to be right now?" to "How do you fill your holes?" to "Explore your experience of emptiness and deficiency."

One of the last questions we engaged was "What's right about *avoiding* feeling empty?" This was perhaps the most surprising and enlightening of the exercises for me. I could name plenty of reasons for not wanting to feel empty, among them that I associated emptiness with loneliness, sadness, disconnection, hopelessness, and fear. Beyond all that, no one in my life had ever suggested that there is any value in feeling empty. Filling myself up—through work and relationships and being a parent, playing sports and going to movies, worrying and planning—had long been the central mission of my life. It had never occurred to me that feeling empty might actually be a route to something deeper and richer within.

"Emptiness can be experienced in very different ways," Maitri explained, after we'd done the exercise. "Often you almost literally fear you'll die if you stay in that emptiness, and in a sense that's true. A given sector of the personality will die if you don't keep trying to fill it up. But there is something deeper. Emptiness feels like a black hole when it's viewed through the prism of the personality. But that same hole is experienced as open and pristine and very peaceful when you are in essence. It may take a leap of faith to let go into this emptiness—whether from courage or desperation. But when you do, it is very spacious, and it's anything but deficient. It is the beginning of opening up to our true selves—to the empty space in which everything arises, to the ground of our fundamental nature."

These exercises had a subtle but cumulative impact on me. Each one gave me a slightly clearer sense about where I was still stuck and how my fixed beliefs fed those patterns. As Maitri put it: "When a machine knows itself, it is no longer possible for it to be a machine." There was also something wonderful about having another person there simply as a presence, listening closely but not interjecting. It made me realize how rarely I felt fully heard—

and how rarely I listened to another person carefully, quietly, and without judgment. Deborah and I have incorporated this active listening exercise into our lives, and it's been remarkably powerful. Having the other person just listen for ten minutes several times a week gives us another level of connection and mutual understanding.

As the weekend came to an end, Maitri made it clear that the work we'd done wasn't much concerned with cathartic breakthroughs, or instant transformations, or even easing our burden. "This path is not about rising above or transcending," she told us. "It's about moving through what is, and a lot of that isn't real pleasant. It's very difficult, it's painful, and there's a lot we'd rather avoid." Ali makes the point even more directly: "We could do meditations, certain exercises and everybody could feel wonderful things. However these will not last unless the person actually confronts his deficiencies, his holes and goes through them. It is not a simple process, nor a short or easy one."

"We're not interested in making people feel better," he told me later. "We're interested in helping them find the truth about themselves. In the process, everything gets deeper." This made enormous sense to me. I was no longer looking for instant catharsis, which experience told me was sure to fade in a matter of days. This work didn't leave me feeling my world had transformed. Rather, it had an impact that grew over time and required patience and attentiveness.

For Ali, the complete life must be embodied in everyday experience. Insight is not sufficient. Conduct matters, too. "Indulgence means permitting what is unhealthy in you to control your actions, even though you already recognize it is unhealthy," he told me. "Spiritual work has to do with actualizing your potential. It needs to be done while we are in the world. Experiencing essence is not that difficult. You can do it through meditation, or by taking psychedelics, or even through an intense experience in life. A lot of the Eastern traditions aren't that much interested in living in the world. They just want to connect with the divine. But to truly *own* your essence—to experience it as who you really are and to behave accordingly—requires moving through the barriers of the psyche, integrating the heart and the mind. This is what I call realization. It means learning to make your inner understandings the source of your external actions. Being accomplished, creative, successful and contributing usefully to the world are expressions of a particular aspect of our essential nature. Finally, it's about living your life from a certain inner center—with love and integrity, openness and awareness. Ultimately, that becomes the work."

Even as this work proceeds, Ali says, a distinctive personality persists. What changes is its character. "In my case," he told me, "I used to be shy and passive, and now I can be quite aggressive. I used to be more afraid of people, and now I enjoy them. I used to be very lazy, and now I'm very active. Even so, it's not like you work on the personality and then go on to something else. Personality obstacles are infinite, and you keep coming back to them."

Like Michael Murphy, Ali concluded that no single virtue—or quality of essence—is sufficient by itself. Completeness depends on balanced development. "Love is just one of the aspects of essence," Ali explained. "We don't want you *just* to be loving. If you have love but you have no will, your love will not be real. If you have will but no love, you will be powerful and strong but without any idea of real humanity. If you have love and will but no objective consciousness, then your love and will may be directed toward the wrong things. Only the development of all the qualities will enable us to become full, true human beings."

CONCLUSION
The Point Is to Be Real

Life is a contest of opposites: birth and death; health and sickness; love and hate; giving and taking; systole and diastole; summer and winter; day and night.
—*E. A. BENNETT*

The path to sainthood goes through adulthood. There are no quick and easy shortcuts. Ego boundaries must be hardened before they can be softened. One must find one's self before one can lose it.
—*M. SCOTT PECK*

The serious problems in life . . . are never fully solved. If ever they should appear to be so it is a sure sign that something has been lost. The meaning and purpose of a problem seems to lie not in its solution but in our working at it incessantly.
—*CARL JUNG*

I'M not the same person I was when I began this book. I don't say that casually. During the first several years of my search for wisdom, I had plenty of insights and revelations, but nothing in my experience fundamentally changed. Only when I began to move out of my head and into my heart did I start to *feel* a change—and to behave differently. These shifts have sometimes been subtle, and I've moved forward only to find myself falling back. But on balance, my life has more depth, breadth, and richness than it has ever had. I have more understanding about where I fall short and what stands in my way. I feel clearer than ever where I'm headed and why I'm here.

My life has a sense of meaning, purpose, and direction that it never had before.

The first and foremost challenge is to be more aware, of myself and others, to make more of my unconscious conscious, to see more of the truth. Seeking the truth is sometimes painful and difficult, but it invariably makes me feel more authentic and more grounded. It's not truth in some absolute sense that I'm after. Nor am I primarily seeking to uncover the truth about others, much as I appreciate it when I sense that people are talking to me honestly, from their hearts. What I'm most committed to is searching for my own truth. Like most people, I still often avoid, or deny, or rationalize, or act out of habit, or look to blame others in an effort to avoid truths that I find unpleasant or threatening.

This capacity for self-deception sometimes seems infinite. Being honest with myself now strikes me less as an end—something I'll finally achieve after enough work—than an ongoing challenge every day. Over time, the attempt to be more broadly aware has enlarged my life. I spend less of my energy defensively, and that frees me to reach out to others more positively and to work more productively. Seeking the truth in the face of my fears has given shape and passion to my search. In turn, I'm convinced that the planet's survival—and evolution—depends on our collective capacity to look within more honestly, and to act more consciously and less defensively in every sphere of our lives.

I've grown less hungry for absolute answers and more skeptical of those who claim to have them. Invariably, these teachers and sages turn out to have short-circuited their own search for truth by choosing up sides, excluding some aspects of a complete life in favor of others. I've met people who are exceptionally successful in their chosen fields but seem utterly disconnected from their hearts or from any committed social or spiritual purpose. I've encountered meditators who can move into transcendent states of consciousness, only to behave awkwardly and even abusively in their everyday relationships. I've come across people who are compassionate and highly self-aware but lack the qualities of logic, discrimination, and will that make it possible to act intelligently and productively in the world. And perhaps the most common imbalance I've encountered is my own—overvaluing the skills of thinking and analyzing, codifying and conceptualizing, and undervaluing those of the heart. To live a complete life requires drawing deeply on all of one's potentials—mind, body, heart, soul, and spirit.

I've learned to value humility. Few teachers I encountered seemed comfortable acknowledging their own shortcomings, fears, and uncertainties. I was moved most by those who remain committed to looking truthfully at their own lives and who have the courage to continue struggling with their own contradictions. At the same time, I struggle not to rush to judgment. Even those I met who failed to fully embody their teachings, or who insisted on their own way to the exclusion of others, often had something valuable to offer. Humility was as much a challenge for me as for those I met. I, too, wished for simple and absolute solutions. But the longer I've stayed at it, the more I see that what works for me isn't necessarily useful for someone else, and that I'm not going to find all of the answers I'm after, no matter how honestly and diligently I search.

I continue to wrestle with life's complexity, paradox, and contradiction. This play of opposites, I'm convinced, is part of any fully lived life, a source of richness rather than an obstacle. I try increasingly to balance the signals I get from my mind, based on logic and analysis, with those I get from my gut, based on intuition and instinct. Too much emphasis on rational analysis short-circuits spontaneity, as well as access to a level of wisdom that is beyond words. At the same time, thinking and reflection are uniquely powerful tools for integrating insights, making critical discriminations, and communicating more effectively.

I try to act better in the world. No amount of insight or wisdom counts for much, I've found, if it doesn't lead to changes in behavior. But even then, the choices are not simple. I've come to share Michael Murphy's belief that all of the virtues are mutually entailed and that no single one is a virtue by itself. For a long time, I valued honesty above all else. I said what I felt because anything less seemed to me inauthentic and hypocritical. If I felt angry or wronged, I didn't try to hide it. My brusque directness often bruised and alienated people, but I convinced myself that I had a noble purpose: telling the truth, even if others did not. But whose *version* of the truth, I came to wonder, and at what cost? Honesty unbalanced by compassion is cruelty. I am still learning that lesson, but I value it more than ever.

For all my searching within, I feel more engaged in the world, not less. In the end, I've found that I'm not seeking to transcend ordinary life. To the contrary, I'm eager to become more embodied, more passionately involved with others, and more willing to treat each moment as if it matters deeply. I have developed a stronger inner observer—the capacity to witness, without so much judgment and identification, the relentless rush of my thoughts and emotions. But the value of this inner observer is not to help me move beyond pain and conflict or experience my sense of a separate self as illusory. Rather, by learning to step back from my ongoing drama—to maintain some equanimity in the face of life's ups and downs—I've been able to explore what stands in my way more freely and deeply.

I'm less judgmental than I once was. I've seen—sometimes with frightening clarity—that judgment serves mostly to separate me from other people and from myself. I've come to understand that I share all of the shortcomings that I find most distasteful in others. Contained in every judgment I make is some difficulty with self-acceptance. I struggle to be discriminating without being judgmental, to live by a clear set of ethical standards without using them as a weapon against others or myself. That doesn't mean I stand by idly when I believe that someone is acting in a way that is hurtful. It does mean avoiding the attitude of moral righteousness, even when I choose to intervene. The more I'm able to move from my head into my heart—to appreciate the pain and struggle and complexity that others face, just as I do—the less I'm inclined to be judgmental.

I see the value of searching for a deeper level of truth but also of accepting the way things are. For the first several years of this search, I focused on trying to change my life. I sought the courage to make choices that I felt were right for me, even when I knew that they wouldn't lead to broad acclaim and might even prompt criticism from others. The decision to write this book—and to make the search for wisdom central in my life—was itself an immense challenge. Friends and colleagues expressed skepticism about the project, and I found it difficult to explain precisely what I was trying to do. But it always *felt* right.

I continue to explore painful issues and to challenge my habitual behaviors. I still often feel that I'm swimming upstream—not just against my own resistance but against the culture's, too. Looking deeply within challenges people to engage their own feelings of emptiness, dissatisfaction, and despair. Most people instinctively avoid such pain at any cost, and the culture provides us with endless ways to anesthetize ourselves—with everything from alcohol and drugs to food, trivial chitchat, obsessive work, and fame. It is easy to get seduced and sidetracked.

There is much to be said for acceptance. All too often, I've tried with a certain desperation to win people over to my vision and my values, rationalizing that I'm only seeking to help them see more of the truth. In my clearer moments, I now recognize that this proselytizing mostly reflects my lingering unwillingness to trust my own choices and a fearful belief that unless everyone sees the world the way I do, I won't be truly safe and secure. Increasingly, however, I've derived more comfort from allowing myself to see things as they truly are than from trying relentlessly to make them over.

More often than not, my attempts to change people have led only to suffering on both sides. I've experienced this most poignantly with my parents. I spent years wishing that they might change and feeling angry and frustrated when they did not. At some level, I've held on to an image of the way I'd like them to be, and the sort of relationship I wished that we could have. I tried to adjust myself to make that happen and sought to reform them as well. In the course of this search, I've found a way to be more truthful with both of them, yet to stop insisting that they change to accommodate me. The effect has been freeing for me, and, I think, for them. Sometimes the greatest value is in letting go. The residue may be some sadness and grief and longing, but I've learned that fully feeling these difficult emotions is part of the process of truly moving through them.

I've found value in learning to control my thoughts and emotions—and in focused attention. When it comes to competing in sports or getting a certain task completed, for example, I'm convinced that the challenge is not to turn attention inward or to open to whatever arises. Rather, it's to marshal very specific positive thoughts and emotions that enhance performance. I've seen how much this improves the level of my tennis and how negative thoughts and emotions undermine my play. More generally, I've seen that the mind, the body, and the emotions are inextricably connected. Negative thoughts often create physical tension, while difficulty physically relaxing interferes with concentration, clarity, and confidence. I also see how emotions such as anxiety and anger can take form as physical symptoms.

One evening, shortly after I began to write the first draft of this final chapter, I felt a sudden sharp pain in my knee. I paid it no special attention and I went to bed figuring that it would be gone by the morning. Instead, I woke up in the middle of the night with throbbing discomfort. By the morning, I found it difficult to walk up and down the stairs. When two days went by with no relief, I began to wonder if I'd torn something in my knee. Had twenty years of jogging every day on paved roads finally caught up with me? I envisioned surgery and crutches, rehabilitation, and the prospect of being sedentary for months. My mind went into overdrive, and the fear fed on itself.

I decided to call a highly respected orthopedist. He named several possibilities about what sort of injury I might have and suggested that I come to see him in a few days if the pain persisted. At that point, he said, he'd take an MRI—an unpleasant and very expensive diagnostic procedure. Our conversation was utterly impersonal. He might as well have been talking about bringing my car in for repair. For this utterly conventional physician, a knee was a knee, the problem was purely physical, and that was that.

But what if it wasn't? What if the throbbing in my knee were sending me a different message? I'd seen with my back how connected physical pain can be to unconscious conflict. This pain in my knee was undeniably real, but what exactly was causing it? I decided to try free-associating, as I sometimes did when I felt a twinge of back pain. My first association in this case was that the pain literally made me feel cut off at the knees, crippled. How paradoxical, I thought. At precisely the moment that I ought to have been feeling most powerful—completing a book that I'd been working on for five years—I instead found myself immobilized and distracted from finishing the job.

I called John Sarno. After carefully describing my symptoms, he laughed. We'd been down this road before. It turned out that he had been seeing more and more patients with very similar complaints. He treats them the same way that he does his back patients—and has been enjoying similar rates of success. "Congratulations, Tony," he told me. "It sounds as if you've successfully managed to move your fear and anxiety from your back to your knee. What's going on in your life?" I felt instantly that the connection he'd made was right. Within a couple of hours, my severe pain had diminished by 25 percent. By the next day, it was gone altogether, just as mysteriously as it had arrived.

Or was it so mysterious? The pain, I concluded, had indeed been sending me a message. Much as I'd discovered in working with dreams, the challenge was translation—in this case, to put the physical symptoms into words. My knee began to hurt, I eventually decided, as a way of telling me that I was ambivalent about finishing my book—frightened particularly by the prospect of facing critical response to something I'd worked on for so long and about which I felt so passionately. I also concluded that the pain was trying to tell me that I was headed in the wrong direction with this last chapter. I'd been trying to write it from a safe and lofty intellectual perch that had no connection to anything I felt in my own life. The aching in my knee literally forced me to get out of my head and come back into my body. Sure enough, the moment I stopped trying to separate what was going on in my body from what was going on in my mind, the pain went away. It had served its purpose.

I listen to my body now more closely than ever. Even when I'm not experiencing physical pain, my body is an accurate barometer of how I'm really feeling. By paying attention to whatever sensations are arising—a tightening in the chest, a dread in the pit of my stomach, an opening in my heart, a clenching in my jaw—I've gained access to a whole new way of knowing myself.

In the course of my search, I spent many hours talking with people whose work focuses on body-based techniques for unlocking the body's armor, freeing up repressed emotions, and increasing self-awareness. I tried many of the techniques myself, but I found most of them oddly unsatisfying. Simply freeing up emotions, without using the mind to connect these feelings to past experience and repetitive patterns, just wasn't sufficient. Much as traditional insight-oriented psychotherapy often undervalues the role of the body and the truth it contains, so the body-based practitioners I came across seemed to undervalue the importance of analysis and insight in the search for wisdom. At the same time, I had another level of resistance to this body-based work. I've only recently begun to feel comfortable and safe enough to explore the very deep and undefended emotions contained in my body. Some of that work lies ahead.

One other experience profoundly influenced my search. A couple of years after I began work on this book, I returned to psychotherapy. I hesitated to write about this at first, because I wasn't sure that I could draw from such a personal experience any universal conclusions. But I finally realized that leaving it out would make this story incomplete. I chose to try psychotherapy again when I became convinced that meditation was not going to provide all the answers I was seeking. Despite my past disappointment and considerable skepticism about its value, I still held out hope that I could derive something unique from the one-to-one relationship that therapy makes possible.

From the first time I met Nathan Schwartz-Salant, he struck precisely the balance I was seeking. Jungian by training but eclectic and nondoctrinaire in his approach, he was at home in his head and in his heart, willing to work both with my psychological issues and with my broader spiritual quest. He plainly cared, he really listened, and he was truly on my side. But he was also tough-minded and fiercely honest, and he wasn't about to let me off the hook. When I deceived myself, however cleverly I might try to mask it, he was quick to notice. Nor was he reluctant to take a stand. When he felt I had acted badly in my life, he said so and pushed me not only to be more aware but to change my behavior. At the same time, he had humility. He wasn't afraid to admit that he'd made a mistake. When I felt *he* had veered off track and told him so, he listened closely and often agreed. I came to trust him, in part because he didn't need to be right. He was a steady source of insight when I couldn't sort out my feelings, and of support when my faith began to flag. Finally, he became a role model for me—someone who seemed enlarged rather than diminished by the willingness to embrace his own contradictions and uncertainties.

Above all else, I've learned to love more freely and more deeply during these past five years. The quality of my closest relationships, including those with friends, has deepened. I'm more able to feel and express my love for those I care most about, even when they make choices that I might not. I see this with my older daughter as she moves into adolescence. I feel how much I want to protect her from the unhappiness that I felt as a child and how much I fear feeling this pain again, through her. My impulse is to try to steer her firmly away from my mistakes—to jump in and fix things. But I also recognize how much of a burden this puts on her. My real job is to resist *my* needs in favor of hers. It's to love her and to let her go, to set certain limits but then to give her plenty of space. Most of all, it is to fully appreciate her and to keep my faith even when her missteps threaten to break my heart.

Far better than offering her advice is living my own life in a way that she senses is truthful and honorable. In turn, I've learned to step back far more than I once did. I don't pretend that I've got all the answers. She struggles, but I also sense something unmistakable. She is blossoming. It's thrilling to watch.

The same is true for Deborah, at another level. For several years, she kept her distance from the waxing and waning enthusiasms that characterized my search. Nearly three years ago, she decided to join me for Helen Palmer's workshop at Esalen. She found the Enneagram work unexpectedly moving and exhilarating. Eventually, she decided that this sort of inner exploration and the chance to share it with others was more compelling to her than the work as a magazine editor that she'd been doing for twenty years. A year before I finished this book, Deborah gave up her job and returned to school to get her master's degree in social work. For the first time in her life, she feels as if she's found a calling. Much as we've each changed in the fifteen years that we've been married, we've ended up on a parallel track that has brought us closer together than ever.

I continue to learn by looking inward and by staying open to others. I'm always trying to broaden my awareness—to see more and to resist less. Putting these insights to work in everyday life is at least equally compelling to me now. Sometimes that simply means trying to be more focused and productive in my work. Other times, it's about being more open and available in my relationships, or simply sitting quietly in meditation or contemplation. More now than ever, I realize that it also means reaching out in service, being useful to others wherever I can.

The road to wisdom is often an obstacle course. During the past five years, I have spent much of my time detouring around New Age popularizers, self-promoting hucksters and charismatic demagogues posing as enlightened teachers. Theirs was not the story I wanted to tell. Instead, I chose to focus on a much smaller group of people who I've come to believe embody an emerging American wisdom tradition. Their ideas, techniques, and practices convinced me that a richer, deeper, and more meaningful life is within reach. Nor is it necessary, I discovered, to drop out, move to an ashram, or renounce material life in order to experience and embody this wisdom.

The capacities and potentials I explored weren't nearly so mystical or arcane or esoteric as I'd long imagined they'd be. Gaining access to them often depends, however, on a subtle level of self-awareness and inner sensitivity. It is plainly possible to cultivate in everyday life the capacities I've described in these pages, but this sort of transformation doesn't occur in a flash, or in the course of a weekend workshop. Real discovery and change, I found, requires sustained and committed practices. Nor does any single practice I encountered address the full spectrum of what it means to be a human being—perhaps least of all those practices that claim to provide absolute answers.

But where does this search for wisdom lead in the end? In the 1960s and me-decade 1970s, critics such as Christopher Lasch and Tom Wolfe disparaged the turn inward and the focus on personal growth as narcissistic and self-indulgent. Where that is so, I'm convinced, the search for wisdom has been distorted, or prematurely aborted. The key issue is balance. Do insights derived from one's inner work lead not just to greater depth and self-understanding, but also to positive changes in behavior? In short, does one's inner exploration ultimately enhance the quality of one's participation in the world?

At the same time, I've found that a sustained, honest effort to look within leads almost inevitably to positive external ends. On one level, nurturing the potentials I've described provides people with new and practically useful skills—whether at work, in their everyday relationships, on the playing field or simply in maintaining physical health and coping with illness. But beyond any practical value, this effort to broaden and deepen self-awareness—the capacity to be conscious of more and to exclude less—has a subtle, cumulative impact. I believe more than ever that profound social transformation—reducing the level of hatred and violence in this country, to take just one example—depends first on addressing the barriers within ourselves.

I'm no longer much drawn to singular paths to wisdom. Instead, I've begun to embrace those people and approaches that emphasize a comprehensive, balanced, and integrated path to a complete life—practices that address the body, mind, and heart as well as the spirit. Much as I see the value of nurturing a full range of human potentials, I've grown more distrustful of any approach that emphasizes one set of capacities to the exclusion of others. I feel most moved by the work of people such as Michael Murphy, Jack Kornfield, Ken Wilber, Helen Palmer, and Hameed Ali precisely because their approaches are multidimensional and inclusive.

We all share extraordinary potentials, but we can also misuse them. Not only can we distort and deny our lower dimensions— our shadow, our instincts, our emotions—we can also distort and deny our higher possibilities—our spiritual dimension, our transpersonal selves, our essential nature. The costs, in either case, are catastrophic. As Abraham Maslow put it, "If you set out to be less than you are capable of being, I warn you, you will be deeply unhappy for the rest of your life."

At the same time, these integrated practices are a source of hope and promise. The flowering of more comprehensive approaches to wisdom, uniting the best of the East and the West, represents a historic first. Never before have we had access to so many technologies of transformation or to so much knowledge about the full spectrum of human possibility. It's not just that there is wisdom to be found in America, but that these comprehensive approaches are emerging primarily in America. Perhaps never before have they been so desperately needed.

ACKNOWLEDGMENTS

Because this book represents a personal journey as much as it does a journalistic one, I feel an especially profound appreciation for the people I encountered along the way. When I set out, I had many questions and very few answers. I spent the first months of reporting looking for people who might give my search direction. Early on, I received a serendipitous letter from Nancy Kaye Lunney, director of programming for the Esalen Institute. She had no idea I was writing a book. Rather, she'd read several magazine pieces I'd written over the years, decided that we had common interests, and was writing to suggest that we meet. I was delighted. Who could possibly be a better source? I spent that first lunch with Nancy grilling her about the most interesting people she'd met in the course of programming Esalen seminars over the past ten years.

A highly discriminating seeker herself, Nancy wasn't easily impressed. She had three suggestions for me. The first was to talk with Michael Murphy, the founder and chairman of Esalen, not only because he'd been a pioneer in the field but because he retains such a passionate and wide-ranging vision of human possibility. Eventually, Murphy became not just a central character in the history I was describing but an extraordinary source of information and a cheerleader in my attempt to make sense of it all.

Nancy Lunney's other two suggestions were Helen Palmer and Hameed Ali—two people whose work I ultimately found especially useful in my own life and whose approaches to wisdom represent pioneering attempts to blend Eastern and Western thinking in comprehensive transformative practices. It was through

Helen that my wife Deborah discovered her new calling—one inspired in part by the Enneagram.

In short, Nancy was three for three. The bonus was that she became a close friend, too.

Catherine Ingram was another source of important insights in those early days. A journalist and seeker herself, Catherine helped point me toward those teachers who have been most influential in importing Buddhism—and Eastern practices in general—to America. Most important, she managed to convince her notoriously reclusive friend Ken Wilber to talk with me. That in itself was a huge service—and no mean feat.

Ken Wilber, in turn, spent many hours helping me to fit a particular practice or tradition or human potential into the larger wisdom picture that I was trying to develop. He is an amazing man. I've never met anyone who knows as much about as many things as Ken does, or who thinks about them so clearly and systematically. Beyond that, Ken became a true soul mate in my continuing search—and a wonderful friend.

When I took my first drawing class with Betty Edwards very early in my reporting, I showed her the proposal that I'd written for this book. In retrospect, it was an embarrassingly thin document that reflected the limited state of my knowledge and experience. Still, Betty responded to my enthusiasm, sensed that I was on to something bigger than I'd yet articulated, and insisted that I had an important book to write. She never lost that conviction. Over the years, she became something of a second mother—loving and supportive, forever able to find kind words for me, even when the ideas I was sharing with her remained muddled and incomplete in my own mind.

I got another kind of inspiration from Elmer Green. At once a scientist and a mystic, he struck me from the first time we spoke as utterly grounded and capable of scientific objectivity but also completely at home with the sort of transcendental experiences that have been a part of his life since childhood. I relished talking with him about my search and finished every conversation richer for the experience. As much as anyone I met, Elmer walked his talk. I also greatly valued my conversations with Dale Walters, Elmer's original partner, and Pat Norris, Elmer's daughter, both of whom are carrying on and advancing the biofeedback work that Elmer and Alyce pioneered in the mid-1960s.

Jerry Alleyne was my tennis teacher before I began work on this book. His insights and his passionate desire to help me experience some of the pleasure that he does in many parts of his life gave me an enormous lift. I sensed immediately that Jerry had figured out at least part of the wisdom puzzle—and far more of it than most people ever do. I met Jim Loehr, too, by virtue of his work in tennis, but I soon recognized that it had much broader applications, just as Jerry's did. Jim also became a good friend and someone with whom I still regularly discuss the ups and downs of our mutual searches.

In a very different way, John Sarno played a role in my eventual decision to write this book. I'm forever grateful that he helped to heal the back pain that plagued me for the two years before we met. Beyond that, it was through Sarno that I saw how powerfully the mind and body are connected—and what exceptional potentials can be tapped by putting that knowledge consciously to use.

In the course of writing this book, I interviewed more than two hundred people but ended up writing about only a fraction of them. Nonetheless, many of them had a significant impact on my thinking. These include Deepak Chopra, Norman Cousins, Jack Engler, Mark Epstein, Lester Fehmi, Don Johnson, Stanley Keleman, Mathew Kelley, Stanley Krippner, Steven LaBerge, Steven Locke, Alexander Lowen, Wes Nisgur, Naomi Remen, Ernest Rossi, Carl Simonton, Brian Weiss, Anna Wise, and Shinzen Young. I'm especially grateful to Joan Borysenko, a pioneer in the mind-body field and an immensely generous and warm-hearted human being.

I also drew on many books in the course of my research. All of them are listed in the bibliography, but two were exceptionally useful. Walter Anderson's *The Upstart Spring* is by far the best history yet written about the early years at Esalen. *Storming*

Heaven by Jay Stevens is the best book I came across about the history of psychedelic drugs in this country. Both of these works transcend the specific stories they tell and capture in rich detail cultural movements of the 1960s and 1970s that have too often been undervalued.

If I had to recommend a half-dozen books to anyone interested in starting out on the path to wisdom, I'd choose *Essence* by A. H. Almaas (or equally, *Diamond Heart: Part One*); *A Path with Heart* by Jack Kornfield; *The Enneagram* by Helen Palmer; *Grace and Grit* or *No Boundary* by Ken Wilber; *Beyond Biofeedback* by Elmer and Alyce Green; and *The Road Less Traveled* by M. Scott Peck. There are many others of more specialized interest, but these six are an extraordinary introduction. I was also deeply moved by Judith Herman's *Trauma and Recovery*, a book that speaks brilliantly not just to victims of physical and sexual abuse but to a much broader group of people who have suffered other, subtler forms of trauma.

My editor, Toni Burbank, inherited this project more than a year after I'd begun my reporting. Immensely knowledgeable about the field, she was a tough critic from the start. In response to her very detailed comments, I did two extensive revisions of the manuscript. Toni's tenacity and intelligence forced me to stretch my heart and my mind. It gives me great pleasure to know that this book finally meets her very rigorous standards. I'm also appreciative to Toni's assistant, Alison Rivers, a positive spirit who made this whole process move more smoothly.

My search was also influenced by people outside the direct scope of this book. Nathan Schwartz-Salant has made an enormous difference in my life, helping me to face even the most painful truths but always doing so with exquisite sensitivity and compassion. I love and admire him as much as I appreciate him.

Several friends played multiple roles during the five years I worked on this book, ranging from providing counsel and support to setting me straight when I fell too hard for some person or technique. I talked the book through on countless morning runs with Steven Weinstock, my best friend these past five years, and nearly as often with Nancy Weinstock, when we all got together for dinner or for a cup of coffee on weekends. Susan Lyne and George Crile were my next-door neighbors for most of the search, and they remain two of my closest and most supportive friends. Mitch Alfus is my oldest friend—we met in the sixth grade—and to our surprise, the mutual search for wisdom has brought us closer together than ever during the past two years. The same has happened with Jane Strong, long one of Deborah's best friends but someone I've only truly gotten to know, love and appreciate during the past few years. John Harper is a very special person, and I feel fortunate to have him in my life.

I'm also thankful for the feedback and support I've gotten from Therese Alfus, Laura Day, Jane Eisen, Michael Fiori, Kathryn Galan, David Hirshey, Gail Koff, David Obst, John Osborne, Vicky Rybka, Cassie Schwartz, Irving Schwartz, Anita Shreve, Susan Squire, and Wally Vincente.

Kathy Robbins has been my agent for more than a decade. No one has been more involved in my work life or more committed to it. Kathy had faith in this book from the start, and it never wavered—even when mine did. Kathy is brilliant and unmatched at what she does. Beyond her skills as an agent, she is also my close friend, confidante, editor, and cheerleader. I cannot imagine having done this book without her, any more than I can imagine life without her. I'm also indebted to Kathy's extraordinary staff, who have made my work life easier and better in innumerable ways.

Finally, there is my family. My children—Kate, thirteen, and Emily, nine—weren't always sure what to make of the book I was writing and the journey Deborah and I have been on. "Why is it," Emily asked one day, "that our family talks so much about feelings?" I got a great kick out of the question, even if I couldn't find a simple answer. In the end, I think that my daughters came to appreciate that I was doing something I believed in passionately, and they valued that. Mostly, though, what they seek from their father is fathering—time, attention, and love. I hope that I've gotten better and better about giving them all three, because only then does the search I've undertaken assume real-life meaning. For their part, they have given me immense joy and taught me a lot about unconditional love.

How fortunate I am to have Deborah in my life. She has made it better in so many ways—by loving me, by believing in me, by listening to me, by prodding me, and by following her own instincts, even when they conflict with mine. It has been thrilling to watch her come so completely into her own and to realize that we have years ahead to share all that we've learned and will learn, separately and together. After eighteen years, she is—more than ever—the love of my life.

BIBLIOGRAPHY

Boldface books are those of special note.

Achterberg, Jeanne. *Imagery and Healing*. Boston: Shambhala, 1985.
———. *Woman as Healer*. Boston: Shambhala, 1990.
Almaas, A. H. Diamond Heart: Book One. Berkeley: Diamond Books, 1987.
———. *Diamond Heart: Book Two*. Berkeley: Diamond Books, 1989.
———. *Diamond Heart: Book Three*. Berkeley: Diamond Books, 1990.
———. ***Essence*. York Beach, Maine: Samuel Weiser, 1986.**
———. *The Pearl Beyond Price*. Berkeley: Diamond Books, 1988.
Anderson, Walter Truett. *Open Secrets: A Guide to Tibetan Buddhism for Western Spiritual Seekers*. Los Angeles: Tarcher, 1979.
———. ***The Upstart Spring: Esalen and the American Awakening*. Reading, Mass.: Addison-Wesley, 1983.**
Assagioli, Roberto, M.D. *Psychosynthesis*. New York: Penguin, 1976.
Barasch, Marc Ian. *The Healing Path*. New York: Tarcher/Putnam, 1993.
Bennett, E. A. *What Jung Really Said*. New York: Schocken Books, 1966.
Benson, Herbert, with Miriam Klipper. *The Relaxation Response*. New York: Avon, 1976.
Benson, Herbert, with William Proctor. *Your Maximum Mind*. New York: Avon, 1989.
The Bhagavad Gita. New York: Penguin, 1962.
Bly, Robert. *Iron John*. New York: Vintage, 1990.
Borysenko, Joan, Ph.D. *Minding the Body, Mending the Mind*. New York: Bantam, 1988.
———. *Fire in the Soul*. New York: Warner, 1993.
Bosnak, Robert. *A Little Course in Dreams*. Boston: Shambhala, 1986.
Boyd, Doug. *Swami*. New York: Paragon House, 1990.
Brennan, Barbara. *Hands of Light*. New York: Pleiades Books, 1987.
———. *Light Emerging*. New York: Bantam, 1993.

Brooks, Charles V. W. *Sensory Awareness*. Santa Barbara, Calif.: Ross Erikson, 1982.

Cade, C. Maxwell, and Nona Coxhead. *The Awakened Mind*. Longmead, Great Britain: Element Books, 1987.

Campbell, Joseph. *The Portable Jung*. New York: Penguin, 1971.

Campbell, Joseph, with Bill Moyers. *The Power of Myth*. New York: Anchor, 1988.

Capra, Fritjof. *The Tao of Physics*. New York: Bantam, 1984.

Carlson, Richard, and Benjamin Shield. *Healers on Healing*. Los Angeles: Tarcher, 1989.

Casteneda, Carlos. *A Separate Reality*. New York: Washington Square Press, 1972.

———. *Tales of Power*. New York: Simon & Schuster, 1974.

———. *The Teachings of Don Juan*. New York: Washington Square Press, 1974.

Chandler, Russell. *Understanding the New Age*. Dallas: Word, 1988.

Chopra, Deepak, M.D. *Ageless Body, Timeless Mind*. New York: Harmony Books, 1993.

———. *Perfect Health*. New York: Harmony Books, 1990.

———. *Quantum Healing*. New York: Bantam, 1989.

———. *Unconditional Life*. New York: Bantam, 1991.

A Course in Miracles. Glen Ellen, Calif.: Foundation for Inner Peace, 1985.

Cousins, Norman. *Anatomy of an Illness*. New York: Bantam, 1981.

———. *Head First: The Biology of Hope*. New York: Dutton, 1989.

———. *The Healing Heart*. New York: Avon, 1984.

Csikszentmihalyi, Mihaly. *Flow*. **New York: Harper & Row, 1990.**

D'Antonio, Michael. *Heaven on Earth*. New York: Crown, 1992.

Dardik, Irving, and Dennis Waitley. *Quantum Fitness*. New York: Pocket Books, 1984.

Deikman, Arthur J., M.D. *The Wrong Way Home*. Boston: Beacon, 1990.

Dienstfrey, Harris. *Where the Mind Meets the Body*. New York: HarperCollins, 1991.

Doore, Gary. *What Survives? Contemporary Explorations of Life After Death*. Los Angeles: Tarcher, 1990.

Dossey, Larry, M.D. *Healing Words*. San Francisco: HarperCollins, 1994.

———. *Recovering the Soul*. New York: Bantam, 1989.

Dychtwald, Ken. *Bodymind*. Los Angeles: Tarcher, 1986.

Edwards, Betty. *Drawing on the Artist Within*. New York: Simon & Schuster, 1986.

———. *Drawing on the Right Side of the Brain.* Los Angeles: Tarcher, 1989.

Eisenberg, David, M.D. *Encounters with Qi.* New York: Penguin, 1985.

Epstein, Gerald. *Healing Visualizations.* New York: Bantam, 1989.

Faraday, Ann. *Dream Power.* New York: Berkeley, 1980.

Feldenkrais, Moshe. *Awareness Through Movement.* New York: HarperCollins, 1972.

Ferguson, Marilyn. *The Aquarian Conspiracy.* Los Angeles: Tarcher, 1980.

Feuerstein, Georg. *Yoga: The Technology of Ecstasy.* Los Angeles: Tarcher, 1989.

Fields, Rick. *Chop Wood, Carry Water.* Los Angeles: Tarcher, 1984.

———. *How the Swans Came to Lake.* Boston: Shambhala, 1992.

Freud, Sigmund. *Civilization and Its Discontents.* New York: Norton, 1930, 1961.

———. *A General Introduction to Psychoanalysis.* New York: Pocket Books, 1971.

———. *On Dreams.* New York: Norton, 1980.

Friedman, Meyer, M.D., and Ray Rosenman, M.D. *Type A Behavior and Your Heart.* New York: Fawcett, 1985.

Friedman, Meyer, M.D. and Diane Ulmer, R.N., M.S. *Treating Type A Behavior and Your Heart.* New York: Fawcett, 1984.

Gallwey, Timothy W. *The Inner Game of Tennis.* New York: Bantam, 1979.

———. *Inner Tennis: Playing the Game.* New York: Random House, 1976.

Garfield, Charles A. *Peak Performance.* New York: Warner, 1985.

Garfield, Patricia. *Creative Dreaming.* New York: Ballantine, 1976.

Gawain, Shakti. *Creative Visualization.* New York: Bantam, 1985.

Gazzaniga, Michael. *Mind Matters.* Boston: Houghton Mifflin, 1988.

Gendlin, Eugene, Ph.D. *Focusing.* New York: Bantam, 1981.

———. *Let Your Body Interpret Your Dreams.* Wilmette, Ill.: Chiron, 1986.

Goldstein, Joseph. *The Experience of Insight.* Boston: Shambhala, 1976.

———. *Insight Meditation.* Boston: Shambhala, 1993.

Goleman, Daniel. *The Meditative Mind.* Los Angeles: Tarcher, 1988.

Goleman, Daniel, Paul Kaufman, and Michael Ray. *The Creative Spirit.* New York: Dutton, 1992.

Green, Elmer and Alyce Green. *Beyond Biofeedback.* Fort Wayne, Ind.: Knoll Publishing, 1977.

Green, Judith Alyce, and Robert Shellenberger. *From the Ghost in the*

Box to Successful Biofeedback Training. Greeley, Colo.: Health Psychology Publications, 1986.

Grof, Stanislav, M.D. *LSD Psychotherapy*. Pomona, Calif.: Hunter House, 1980.

Grof, Stanislav, M.D., and Christina Grof, eds. *Spiritual Emergency*. Los Angeles: Tarcher, 1989.

————. *The Stormy Search for the Self*. Los Angeles: Tarcher, 1990.

Hall, Calvin S. *A Primer of Freudian Psychology*. New York: Penguin, 1982.

Hall, Calvin S., and Vernon J. Nordby. *A Primer of Jungian Psychology*. New York: New American Library, 1972.

Harman, Willis, and Howard Rheingold. *Higher Creativity*. Los Angeles: Tarcher, 1984.

Harner, Michael. *The Way of the Shaman*. New York: Bantam, 1982.

Herman, Judith Lewis, M.D. *Trauma and Recovery*. New York: Basic Books, 1992.

Herrigel, Eugen. *Zen in the Art of Archery*. New York: Vintage, 1971.

Hillman, James. *The Dream and the Underworld*. New York: Perennial Library, 1979.

Hoffman, Edward. *The Right to Be Human: A Biography of Abraham Maslow*. Los Angeles: Tarcher, 1988.

Horney, Karen, M.D. *Self-Analysis*. New York: Norton, 1942.

Houston, Jean. *The Possible Human*. Los Angeles: Tarcher, 1982.

Huffington, Arianna. *The Fourth Instinct*. New York: Simon & Schuster, 1994.

Hurley, Kathleen, and Theodore Dobson. *My Best Self: Using the Enneagram to Free the Soul*. San Francisco: HarperCollins, 1993.

Hutchison, Michael. *Megabrain*. New York: Ballantine, 1986.

————. *Megabrain Power*. New York: Hyperion, 1994.

Huxley, Aldous. *The Doors of Perception*. New York: Perennial Library, 1954.

————. *The Perennial Philosophy*. New York: Perennial Library, 1944.

Huxley, Laura. *This Timeless Moment*. San Francisco: Mercury House, 1968.

James, William. *The Varieties of Religious Experience*. New York: Collier Books, 1961.

Johnson, Don. *Body*. Boston: Beacon Press, 1983.

Joy, W. Brugh. *Joy's Way*. Los Angeles: Tarcher, 1979.

Jung, Carl. *Man and His Symbols*. New York: Dell, 1968.

————. *Modern Man in Search of a Soul*. New York: Harcourt Brace, 1936.

Kabat-Zinn, Jon. *Full Catastrophe Living*. New York: Delacorte Press, 1990.

———. *Wherever You Go There You Are*. New York: Hyperion, 1994.

Keen, Sam. *Faces of the Enemy*. New York: HarperCollins, 1991.

———. *Fire in the Belly*. New York: Bantam, 1992.

Keleman, Stanley. *Embodying Experience*. Berkeley: Center Press, 1987.

———. *Your Body Speaks Its Mind*. Berkeley: Center Press, 1975.

Keyes, Margaret Frings. *Emotions and the Enneagram*. Berkeley: Molysdatur Publications, 1988.

Kornfield, Jack. *A Path with Heart*. New York: Bantam, 1993.

Kornfield, Jack, and Paul Breiter. *A Still Forest Pool*. Wheaton, Ill.: Quest, 1985.

Kornfield, Jack, and Joseph Goldstein. *Seeking the Heart of Wisdom*. Boston: Shambhala, 1987.

Krippner, Stanley, Ph.D., ed. *Dreamtime and Dreamwork*. Los Angeles: Tarcher, 1990.

Krishnamurti. *You Are the World*. New York: Harper & Row, 1972.

Kuhn, Thomas. *The Structure of Scientific Revolutions*. Chicago: University of Chicago Press, 1962.

LaBerge, Stephen. *Lucid Dreaming*. New York: Bantam, 1985.

Langer, Ellen J. *Mindfulness*. Reading, Mass.: Addison-Wesley, 1989.

Lao-tzu. *Tao Te Ching*. New York: Vintage, 1972.

Leary, Timothy. *Flashbacks*. Los Angeles: Tarcher, 1983.

Leonard, George. *Mastery*. New York: Dutton, 1991.

———. *The Silent Pulse*. New York: Dutton, 1978.

———. *The Transformation*. Los Angeles: Tarcher, 1972.

———. *Walking the Edge of the World*. Boston: Houghton Mifflin, 1988.

LeShan, Lawrence. *Alternate Realities*. New York: Ballantine, 1976.

———. *Cancer as a Turning Point*. New York: Dutton, 1989.

———. *How to Meditate*. New York: Bantam, 1975.

———. *The Medium, the Mystic and the Physicist*. New York: Ballantine, 1975.

———. *The Science of the Paranormal*. Wellingborough, Northamptonshire: Aquarian Press, 1987.

———. *You Can Fight for Your Life*. New York: Evans, 1977.

Levine, Stephen. *A Gradual Awakening*. New York: Anchor, 1979.

———. *Who Dies*. New York: Anchor, 1982.

Lilly, John, *John Lilly, so far*. Los Angeles: Tarcher, 1990.

Locke, Steven, and Douglas Colligan. *The Healer Within*. New York: Dutton, 1986.

Loehr, James E. *The Mental Game.* Lexington, Mass.: Stephen Greene Press, 1990.

———. *Mental Toughness Training for Sports.* Lexington, Mass.: Stephen Greene Press, 1982.

———. *Toughness Training for Life.* New York: Dutton, 1993.

Lowen, Alexander. *The Betrayal of the Body.* New York: Macmillan, 1967.

———. *Bioenergetics.* New York: Penguin, 1975.

———. *The Spirituality of the Body.* New York: Macmillan, 1990.

Mahesh, Maharishi Yogi. *Transcendental Meditation.* New York: Signet, 1968.

Marrone, Robert. *Body of Knowledge.* Albany, N.Y.: State University of New York Press, 1990.

Maslow, Abraham. *The Farther Reaches of Human Nature.* New York: Penguin, 1971.

———. *Religions, Values and Peak Experiences.* New York: Viking, 1970.

———. *Toward a Psychology of Being.* Princeton, N.J.: Van Nostrand, 1962.

Mindell, Arnold. *The Dreambody in Relationships.* London: Routledge & Kegan Paul, 1987.

Moore, Thomas. *Care of the Soul.* New York: HarperCollins, 1992.

Moyers, Bill. *Healing and the Mind.* New York: Doubleday, 1993.

Murphy, Michael. *An End to Ordinary History.* Los Angeles: Tarcher, 1982.

———. **The Future of the Body. Los Angeles: Tarcher, 1992.**

———. *Golf in the Kingdom.* New York: Delta, 1972.

———. *Jacob Atabed.* New York: Bantam, 1979.

———. *The Physical and Psychological Effects of Meditation.* Big Sur, Calif.: Esalen Institute, 1988.

Murphy, Michael, and Rhea White. *The Psychic Side of Sports.* Reading, Mass.: Addison-Wesley, 1978.

Naranjo, Claudio. *Ennea-Type Structures.* Nevada City, Calif.: Gateways Publishers, 1990.

———. *How to Be.* Los Angeles: Tarcher, 1989.

Norris, Patricia, and Garrett Porter. *Why Me?* Walpole, N.H.: Stillpoint Publishing, 1985.

Ornish, Dean. *Stress, Diet and Your Heart.* New York: New American Library, 1982.

———. **Dr. Dean Ornish's Program for Reversing Disease. New York: Random House, 1988.**

Ornstein, Robert. *The Psychology of Consciousness*. New York: Penguin, 1973.

Palmer, Helen. *The Enneagram*. San Francisco: Harper & Row, 1988.

Peck, M. Scott. *Further Along the Road Less Traveled*. Simon & Schuster, 1993.

————. *People of the Lie*. New York: Simon & Schuster, 1983.

————. *The Road Less Traveled*. New York: Simon & Schuster, 1978.

Perls, Fritz. *The Gestalt Approach and Eyewitness to Therapy*. New York: Bantam Books, 1973.

————. *Gestalt Therapy Verbatim*. Highland, N.Y.: The Center for Gestalt Development, 1969.

Prigogine, Ilya. *Order Out of Chaos*. New York: Bantam, 1984.

Progoff, Ira. *At a Journal Workshop*. New York: Dialogue House Library, 1975.

Ram Dass. *Be Here Now*. New York: Crown Publishing, 1971.

————. *Grist for the Mill*. Santa Cruz, Calif.: Unity Press, 1976.

————. *Journey of Awakening*. New York: Bantam, 1978.

————. *The Only Dance There Is*. New York: Anchor, 1970.

Reich, Wilhelm. *Character Analysis*. New York: Farrar, Straus & Giroux, 1980 (originally published in 1949).

Ring, Kenneth. *Life at Death*. New York: Coward, McCann & Geoghegan, 1980.

Riso, Don Richard. *Personality Types*. Boston: Houghton Mifflin, 1987.

————. *Understanding the Enneagram*. Boston: Houghton Mifflin, 1990.

Rohr, Richard, with Andreas Ebert. *Discovering the Enneagram*. New York: Crossroad, 1992.

Rossi, Ernest Lawrence. *The Psychobiology of Mind-Body Healing*. New York: Norton, 1986.

Rutter, Peter. *Sex in the Forbidden Zone*. Los Angeles: Tarcher, 1989.

Samuels, Mike, M.D., and Nancy Samuels. *Seeing with the Mind's Eye*. New York: Random House, 1975.

Sarno, John E. *Healing Back Pain*. New York: Warner, 1991.

————. *Mind Over Back Pain*. New York: Morrow, 1984.

Schutz, William C. *Joy*. New York: Grove Press, 1967.

Seligmann, Martin E. P. *Learned Optimism*. New York: Knopf, 1990.

————. *What You Can Change and What You Can't*. New York: Knopf, 1993.

Siegel, Bernie S. *Love, Medicine and Miracles*. New York: Harper & Row, 1986.

————. *Peace, Love and Healing*. New York: Harper & Row, 1989.

Simonton, Carl. *The Healing Journey*. New York: Bantam, 1992.

Simonton, Carl, Stephanie Simonton-Mathews, and James L. Creighton. *Getting Well Again*. New York: Bantam, 1980.

Smith, Huston. *The Religions of Man*. New York: Harper & Row, 1986.

Sontag, Susan. *Illness as Metaphor*. New York: Farrar, Straus and Giroux, 1977.

Speeth, Kathleen Riordan. *The Gurdjieff Work*. Los Angeles: Tarcher, 1989.

Spiegel, David. *Living Beyond Limits*. New York: Times Books, 1993.

Springer, Sally, and Georg Deutsch. *Left Brain, Right Brain*. New York: W. H. Freeman, 1981.

Stevens, Jay. *Storming Heaven*. New York: Perennial Library, 1987.

Stevenson, Ian, M.D. *Children Who Remember Previous Lives*. Charlottesville, Va.: University of Virginia Press, 1987.

Suzuki, Shunryu. *Zen Mind, Beginner's Mind*. New York: Weatherhill, 1970.

Tart, Charles T., ed. *Altered States of Consciousness*. New York: Anchor, 1969.

——. *Open Mind, Discriminating Mind*. New York: Harper & Row, 1989.

——. *States of Consciousness*. New York: Psychological Processes Incorporated, 1975.

——, ed. *Transpersonal Psychologies*. New York: Harper & Row, 1975.

——. *Waking Up*. Boston: Shambhala, 1987.

Tavris, Carol. *Anger: The Misunderstood Emotion*. New York: Simon & Schuster, 1982.

Taylor, Jeremy. *Dream Work*. New York: Paulist Press, 1983.

Trungpa, Chogyam. *Cutting Through Spiritual Materialism*. Boston: Shambhala, 1973.

Ullman, Montague, and Nan Zimmerman. *Working with Dreams*. Los Angeles: Tarcher, 1979.

Vaughn, Frances E. *Awakening Intuition*. New York: Anchor, 1979.

Walsh, Roger N. *The Spirit of Shamanism*. Los Angeles: Tarcher, 1990.

——. *Staying Alive*. Boston: New Science Library, 1984.

Walsh, Roger N., and Frances E. Vaughan. *Beyond Ego*. Los Angeles: Tarcher, 1980.

——. *Paths Beyond Ego*. Los Angeles: Tarcher/Perigee, 1993.

Watts, Alan. *Psychotherapy East and West*. New York: Vintage, 1961.

——. *The Wisdom of Insecurity*. New York: Vintage, 1951.

Weil, Andrew. *The Natural Mind*. Boston: Houghton Mifflin, 1972.

Weiss, Brian L. *Many Lives, Many Masters*. New York: Simon & Schuster, 1988.

————. *Through Time into Healing.* New York: Simon & Schuster, 1992.

Wilber, Ken. *Eye to Eye.* Boston: Shambhala, 1983.

————. **Grace and Grit. Boston: Shambhala, 1991.**

————. **No Boundary. Boston: New Science Library, 1979.**

————. *Sex, Ecology and Spirituality.* Boston: Shambhala, 1995.

————. *The Spectrum of Consciousness.* Wheaton, Ill.: Quest, 1977.

Wilber, Ken, Jack Engler, and Daniel Brown. *Transformations of Consciousness.* Boston: New Science Library, 1986.

Williams, Redford. *The Trusting Heart.* New York: Times Books, 1989.

Williams, Redford, and Virginia Williams. *Anger Kills.* New York: Times Books, 1993.

Williamson, Marianne. *A Return to Love.* New York: HarperCollins, 1992.

Zweig, Connie, and Jeremiah Abrams. *Meeting the Shadow.* Los Angeles: Tarcher, 1991.

NOTES

INTRODUCTION

page 1   *What does a life of:* M. Scott Peck, *The Road Less Traveled* (New York: Touchstone, 1978), 51.

page 1   *One does not become:* Connie Zweig and Jeremy Abrams, eds., *Meeting the Shadow* (Los Angeles: Tarcher, 1991).

CHAPTER ONE

page 19   *Our normal waking consciousness:* William James, *The Varieties of Religious Experience* (New York: Collier Books, 1961), 215.

page 19   *It is because we don't know:* Aldous Huxley, *The Perennial Philosophy* (New York: Perennial Library, 1994), 14.

page 29   *I had an apartment:* Ram Dass, *Be Here Now* (New York: Crown, 1971), unpaginated.

page 30   *activist research projects which will:* Timothy Leary, *Flashbacks* (Los Angeles: Tarcher, 1983).

page 30   *The nature of life:* Ram Dass, *Be Here Now.*

page 30   *The journey lasted:* Leary, 32.

page 32   *It was as if:* Ram Dass, *Be Here Now.*

page 32   *Although everything:* Ibid.

page 36   *It was a daring, dangerous experiment:* Leary, 107.

page 36   *A separate follow-up program:* Ibid., 111.

page 36   *The history of the project:* Jay Stevens, *Storming Heaven* (New York: Perennial Library, 1987), 160.

page 37   *It is probably no accident:* Ibid., 160.

page 38   *Twenty years later, a researcher:* Rick Doblin, "Pancke's 'Good Friday Experiment': A long-term follow-up," *Journal of Transpersonal Psychology* vol. 23, no. 1 (1991): 1–28.

page 39   *To be shaken out of the:* Aldous Huxley, *The Doors of Perception* (New York: Perennial Library, 1954), 73.

pages 39–40   *I am very fond of Tim:* Walter Truett Anderson, *The Upstart Spring* (Reading, Mass.: Addison-Wesley, 1983), 74.

page 40   *I felt in my heart:* Stevens, 161.

page 41   *It tears my heart to see:* Ibid., 189.

page 43   *I felt strongly:* Stanislav Grof, M.D., and Christina Grof, *The Stormy Search for the Self* (Los Angeles: Tarcher, 1990), 22.

pages 43–44   *Difficult symptoms that had resisted months:* Ibid., 24.

page 44   *may actually be the organism's radical:* Ibid., 24.

page 44   *What actually seemed to die:* Stanislav Grof, M.D., *The Adventure of Self-Discovery* (Albany, N.Y.: State University of New York Press, 1988), 30.

page 44   *Worldly ambitions, competitive drives:* Stanislav Grof, M.D., *LSD Psychotherapy* (Pomona, Calif.: Hunter House, 1980), 72.

page 53   *I felt this extremely violent pain:* Ram Dass, *Be Here Now.*

page 63   *It's very easy to break attachments:* Ram Dass, *The Only Dance There Is* (New York: Anchor Books, 1970), 1.

page 63   *The essence of civilization:* Ram Dass, *Be Here Now.*

page 63   *Thoughts keep us separate:* Ibid.

page 64   *But by the early 1970s:* Colette Dowling, "Confessions of an American Guru," *The New York Times Magazine* (4 Dec. 1977): 141.

page 64   *He appeared to have changed:* David C. McClelland,

Motives, Personality and Society (New York: Praeger, 1984), 188.

page 65   *I was . . . getting caught in more:* Ram Dass, *Grist for the Mill,* (Santa Cruz, Calif.: Unity Press, 1976), 63.

page 65   *You don't have to go to India:* Ibid., 63.

page 65   *If she were a charlatan:* Dowling, 142.

page 66   *Surrender and devotion was:* Ram Dass, *Grist for the Mill,* 63.

page 67   *Once you are in them:* Ram Dass, "Egg on my Beard," *Yoga Journal* (1976): 11.

page 67   *One reason for the Joya fiasco:* Ibid., 10.

page 67   *Some seemed to have been hurt:* Ram Dass, *Grist for the Mill,* 72.

page 68   *The spiritual journey:* Ram Dass, "Is Enlightenment Good for Your Mental Health?" *Common Boundary* (Sept.–Oct. 1988): 7.

page 68   *The realities which we thought:* Ram Dass, *Grist for the Mill,* 54–57.

CHAPTER TWO

page 73   *We fear our highest:* Abraham Maslow, *The Farther Reaches of Human Nature* (New York: Penguin, 1971), 34.

pages 75–76   *he had just finished his seventh:* Michael Murphy, *The Future of the Body* (Los Angeles: Tarcher, 1992).

page 87   *cruel, ignorant and hostile:* Edward Hoffman, *The Right to Be Human: A Biography of Abraham Maslow* (Los Angeles: Tarcher, 1988), 7.

page 87   *The whole thrust of my:* Ibid., 9.

page 88   *Every age but ours:* Abraham Maslow, *Toward a Psychology of Being* (Princeton, N.J. Van Nostrand, 1962), 5.

page 89   *The physiological needs:* Abraham Maslow, "A Theory of Human Motivation," *Psychological Review* 50 (1947): 375–77.

page 90   *are devoted to some task:* Ibid., 291.

page 90   *passionate, selfless and profound:* Ibid., 301.

page 91   *As Leary later recounted:* Leary, 111.

page 94   *snubbed by Freud:* Anderson, 93.

page 95   *We live in patterned:* Fritz Perls, *Gestalt Therapy Verbatim* (Highland N.Y.: The Center for Gestalt Development, 1969), 29, 38.

page 96   *Chickenshit:* Anderson, 145.

page 96   *A little bit of honesty:* Fritz Perls, *The Gestalt Approach and Eyewitness to Therapy* (New York: Bantam 1973), 127.

page 97   *I do my thing:* Perls, *Gestalt Therapy Verbatim*, 5.

page 98   *Helpful understanding of others:* Murphy, 559–61.

page 99   *If there is one:* William C. Schutz, *Joy* (New York: Grove Press, 1967), 15.

page 102   *That heart broke me up:* Leo Litwak, "Joy Is the Prize." *The New York Times Magazine* (12 Sept. 1967): 28.

page 104   *The people who are most prone:* Carol Tavris, *Anger: The Misunderstood Emotion* (New York: Touchstone, 1982), 129.

page 104   *Encounter is like:* Calvin Tomkins, "New Paradigms, *The New Yorker* vol. 51, no. 46 (5, Jan. 1976): 61.

page 107   *This is just like school:* Hoffman, 234.

page 108   *I must urge you:* Ibid., 291–92.

page 108   *Maslow sat down to write:* Ibid., 329.

page 110   *We have first to penetrate:* Robert Assagioli, M.D., *Psychosynthesis* (New York: Penguin, 1976), 22–24.

CHAPTER THREE

page 117   *We have been inhibited:* Elmer Green and Alyce Green, *Beyond Biofeedback* (Fort Wayne, Ind.: Knoll, 1977), 2–3.

page 117   *Wherever limitations recede:* Ibid., 154.

page 119   *a bridge between the conscious:* Ibid., 68.

page 122   *If you feel that you know a truth:* Ibid., 7.

page 124   *Such compliance [leads] ultimately:* Ibid., 294.

page 126   *The sensations ranged from:* Wolfgang Luthe, "Autogenic Training: Method, Research and Application in Medicine," in *Altered States of Consciousness,* ed. Charles Tart (New York: Anchor, 1969), 321.

page 132   *It is most amazing that:* Green and Green, *Beyond Biofeedback,* 207.

page 134   *ethical, social, economical:* Katherine Webster, "The Case Against Swami Rama of the Himilayas," *Yoga Journal* (Nov./Dec. 1990): 59–94.

page 135   *Sex with a guru:* Ibid., 60, 64.

page 136   *Nearly half of the students:* Jack Kornfield, "Sex Lives of the Gurus," *Yoga Journal* (July/August 1985): 26–28.

page 136   *a pattern of denial:* Katy Butler, "Encountering the Shadow in Buddhist America," *Common Boundary* (May/June 1990): 14–22.

page 137   *Out of a love for truth:* William Rodarmor, "The Secret Life of Swami Muktananda," *The CoEvolution Quarterly* (Winter 1983): 110–11.

page 137   *A lot of people have confused:* Webster, 62.

page 139   *three Indian researchers:* C. Tart ed. Akira Kasamatsu and Tomio Hirai, "An Electroencephalographic Study on the Zen Meditation," in C. Tart, op. cit., 510–14.

page 139   *a study of forty-eight Zen Buddhist:* B. K. Ananda, G. S. Chhina, and B. Singh, "Some Aspects of Electroencephalographic Studies in Yogis," in C. Tart, op. cit., 515–18.

page 140   *he began producing:* Green and Green, *Beyond Biofeedback,* 231–32.

page 141   *Researchers:* Elmer Green, *Biofeedback and States of Consciousness,* eds. Benjamin Wolman and Montague Ullman (New York: Von Nostrand, 1986), 563.

page 147   *The state of deep:* Green and Green, *Beyond Biofeedback,* 143, 146.

page 149   *Visualization coupled with:* Elmer Green, "Alpha-Theta Brainwave Training: Instrumental Vipassana?" (Paper delivered at Montreal symposium, 22 June 1973), 7.

page 149   *the chemist Friedrich Kekule:* Green and Green, *Beyond Biofeedback,* 126.

page 150   *Even Albert Einstein:* Elmer Green, Alyce Green, and E. D. Walters, "Brainwave Training, Imagery, Creativity and Integrative Experiences," Biofeedback Research Society Conference (Feb. 1974): 1–4.

page 150   *It was a level of mind:* Green and Green, *Beyond Biofeedback,* xvi.

page 150   *It meant:* Ibid., xviii.

pages 154–55   *The Self is always willing:* Green, "Alpha-Theta Brainwave Training," 4.

CHAPTER FOUR

page 159   *Clarity, insight or understanding:* Krishnamurti, *You Are the World* (New York: Harper & Row, 1972), 72.

page 159   *At these moments:* Betty Edwards, *Drawing on the Artist Within* (New York: Simon & Schuster, 1986), 222.

page 164   *These sorts of anecdotal:* Sally Springer and Georg Deutsch, *Left Brain, Right Brain* (New York: W. H. Freeman & Co., 1981), 8.

page 165   *If it should be proven:* Robert Ornstein, *The Psychology of Consciousness* (New York: Penguin, 1973), 100.

page 166   *By 1970:* Jerry Levy, "Right Brain, Left Brain: Fact and Fiction," *Psychology Today* (May 1985): 33–44.

page 168   *The intellect is an organ:* J. E. Bogen, M.D., "Some Educational Aspects of Hemispheric Specialization," *UCLA Educator* (Spring 1975): vol. 17, no. 2.

page 168   *The main theme to emerge:* Betty Edwards, *Drawing on the Right Side of the Brain* (Los Angeles: Tarcher, 1989), 29.

page 169   *powerful brain functions:* Ibid., xiii.

page 174   *At this point:* Springer and Deutsch, 299.

page 174   *Since the late 1970s:* Edwards, *Drawing on the Right Side,* xiv.

page 175   *The fact is that Edwards':* Springer and Deutsch, 299.

page 179   *We must overcome:* Edwards, *Drawing on the Right Side,* 127.

page 185   *five stages of creativity:* Lucia Cappacchione, *The Power of Your Other Hand* (North Hollywood: Newcastle, 1988), 73.

page 185   *four stages as "preparation":* Daniel Goleman, Paul Kaufman, and Michael Ray, *The Creative Spirit* (New York: Dutton, 1992), 23.

page 186   *The deliberate giving over:* Edwards, *Drawing on the Artist,* 223.

page 187   *One becomes more creative:* Ibid., 230.

page 189   *By means of drawing:* Ibid., 111.

page 190   *Drawing gives one a feeling of:* Ibid., 231.

CHAPTER FIVE

page 193   *The great majority:* Norman Cousins, *Anatomy of an Illness* (New York: Bantam, 1981), 65.

page 193   *The witch doctor succeeds:* Ibid., 69.

page 195   *The annual cost of treating:* Gina Kolata, "Study Raises Serious Doubts About Commonly Used Methods of Treating Back Pain," *New York Times,* 11 July 1994, sec. C1.

page 196   *an extraordinary study:* Ibid.

page 196   *The temptation is there:* Ibid.

page 198   *It's a bit like blowing:* John E. Sarno, *Mind Over Back Pain* (New York: Putnam, 1987), 73.

page 198   *That tells you that:* E. Rosenthal, "Chronic Pain Fells

Many Yet Lacks Clear Cause," *New York Times,* 29
Dec. 1992, C1, C-3

page 200   *the nonspecific response:* Steven Locke and Douglas
Colligan. *The Healer Within* (New York: Dutton,
1986), 62.

pages 201–2   *The cases are so frequent:* Lawrence LeShan. *Cancer
as a Turning Point* (New York: Dutton, 1989), 9–10.

page 204   *Nothing can be more:* Lawrence LeShan. *You Can
Fight for Your Life* (New York: Evans, 1977), 108.

page 204   *fully half of his patients:* Ibid., 30.

page 207   *There is some utility:* Redford Williams, *The Trusting
Heart* (New York: Times Books, 1989), 48.

page 209   *The true 'toxic' factor:* Meyer Friedman, "Type A
Behavior: A Frequently Misdiagnosed and Rarely
Treated Medical Disorder," *American Heart Journal,*
vol. 115, no. 4: 930–936.

page 209   *Friedman's most compelling study:* Meyer Friedman,
Treating Type A Behavior and Your Heart (New
York: Fawcett, 1984), 146–47.

page 210   *No drug, food or exercise:* Ibid., 149.

page 211   *tended to gain weight:* Williams, 113.

page 211   *A long term study:* Ibid., 66.

page 211   *recently divorced women:* Locke and Colligan, 72.

page 211   *strong social connections:* Redford Williams, et al.,
"Prognostic Importance of Social and Economic Re-
sources Among Medically Treated Patients with An-
giographically Documented Coronary Artery
Disease," *JAMA,* vol. 267, no. 4 (22/29 Jan. 1992):
520–24.

page 212   *They were also denying less:* David Spiegel, et al.,
"Effect of Psychosocial Treatment on Survival of
Patients with Metastatic Breast Cancer," *Lancet* (14
Oct. 1989): 888–91.

page 212   *Peace of mind sends the body:* Bernie S. Siegel, *Love,
Medicine and Miracles* (New York: Harper & Row,
1989), 17.

page 213   *To his astonishment:* Spiegel, et al., 889.

page 213   *Only three of the 86 women:* Ibid., 889.

page 218   *Chronic pain patients:* Jon Kabat-Zinn, et al., "Four-Year Follow Up of a Meditation-Based Program for the Self-Regulation of Chronic Pain," *The Clinical Journal of Pain,* vol. 2, no. 3 (1986): 159–73.

page 218   *When we learn:* Jon Kabat-Zinn, *Full Catastrophe Living* (New York: Dalacorte Press, 1990), 19.

page 220   *describes the state:* Jeanne Achterberg, *Imagery and Healing* (Boston: Shambhala, 1985), 23.

page 220   *The imagery of the right side:* Ibid., 123–24.

page 221   *The immune system:* Ibid., 191.

page 224   *More extraordinary still:* Eugene Peniston and Paul Kukolsky, "Alpha-Theta Brainwave Training and B-Endorphin Levels in Alcoholics," *Alcoholism: Clinical and Experimental Research,* vol. 13 (1989): 271–79.

page 225   *thirty months later:* Eugene Peniston, Paul Kukolsky, et al., "EEG Alpha-Theta Brainwave Synchronization in Vietnam Theater Veterans with Combat-Related Post-Traumatic Stress Disorder and Alcohol Abuse," *Advances in Medical Psychotherapy,* vol. 6 (1993): 37–50.

page 227   *Ornish reported in:* Dean Ornish, et al., "Can lifestyle changes reverse coronary heart disease?" *Lancet* (21 June 1990): 129–33.

page 228   *The more inwardly defined:* Dean Ornish, *Dr. Dean Ornish's Program for Reversing Heart Disease* (New York: Random House, 1988), 87.

CHAPTER SIX

page 235   *Nothing clutters the soul:* Norman Cousins, *Head First: The Biology of Hope* (New York: Dutton, 1989), 311.

page 235   *In every contest:* Pat Riley, *The Winner Within* (New York: Putnam, 1993), 254.

page 236	The *"inner game"*: Timothy Gallwey, *The Inner Game of Tennis* (New York: Bantam, 1979), introduction.
page 238	*the term 'flow' to*: Mihalyi Csikszentmihalyi, *Flow* (New York: Harper & Row: 1990), 41.
page 238	*In a threatening*: Ibid., 206.
page 238	*To still the mind*: Gallwey, 104, 106.
page 238	*When the player*: Ibid., 8–9.
page 257	*Toughness is the ability*: James Loehr, *Mental Toughness Training for Sports* (Lexington, Mass.: Stephen Greene Press, 1982), 1.
page 257	*exhibit a highly refined*: James Loehr, *Toughness Training for Life* (New York: Dutton, 1993), 64.
page 258	*Poor nutrition, thirst*: Ibid., 70.
page 258	*How you really*: Loehr, *Mental Toughness Training for Sports*, 16.
page 258	*Emotions respond much like*: Ibid., 22.
page 258	*Converting bad habits*: Ibid., 178.
page 259	*Could the military succeed*: Loehr, *Toughness Training for Life*, 133.
page 259	*You never see any*: Ibid., 134.
page 259	*Of all the virtues*: Csikszentmihalyi, 200.
page 265	*Optimal experience*: Ibid., 69.
page 267	*If you don't*: Loehr, *Toughness Training for Life*, 28–29.

CHAPTER SEVEN

page 269	*It is certainly true*: Montague Ullman and Nan Zimmerman, *Working with Dreams* (Los Angeles: Tarcher, 1980), 53.
page 269	*From the standpoint*: Stanley Krippner, Ph.D., ed. *Dreams and Dreaming* (Los Angeles: Tarcher, 1993), 8.
page 271	*Dream symbols are the*: Carl Jung, *Man and His Symbols* (New York: Dell, 1968), 37.

page 271   *It ought not to matter:* Carl Jung, *The Practice of Psychotherapy* (Princeton: Princeton University Press, 1931), 42–43.

page 272   *reveals in the clearest:* Ann Faraday, *Deam Power* (New York: Berkeley, 1980), 129.

page 272   *The goal of dream interpretation:* Calvin Hall, *The Meaning of Dreams* (New York: McGraw-Hill, 1966), 214.

page 272   *On the whole, the dreamer:* Faraday, 130.

page 273   *Dreams are not mysterious:* Hall, 120.

page 278   *Do we throw away:* Jeremy Taylor, *Where People Fly and Water Runs Uphill* (New York: Warner, 1992).

page 280   *These ugly, scary, dark:* Ibid., 109.

page 280   *When we admit:* Ibid., 181.

page 296   *I believe that everyone:* Taylor, 96.

page 296   *All dreams:* Ibid., 50.

page 298   *no matter how it appears:* Ibid., 183.

page 298   *In order for the personality:* Ibid., 182–83.

page 300   *When read correctly dream:* Ullman and Zimmerman, 8.

CHAPTER EIGHT

page 305   *Many people have taken:* Rick Fields, *How the Swans Came to the Lake* (Boston: Shambhala, 1992), 374.

page 305   *Look at every path closely:* Jack Kornfield, *A Path with Heart* (New York: Bantam, 1993), 12.

page 307   *We are dominated by:* Assagioli, 22.

page 307   *What we want to do:* Joseph Goldstein, *The Experience of Insight* (Boston: Shambhala, 1976), 24.

page 311   *Joseph was famous:* Fields, 318–19.

page 314   *My meditation had:* Kornfield, *A Path with Heart*, 7.

page 316   *We can deceive:* Chogyam Trungpa, *Cutting Through Spiritual Materialism* (Boston: Shambhala, 1973), 3.

page 317   *Whenever we begin:* Ibid., 14.

page 317   *What was needed was:* Fields, 316.

page 321　　*The mind stops grasping:* Goldstein, *The Experience of Insight,* 22.

page 321　　*If we are engaged in:* Jack Kornfield and Joseph Goldstein, *Seeking the Heart of Wisdom* (Boston: Shambhala, 1987), 7.

page 321　　*not speaking what is:* Goldstein, *The Experience of Insight,* 10.

page 321　　*causing suffering to:* Ibid., 11.

page 321　　*doing that kind of work:* Ibid., 12.

page 321　　*to be persistent:* Ibid., 13.

page 322　　*Doubt . . . is counteracted:* Roger N. Walsh and Frances Vaughn, *Beyond Ego* (Los Angeles: Tarcher, 1980), 131.

page 322　　*Every act of condemning:* Goldstein, *The Experience of Insight,* 57.

page 323　　*he published perhaps the:* Roger Walsh, "Initial Meditative Experiences," parts 1 and 2, *Journal of Transpersonal Psychology,* vol. 9, no. 2 (1977): 151–92; vol. 10, no. 1 (1978): 1–28.

page 323　　*I was lost in fantasy:* Ibid., vol. 10, no. 1, 154.

page 332　　*They hope to rise above:* Kornfield, *A Path with Heart,* 53.

page 332　　*In the end spiritual life:* Ibid., 11.

page 333　　*When we have not completed:* Ibid., 41.

page 336　　*No matter how tremendous:* Ibid., 141.

page 336　　*If liberation is the central:* Joseph Goldstein, *Insight Meditation: The Practice of Freedom* (Boston: Shambhala, 1993), 9–10.

CHAPTER NINE

page 339　　*To know that:* Green and Green, *Beyond Biofeedback,* 299.

page 339　　*The ultimate metaphysical secret:* Ken Wilber, *No Boundary* (Boston: New Science Library, 1979), 31.

page 344　　*The concept of self-actualization:* Anthony Sutich, *Journal of Transpersonal Psychology,* vol. 8, no. 1, 7.

page 344   *The fully developed:* Abraham Maslow, "The Farther
               Reaches of Human Nature," *Journal of Humanistic
               Psychology* (Spring 1969).

page 345   *The more I think of it:* Anthony Sutich, *Journal of
               Transpersonal Psychology,* vol. 8, no. 1 (1976): 16.

page 345   *In my experience:* Roger N. Walsh and Frances
               Vaughan, *Paths Beyond Ego* (Los Angeles: Tarcher/
               Perigee, 1993), 100.

pages 345–46   *The common denominator:* Ibid., 102.

page 346   *This data cannot be:* C. Tart, ed., *Altered States of
               Consciousness,* 7.

page 348   *I fashioned a self:* Ken Wilber, "Odyssey: A Personal
               Inquiry," *Journal of Humanistic Psychology,* vol. 22,
               no. 1 (Winter 1982): 57–90.

page 348   *It was as if my previous:* Ibid., 58.

page 349   *I was not doing this:* Ibid., 59.

page 350   *I had spent my entire life:* Ken Wilber, *Grace and
               Grit* (Boston: Shambhala, 1991), 12.

page 351   *When I was writing:* Ibid., 58.

page 353   *To be part of a larger:* Ibid., 70.

page 354   *First, Spirit, or God:* Ibid., 79.

page 360   *The aim is to remember:* Wilber, "Odyssey: A Per-
               sonal Inquiry," 81.

page 363   *Since prerational and transrational:* Ken Wilber, *Eye
               to Eye* (Boston: Shambhala, 1983), 216.

page 363   *exists to this day in both:* Ibid., 216.

pages 367–68   *When I put my arm around:* Wilber, *Grace and
               Grit,* 7.

page 368   *These tumors are the Nazis:* Ibid., 33.

pages 368–69   *Was there some secret death wish:* Ibid., 48.

page 369   *Since nobody knows what:* Ibid., 51.

page 369   *Certainly I worked hard to achieve:* Ken Wilber,
               "Attitudes and Cancer: What Kind of Help Really
               Helps?" *Journal of Transpersonal Psychology,* vol.
               20, no. 1 (1988): 49–59.

page 370   *As men often do:* Wilber, *Grace and Grit,* 141.

page 370   *The strong taste I had:* Ibid., 141.

page 370   *I felt I had lost all control:* Ibid., 140.

page 371   *If anything the events:* Ibid., 172.

page 372   *This growing acceptance:* Ibid., 360.

page 372   *Treya's facing a potentially:* Ken Wilber, "On Being a Support Person," *Journal of Transpersonal Psychology,* vol. 20, no. 2 (1988): 141–59.

page 372   *she had returned to her roots:* Wilber, *Grace and Grit,* 307.

page 373   *Only the balance of the two:* Ibid., 367.

CHAPTER TEN

page 375   *Man's higher nature rests:* Kathleen Riordan Speeth, *The Gurdjieff Work* (Los Angeles, Tarcher, 1989), 50.

page 375   *The goal of man is Truth:* A. H. Almaas, *Diamond Heart: Book One* (Berkeley: Diamond Books, 1987), 89.

page 379   *As his powers of attention:* Speeth, 9.

page 379   *It must be understood:* P. D. Ouspensky, *In Search of the Miraculous* (New York: Harcourt, Brace & World, 1949), 232.

page 380   *The hope is that by naming:* Helen Palmer, *The Enneagram* (New York: Harper & Row, 1988), 25.

page 383   *The fact that the Enneagram:* Ibid., xiii.

page 383   *When the nature of my type:* Ibid., xiii.

page 389   *We lose the essential:* Ibid., 26.

page 393   *It can be astounding:* Ibid., 21.

page 396   *Above all a fearful person:* Ibid., 267, 269.

page 397   *They have sensitive:* Ibid., 276.

page 399   *Threes can project:* Ibid., 144–48.

page 407   *The effectiveness of psychotherapy has been:* A. H. Almaas, *Diamond Heart: Book One,* 34.

page 411   *It is as if they are different:* A. H. Almaas, *Essence* (York Beach, Maine: Samuel Weiser, 1986), 148.

page 412   *Many people do not:* Ibid., 26.

page 412   *The personality will do:* Ibid., 44.

page 412   *This need is literally in:* Ibid., 46.

page 414   *What you fill the holes with:* A. H. Almaas, *Diamond Heart: Book One,* 29–30.

page 414   *They think the hole:* Ibid., 20.

page 414   *People don't know:* Ibid., 50.

page 415   *A person who is this essence:* A. H. Almaas, *Essence,* 25.

page 419   *We could do meditations:* A. H. Almaas, *Diamond Heart: Book One,* 27.

page 420   *Love is just one:* Ibid., 55.

CONCLUSION

page 421   *Life is a contest:* E. A. Bennett, *What Jung Really Said* (New York: Schocken Books, 1966), 92.

page 421   *The path to sainthood:* Peck, 97.

page 421   *The serious problems in life:* Carl J. Jung, *The Structure and Dynamics of the Psyche* (New York: Pantheon, 1960), 393–94.

INDEX

463